Intercultural Communication

A New Approach to International Relations and Global Challenges

Houman A. Sadri
Madelyn Flammia

continuum

2011

The Continuum International Publishing Group
80 Maiden Lane, New York, NY 10038
The Tower Building, 11 York Road, London SE1 7NX

www.continuumbooks.com

Library of Congress Cataloging-in-Publication Data
Sadri, Houman A.
Intercultural communication : a new approach to international relations and global
challenges / Houman A. Sadri, Madelyn Flammia.
    p. cm.
  Includes bibliographical references and index.
  ISBN-13: 978-1-4411-3352-6 (hardcover : alk. paper)
  ISBN-10: 1-4411-3352-6 (hardcover : alk. paper)
  ISBN-13: 978-1-4411-0309-3 (pbk. : alk. paper)
  ISBN-10: 1-4411-0309-0 (pbk. : alk. paper)
  1. Intercultural communication. 2. Communication, International.
3. International cooperation. 4. International relations. 5. Nonverbal
communication. 6. Visual communication. 7. Culture and globalization. I. Flammia,
Madelyn. II. Title.
  GN345.6.S23 2011
  303.48'2—dc22   2010033020

ISBN: HB: 978-1-4411-3352-6
        PB: 978-1-4411-0309-3

Typeset by Pindar NZ, Auckland, New Zealand
Printed and bound in the United States of America

Contents

viii   Contents

Dedication

This book is first and foremost dedicated to all those unknown global citizens whose contributions to humanity are often not acknowledged, but who continue their service by feeding, sheltering, clothing, counseling, educating, and/or protecting others, especially the unprivileged. Also, we would like to dedicate this work to those individuals who go beyond what they know to learn about diverse cultures, to understand human uniqueness and commonalities, to communicate with others without prejudice, and to produce mindful solutions for making a better community for all. We can learn from them, and we wish them all the best. And let's hope that we succeed in making a better living and working environment for all of us.

Preface

The World War II generation often speaks of the devastation of the Japanese attack on Pearl Harbor on December 7, 1941, which changed the direction of American history. It showed that the United States was no longer isolated from the rest of the world. The American Civil Rights generations remind us about the shocking impact of the late Reverend Martin Luther King's assassination, which led some to question the value of his preaching about the peaceful nature of the struggle to gain equality. Reverend King's larger-than-life legacy, however, led to the final success of the non-violet movement to secure civil rights for people of color.

Along the same lines, September 11, 2001, had a similar effect on ordinary U.S. citizens by showing that intercultural conflict is not a phenomenon that occurs only on foreign soil. This tragic event forever changed the face of international communication and intercultural relations for Americans. In such an environment, the study of intercultural communication and international relations reached new heights. Experts reorganized concepts, theories, and methods and provided us with tools to understand the causes and effects of the tragedy. Moreover, studies were launched to address questions about cultural imperialism, ethnic profiling, hate crimes, the globalization process, human rights violations, political exploitation, religious intolerance, and social marginalization.

Concentrating on domestic issues, intercultural communication is one discipline within the field of communication. Its focus is on challenges within organizations consisting of people from diverse ethnic, racial, religious, and social backgrounds. Also known as cross-cultural communication, this discipline aims to comprehend how individuals from diverse cultures behave, communicate, and perceive their environment as well as interact with one another. Beyond language differences, intercultural communication involves understanding diverse cultures to comprehend different behaviors. Thus, the field involves anthropology, cultural studies, international business, political science, psychology, and sociology.

Despite their interdisciplinary nature, departments (or schools) of communication are not the only academic programs that can lay claim to intercultural communication. The field of international relations (IR) also asserts a natural jurisdiction over intercultural communication, especially when the communications cross national boundaries. For IR specialists, communication is a natural element of diplomacy, negotiation, and signaling. Diplomacy entails diplomats communicating their national concerns with their counterparts and persuading others to support or comply with their policy goals. The personal ability to persuade others is associated with soft power. This ability is not exclusively for diplomats anymore, especially since the internet has empowered ordinary individuals with opportunities to effect change. There are numerous studies about how politics affects communication and vice versa. Focused on the notion of soft power, IR studies fill a major gap in the cross-cultural communication literature by illustrating how the interactions among cultures, communications, and power impact the lives of individuals as well as the conditions of groups, organizations, nations, and even the global community. In this regard, Joseph Nye's body of works on soft power requires special attention.

For years, the scholars and practitioners of international communication have demanded professional recognition in academic associations, especially in the International Studies Association (ISA), the largest professional organization of IR experts in the world. In 2000, the subfield of international communication was publically recognized, when the ISA officially chartered the International Communication Section. The Section website clearly states that this subfield generally entails topics about cultural dimensions of international studies, the role of the media in foreign policy, the impact of information technologies in world politics, and information in the global society. All these topics involve soft power, which is a focus of our study.

In an increasingly interdependent world, realities demonstrate that neither IR nor communication have exclusive dominion over the subfield of intercultural communication. Considering that it is progressively more difficult to separate domestic and international issues, the fields of communication and IR actually provide complementary perspectives about complex intercultural issues. One major challenge is that neither discipline has integrated the concepts, theories, and methods of both fields to provide a comprehensive perspective on intercultural puzzles. Moreover, for recognized intercultural problems, each discipline has taken a different approach to formulating and offering relevant solutions. Last, but not least, the majority of communication and IR studies focus mainly on either individual, group, national, or global levels of analysis and ignore the interactions among different actors at the different levels of a study. These shortcomings do not allow us to understand the real nature of intercultural conflicts, to identify the main elements of such intercultural challenges, and to avoid the pitfalls or to offer relevant solutions to address them.

In this book we aim to address such shortcomings in the literature of both communication and IR. Thus, the purpose of our work is threefold: (1) to offer a truly interdisciplinary approach that integrates the strengths of both fields to help us better understand the nature of intercultural communication in the twenty-first century; (2) to identify the domestic and foreign cultural causes of conflict from a fresh perspective; and (3) to bridge theory and practice of intercultural communication in both fields in order to offer reliable solutions for cultural clashes in a global village.

This work is best described as a research effort that provides a fresh look at intercultural communication from the combined perspective of international relations and communication. However, our target audience is not limited to the academic community. That is why we did not publish this work with a university press, which markets ideas mainly in the academic community. Instead we worked with a well-respected private publisher with a reputation for marketing innovative interdisciplinary manuscripts internationally to professionals who realize they need both knowledge and skills to function in culturally diverse work environments. We also provide a companion website with supplementary materials for better comprehension of challenging concepts, theories, and methods. Thus, some may chose to adapt this text for diversity, protocol, or cross-cultural workshops and professional training. Others may choose it for a college course.

This book is the result of our collaborative research, teaching, and service activities over more than a decade at the University of Central Florida (UCF). Our home institution is currently the second largest university in the United States in terms of enrollment. With more than 56,500 students, UCF is a comprehensive metropolitan university, whose staff, faculty, and students truly represent diversity in terms of their cultural, economic, ethnic, religious, and political perspectives. Beyond our multicultural background and education, UCF is a great academic environment where one can work with cross-cultural, diverse teams to gain professional experience.

Beyond the sacrifices of our families to provide us with time and opportunity to complete this project, our work could not have been finished without the help of our colleagues, departments, and colleges at UCF. Houman Sadri has a special appreciation for the support of Robert Bledsoe, Kerstin Hamann, Roger Handberg, Waltraud Morales, and Consuelo Stebbins. He also thanks Phillip Pollock for his insightful comments on Chapter 8, on media, and Terri Fine for commenting on Chapter 10, about global citizenship. Madelyn Flammia would like to express her thanks for the support of her colleagues, Yvonne Cleary, Rosie Graziani, Patrick Murphy, Carol Saunders, and Darina Slattery. She would also like to thank Daniel Voss, whose guidance and expertise helped shape Chapter 9.

Both authors express their gratitude to Marie-Claire Antoine (Continuum Publishing Senior Commissioning Editor) for her endless efforts to produce a quality book. The authors are also grateful to Jerry Klein and Chad Binette (from UCF News & Information) for securing relevant pictures for different chapters. Both authors would like to thank their colleagues, Valarie King, Angel Cardec, and Diana Wilson-Mosley, for their support and guidance. Moreover, they express thanks to a number of UCF students who helped in the last few years as research assistants and manuscript commentators, including Jou-Ying Chen, Albert Citron, Patrick Hayes, Rachel Hobbs, Zachary Johnson, Cherie Parker, Catharine Rash, Joseph Rosenberg, Nicholas Schenk, Mary Shrum, Sabrina Stein, Michael Tipton, Evelyn Tonn, Jennie Zilner, and especially Stephanie Rash for her generous assistance until the final submission deadline.

Last, but certainly not least, both authors wish to express their sincere appreciation to the Fulbright International Educational Exchange Program. With the support of Gary Garrison (of the Council for International Exchange of Scholars), Sadri benefited from two Fulbright research grants providing him with unique experiences during his residency, one before and the other after September 11. Flammia led a Fulbright–Hays group to the Caribbean, and has many interesting stories about her cross-cultural experience. Sadri is also grateful to the US State Department, the Department of Education, Rotary International, the International Research and Exchange Board (IREX), the Nile Foundation (Orlando), Istanbul Center (Atlanta), and the Russian International Studies Association (Russia) for funding his extensive research trips to other regions of the world. However, these organizations are not responsible for the ideas presented by the authors of this book.

We have tried to avoid overwhelming readers with a heavy discussion of IR methodology and theories. However, a careful observer may easily notice the use of Kenneth Waltz's methodological view, as we discuss intercultural communication at different levels of analysis in IR. In fact, special effort is made to bring more attention to the individual level-of-analysis as we explain verbal communication, non-verbal communication, and visual communication in Chapters 5, 6, and 7 respectively. These are not typical topics in the mainstream IR literature. Moreover, issues associated with state level-of-analysis as well as international level-of-analysis are addressed, especially in their relation to an individual level.

Although this is not a pure theory book, we did not ignore the discussion of significant theories. In Chapter 3, we introduce social science and interpretive approaches used in the communication field, while we address the critical and dialectical approaches in the next chapter. This dialogue is indirectly connected to mainstream IR theories (realism and liberalism) and critical theories (feminism and structuralism). We discuss how IR theories overlap with those in the communication field about the intercultural communications subfield. Thus, our preliminary effort here should open more opportunities for other scholars to fill other gaps in the literature.

A theme of this work is that conflict in any form is a costly affair. Thus, cooperation is not just a politically correct behavior, but it also makes sense in business and economic terms. Conflicts waste valuable human resources and scarce natural resources in addition to wasting time and costing money. To avoid unintended conflicts, we propose methods such as being mindful of the environment and informed about cultural issues, as well as negotiating via direct communication with counterparts. In other words, we generally recommend what some (e.g. Turkish spiritual leader Fethullah Gulen and former President Khatami of Iran) called the "dialogue of civilizations" approach, which directly challenges the "clash of civilizations" idea of Samuel Huntington. Nevertheless, this book is not a comprehensive test of Huntington's controversial thesis, and we do not aim to disprove it here.

To achieve the earlier mentioned objectives, this book is divided into four interrelated parts. In Part I, we begin with the foundations of intercultural communication when we discuss the significance of the field for the global community, and then we proceed with an explanation of its core concepts. Part II covers a discussion of major theories of intercultural communication in two consecutive chapters. Using an interdisciplinary approach, we borrowed ideas and perspectives from political science, communication, anthropology and psychology. In Part III, we introduce intercultural communication processes and technologies, as we continue with different types of communication from verbal to non-verbal and finally visual in separate chapters. In Part IV, we discuss the major issues of the field. We begin with a description of the main ethical issues and end with an examination of the notion of global citizenship.

We hope that you enjoy reading this work, which entails many practical examples to make complex ideas and situations easier to comprehend. We seek and appreciate your reflections and suggestions. We hope that you offer us ideas about improving the quality of this modest attempt to integrate the fields of IR and communication and examine their overlap in the form of intercultural communication. Finally, we hope that you find helpful our practical ideas and plans for those who need to adjust to the new culturally and globally diverse work environment. Let's make a better living and working environment for all of us.

Houman A. Sadri and Madelyn Flammia
Orlando, Florida
December 2010

FOUNDATIONS OF INTERCULTURAL COMMUNICATION IN A GLOBAL SOCIETY

I

Introduction: Assessing Your Knowledge of Intercultural Communication

The first part of this book introduces you to the study of intercultural communication. In Chapter 1, we discuss the significance of the study of intercultural communication to our society today. In Chapter 2 we introduce the core concepts of the field of intercultural communication and explain that we approach the field with a focus on the issue of power and the challenges of conflict and cooperation in our global community. In order to understand these issues, we draw upon concepts from a subfield of political science — international relations.

Some of you may come to this book already possessing a great deal of knowledge about intercultural communication. You may have gained knowledge of intercultural communication through experiences you have had either socially or at work. You may have lived or studied abroad. Perhaps you are pursing a field of study that naturally involves a global perspective, like international business or foreign languages. You may know a lot about intercultural communication because of your family background. However, we believe that even if you have not had any of the experiences we list above, you may already know more than you realize about effective intercultural communication.

Before we begin our formal discussion of the field of intercultural communication, we ask you to answer the following questions and reflect on your current level of experience and knowledge.

1. Are you a first-generation American (meaning that one or both of your parents came to the United States from another country)?
2. Does your immediate or extended family practice customs and celebrate holidays not practiced or observed by the majority of people in the US?
3. Do you speak a language(s) other than English?
4. Have you ever lived in another country for an extended period of time (longer than a couple of weeks of vacation)?
5. Do you have roommates or co-workers who are from other cultures?
6. Do you read (in print or online) non-US newspapers or listen to or watch non-US news broadcasts (traditional, cable, or on the internet), television shows, or international music on a regular basis?
7. Do you know the proper way to greet someone from at least one of these cultures — Indian, Japanese, Middle Eastern?
8. Do you know at least two gestures commonly used in the United States that are considered obscene in other cultures?
9. Can you name a culture in which making eye contact with one's elders is considered disrespectful?

10. Can you name a culture in which handshakes between members of the opposite sex are taboo?

Your answers to these questions will help you reflect upon your current level of intercultural awareness. You may be surprised to discover how much you already know. However, you do not need any previous experience with or knowledge of intercultural communication to benefit from reading this book. By the way, if you are curious, the answers to questions 7 through 10 will be covered in subsequent chapters of this text.

As you begin your study of intercultural communication, we suggest to you that such study is a vitally important undertaking for all of us in our global community today. It is also a journey of discovery to learn more about the other peoples of the earth, near and far, and about yourself. We invite you to begin your journey now with Chapter 1, which describes the many ways that our world is truly one interconnected community, a community in which you are called to play a meaningful and engaged role as a global citizen.

The Significance of Intercultural Communication in a Global Society

1

Views of Our Global Community

There are more than 1,000 KFC restaurants in China, and they are increasing at a rate of 200 per year. A new KFC opens in China almost every other day.[1]

Films from Bollywood, the film capital of India, reach up to 3.6 billion people around the world — a billion more than the audience for Hollywood. Some Bollywood films, like the popular "Slumdog Millionare," have grossed millions in the United States.[2]

The final text of the UNESCO Treaty on cultural diversity was adopted in June 2005. The treaty would allow nations to subsidize their own local cultural productions and impose limits and tariffs on imported cultural products like films, TV shows, music, or books. The aim of the treaty is to curtail the spread of American popular culture.[3]

"The average Nigerian youth tends to want to be as westernised as much as his or her present circumstances allow. Because smoking cigarettes is common in the Western societies of Europe and America he or she feels that smoking should be cultivated, to make him or her belong. This partly fuels the intense peer pressure that leads youths to smoke because they do not want to be left out. The idea that smoking is a Western thing is conveyed mainly through films, music, and advertisements."[4]

The Zapatista Army of National Liberation is an anti-globalization movement in Mexico that seeks to maintain their unique agrarian traditions and a system of communal property in the face of the North American Free Trade Agreement.[5]

A survey in the International Herald Tribune said that "66 percent of consumers polled in Germany said they were less likely to buy US product as a result of their opposition to US foreign policy."[6]

Those who argue in favor of cultural identity and against globalization, betray a stagnant attitude towards culture that is not borne out by historical fact. Do we know of any cultures that have remained unchanged through time? To find any of them one has to travel to the small, primitive, magical-religious communities made up of people who, due to their primitive condition, become progressively more vulnerable to exploitation and extermination.[7]

Red and blue are states of mind, not actual states. Red and blue aren't absolute predictors of political leanings, either. There are plenty of blue cities in red states, red enclaves in blue states, red-leaning governors of blue states, people who vote Republican but are of a blue state of mind, and so on. It's not as simple as liberal vs. conservative, elite vs. populist, urban vs. rural, religious vs. nonreligious, educated vs. uneducated, rich vs. poor — if it were, the terms "red" and "blue" wouldn't have taken off as the best shorthand for a divided America.[8]

The Italian garment industry is facing increased competition from China, but also, like the rest of the world recognizes China as a growing market. "China is both a problem and an opportunity . . . It's indisputable that every garment produced in China is a garment less made in Italy but, at the same time, China's average income rate and taste level are growing steadily."[9]

Most immigrants today are from Latin America and Asia, and it is projected that by 2050 the US population will be only 50.1 percent European-American desent.[10]

Somebody would look at Pizza Hut in Thailand and say this is American cultural imperialism . . . But wait a minute — where did pizza come from? We're a country of immigrants. Our culture is constantly changing, and we often repackage things that were cultural exports to this country.[11]

In Talibanized Afghanistan, in 1997, all aspects of culture — movies, music, photographs, art — were strictly forbidden. Yet smuggled copies of "Titanic" (which many an American pastor preached against) found their way into Afghan homes. The movie was so popular that young men in the capital of Kabul wanted their hair cut in the style of star Leonardo DiCaprio. At weddings, cakes were shaped like the Titanic.[12]

Americans, after all, did not invent fast food, amusement parks, or the movies. Before the Big Mac, there were fish and chips. Before Disneyland, there was Copenhagen's Tivoli Gardens (which Walt Disney used as a prototype for his first theme park, in Anaheim, a model later re-exported to Tokyo and Paris).[13]

Donald Trump is planning a Chinese version of his hit reality TV show The Apprentice. Beijing real-estate mogul Pan Shiyi will be the host and do the hiring and firing.[14]

We live in an increasingly complex, diverse, divisive, and global society. As the international system is saturated with natural competitions and struggles for power, much of our entertainment media today is fueled by the spirit of competition. For example, in addition to situation comedies and dramas, some of the most popular television shows now are reality-based programs like *Survivor* and *The Apprentice*. These shows pit contestants against one another in a no-holds-barred contest to win the prize money or the job. Others, such as the *Surreal Life*, force a group of very dissimilar celebrity roommates to live together in what the producers of the show describe as "a twisted sociological lab experiment in communal living."[15] We seem to enjoy seeing people compete with one another; we find competition and even conflict entertaining. This focus on competition and conflict is perhaps why some scholars argue that international anarchy continues to prevail.

On a daily basis, the news media bombard us with both political information and opinions that highlight competition and conflict in our political system. A good example is the major television networks' Sunday news magazines, like NBC's *Meet the Press* and CBS's *Face the Nation*, during which the media reporters often set one political figure against another, show the political rivalry within the US Congress, or put forward an issue for debate among competing leaders or rival media members. These practices have led some to suggest that the media is the fourth branch of government, and that the national media has three major tasks: gatekeeper, scorekeeper, and watchdog.

We are also seeing great political sophistication and also polarization within our nation. Americans used to identify themselves with only one political party. Today, however, Americans display a much more sophisticated and complex array of ideas and identifications, and do not necessarily limit themselves to only one political party. This is not to suggest that political parties are not important, although many argue that the power of political parties has declined in America since the nineteenth century. Nevertheless, it is hard (if not impossible) to force a typical American into a pre-constructed political party box, when he/she may vote for a Democratic President and a Republican member of Congress. Moreover, an American who shows a pro-business Republican attitude may also vote for the protection of the environment — a Green characteristic often associated with the Democratic Party.

Some of the causes of conflict within our nation have to do with differing opinions about the role we should play in world affairs: This is directly impacted by how we view the international system. We are engaged in a conflict in Iraq. We are concerned about the proliferation of nuclear weapons in states like Iran and North Korea. We are focused on homeland security in the wake of the events of September 11, or 9/11. All of these issues and a host of others involve our relationships with other nations or at least with their governments. This is why it is so important to study international relations (IR) in association with intercultural communication. We also have many contacts with members of other nations that are based on cooperation and collaboration. We participate in world events like the Olympics. We provide aid to victims of natural disasters like the 2004 tsunami and Haiti's 2010 earthquake. Americans play a role in many international organizations at the global (or international system) level, the national level, and at the individual level — a typology borrowed from a prominent scholar of international politics, Kenneth Waltz.

We have a diverse society composed of members of multiple cultural groups. Despite minor anti-immigrant sentiments, Americans have traditionally been a *nation* (a concept generally defined as a group of people with common characteristics that want to be independent) that welcomed immigrants. The US has also played a significant role in world affairs throughout its history. Nowadays, via the revolution in communication(s) technology, American popular culture spreads all over the globe at a faster pace than ever before. This presents America's *soft power* (often defined as the non-military capability of a state to influence others), whose effects tend to be more enduring than the US military might. Some nations fear the spread of American popular culture because they see it as a corrupting force. However, the argument could also be made that the reason for the global appeal of American culture is due at least in part to the fact that Americans are such a culturally diverse nation. Further, amid all the concern about the exporting of American popular culture, the US is also increasingly importing culture from other nations. Such global reciprocity is essential to the understanding of the rules regarding intercultural communication. For these and many other reasons, we are continually faced with challenges related to communication across cultures both domestically and internationally.

What's the Difference between Multicultural and Intercultural?

The term *multicultural* refers to nations that have diverse cultural groups, usually as a result of immigration, while the term *intercultural* refers to the diversity among separate nations. We frequently hear people refer to US society as multicultural. Certainly, the United States is culturally diverse, and has always taken pride in the fact that it entails a nation of immigrants. Some people attribute America's strength as a *state* (a concept generally defined as a political/legal unit that includes at least a nation, territory, government, sovereignty, and diplomatic recognition) to its cultural diversity, which is a source of pride for many Americans. Earlier in US history, when a majority of the immigrants came from European nations, there was an emphasis on cultural assimilation; that is, immigrants were urged to "become Americans" and leave behind their cultural identities. The "melting pot" was the metaphor used to describe a nation where immigrants all blended together to become one as Americans. Historically, many nations have dealt with immigrants by requiring that they assimilate to the majority culture; this approach is sometimes referred to as *monoculturalism*.

Today, we have moved away from the "melting pot" view of immigration, and have adopted a policy of multiculturalism (sometimes referred to as the "salad bowl" approach). The term multiculturalism refers to the view that immigrants should preserve their cultures and that all the different cultures within a state should interact peacefully; all cultural groups should be treated with respect as equals. Such ideas are currently and often associated with the liberalism perspective in international relations literature. The term "multiculturalism" was first used in 1957 to describe Sweden. Then in the late 1960s in Canada the *Report of the Royal Commission on Bilingualism and Biculturalism* recommended the implementation of an official government policy of multilingualism and multiculturalism.[16] While multiculturalism is a viewpoint regarding immigrants, in many states, it has also become an official social policy, as it is in both Australia and Canada. Although multiculturalism is practiced in the US, it is not an official policy at the federal level.

In Canada and Australia, some of the governmental policies that are associated with multiculturalism include the granting of dual citizenship; support for newspapers, television, and radio in minority languages; support for minority festivals, holidays, and celebrations; and acceptance of traditional outfits in schools, the military, and in society in general. For example, in Australia, the government-funded Special Broadcasting Service (SBS) provides multilingual and multicultural radio and television services to educate and entertain all Australians and also to reflect the diversity of the society.[17]

Like the term multiculturalism, the term intercultural refers to interactions among members of diverse cultures. However, when we use the term intercultural we are usually referring to cultural diversity among nations rather than among cultural groups within a single nation. For example, we would describe cities like New York or Montreal that have diverse cultural groups living in them as multicultural; an event like the Olympic Games brings together individuals from many different nations, and we would describe the Games as intercultural.

Mostly ignored by IR theorists, cultural differences, whether they occur among diverse groups within a nation or between two or more individuals from different nations, present both challenges and opportunities for communication. Cultural differences have the potential to lead to misunderstanding, miscommunication, dispute, and even conflict. Sometimes diverse cultural groups within a nation will come into conflict with one another; one example is the tensions that exist in cities like New York, Chicago, and Los Angeles

Figure 1.1 An event like the Olympic Games is the scene of many intercultural encounters. The Olympic Village is composed of athletes from all over the world who come to compete with one another. Spectators, too, come from far and wide to witness this international event and to interact with members of diverse cultures.

among diverse ethnic groups that include Hispanic Americans, African Americans, Asian Americans, Arab Americans, and European Americans. With some reservations, one may even posit that such domestic conflicts are a microcosm of many global conflicts. These tensions are related to cultural differences, particularly differences in languages, values, lifestyles, and world views. Violence has resulted from these tensions. However, cultural differences can also open up opportunities for collaboration, cooperation, and learning. People can learn from their differences and create something together that is greater than they could produce separately. International cooperation has the potential to lead to advances in technology and to our ability as a global community to combat world environmental and health concerns. Many corporations have global teams of employees working together. We have seen international cooperation in space exploration, in searching for cures to diseases, in seeking to preserve our environment, and in times of crisis. At times, people come together as part of international organizations, often called intergovernmental organizations (IGOs), like the United Nations or as part of nongovernmental organizations (NGOs) that consist of ordinary individuals rather than government officials, like Amnesty International and Doctors Without Borders (see Chapter 2). Often cooperation among cultures leads to great accomplishments and to significant humanitarian efforts. In fact, there are the interactions among cultures and nations that contribute to the modern meaning of the international relations (IR) field. The latter implies relations among ordinary people and nations, beyond the regular ties between government officials and states. This discussion refers to the debate between the traditional *State Centric Model* and the modern *Complex Interdependence Model*, as explained later (see Chapter 10).

What Is Intercultural Communication?

To define intercultural communication, we will begin with a definition of communication. Communication is a complex term for which there are numerous definitions. However, most definitions agree that communication is a symbolic process by which people create shared meanings.[18] Intercultural communication occurs when the people creating shared meanings have different cultural perspectives and values. Typically, it is the differing world views of members of different cultures that make intercultural communication challenging. Intercultural communication may occur between individuals; it occurs when you travel abroad and talk with someone in a culture that is different from your own. Intercultural communication may also occur between groups of people or within nations; for example, an intercultural encounter would occur when a group of US doctors who are specialists in emergency care travel to Brazil and meet with their counterparts at a Brazilian hospital to exchange knowledge and techniques. Of course, intercultural communication also occurs between and among states, often through global intergovernmental organizations like the United Nations, through alliances, like the North Atlantic Treaty Organization (NATO), and via regional arrangements, like the North American Free Trade Agreement (NAFTA). With more than 5,000 NGOs in the world, a great deal of intercultural communication happens outside of the official governmental channels and among ordinary people, who can be called "citizen diplomats" (see Chapter 2 for a fuller discussion of citizen diplomats).

The study of intercultural communication is a subfield of the larger area of international and/or communication studies. Most US colleges and universities have schools and/or departments devoted to study of the field of international relations (also known as international studies) and/or communication. It was the development and proliferation of communication technologies such as the telephone, radio, television, satellites, and computer technology that led to the study of international communication becoming a major topic of interest in the twentieth century. However, early studies were dominated by the study of advertising, and it was not until after World War II that the study of international communication gained recognition as an important scholarly pursuit.[19] The subfield of intercultural communication also came into its own after World War II with the development of the Foreign Service Institute (see Part II Introduction).

Although the study of intercultural communication is sometimes housed within the communication discipline, scholars from many other disciplines also focus on intercultural communication. The study of intercultural communication is incorporated into the fields of international studies, political science, psychology, linguistics, sociology, anthropology, comparative literature, education, technical communication, and history. Of course, in each discipline the study of intercultural communication is subordinated to the study of the discipline, and it is approached differently in each. For example, in political science, the field of international relations is directly concerned with the role of intercultural communication in the political relations among nations. In war and peace studies, the role of communication in soft power is essential to maintaining peace in a region. In sociology, scholars view intercultural communication as one of many social factors. In education, scholars are concerned with preparing students to function in a global society and with multicultural issues in the classroom. In technical communication, scholars focus on the preparation of documentation that can meet the needs of diverse audiences internationally and on the use of communication technologies across cultures. Just as many other fields incorporate the study of intercultural communication in some fashion, in this book, we will study intercultural communication from the perspective of the field of international relations, particularly in terms of the issues of soft power and conflict/cooperation. We believe that these issues are crucial ones in today's global society.

Do We Live in a Global Society?

What does it mean to say that we live in a global society? Certainly, many factors have combined to increase the ease and frequency of international communication among members of different cultures. These factors include developments in international politics; advances in transportation systems and in telecommunications; increased social challenges related to health, the environment, and security; increased opportunities for international cooperation; changing immigration trends; as well as the rise of e-commerce and multinational corporations whose growing power challenges many governments.

Increased mobility

While international travel is nothing new and dates back to well-known travelers in history like Marco Polo, today the peoples of the world are much more mobile. Because of advances in transportation systems, a trip that would once have taken days now takes a matter of hours. Ease of mobility together with an increase in international business ventures has led to increased business travel. A worldwide growth in tourism means that more and more people are traveling for pleasure and many of them to destinations farther from home than in the past. The World Tourism Organization reports significant changes in the world's top tourism destinations in the past ten years, most notably the growth of tourism to China and Hong Kong. China has become the world's fourth most visited destination.[20] These changes in the frequency and speed with which individuals travel mean that people today are often in contact with members of other cultures.

Technological advances

Even those individuals who choose to stay at home experience many opportunities for intercultural contact. The development of new technologies like the internet, email, and collaborative software programs has enabled international communication among individuals, non-governmental organizations (NGOs), and businesses all over the world. As Thomas Friedman says in *The Lexis and the Olive Tree*, "thanks to the Internet, we now have a common, global postal system, through which we can all send each other mail. We now have a common global shopping center, in which we can all buy and sell. We now have a common global library, where we can all go to do research . . ."[21] It is not unusual today for individuals from different nations to establish friendships, and even to develop romantic relationships, online. The internet and new courseware technologies have also made possible distance education and the rise of "virtual universities," composed of faculty and students who never meet face-to-face. Similarly, many corporations now rely on global virtual teams. Multinational corporations like VeriFone use virtual teams to run their daily business operations. Microsoft is one of many organizations that service global clients by using virtual teams for customer sales and support.[22]

Whether its political implications are positive or negative, popular culture is also spread via the internet and global communication media. Many television programs, films, recordings, and other cultural artifacts that might once have been consumed only by members of the culture where they originated are now widely available to other cultures around the world. Many popular programs are also taken from one culture and adapted to another culture as in the case of the Chinese version of *The Apprentice*, the Indian version of *Dancing with the Stars*, the American version (i.e. *American Idol*) of the British program *Pop Idol*, and the Russian version of *Skating with Celebrities*.

Shared global concerns

At the same time that international communication has become easier and more prevalent than ever before, many social and political factors have developed to make the need for meaningful communication across cultures a vital one for all peoples of the world. The world faces many challenges that cannot be solved by any one nation or state alone and that have the potential to affect every person on the planet. Such challenges require what political scientists call "collective action." Some of the most prominent of these challenges are rising population growth and diminishing natural resources, ecological concerns including global warming and the destruction of the rain forest, and issues related to world health, most notably the AIDS epidemic. In addition to these challenges, none of which developed overnight, we face increased concerns about terrorist actions in the wake of 9/11, the Madrid bombings, and the London bombings. What is evident from these global concerns is that meaningful cross-cultural communication is vital for the survival of humanity.

Clearly, what happens in one part of the world has the potential to affect other parts of the planet. In international relations literature, this phenomenon is called "interdependence," which necessitates that states and nations cooperate, regardless of their political agendas. Epidemics, natural disasters, and environmental pollution do not respect national boundaries. There are many promising instances of international cooperation to address the challenges we face. For example, there are many non-governmental organizations working hard to safeguard the environment and to fight epidemics and other health issues. Some of the organizations working to protect our environment include Greenpeace, the International Center for the Environmental Management of Enclosed Coastal Seas, and the International Coral Reef Association. Similarly, organizations like the International Red Cross, the Pan American Health Organization (PAHO), and the Peace Corps are devoted to improving world health both through education and prevention efforts, and by assisting victims of war, famine, and disease.

Related to concerns about the environment and world health is the issue of *sustainable development*. The United Nations World Commission on

Environment and Development (WCED) defines sustainable development as "development that meets the needs of the present without compromising the ability of future generations to meet their own needs."[23] Sustainable development is a global issue that can only be addressed by cooperation among the states of the world, since the trade, economic policies, and natural resources management of individual states will impact the whole. Effective communication among leaders in government, industry, and NGOs is necessary to implement policies that will benefit the global economy, the environment, and society.[24] Meetings like the Earth Summit 2002 bring together leaders from government, business, and the private sector to address these global concerns. As a result of the numerous international and intercultural interactions that take place within the global community, the use of soft power is essential to avoiding conflict as well as providing clarity in communication.

Opportunities for international cooperation

Cooperation across cultures may also occur at more local levels with exchange programs and linkages. For example, many study-abroad programs give individual college students and faculty the opportunity to study and teach at universities in other countries. Such individual efforts can do much to increase understanding across cultures; we should not underestimate the ability of effective communication among individuals to enhance cooperation among cultures. In Chapter 2, we will introduce the concept of the "citizen diplomat" to demonstrate the power of private citizens to contribute to global understanding. This is one of the major topics in the field of international relations.

At the level of local government, cities around the world participate in Sister Cities International (SCI), which teams a city in one country with a city of comparable size in another country. SCI has its headquarters in Washington, DC. The Sister Cities movement was developed by President Dwight D. Eisenhower in 1956 during a White House summit on citizen diplomacy. The movement was started as a way to promote world peace in the wake of World War II. Sister City programs are locally based and run by the municipal governments in collaboration with citizen volunteers. Each community together with its sister city determines what type of projects and activities they want to pursue. These activities may include humanitarian assistance, economic development, and youth exchanges; the purpose of the partnerships is to "increase global cooperation, promote cultural understanding, and stimulate economic development."[25]

Immigration trends and diversity

Certainly, trends in immigration have also contributed to the global nature of our society. Many countries are experiencing increasing numbers of immigrants. For example, as US immigration trends change so do the demographics of the US population. Earlier in US history, the majority of immigrants came

Figure 1.2 The U.S. workforce is becoming increasingly diverse. Even Americans who do not travel abroad may find that they will encounter many intercultural communication challenges at work. Developing intercultural communication skills will help them succeed within our nation's diverse workforce.

from European countries. Today, approximately 69.4 percent of the US population is European American.[26] However, most immigrants today are from Latin America and Asia, and it is projected that by 2050 the US population will be 50.1 percent European American,[27] 14.6 percent African American, 8.0 percent Asian, and 24.4 percent Hispanic.[28] These demographic shifts are creating a change in the US workforce, which is becoming increasingly diverse.

As the workforce changes, Americans will face many of the same challenges at work that they face when communicating with members of other cultures internationally. Many businesses have recognized the need for diversity training. Similarly, many colleges and universities offer courses that focus on understanding the diversity of the many cultures that co-exist within the United States. Diversity training will become increasingly important as major shifts in the demographics of the workforce come to pass (see Part II Introduction).

MEDIA IMPACT
The Influence of the Tobacco Industry on Youth Addressed through International Cooperation
Dr. Marvin E. Goldberg of Pennsylvania State University studied the smoking patterns of 1,300 high school students in Thailand. He found that Thai teenagers who smoke are more likely to have been exposed to Hollywood movies. Goldberg says that teens in developing countries admire "Hollywood-made teenagers" and want to emulate them. The influence of smoking in movies has been noted in several other countries as well. Some teenagers in Nigeria have spoken out about this influence. One high school student in Lagos, Nigeria, is quoted as saying: "I love American films . . . but I wonder why must there be so much smoking in them, I don't want my friends to imitate this to be like Americans."

However, Hollywood is not the only moving-making capital that is responsible for this negative influence on teens. Bollywood, the center of India's film industry, has also turned out a large number of films that depict glamorous stars smoking cigarettes. In fact, according to a World Health Organization (WHO) survey, three out of four films produced by Bollywood during the past decade depict smoking, and teenagers who watch these movies are three times as likely to smoke. These facts are particularly troubling since one-third of the estimated three million people who die every year from tobacco-related causes are in India.

International organizations like the Smoke Free Movies Action Network are striving to ban depictions of smoking from films that are targeted to youth. Other organizations like the Global Youth Action Network and UNICEF's Voices of Youth are working to raise awareness and to combat the negative effects of media portrayals of tobacco use on the younger generation. Like many challenges facing our world today, the issue of the influence of the tobacco industry on the youth of the world is one that is most effectively addressed through international cooperation.

Sources: Rory McCarthy, "Bollywood Blamed for Teenage Smoking," *The Guardian*, February 17, 2003; World Health Organization Report (WHO), "'Bollywood': Victim or Ally? A WHO Study on the portrayal of tobacco in Indian Cinema," by Strategic Mediaworks, February 21, 2003.

International business and the global economy

Of course, beyond the increased diversity within any one country's workforce, there is the inescapable fact that today nearly all business is at some level international business. Many American multinational corporations including Ford, GM, Texaco, Dow Chemical, Philip Morris, Coca-Cola, and Eastman Kodak make a significant percentage of their sales outside the United States; they also have plants located in many other countries. Moreover, the same is true of many large non-US corporations like Sony and Michelin.[29] The rise of e-commerce, the flattening of traditional corporate structures, and the loosening of boundaries between markets have all contributed to a global marketplace that is not restricted by national boundaries. In his book *The Lexus and the Olive Tree*, Pulitzer Prize-winning reporter Thomas Friedman refers to the global marketplace as an "Electronic Herd" of "often anonymous stock, bond and currency traders and multinational investors, connected by screens and networks."[30] The global marketplace means that the world economy is interconnected, and what happens to one country's economy has the potential to affect the economies of other countries. This is the same process that Robert Keohane and Joe Nye called "Interdependence," in their classical work titled *Power and Interdependence*. The Asian financial crisis of 1997 started with a weakening of the economy of Thailand, but it spread to other Asian nations. Indonesia, The Philippines, Hong Kong, South Korea, and Malaysia were all affected by the crisis. Even the United States and Japan were affected, although to a lesser degree, because of the efforts of the United States, other major Western powers, and the International Monetary Fund to remedy the negative impacts of the crisis. However, the Asian flu did precipitate a mini-crash of the US stock market in October 1997. The Asian monetary crisis also contributed to the Russian and Brazilian crises in 1998 because of the reluctance of banks to lend to emerging states after the crisis. Moreover, the 1998–99 currency crisis resulted in problems for the Argentinean economy that lasted into 2002.

International politics

Like the global economy, international politics involves the interrelationship of states; typically, political relations among states include a range of activities from diplomacy, cooperation, and alliances, to disputes, conflict, and war. In general, any international relationship can be either cooperative or conflictual in nature. The actions of governments and political leaders can have repercussions not just for individuals living within a particular state, but potentially for all people in the world. These actions may be aggressive, as when one nation or state invades another seeking to seize territory and/or resources; of course, from a historical perspective the invading nation or state may perceive its action as reclaiming its rightful territory. Such actions may also be aimed at enhancing cooperation, as when governments send aid to less developed countries (LDCs). Enhancing international cooperation, and focusing on the benefits of soft power, two of the themes of this book, can benefit us all, not merely by avoiding violent and destructive conflict, but by making possible collaborative efforts to address global challenges. Today, cooperation is not just the politically correct avenue to take in modern international relations; it also makes good business sense since conflicts are typically expensive in terms of human loss, wasted resources, and misused scarce capital.

Our global community

We live in a world in which even superpowers such as the United States cannot resolve all global challenges without the cooperation of others. This situation is due to the fact that no matter how powerful a state is, no state is able to control everything. Further, many modern challenges are international as opposed to national in nature. Despite the lack of a global government, states tend to recognize each other's sovereignty (a key assumption of the Realist School) and organize themselves for the collective action to work according to neorealism. The greenhouse effect, which is associated with the increasing intensity of the hurricane seasons, is not just an American environmental challenge, even though we Americans contribute more than our fair global share to the production of CO_2. We need to address this problem, but we cannot do it alone. Beyond such environmental problems are global medical crises from the movement of HIV and AIDS from Africa to the rest of the world, to the movement of bird flu and swine flu from Asia to the other parts of the globe.

In terms of global terrorism and security, we also need the help of others to manage the problem at hand, even though the United States has the most professional and powerful military machine on the planet. If our military might was the solution, we would have solved the problem of the al-Qaeda terrorist network and Iraq crisis years ago, as top American military leaders have observed. In fact, the relative success of the "surge strategy" was not really because of quantitatively increasing our forces by 30,000 troops in Iraq. The recent success is mainly due to the changing quality of our operation as US military leaders began to listen to local Iraqi demands, emphasizing common values and challenges, and implementing shared ideas. Thus, we should be more modest in our typically exaggerated military power claims, less nationalistic in our general approach to issues, and more culturally mindful of others to meet such challenges beyond the control of our national abilities and ingenuity. These are some concerns of international relations.

As global citizens in the twenty-first century, we live in a society where we can easily communicate with members of other cultures, where we can travel quickly to other countries, where popular culture and other ideas are rapidly disseminated via the internet and mass media. We also live in a society of dwindling natural resources and rising population, where we face many challenges related to world health and sustainable development of our environment. We also face challenges related to conflict within and among nations or states and to acts of terrorism. Precisely what relevance does the study of intercultural and international communication have to our existence in this global society?

Why Is Intercultural Communication Important?

Intercultural and international communication has relevance to our lives now more than at any other time in history. Recently, the Association of American Colleges and Universities Presidents' Campaign for the Advancement of Liberal Learning stated: "Especially since September 2001, Americans have been catapulted into a powerful sense of engagement with peoples, places, histories, and ideologies that many of us previously knew only dimly. Our entire society is now caught up in quests for deepened understanding, and in re-examinations of the most basic questions about social trust, civic duty, international justice, world cultures, and sustainable health."[31] Of the four aims of liberal education cited in the Campaign, two have to do with intercultural knowledge: "expanding cultural, societal, and scientific horizons," and "cultivating democratic and global knowledge and engagement."[32] The study of intercultural and international communication has great relevance for all citizens; however, students and professionals are especially well positioned to appreciate the importance of intercultural communication and connections to help them value the past, understand the present, and prepare for the future.

Valuing the past

Our world changes rapidly, and you may find yourself struggling to keep up with the demands of work, family, and school with little time to reflect on the past or the future. However, the study of international communication can provide you useful insights into current situations and help you prepare to address the future. Many world situations that exist today have their roots far back in history. Many conflicts among states; between nations or ethnic groups or even within states have a long and complex history behind them. Conflicts between nations or ethnic groups are often rooted in historical disputes over territories or natural resources. Many ethnic (or nationality) conflicts center on the desire to gain territory or redraw borders, often with the goals of establishing one group as a separate state. These types of conflicts have fueled many wars, such as the ones between Armenia and Azerbaijan and between India and Pakistan. Religious differences are another source of conflict between individuals, groups, nations, and states; the longstanding conflict in Ireland between Catholics and Protestants is one example of a conflict fueled by religious differences. Other conflicts are related to a desire by one nation or group to be free from the domination of another; many wars have been fought to break free from colonial rule, including the American Revolution against British rule and the Algerian Revolution against French rule.

When we have an understanding of the influence of the past on current situations we can communicate much more effectively with members of other cultures and prevent avoidable conflicts. Any time we can understand the perspective of another person, we are much more likely to be able to have a meaningful exchange with that person. Then we can identify common values and concerns to succeed in achieving results at minimum cost. We cannot expect to be successful in our business and social dealings with members of other cultures if we do not have an appreciation of their world views. Additionally, you may even find that study of other cultures will give you a better understanding of your own ideas and world view as one viewpoint among many.

Understanding the present

The greatest personal benefit you are likely to derive from the study of international relations, especially intercultural communication, is self-knowledge. Many individuals find that they gain a much better understanding of the grammar of their native language when they undertake the study of a foreign language. In a similar way, studying other cultures will lead people to better understand their own cultures. Often, we do not set out with the intention of learning about other cultures, but our life experiences give us the opportunity to do so. We might be assigned roommates or have co-workers who are from other cultures. Some individuals may even grow up in multicultural families with parents who come from two different cultures. Whatever our background, the exposure to other cultures is a great opportunity for personal growth in a global world.

Individuals can only truly become aware of their own culture and their own identity in comparison to that of other cultures when they set aside the notion that their culture is the norm and begin to see the values, beliefs, and rituals of their culture as one way of doing things — not the "right" or the "only" way. The more we learn about the deeper levels of other cultures the more clearly we can see the reasons for cultural differences that may not make sense to us at a superficial level. It is only by learning about other cultures via using "mindful" international relations and communication that we can develop a mature appreciation of our own culture and our relationship to it.

Life experience and socialization are certainly the most natural ways to learn about other cultures. For instance, one of the authors grew up in a multicultural family in Iran and came to the United States as a youth; his life is enriched by both cultures and also by his extensive travels around the world. His fluency in several languages has enhanced his ability to view the world from many different perspectives. The other author was raised in a traditional American family of European extraction; however, the great contrast between her Italian father's collective approach to family life and the rugged individualism of her mother's New England Yankee background led to many cultural clashes within the family that sparked her interest in studying communication across cultures. We all begin our study of culture from our unique individual perspectives. The only real prerequisite is the willingness to step beyond our belief that our culture's way is the "right" way. In other words, as we begin our study of intercultural and international communication, we need to adopt a "mindful" approach, which is a prerequisite for international studies, without holding to the cultural superiority of our own values.

As a professional (in the work force) or a student (not yet in the workforce), you should know that the business world today changes rapidly and knowledge of international and intercultural communication will be a great asset to you in your career; in fact, your success may depend upon it. Corporations face challenges related to marketing products globally, to developing international user interfaces, to managing culturally diverse employees, and to managing global virtual teams. There are many well-known examples of international marketing campaigns that went spectacularly wrong. When Frank Purdue, chicken entrepreneur, wanted to use his slogan, "It takes a tough man to make a tender chicken" for a Spanish-speaking market, it was translated as "It takes a virile man to make a chicken affectionate."[33] When introducing its Big John products in French Canada, Hunt-Wesson translated the name as "Gros Jos," before finding out that the phrase is a slang term for "big breasts."[34] While these errors may strike us as humorous, for the companies involved they are very serious indeed and can lead to loss of income and, in some cases, to loss of credibility for the product and the company.

Many high-technology products rely on user interfaces developed within the United States; however, in order for these products to be marketed and sold internationally, designers must develop interfaces that can be used by members of other cultures. There are a myriad of issues involved beyond a good translation that avoids the kind of unintentional meanings found in the advertising campaigns cited here. Designers must recognize differences related to visual language; to references to the physical world, particularly the use of metaphors; and to cultural values, norms, and taboos. For example, when the Macintosh computer used a drawing of a figure that was half cow and half dog — called a moof — as an icon in one of its programs there was a negative reaction from many followers of the Hindu religion, in which the cow is a sacred symbol.[35]

In the global marketplace, managers may find themselves managing employees from diverse cultural backgrounds. Traditionally, managers use "a home-country standard as a reference point when managing international activities."[36] When North American managers are sent to work at locations outside the United States, they must adapt their management styles to the culture within which they are working. The most common reason for the failure of international business ventures is not related to lack of professional or technical expertise, but to a lack of effective international and intercultural communication.[37] In recognition of this problem, many business schools in American universities as well as many corporations have developed formal training programs in multinational and multicultural business practices.[38]

Another challenge faced by managers in the global marketplace is the challenge of managing global virtual teams. Today many managers are charged with the task of leading a diverse group of individuals who are geographically remote and who conduct all their work through the use of collaborative technologies that allow them to share data and work on projects together without having any face-to-face meetings. In order to manage these new work groups, managers must not only understand the cultural values of their team members, but must know how to ensure effective communication and to manage conflict in a completely virtual environment. Although managers of global virtual teams need to have a great deal of knowledge and many diverse skills, one of their greatest needs is likely to be knowledge of international and intercultural communication.

Even in your personal life, you may have many encounters with members of other cultures via the internet and other communications technology that will be enhanced by your knowledge of intercultural communication. In the last two decades, rapid advances in computer technology and in the telecommunications industry have dramatically changed the way many people live their lives. Technological advances have dramatically increased individuals' opportunities to engage in international and intercultural communication. Email, internet chat rooms, instant messaging, and personal websites are all media that can be used by individuals to communicate with members of other cultures. E-commerce has made it possible for multinational companies, small domestic firms, and individual entrepreneurs to sell their goods and services via websites and for citizens around the world to shop electronically. The internet has also made it possible for researchers to share information quickly and easily. Distance education has been made possible by courseware like Webcourses, Blackboard, and ANGEL. Today students can take courses in universities that are halfway around the world from them without ever leaving their homes. In some instances, students can complete an entire degree program via distance education.

Use of the World Wide Web has grown dramatically during the past decade. It has made possible the linking of diverse regions around the globe that were once separated by geography, space, and time. However, increased opportunities for contact with members of other cultures does not ensure knowledge of effective methods of international and intercultural communication. The growth of the web and of other computer-mediated means of communication has greatly increased the need for intercultural and international communication. Without some background in intercultural and international communication, many people may find themselves experiencing the equivalent on a personal level of what companies unprepared for international business have experienced on the corporate level. As a result, individuals may find that their messages are misunderstood or, worse still, are perceived as offensive. Obviously, miscommunication can also occur in face-to-face communication encounters, but as we shall see in our discussion on non-verbal communication (Chapter 6) computer-mediated communication lacks many of the cues we typically rely on to convey meaning. Thus, intercultural communication knowledge and skills are useful at all levels of analysis, from global and regional levels to corporate, group, and even individual (or personal) levels of analysis.

Preparing for the future

As we work to address global issues, like pollution and epidemics, we all hope to create a future that will be free from many of the ills that plague society today. Knowledge of intercultural and international communication is crucial to our ability to address these issues. Addressing global challenges related to world health and the environment is crucial to our survival on the planet; they are simply too large to be addressed by any one nation or state alone. It is imperative that states, nations, and individual citizens work together to address these issues; in order to do so, people from around the world must be able to communicate with one another. To quote the former UN Secretary-General Kofi Annan speaking about the challenges that we face in the twentieth-first century:

> The idea that there is one people in possession of the truth, one answer to the world's ills, or one solution to humanity's needs has done untold harm throughout history — especially in the last century. Today, however, there is

a growing understanding that human diversity is both the reality that makes dialogue necessary and the basis for that dialogue.

We understand, as never before, that each of us is fully worthy of the respect and dignity essential to our common humanity. We recognize that we are the products of many cultures, traditions, and memories; that mutual respect allows us to study and learn from other cultures; and that we gain strength by combining the foreign with the familiar.[39]

We cannot use our combined strength to address global issues unless we have the ability to communicate effectively. We face many challenges, including these key international, and increasingly global, issues: overpopulation, world hunger, depletion of natural resources, global warming, world health issues, and terrorism.

The world population is now at 6.5 billion and growing. An increasing world population creates problems related to the environment and to world hunger. As the world population increases so too does the consumption of natural resources. These resources are being used much more rapidly than the rate at which they can be replaced. It currently takes 14.4 months to replenish the resources that we use in 12 months.[40] In *Eco-Economy*, Lester R. Brown of the Earth Policy Institute points to this problem, "Evidence of the intensifying conflict between the economy and the ecosystem of which it is a part can be seen not only in the dust bowl emerging in China, but also in the burning rain forests in Indonesia, the collapsing cod fishery in the North Sea, falling crop yields in Africa, the expanding dead zone in the Gulf of Mexico, and falling water tables in India."[41] In addition to depleting natural resources, our consumption of energy, particularly in the form of fossil fuels, is causing air pollution and worsening global warming. Global warming in turn can cause many additional problems like rising sea levels, droughts, and other disruptions of the climate.[42]

We also face serious problems in the area of world health. Many LDCs lack the access to basic healthcare that is available to individuals in developed countries (DCs). According to the World Health Organization, in the year 2000 an estimated 2.4 billion people had no access to basic sanitation and 1.1 billion lacked access to a safe water supply.[43]

Of course, the AIDS epidemic is the single greatest challenge in terms of global health. The rising number of deaths caused by AIDS "marks a tragic new development in world demography"[44] and the implications of the AIDS epidemic go beyond the staggering death toll of approximately 14 million. In Botswana, for example, life expectancy fell from 61 years in 1990 to 44 years in 1999. In addition to lowering the life expectancy in many nations, HIV/AIDS also reduces fertility and creates a large number of orphans — an estimated 7.8 million in Africa as of 1997.[45] The devastation of the AIDS epidemic in developing countries is staggering and is undoing much of what was accomplished there in the last decade.

Another kind of devastation is inflicted by the violent actions of terrorists. Since the September 11 terrorist attacks on the World Trade Center in New

York City and the Pentagon in Washington, and the more recent bombings in Madrid and London, we are all aware of the need for increased security to protect citizens — a tenet of hard power. Beyond the use of the military in countering terrorism, however, we need to seek non-violent methods of ensuring safety and preventing terrorist actions if we wish to avoid escalating violence around the world. The causes of global terrorism are not simplistic, but very complex. Similarly, the means of preventing such actions are also likely to involve many considerations and require a great deal of cooperation among nations. All of the global challenges that we face in the twentieth-first century have one common thread running through them — they are issues that cannot be addressed without cooperation among culturally diverse peoples. That cooperation will require an understanding of political and economic issues and the ability to communicate effectively with members of other cultures.

How Do We Study Intercultural Communication?

As a subfield of international relations (that some call international studies), intercultural and international communication is inherently interdisciplinary, although some consider it only a part of the field of communication. The intercultural field developed in the period following World War II when the US government suddenly reoriented its foreign policy posture from "international isolationism" to "global engagement." Soon, Washington created the Foreign Service Institute to train diplomats who were being sent abroad. The Institute brought together linguists, anthropologists, and psychologists to develop the training programs, and naturally these scholars drew upon their respective disciplines in their work on intercultural communication.

The influence of these three disciplines is still evident in the classical research techniques used today. The field of linguistics contributed an understanding of the relationship between language and other cultural systems; anthropology contributed the recognition of cultural patterns and realization of the importance of non-verbal communication; and psychology contributed the role of human cognition in understanding and categorizing the patterns of behavior of cultures. Nevertheless, the contributions of anthropology, linguistics, and psychology do not dominate the entire field of intercultural and international communication, which is also enriched by the works of political science and international studies. In fact, the largest global academic and professional association of international relations, the International Studies Association (ISA), relatively recently designated international communication as one of its major subfields and organizational sections (see http://icomm.igloogroups.org). This book is a new effort to reorganize the literature of international communication in order to illustrate the significant recent contributions of the scholars of international relations and/or studies.

All intercultural and international communication scholarship can be divided into two broad categories: etic scholarship, that is scholarship based on a researcher-imposed structure and **emic** scholarship, that is scholarship based on understanding a given culture from the perspective of members of that culture. Both approaches have validity. Often, etic scholarship is quantitative in nature; it involves gathering data, particularly data based on comparisons of cultures with respect to some quality or predetermined category developed by the researchers. In contrast, emic scholarship is typically more interested in gathering qualitative information, which is often presented in the form of ethnographies and other narratives. There are four primary approaches to the study of intercultural communication; they are the social science approach, the critical approach, the interpretive approach, and the dialectical approach.

The **social science approach** is based on the assumptions that human behavior is predictable and that there is a describable external reality. Many international relations and/or studies scholars using the social science approach seek to describe and predict human behavior, and they tend to rely on quantitative methods, although not exclusively. While the quantitative methods became popular in the 1960s, there is a resurgence of emphasis on fine qualitative work in social sciences in recent years. The **interpretive approach** is based on the premise that human beings construct their reality and that communication is a subjective experience. Scholars using the interpretive approach are interested in describing human behavior, which they believe to be unpredictable and creative; they believe that culture is both created and perpetuated through the means of communication. The interpretive approach uses qualitative research methods that include field studies, ethnographies, observations, and participant observations. Researchers using the **critical approach** are particularly interested in the historical context of communication and in understanding the role that power and power relationships play in communication. The critical approach focuses on subjective reality and on the importance of studying the context in which communication occurs.

The **dialectical approach**, developed by Martin, Nakayama, and Flores, stresses the processual, relational, and contradictory nature of intercultural communication.[46] There are six dialectics: cultural–individual, personal–contextual, differences–similarities, static–dynamic, history/past–present/future, and privilege–disadvantage. These dialectics are related to the four building blocks of intercultural communication: culture, communication, context, and power. The dialectical approach brings together the strengths of the social science, critical, and interpretive approaches and makes it possible to study the many contradictory aspects of intercultural communication. While not a specific theory in the way that the other approaches are, the dialectical approach is a perspective from which to study intercultural communication encounters. Regardless of the approach we take to the study of intercultural communication, it is important that we do so with mindfulness.

The Role of Mindfulness in Intercultural Communication

Various definitions of the concept of mindfulness can be found in East and South Asian religion and philosophy. In this textbook we will use the definition of mindfulness posited by Ellen Langer. In *Mindfulness*, Langer defines mindfulness as a state of mind in which a person is open to new information, is continually creating new categories, and is open to new perspectives. A mindful individual is focused on the process rather than the outcome in any interaction.[47]

A mindful approach to the study of intercultural and international communication means that we will approach information about other cultures with an open mind and that we will break free of stereotypical categorizations of members of cultures that are different from our own. In turn, we overcome our own ethnocentrism to create a more understanding and peaceful world. We will also strive to see the world from the perspectives of other cultures. This approach can go a long way toward decreasing and even preventing unintentional conflict. As Langer states:

> The consequences of trying out different perspectives are important. First we gain more choice in how to respond. A single-minded label produces an automatic reaction, which reduces our options.[48]

This is also a major concern in the decision-making process of the fields of international relations and political science. Moreover, to understand that other people may not be so different allows us empathy and enlarges our range of responses. We are less likely to feel locked into a polarized struggle. The importance of mindfulness in intercultural and international communication has been thoroughly discussed by Stella Ting-Toomey. In *Communicating Across Cultures*, she talks about the benefits of being a mindful intercultural communicator, which include creating a feeling of "being understood, supported, and respected" in the individual(s) with whom you are communicating.[49] Ting-Toomey's work emphasizes the need to go beyond our preconceived notions, to strive to gain knowledge about other cultures, and to acquire skills for effective communication and conflict resolution.[50]

In this work, we use Langer's definition of mindfulness and Ting-Toomey's description of the mindful intercultural communicator. We define mindful intercultural and international communication as interactions with members of other cultures in which an individual strives to understand the cultural values, beliefs, and norms of other parties and to use that understanding to adapt his/her communication style to achieve a meaningful exchange and a win-win result. In other words, rather than use one's own preferred style of communication, a mindful intercultural and international communicator will adapt to the style of the other individual, group, or nation involved in the

Figure 1.3 Respect for differences is an important component of mindful intercultural communication. Additionally, it is important to maintain an open mind and strive to see the world from the different perspectives of other cultures. Such an approach to communication can go a long way toward reducing misunderstandings and preventing conflict.

communication encounter. For example, if a US student is communicating with an international student from Japan, rather than begin a conversation abruptly, a common practice in the United States, he/she will begin with a formal greeting, since that would be the way the Japanese student would be used to starting a conversation.

Mindfulness is primarily a question of *awareness*. This is not necessarily a new discovery. Nowadays in contemporary political science literature, it is very fashionable to advocate political "awareness" as a starting point for any political action and solution. If we are aware of the need to be sensitive to and respectful of differences among cultures we will be more likely to carry out the necessary steps to gain the knowledge required to communicate mindfully. Individuals with no knowledge of other cultures but with an awareness of the importance of intercultural communication can begin their journey to becoming mindful intercultural and international communicators with this book. We are sure that the journey will be both personally and professionally enriching and will be good preparation for the challenges of global citizenship in the twenty-first century.

An Overview of This Book

Throughout this book we will emphasize the importance of taking a mindful approach to the study of intercultural and international communication. We also have chosen to approach the study of intercultural communication from the perspective of the field of international relations (also called international studies), that is, we focus on issues of soft power and conflict/cooperation throughout the book. We will also examine the role of the citizen diplomat, a new concept from international relations, in our global community. We believe that an understanding of these key issues in international relations will enrich our study of communication across cultures and will provide useful insights to help us address the many challenges of global citizenship in the twenty-first century.

This book has 10 chapters and following this chapter we begin with an overview of the core concepts of intercultural and international communication in Chapter 2. Then in Part II, the next two chapters are devoted to approaches to the study of intercultural and international communication: Chapter 3, "Social Science and Interpretive Approaches" and Chapter 4, "Critical and Dialectical Approaches."

In Part IV, the next four chapters focus on intercultural and international communication process and technologies. Chapter 5 discusses verbal communication and examines linguistic differences, translation, multilingualism, and the language of conflict management. Chapter 6 focuses on non-verbal communication and the influence of cultural values on body language, gestures, and the conception and use of space and time. Chapter 7 covers the role of visual communication in intercultural communication and examines how culture influences perception and the use of graphic images. Chapter 8 discusses the effect of mass communication on intercultural and international communication with particular attention to the relationship between media and power and the global impact of US popular culture.

In Part IV, the last two chapters focus on issues in intercultural and international communication. Chapter 9 examines ethical issues as they relate to culture. We discuss ethnocentrism, ethical issues and power, and the dialogical approach to studying ethics. Finally, Chapter 10 concludes by discussing the role of international relations and intercultural communication in shaping the future of our world. Specifically, we give a call to action for the engagement of citizen diplomats and other mindful intercultural communicators to play their parts in addressing global concerns. We take a look at significant contemporary international relations issues and challenges, such as the politics of war and peace, with particular attention to concerns about terrorism, the global economy, and sustainable development.

This book aims to provide a fresh outlook about intercultural communication from the perspective of international relations. It is prepared as a readable research manuscript for general public consumption. Beyond scholars and academics, our target audiences are the professionals in the business, government, and non-profit communities, especially those who already have a basic knowledge of international relations. For professionals who choose this work for classroom or workshop purposes, we have also prepared a companion website that includes extensive supplementary materials in order to make the concepts, theories, and methods presented easier to comprehend and use. Each supplementary chapter section includes questions for discussion and exploration to guide your reflection on the material presented. We suggest writing and research assignments to use for further exploration of the topics discussed. Finally, each chapter includes a case study for you to analyze in light of the concepts, theories, and guidelines presented. Your development as an intercultural and international communicator is an exciting journey, and we wish you well as you begin it.

References

1. "KFC and McDonalds — A Model of Blended Culture," *China Daily*, www.chinadaily.com.cn/english/doc/2004-06/01/content_335488.htm, posted June 1, 2004, accessed September 5, 2005.
2. John H. Brown, "Is the U.S. High Noon Over? Reflections on the Declining Global Influence of American Popular Culture," *English* 7(February 2004), http://eng.1september.ru/2004/07/3.htm, accessed November 7, 2010.
3. Brigitte Pellerin, "Can Pop-Cultural Imperialism Be Stopped?," Global Envision, www.globalenvision.org/library/33/775, posted July 6, 2005, accessed November 7, 2010.
4. Chibuzo Odigwe, 3rd year medical student, University of Calabar, Nigeria, "Smoking in Nigeria: Is it Time for a Rethink?" *Student BMJ* 11(August 2003), http://archive.student.bmj.com/issues/03/08/life/294.php, accessed November 8, 2010.
5. Max Borders, "Zapatistas: Rebels with a Confused Cause," Global Envision, www.globalenvision.org/library/3/721, posted January 26, 2005, accessed November 7, 2010.
6. Eric Pfanner, "On Advertising: Anti-U.S. Ads Break Taboo Over Politics," *International Herald Tribune*, www.nytimes.com/2004/01/19/business/worldbusiness/19iht-ad19_ed3_.html, posted January 19, 2004, accessed December 22, 2010.
7. Peruvian writer Mario Vargas Llosa in Joseph Nye, "Globalization is not Americanization," *Taipei Times*, October 22, 2004, 9, www.taipeitimes.com/News/editorials/archives/2004/10/22/2003207970/1, accessed November 7, 2010.
8. Anne E. Kornblut, "Red or Blue—Which Are You?" *Slate*, www.slate.com/id/2103764, updated July 14, 2004, accessed September 5, 2005.
9. Paolo Gerani, Creative Director of Iceberg and Executive Vice President of Gruppo Gilmar quoted in Allessandri Ilari, "'Made in Italy' Looks to 'Made in China,'" *Women's Wear Daily*, February 19, 2004, 12–13, www.wwd.com/wwd-publications/pdf/wwd-2004-02-19.pdf?id=696873, accessed November 7, 2010.
10. U.S. Census Bureau, 2004, "U.S. Interim Projections by Age, Sex, Race, and Hispanic Origin: 2000–2050," www.census.gov/ipc/www/usinterimproj, posted March 18, 2004, accessed September 5, 2005.
11. Joseph Nye, Harvard University in Scott Galupo, quoted in "U.S. Pop Culture Seen as Plague; Damage, Influence May Be Exaggerated," *The Washington Times*, www.washingtontimes.com/news/2004/dec/30/20041230-114327-7178r/?page=5, posted December 30, 2004, accessed November 7, 2010.
12. Chareles Paul Fruend, Senior Editor of Reason Magazine in Scott Galupo, quoted in "U.S. Pop Culture Seen as Plague; Damage, Influence May Be Exaggerated," *The Washington Times*, www.washingtontimes.com/news/2004/dec/30/20041230-114327-7178r/?page=7, posted December 30, 2004, accessed November 7, 2010.
13. Richard Pells, "American Culture Goes Global, or Does It?" *The Chronicle of Higher Education*, April 12, 2002, http://202973-web3.chronicle.com/article/American-Culture-Goes-Global/23671, accessed September 5, 2005.
14. UPI News Service, "Donald Trump Planning Chinese Version of the 'Apprentice,'" Reality TV World, www.realitytvworld.com/news/donald-trump-planning-chinese-version-of-the-apprentice-1004320.php, posted August 22, 2005, accessed November 7, 2010.
15. *The Surreal Life* Season 5, VH1, www.vh1.com/shows/dyn/the_surreal_life_5/series_about.jhtml, accessed September 5, 2005.
16. Elspeth Cameron, ed., *Multiculturalism and Immigration in Canada: An Introductory Reader* (Toronto, ON: Canadian Scholars' Press, 2004), p. 79.
17. John Henningham, ed., *Institutions in Australian Society* (Oxford: Oxford University Press, 1995), p. 263.

18. Stephen W. Littlejohn, *Theories of Human Communication*, 7th ed. (Belmont, CA: Wadsworth/Thomson Learning, 2002).
19. Ibid.
20. World Tourism Organization, *UNWTO World Tourism Barometer: Interim Update, April 2010*, www.unwto.org/facts/eng/pdf/barometer/UNWTO_Barom10_update_april_en_excerpt.pdf, accessed November 7, 2010.
21. Thomas L. Friedman, *The Lexus and the Olive Tree* (New York: Anchor Books, 2000), p. 141.
22. Sirkka L. Jarvenpaa and Dorothy E. Leidner, "Communication and Trust in Global Virtual Teams," *Organization Science* 10 (1999), 791.
23. World Commission on Environment and Development (WCED), *Our Common Future* (Oxford: Oxford University Press, 1987), p. 43.
24. International Institute for Sustainable Development (IISD), www.iisd.org/about/faq.asp, accessed September 2, 2005.
25. Sister Cities International, www.sister-cities.org/about/faqs.cfm, accessed September 7, 2005.
26. U.S. Census Bureau, March 18, 2004.
27. Ibid.
28. Ibid.
29. Benjamin R. Barber, *Jihad vs McWorld* (New York: Ballantine Books, 1996), p. 57.
30. Friedman, p. 113.
31. Carol Schneider, President of Association of American Colleges and Universities (AACU), "Presidents' Campaign for the Advancement of Liberal Learning," *Journal of the National Collegiate Honors Council*, 2002, 33, http://digitalcommons.unl.edu/cgi/viewcontent.cgi?article=1096&context=nchcjournal, accessed August 31, 2005.
32. Schneider, p. 34.
33. Gary P. Ferraro, *The Cultural Dimension of International Business*, 4th ed. (Upper Saddle River, NJ: Prentice Hall, 2002), p. 8.
34. Lingo Systems, *The Guide to Translation and Localization* (Portland, OR: Lingo Systems, 2000), p. 5.
35. Tony Fernandes, *Global Interface Design* (Chestnut Hill, MA: AP Professional, 1995), p. 113.
36. Ben L. Kedia and Ananda Mukherji, "Global Managers," in David C. Thomas, ed., *Readings and Cases in International Management: A Cross-Cultural Perspective* (Thousand Oaks, CA: Sage, 2003), p. 9.
37. Ferraro, p. 7.
38. Mary O'Hara-Devereaux and Robert Johansen, *Global Work: Bridging Distance, Culture, and Time* (San Francisco, CA: Jossey-Bass, 1994), pp. 118–19.
39. Kofi A. Annan, "Strategies for World Peace: The View of the UN Secretary-General," *The Futurist*, May/June 2002, 18–21.
40. Jeffrey Kluger and Andrea Dorfman, "The Challenges We Face," *Time*, www.time.com/time/2002/greencentury/enopener.html, posted August 18, 2002, accessed November 7, 2010.
41. Lester R. Brown, *Eco-Economy* (New York: W. W. Norton & Company, 2001), p. 50.
42. Kluger and Dorfman, 2002.
43. World Health Organization, "Flagging Global Sanitation Target Threatens Other Millennium Development Goals," *WHO Bulletin*, 82 (2004), 160–238.
44. Lester R. Brown and Brian Halweil, "Breaking Out or Breaking Down," *World Watch*, September/October 1999, 20–9.
45. Ibid.
46. Judith N. Martin, Thomas K. Nakayama and Lisa A. Flores, "A Dialectical Approach to Intercultural Communication," in Judith N. Martin, Thomas K. Nakayama, and Lisa A. Flores, eds., *Readings in Intercultural Communication*, 2nd ed. (Boston, MA: McGraw-Hill, 2002), pp. 3–13.
47. Ellen J. Langer, *Mindfulness* (Reading, MA: Addison-Wesley, 1989), pp. 61–79.
48. Langer, p. 71.
49. Stella Ting-Toomey, *Communicating Across Cultures* (New York: The Guilford Press, 1999), pp. 46–54.
50. Ibid., pp. 50–4.

Core Concepts of Intercultural Communication in a Global Community

2

Three students in a business communication course at a large metropolitan university are teamed by their professor to work together on a research project. Miguel is a sophomore student who is from El Salvador; Charlie is a Chinese-American junior from New York City; and Yemi is a junior student from Nigeria. The students are given a deadline for the project by their professor. Together they select a topic, divide up the workload, and schedule several meetings to work on the project throughout the semester, with one big meeting at the end of the term to compile their individual work into the final project. In the final meeting, the students end up working all night putting the project together. They do not get a very good grade on the project. Their professor says that the main reason for the low grade is the lack of cohesiveness of the project; it reads like three separate documents rather than an integrated whole. Individually, the three students earn good grades in all their classes, and so they are all frustrated by the group experience, particularly by the low grade. Each student has a different perspective on why the project did not turn out well and failed to earn them a good grade.

Miguel is a very creative person and does not like the fact that Charlie became the self-appointed leader of the group. He felt that his ideas were not given enough consideration when they initially discussed the project topic and that the project would have been more successful if the three of them had been more collective in their approach and had worked together rather than doing all the work separately and then just trying to paste it together at the end. Miguel feels that the group lacked a collaborative spirit and that Charlie acted like his boss at work, constantly noting the fact that he was a few minutes late for meetings and other unimportant points. Miguel is disappointed that the three of them did not spend more time getting to know one another. He liked Yemi's sense of humor, and got irritated when Charlie interrupted Yemi's stories about Nigeria to bring them back to the topic at hand. He was also disappointed that Yemi did not do as much research as he and Charlie did, but he still likes Yemi, whereas he is angry with Charlie.

Charlie has never liked working in teams, although he knows he will have to do so in his career in the business world. He believes that the only way to get a good grade on a group project is for one person to take control and do most of the work. He feels that discussing ideas at length is a waste of time, because he is not genuinely interested in the teammates' ideas and secretly wants to champion his own ideas. He has a busy schedule and resents it when other people show up late for meetings or waste time in meetings talking about irrelevant topics. He respects Miguel for doing his fair share of the work, but is constantly annoyed by his showing up late. He is disappointed that Yemi did not do as much work as he and Miguel did.

Yemi takes great pride in being Nigerian and was very insulted when Charlie initially perceived him as an African American. He is further insulted when Charlie repeatedly makes it clear that he has no interest in hearing Yemi's stories about his life in Nigeria. Yemi, like Miguel, resents Charlie's taking the lead on the team and acting as though he is the boss of his teammates. Yemi has difficulty making himself work on the project because he has such negative feelings about his relationship with Charlie. He likes Miguel, who laughs at his jokes, but does not like the fact that Miguel seems to go along with Charlie's ideas for the project. Yemi misses a feeling of camaraderie with his teammates; he does his best to establish it by telling stories and using humor, but he feels that his attempts are not being valued by the other students, and, finally, in frustration he gives up on the project. He does a minimal amount of work, because his heart is not in the project at all.

Although some of the problems the students experienced working on this group project could occur among a group of students who are all members of the same culture, many of the problems that Miguel, Charlie, and Yemi experienced are directly related to cultural differences. When individuals have different cultural values, they are likely to experience challenges when communicating with one another. The more you know about different cultures, the better prepared you will be to communicate with members of cultures that are different from your own.

Defining "Culture" Today

Culture is a complex term and one that is difficult to define. Literally hundreds of definitions of culture have been created by theorists in different disciplines. Despite the disparity in definitions of culture, most of them do agree on certain key characteristics of culture. These characteristics are that culture is learned, that it involves the shared perceptions and values of large groups of people, that culture is expressed as behavior, and that it is dynamic and adaptive. One useful definition that encompasses all these aspects of culture is L. Robert Kohls' definition from *Survival Kit for Living Overseas*: "Culture is an integrated system of learned behavior patterns that are characteristic of the members of any given society. Culture refers to the total way of life of particular groups of people. It includes everything that a group of people thinks, says, does, and makes — its customs, language, material artifacts, and shared systems of attitudes and feelings. Culture is learned and transmitted from generation to generation."[1]

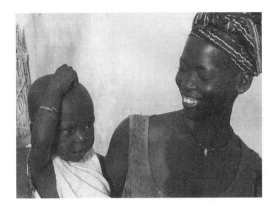

Figure 2.1 This baby will learn the Nigerian culture from his parents, his extended family, and his community. We should bear in mind that culture is learned and that when a baby is born it is not genetically programmed for a particular culture. Children learn their culture unconsciously rather than as a set of rules. Most children learn their culture as the way the world is and the way people should behave.

Culture is learned

When babies are born they are equally open to learning any culture; they are not genetically programmed for a particular culture. A baby born in Sweden of two Swedish parents learns the Swedish culture as she grows up; if that same baby were taken to Greece immediately after being born to be raised by Greek foster parents, she would learn the Greek culture. Most children learn their culture from their immediate and extended families and from the larger community around them. Children learn their culture in the same way that they learn their native language — naturally and unconsciously. They don't need to study books on the language or listen to tapes in a language lab — because they learn their language as part of their daily interaction with their families and communities. The same type of learning is true for culture. Children learn that there are times when it is inappropriate to smile, to speak, or to laugh. They learn that it is acceptable to interact in some ways and that other behaviors are taboo. In some cultures children learn to show respect by casting their eyes down when addressing an elder; children in other cultures are taught that in order to be seen as honest and forthright they must look people directly in the eyes when communicating with them.

However, because children learn their culture so unconsciously, they do not learn it as a set of rules that could easily be exchanged for another set of rules in another culture. More often children learn their culture as the way the world is and perceive that the way individuals in their culture behave is the one correct way to behave. This is where ethnocentrism may lead to misunderstanding and conflict. In fact, anthropologist Edward T. Hall has said that "[c]ulture hides much more than it reveals, and strangely enough what it hides, it hides most effectively from its own participants."[2] He states that culture controls our lives to a great extent precisely because it is so unconscious. In order to become mindful intercultural communicators as adults, it is necessary that we go beyond our initial perceptions of our own culture — whichever culture that may be — as the one right way of being in the world. For example, we need to realize that just because our culture believes that making eye contact is a sign of honesty, it does not mean that someone from another culture who does not make eye contact with us must therefore be dishonest. Just as Western scholarship has dominated the IR field, so have superficial values attributed to "Western" culture. Ideas of colonization and power politics are ingrained in these frameworks and may be unconsciously reflected in our own conceptions of intercultural relations. Thus, to avoid unwanted conflicts, one must be mindful.

Culture is the shared perceptions and values of the group

A given culture is a set of perceptions that is shared by a group of people. These perceptions are cultural patterns of beliefs, values, and social norms. Cultural patterns have to do with a shared understanding of what the world is like, what kinds of behavior are appropriate, and what is defined as good or bad. Often, we speak of a national culture, and many cultures are characterized in relation to nations — such as the Japanese culture, the German culture, and the Korean culture. However, a culture does not necessarily have to be a group of people who share the same national boundaries, government, and laws. This reflects the idea of transnational representation in the IR field. Further, many nations are multicultural, having numerous cultural groups living within their borders, as indicated in the previous chapter. Moreover, some states are nation-states (mainly consisting of one nation), while others are multi-national states (entailing more than one nation).

We may also hear people refer to co-cultural groups. These are groups of people who live within a dominant culture in a society, but who also have membership in a group which does not share all the beliefs and perceptions of that society. The deaf community in America would be an example of a co-cultural group; they are part of American society, but they have a unique set of perceptions that differ from dominant American culture.

Culture is expressed as behavior

An individual's cultural beliefs and values are often expressed in his behavior, which political scientists have aimed to explain with little success. The cultural patterns that we learn when we grow up in a given culture lead us to adopt certain methods of expressing ourselves in society. Our verbal and non-verbal communication behaviors are dictated in a large part by our cultural conditioning. In IR, ideology is most effective when it is invisible, or when ideas become so deeply internalized that people consider them "common sense" or natural. Similarly, the way we interpret and use visual signs and symbols, as well as the way we use communication technology, are a result of our cultural background.

Japanese students sit quietly in class and listen dutifully to everything that their teachers say without question. Their behavior is a result of cultural conditioning that teaches them to show respect by silence and that it is important to defer to their teachers' authority. Students in the United States often ask questions of their teachers and feel free to disagree with them, and American students are vocal and lively in class. Their behavior is a result of different beliefs about the appropriate student–teacher relationship and the value placed on inquiry and independent thought in the United States. In IR, a major criticism against the realist school is that realism fails to consider the different sets of beliefs, ideologies, and collective cultural identities that prompt sovereign states to behave the way that they do. The supporters of the realist school tend to ignore the fact that the rationality assigned as the reason behind states' actions depends on the cultural context.

Culture is dynamic and adaptive

Human society has evolved over time from the earliest hunter-gatherer groupings of primitive peoples. As society continues to evolve, so will the cultures of the world. Cultures may change as a result of exposure to new ideas from outside, contact and conflict with other cultures, technological innovations and scientific progress, and internal variables and conflicts. Superficial levels of culture, such as the adoption of new fashions, cuisine, architecture, or technologies are more easily changed; the deep structure of a culture, such as the value placed on the past and ancestors, moral values, and religious beliefs is much more resistant to change.

As technological innovations are developed, cultures will adapt to them and integrate them into their lives. With the proliferation of email and the internet, a set of guidelines for behavior online, referred to as netiquette, has been developed. Diverse cultures have different ways of adapting to and using new technologies.

High and low culture

In many Western societies, a distinction has been made between high culture and low culture. High culture refers to activities enjoyed by affluent members of society, such as ballet, opera, classical music, fine art, live theatre, and classic works of literature. These activities are believed to be appreciated only by the elite members of society, who are highly educated. The consumption of high culture serves to set the elite above the masses, who enjoy low culture. Traditionally, high culture is considered to have a value that transcends time and place; cultural artifacts like Beethoven's symphonies, Picasso's paintings, and Shakespeare's plays have a lasting value that can speak to people in any time period and any culture. These works are preserved in museums and libraries and are studied in colleges and universities.

Low culture, on the other hand, tends to be more ephemeral and relevant only to a particular society in a particular place and time. Low culture refers to those activities enjoyed by the masses, such as television talk shows, soap operas, game shows, and video games. These activities are believed to appeal to the less educated and affluent members of society. However, distinctions between high and low culture are much less sharply demarcated in modern Western societies. Beginning in the 1960s, many societal changes led to a breakdown in the distinction between high and low culture.

The original categorization of high and low culture in Western societies grew out of the European tradition, wherein aristocrats distinguished themselves from the masses by enjoying more rarified forms of entertainment not available to the less wealthy and educated "common person." They did so, at least in part, as a way to establish themselves as socially superior. Furthermore, because of their positions of wealth and privilege, they were able to influence the categorization of some activities as "superior" to others.

Today, sharp distinctions do not exist between consumers of high and low culture. One reason for this change is technological developments that have led to the explosion of new entertainment media. Another reason is that social changes have led to the weakening of institutionalized cultural authority.[3] Universities and colleges traditionally served to perpetuate the privileging of high culture, but today they recognize the value of low culture, now referred to as popular culture. Although some elitism still exists in the academic world, there has been a movement away from an elitism based on European culture; universities have developed programs to study previously marginalized groups and to study popular culture (see Chapter 8).

National cultures

Often when we talk about culture, we seem to be using the term *culture* synonymously with the term *nation*. When we speak about Nigerian culture, we are usually referring to those individuals who are citizens of the nation of Nigeria. However, the terms *culture* and *nation* are not equivalent in meaning. It might be more accurate to speak of majority cultures (see Chapter 4 for a fuller discussion of majority and minority cultures); typically the majority of the people living in one nation are members of the same cultural group. The majority of the people living in Venezuela are Venezuelans; however, Venezuela is a multicultural nation with many citizens of Spanish, Italian, Portuguese, Arab, and German descent. The United States is certainly a good example of the distinction between the terms *culture* and *nation*; the US is a single nation, but it is inhabited by citizens who represent a large number of cultural groups. Of course, one reason for the great cultural diversity of the US is the fact that it is an immigrant nation. However, most nations are composed of more than one cultural group, including those nations, like Japan, that are typically considered to have a homogeneous population. Even in Japan there are citizens who are of Okinawan, Korean, and Chinese descent.

Therefore, when we speak of a nation we are referring to a group of people as a political entity. A nation is a group of people with common characteristics who want to be independent; they are a politically organized body of people who are under one government. Their behavior is regulated by a system of laws that govern the election of leaders, economic activity, their military, and their system of justice. In the field of political science, a more precise term would be *nation-state*, which is a state (as defined in Chapter 1, p. 8) that mainly consists of one nation (as defined in Chapter 1, p. 7). A nation-state is a political unit with a territory that has boundaries that are internationally recognized, and has its own government that answers to no higher authority. A nation-state has sovereignty over its territory, that is, it has the right to make and enforce laws, collect taxes, regulate trade, and create social institutions. The sovereignty of a nation-state is recognized by other states through diplomatic relations and by membership of international bodies like the United Nations.[4] Frequently, the majority of the people in a given nation-state are all members of the same cultural group. However, nation-states are not defined solely in terms of cultural homogeneity. Further, some cultural groups are without a nation-state to call their own, like the Kurds. When cultural groups do not have a homeland, their efforts to create one may be a source of conflict. Kurdish nationalists have sought to carve a Kurdish state out of part of Turkey, Iraq, Iran, and Syria. However, these states refuse to voluntarily surrender any territory, and as a result Kurdish guerilla armies have fought Iraqi, Iranian, and Turkish military forces. Thus, the Kurds are a nation without a state, while the Turks are a nation with a state — the Republic of Turkey.

Race and ethnicity

Like national identity, racial and ethnic identities are complex categorizations. We need to examine notions of race and ethnicity in detail and to clarify their meaning.

Race

Historically, racial categorization has been used to meet many social and political ends. The term *race* is commonly used to categorize people based on physical characteristics such as skin color and eye shape. However, the notion that there is a biological basis for making distinctions among racial groups is no longer considered valid by most scientists. In fact, the American Anthropological Association has stated that the US government should stop using the term *race* when collecting federal data since the term has no scientific validity. There are many reasons why using a biological basis for classifying racial groups is not valid. Racial categories are not consistent from one nation to another, and even within the United States they have varied greatly over time. While the US makes distinctions between white and black races, in some nations, like Brazil, there are a wide range of racial categories in between black and white. Further, an examination of the categories used in the US Census since its inception in 1790 reveals the changing nature of conceptions of race. The seventh US Federal Census conducted in 1850 asked for "color" and gave three choices: white, black, and mulatto. By the tenth Federal Census conducted in 1880, the categories had expanded to include five choices: white, black, mulatto, Chinese, and Indian.[5] The twenty-second Federal Census conducted in 2000 asked two questions regarding race/ancestry and acknowledged that "the race categories include both racial and national-origin groups":[6]

1. Is the person Spanish/Hispanic/Latino?
   - No, not Spanish/Hispanic/Latino
   - Yes, Mexican, Mexican American, Chicano
   - Yes, Puerto Rican
   - Yes, Cuban
   - Yes, other Spanish/Hispanic/Latino (write in group)

2. What is the person's race?
   - White
   - Black, African American, Negro
   - American Indian or Alaska Native (write in tribe)
   - Asian Indian
   - Chinese
   - Filipino
   - Japanese
   - Korean
   - Vietnamese
   - Native Hawaiian
   - Guamanian or Chamorro
   - Samoan
   - Other Pacific Islander (write in race)
   - Other race (write in race)[7]

Racial categorization, rather than being a matter of biology, is primarily a social and political construction. Often, racial distinctions are used to justify and to enforce social and economic disparities among people. For example, during the peak years of immigration into the United States, many non-Anglo-Saxon cultural groups (notably Irish, Greeks, Italians, and Jews) were categorized as racial "mongrels" and were labeled as non-white. During this period, America was dominated by Anglo-Saxon Protestants who wanted to remain in control and avoid being "overrun" by the immigrants; one way for them to maintain control and superiority was by categorizing the newcomers as a subordinate group. In "The Illogic of American Racial Categories," Paul R. Spickard explains that "[f]rom the point of view of the dominant group, racial distinctions are a necessary tool of dominance. They serve to separate the subordinate people as 'Other.'"[8] As more immigrants came to the US and the Anglo-Saxons feared that they would no longer be a majority, the definition of "white" was changed to include immigrants of European descent.

Generally, individuals in power determine racial categorizations in order to maintain or expand their power. If races are seen as distinct types, those in power can also enforce the notion of the superiority of one racial group over another. Europeans arranged the peoples of the world in a hierarchical structure based on race, putting Caucasians at the top.[9] Historically, these racial distinctions have been used to justify discrimination, segregation, and oppression. Such uses of racial distinctions can also create many communication challenges between individuals in the groups that have been so categorized, as in the case of racism in the United States.

MEDIA IMPACT
Model Minority Image is Harmful to Asian Americans

Communication scholars have frequently called attention to stereotypical depictions of co-cultural groups in the media. Usually, these stereotypes portray members of minority groups very negatively. However, even a stereotype that idealizes the positive qualities of a co-cultural group can have a harmful impact. Paek and Shah conducted a quantitative analysis of the depictions of Asian Americans in U.S. magazine advertising. They found that Asian Americans are frequently portrayed as affluent, well educated, and proficient with technology. This "model minority image" presents Asian Americans as having a "superior work ethic, high levels of educational achievement, and a highly refined business and economic sensibility." At first, such a representation may seem to be favorable. However, Paek and Shah explain how such "positive" stereotyping can be just as harmful as negative depictions.

Depictions of co-cultural groups in the media have the power to create and perpetuate racial characterizations within a society. Such characterizations serve the majority culture by maintaining the existing social hierarchy with the dominant culture at the top. In most cases, the depictions used to maintain the status quo portray members of co-cultural groups as inferior to the dominant culture in some way.

So how can positive depictions be harmful? One reason the model minority image is harmful is that it presents an inaccurate image. While many Asian Americans are successful, there are also many who are poor. The stereotype does not represent the diversity within Asian America. Economic success varies greatly across the different ethnic groups of Asian Americans; for example, Japanese and Asian Indians have incomes that are nearly three times the incomes of Cambodians and Hmong. In fact, the Asian American community is "becoming increasingly polarized into two distinct groups: the 'uptown' Asian Americans and the 'downtown' Asian Americans." Additionally, the stereotype may serve to limit career opportunities for Asian Americans who are portrayed as hard working, but somewhat passive and complacent. Therefore, while they make good workers, they are not seen as management material. Finally, the portrayal of Asian Americans as the "model minority" also serves to reinforce negative stereotypes of other co-cultural groups as "dull and lazy." The implication being that if Asian Americans can succeed then others should be able to do so as well. These comparisons have the potential to exacerbate social conflict among co-cultural groups.

Sources: Hye Jin Paek and Hemant Shah, "Racial Ideology, Model Minorities, and the 'Not-So-Silent Partner:' Stereotyping of Asian Americans in U.S. Magazine Advertising," *The Howard Journal of Communications* 14 (2003), 225–43; X-H. Yin, "Asian Americans: The Two Sides of America's 'Model Minority,'" *Los Angeles Times* (May 7, 2000), M1–3.

However, it should be noted that identification with a constructed racial type can also have a positive impact. While racial categories are sociopolitical constructs rather than biological absolutes, there is a biological component to race, at least in terms of physical characteristics that differ among peoples. Identification with a racial group can give individuals a sense of belonging and sharing a common experience and history with others. Racial identification as a socially constructed identity can be a source of pride and can lead to group solidarity.

As social conditions change, so do our conceptions of race. One significant change has been the increasing number of multiracial individuals who do not fit into one reductive racial categorization. Currently, there are two national organizations in the United States devoted to mixed-race recognition: the Association of Multi-Ethnic Americans (AMEA) and Project RACE (Reclassify All Children Equally). Changing perceptions of racial identity are also evidenced by Tiger Woods describing himself as a "Calablasian,"[10] and by James McBride's novel about his mixed racial heritage entitled, *The Color of Water: A Black Man's Tribute to His White Mother.*

Ethnicity

Race and ethnic identity are sometimes treated as if they are one and the same thing. The 2000 US Federal Census asked individuals to select their race from a list that included ethnic identities (Japanese, Vietnamese) as well as racial categories. In general, racial identity is the primary means used by individuals to classify others; however, racial identity is also usually a category constructed solely by others, whereas ethnic identity is constructed both by oneself and others.[11] In general, race is a much broader term than ethnicity; for example, Caucasian is a broad category encompassing individuals of many different ethnicities. However, in some cases, race and ethnicity are more closely aligned with one another, as in the history of African Americans. The distinct culture of the African American people is unique and quite different from the culture of other black people, such as Caribbean, South American, or African blacks.

It should also be noted that the terms *culture* and *ethnicity* are not synonymous with one another. An *ethnic group* is composed of individuals who share the same origins and history; typically, members of an ethnic group will share a language, customs, family names, religion, values, and traditions. Unlike a nation, an ethnic group does not aim to be independent and to have its own state. Ethnic groups share an identity that is distinct from the majority culture of the state in which they live. Often, they share a link with a culture in another location. For example, Madelyn is an Italian American whose link with her Italian heritage is strong, since her father was born in Italy. For many Americans, identification with their roots is important; they describe themselves as Chinese American, Iranian American, Irish American, and so on. However, even as they seek to maintain their heritage, they are also part of the American culture. Therefore, in the US, while a person's ethnicity may be Jamaican or Bulgarian, his or her nationality and culture is American.

For members of other cultures, the link between ethnicity and culture may be more direct. For example, the three major ethnic groups that composed the former Yugoslavia — Slovenians, Croatians, and Serbians — were forced into one nation-state after World War II.[12] It is also possible for an ethnic group to have members who belong to many different cultures, as is the case with Jewish people, who may be Americans, Greeks, Russians, and so on.

Co-cultural groups

In each society there is a majority culture, a dominant cultural group that is in power, and various co-cultures, non-dominant cultural groups. The majority culture may not be a numerical majority within the society, but it is the group that has power over the major social institutions: church, government, education, military, mass media, and banking. For example, white males of European ancestry are the majority culture in the US even though they are outnumbered by co-cultural groups within society. The majority culture within a nation has control over the flow of information in the society and can shape cultural messages and perpetuate values, beliefs, and traditions through their control of social institutions. All cultures have a majority or mainstream culture within them that influences communication patterns and other behaviors within the society.

For example, white heterosexual males in the United States are the dominant group, and they have the power to shape the norms and values of US society. However, there are also many co-cultural groups within US society. Transnational and co-cultural representation plays a significant role in intercultural communication and IR. These co-cultural groups, sometimes referred to as minorities, include women, African Americans, Asian Americans, homosexuals, individuals with disabilities, and many other groups who are in some way disempowered in society. Members of co-cultural groups face many challenges related to communication, particularly communication with members of the majority culture. They must determine whether or not to adopt the communication styles used by the dominant groups or to use their own styles of communication. For example, an African American male may choose to speak in Standard English when at work, but may speak to friends and family using African American Vernacular English. A fuller discussion of communication accommodation theory is included in Chapter 3.

Dominant Intercultural Communication Theories Today

Culture is composed of patterns of shared perceptions and beliefs that determine the world view and the behavior of members of the cultural group. These cultural patterns have to do with ideas about what is good and what is bad, about what is true and what is false, and about the appropriate way to interact with other members of society. Cultural values determine the kinds of behaviors that are rewarded in society and the kinds of behaviors that are considered to be taboo. If one culture believes that it is wrong for an unmarried woman to have a child, a woman who does so may face ostracism from society. Another culture, however, may consider such behavior perfectly acceptable and offer support systems to help unmarried mothers.

Cultural values and beliefs determine how individuals interact in society, how they dress, and how they express themselves. In Arab culture, there is a strict taboo against men and women displaying intimacy in public, even between a husband and wife.[13] In Latin American cultures, a greeting is displayed by a kiss on the cheek between the same and opposite sexes, so open displays of affection between men and women and between same-sex partners are accepted. Similarly, because of the emphasis placed on modesty, women in some cultures are required to cover their bodies from head to toe when in public, while women in other cultures are free to dress as they please.

These beliefs, values, and norms influence how people use verbal and non-verbal communication. In many instances, deeply held cultural values (the importance of modesty, for example) influence more superficial aspects of culture (i.e. clothing choices). The Iceberg Model of culture is useful to help understand the various levels of a culture. Essentially, the model suggests that much of what we can observe superficially in any culture is determined by more deeply held values and beliefs. When studying other cultures, it is helpful to understand how visible behaviors are controlled by values and beliefs that are often buried far beneath the surface. Therefore, while fashion would be a visible behavior in any culture, the reasoning behind various styles (i.e. women covering their entire bodies in one culture versus the ability to dress freely in another culture) relates to values beneath the surface — in one culture, a strong value is placed on modesty; in the other, an equally important value is placed on an individual's right to self-expression.

There are several dominant theories that influence our study of intercultural communication; although many of them originated years ago they serve as the basis for much current research and for our understanding of patterns of behavior across cultures. All of these theories are *etic* approaches to the study of intercultural communication, that is, they are constructs developed by researchers to study cultures usually by comparing them with respect to some particular quality or predetermined category. In contrast, an *emic* approach to studying intercultural communication focuses on understanding a given culture from the inside, that is, from the perspective of members of that culture. Both approaches have validity. We discuss emic approaches to intercultural communication more fully in Chapter 3.

Kluckhohn and Strodtbeck's value orientations

The work of Florence Kluckhohn and Fred Strodtbeck is important to our understanding of how cultures develop their value systems. Kluckhohn and Strodtbeck studied the cultural values of European Americans, Hispanics, and Native Americans. They posited the fact that all cultures must answer the following questions about the world around them:

- What is the relationship of humans to nature?
- What is the orientation to time?
- What is human nature?
- What is the preferable form of human activity?
- What is the social relationship of humans with one another?[14]

These questions are universal for all human beings, although different cultures address them differently. The way a culture answers these questions is part of its deep structure; these deep-structure values are passed from one generation to the next. These value orientations have a significant influence on how members of a culture behave. Kluckhohn and Strodtbeck found three possible solutions to each of the five questions.

The relationship of humans to nature
There are three solutions to the question about the relationship of humans to nature: some cultures believe humans are subservient to nature, some believe humans are in harmony with nature, and others believe that humans can have mastery over nature. Some Polynesian cultures believe that human beings are subjugated to nature and that they should respect nature's forces, such as floods, earthquakes, and volcanic eruptions and be humbled by them. Native American culture, on the other hand, emphasizes the importance of living in harmony with nature; they believe that human beings are one with nature and that all living creatures are our brothers and sisters. In contrast, the Western cultures believe that humans may dominate nature and are destined to control the forces of nature, as they have tamed nature with their inventions.

Table 2.1 Kluckhohn and Strodbeck's value orientations

Orientation Range of Cultural Responses to Universal Questions		
Relationship of humans to nature	Humans are subjugated to nature	Humans are in harmony with nature	Humans can have mastery over nature
Temporal	Past-orientation	Present-orientation	Future-orientation
Human nature	Humans are basically good	Humans are a mixture of good and evil	Humans are basically evil
Activity	Doing	Being	Becoming
Relationship of humans to one another	Collateral	Individualistic	Lineal

Table 2.1 displays the five questions that researchers Kluckhohn and Strodtbeck believe all cultures must answer about the world around them. For each of the five questions, they offer three possible answers. Kluckhohn and Strodtbeck believe that the way a culture answers these key questions influences the values that a culture passes on from one generation to the next.

Temporal orientation

Some cultures focus on the past, others focus on the present, and still others focus their attention on the future. Cultures with a *past-orientation* are likely to have a great respect for history and to honor their ancestors. *Present-oriented* cultures are those cultures that place a great emphasis on enjoying life today and on the value of spending time with family and friends. *Future-oriented* cultures are those cultures that are concerned with realizing short-term goals and planning for future success and profit. Asian cultures have a past-orientation with their worship of ancestors and their belief in the value of history to teach important lessons. Latin American cultures place a great emphasis on interpersonal relationships and believe in the importance of enjoying the present moment. The American culture is future-oriented, at least in the short term, with its emphasis on progress and planning for the future.

Human nature

Some cultures believe that human beings are basically all good, others believe that they are a mixture of good and evil, and still others believe that humans are essentially evil by nature. These beliefs have a significant influence on how societies are structured and how people interact with one another. In IR, the traditionally dominant "realism" perspective has a pessimistic outlook on human nature. Cultures that believe in the essential goodness of humans, like the Native American culture, are much more likely to be trusting in their interactions with other people, even with individuals who are unknown to them. In the United States, there is a belief that there is a mixture of both good and evil in human nature. Americans tend to believe that a combination of environment and individual willpower determines the nature of an individual's character — for good or ill. Finally, some societies assume that human beings are essentially evil, leading to strict laws and religious codes (e.g. the Judo-Christian religions) that attempt to keep this evil nature in check.

Activity orientation

There are three possible orientations to human activity: *doing, being,* and *becoming.* The doing orientation focuses on the importance of accomplishment and on completion. In contrast, the being orientation focuses on enjoying life and living with openness and exuberance. The becoming orientation is a spiritual approach to life in which individuals seek to develop themselves spiritually by their actions. The American orientation to activity is definitely a doing orientation. There is a large emphasis on achievement, whether it is in school, in sports, or in the business world. Being productive and earning a good salary are valued in this orientation. In IR literature, this is often associated with notions of "power struggle" and increasing one's level of power. The Greek culture has a being orientation, where more value is placed on experiencing life and interacting with family and friends than is placed on accomplishment or monetary success. Native American culture is an example of the becoming orientation, where the value placed on spiritual development is greater than the value placed on material success or recreation.

The relationship of humans to one another

The relationship of humans to one another may be *collateral, individualistic,* or *lineal* in its orientation. A collateral orientation bases relationships on group ties and places the importance of the group before the individual's rights; an individualistic orientation places the rights of the individual above the importance of group harmony and cohesion; and a lineal orientation bases relationships on social structures that are passed down from one generation to the next such as social class or family background. The Korean culture is collateral in its orientation to relationships; group harmony is an important value and individuals do not wish to stand out from the group. In contrast, the American culture places a great value on autonomy; individuals are free to assert their opinion, even if they go against the group consensus. An example of a lineal relationship among humans is the rigid Indian caste system, where individuals are born into a particular level of society with no opportunity for social mobility.

Hofstede's cultural value dimensions

Geert Hofstede's theories on intercultural communication come out of his work as the founder and manager of the personnel research department for IBM in Europe. He created a survey to measure the cultural values of employees as they related to work situations. His initial study encompassed 72 countries, 38 occupations, and 20 languages. A total of 116,000 employees were interviewed twice (in 1968 and then in 1972). The core value dimension that Hofstede examined was Individualism versus Collectivism. In collective societies group loyalty and group harmony are highly valued, while in individualistic societies, freedom, independence, and self-sufficiency are prized.

In the 1980s, and again in 1991, Hofstede revisited his research and delineated five organizational patterns across a diverse range of cultures: Individualism versus Collectivism, Power Distance, Uncertainty Avoidance, Masculinity versus Femininity, and the Confucian Dynamism dimension. Hofstede referred to culture as "software of the mind" because he believed that cultural patterns program us to exhibit certain behaviors.

The Individualism / Collectivism dimension

Hofstede's core cultural value dimension, Individualism versus Collectivism, has to do with the individual's relationship to society. These polar values play a significant role in a wide range of societies around the world. One may easily observe the impact of individualism in the general principles of US foreign policy in terms of empowering individuals and promoting representative democracy. In an individualistic society, the individual is valued over the group and there is an emphasis on individual rights, freedoms, and needs. In an individualistic society, people are expected to take care of themselves and there is no strong social cohesion. In collective societies, on the other hand, the group is valued over the individual and there is an emphasis on the individual's responsibility to the group and on the rights and needs of the group.

Put simply, individualistic societies are "I" societies (like the US) and collectivistic (like China) societies are "we" societies. In cultures with a strong individual orientation, the autonomy and self-reliance of the individual is fostered. In cultures with a strong collective orientation, values of loyalty and harmony are fostered. Because many other cultural value dimensions are informed by an orientation either toward the importance of the individual or the importance of the group, the dimension of individualism/collectivism is the core value dimension through which all of the other value dimensions may be understood.

The Power Distance dimension

The Power Distance dimension relates to the way in which members of a culture respond to an unequal power distribution within society. The inequality may be seen in the workplace, the class structure within a society, and also in relationships within the family between parents and children. In cultures with high power distances, power is centralized within an organization and employees tend to fear their bosses; bosses tend to be paternalistic towards their subordinates, as is the case in almost all Middle Eastern societies. Additionally, children are taught to respect their elders and a major emphasis is placed on children's obedience. Employees and children are expected to do what they are told, and creative thinking and individual freedoms are not encouraged. In general, individuals in cultures where high power distances exist are likely to accept an unequal distribution of power, a hierarchical structure of social institutions, and a reward system based on seniority, rank, status, and age.

Cultures with low power distances reward individual initiative and innovation. Employees feel free to question and even contradict their employers. Bosses tend to have a more democratic management style that allows employees to make suggestions. Children are encouraged to express themselves freely and speak their minds. Families have a democratic decision-making process in which children are consulted, as is the case in many Canadian households. In general, equality is greatly valued in low power distance cultures and rewards systems are based on individual merit rather than status or seniority.

The Uncertainty Avoidance dimension

The Uncertainty Avoidance dimension relates to the extent to which members of a culture feel threatened by the unknown and how strongly they try to avoid situations that force them to deal with uncertainty. In cultures with strong uncertainty avoidance, people view unknown situations as dangerous and tend to avoid these situations as much as possible. In such cultures, innovation is discouraged, and work and family situations tend to be highly structured. Teachers are expected to have all the answers, and students are most comfortable in structured learning situations.

In cultures with weak uncertainty avoidance, on the other hand, uncertainty is accepted as a normal part of life, and curiosity and innovation are encouraged. Members of cultures with weak uncertainty avoidance are comfortable with ambiguity and risk taking. Teachers are allowed to say "I don't know," and students enjoy discussion and open-ended learning situations. At work, conflict is tolerated and employees are motivated by achievement more than conformity and harmony.

The Masculinity/Femininity dimension

In his research, Hofstede found significant organizational differences between male and female behavior, from which he developed the Masculinity/Femininity dimension. Masculine societies are those societies in which gender roles are rigidly defined in a stereotypical fashion. For example, men are supposed to be aggressive and focused on achievement and monetary success while women are supposed to be passive and nurturing and focused on family life and relationships. By contrast, feminine societies are those in which gender roles are flexible, and both men and women are supposed to be nurturing and concerned with the quality of life.

In a masculine organization, work goals center on achievement, recognition, advancement, and an opportunity to earn a high salary. In a feminine organization, on the other hand, work goals focus on the quality of working relationships, respect from employers and peers, and long-term job security. Further, a masculine workplace's primary focus is on the success of the organization, while a feminine workplace tends to put environmental issues before business achievements.

The Confucian Dynamism dimension

The Confucian Dynamism dimension is used to explain some of the distinctive aspects of the East Asian cultures, specifically China, Hong Kong, Taiwan, Japan, and South Korea. The primary values associated with these cultures are related to Confucian philosophy. Confucius was a Chinese philosopher and teacher who lived from 551 to 479 BC. His practical code of conduct puts emphasis on a societal structure that is hierarchical and on one's duty to familial roles. Confucianism is the basis for Chinese values, beliefs, and traditions. The Confucian Dynamism dimension includes a long-term orientation, status-oriented relationships, thriftiness, a sense of shame, and the importance of collective face-saving; collectivism and high power distances are a key part of this value dimension.

Confucian philosophy emphasizes the importance of respect for elders and obedience to superiors. It emphasizes the need to fulfill one's role and meet one's obligations with virtue. One significant aspect of this dimension derived from Confucianism is the concept of face and the need to save face. Face is a person's social self-esteem. Saving face would be taking actions to avoid public embarrassment or disgrace. In a collective society, all members of society should act in such a way to avoid causing any member of the group or the group itself embarrassment or shame — from "loss of face."

The combination of values of thriftiness and perseverance in pursuing goals together with a long-term orientation to life have made possible the economic growth of the Pacific Rim, specifically the Five Dragons (Hong Kong, Taiwan, Singapore, Japan, and South Korea).

Hofstede's definition of culture

Based on his extensive body of research, Hofstede defines culture as "mental programs" or "patterns of thinking, feeling, and acting" that function like "software of the mind." He argues that culture is unavoidably a collective phenomenon insofar as our culture is learned from and shared with the people in our social environment. He calls culture "the collective programming of the mind which distinguishes the members of one group or category of people from another."[15] Hofstede emphasizes the fact that culture is a mental programming and that culture is learned. For this reason, different life experiences can also lead to different programming. Our culture is reflected in the meanings we assign to various aspects of life and our world view. Our culture determines what we consider to be good and bad, true and false, and beautiful and ugly.

Hofstede points out that management ideas and theories are not universal. He states that a society's business organizations and social institutions (and we add governmental policies) reflect its cultural values, and theories of business management should take into account the differences in value systems that exist among countries.[16] A manager cannot coordinate the actions of employees without a deep understanding of their values and beliefs. Although Hofstede's focus is on business and management applications of studying cultural values, his work has a broader application to the study of cultural differences, which has certainly influenced those theorists who have come after him.

His core dimension of collectivism versus individualism to some extent informs all subsequent discussions of cultural differences. Hofstede has noted that developed countries mostly tend to be individualistic; he explains this phenomenon in relation to Adam Smith and the roots of modern day capitalism, which is motivated by self-interest. For some collective countries, an emphasis on self-interest is not culturally acceptable; when individuals do succeed, they are expected to spend part of their earnings to help their extended families.

Hofstede also relates the emphasis on self-interest in individualistic countries to Maslow's "hierarchy of needs" in which "self-actualization" sits at the top of the pyramid and is considered the highest-level need. He points out the fact that the need for self-actualization may not be highest in collective societies. Maslow's work is biased and represents the perspective of the American individualistic culture; it is not necessarily universal in its interpretation of needs. For collective cultures, the highest need may be group harmony, membership and belonging to an in-group, and loyalty to that group.

For individualistic cultures, the work relationship is viewed as one of mutual advantage; it is calculative in that both the employer and the employee have something to gain from it. In general, business is conducted in such a way that everyone is treated equally, and there is an avoidance of nepotism. In collective cultures, on the other hand, the employer–employee relationship is more familial and has a moral component; there is an emphasis on loyalty on the employee's side and obligation on the employer's side. Better deals are given to members of one's in-group, personal relationships are given priority, and finding jobs for relatives is the norm.

In general, in collective cultures there is a blurring of the lines between family and work and also between business life and social life. In order to do business with someone in a collective culture, it is first important to develop a personal relationship and developing this trust takes time. Members of individualistic cultures tend to want to move more quickly and to keep their professional and personal lives separate. In a collective culture, it is not unusual for gifts to be given to business associates in order to secure business; these gifts would be seen as bribes in an individualistic culture and would be considered unethical.

Another difference is that members of individualistic cultures communicate directly and openly, while in collective cultures communication is much more focused on following predetermined social scripts for interaction. In collective cultures it is important not to violate social rules or disrupt group harmony. Disagreements tend to be more indirect, and in general confrontation is avoided. It is important that each member of the group be allowed to maintain his/her dignity, and dignity is based on the relationship the individual has to the group. Face-saving is a major consideration when communicating with one another. Often when there is conflict, loss of face is avoided by having a third party intervene rather than allowing open conflict to take place.

Just as individualistic countries tend to be more economically developed, they also tend to have low power distances. Power distance in a culture is usually consistent across various areas of life: family, school, and work. Cultures with a low power distance do not have a rigid separation between superiors and subordinates. Individual freedom is emphasized, and the individual can challenge authority, whether that authority is the parent, the teacher, or the employer. In cultures with a low power distance, good employers are those who ask for input from their employees. Employees are free to file grievances against employers for unfair treatment without fear of reprisal.

In cultures with a high power distance, by contrast, children are expected to obey parents without question and to be respectful and loyal at all times. Similarly, students are expected to revere teachers as sources of wisdom; students listen passively to lectures and do not challenge teachers. The same pattern of behavior also exists between employee and employer. Employers have paternalistic relationships with their employees, and employees are very loyal to their superiors. An employer's power is more absolute and it is much more difficult for employees to seek redress for unfair treatment; complaints against an employer may lead to reprisals.

In high power distance countries, differences in status are highly visible and subordinates are expected to respect those with higher status — a status that is usually based on wealth, rank, ancestry, and age. There is a great respect for elders both within the family and in the workplace. By contrast, in low power distance countries age is often seen as a negative, and people try to appear younger than they are. Status is much more likely to be tied to personal achievement than to rank, age, or ancestry. Differences in status are generally underplayed because they are not considered desirable.

In cultures with high uncertainty avoidance, fixed rules and rigid social codes are the norm. Members of these cultures want rules to satisfy their emotional need for order and predictability in society. Law and order are important symbols in these cultures, and people agree with the existence of rules even if they transgress them. People in these cultures are made anxious by situations in which there are no clear-cut rules for behavior.

By contrast, people in cultures with low uncertainty avoidance can be comfortable in situations with no rules; they are also more open to changing existing rules. Cultures with low uncertainty avoidance certainly have rules, but the rules are seen more as a matter of convenience than rigid, unchangeable standards. Within cultures that have high uncertainty avoidance, organizations tend to have very formal structures, and there is generally a ritualization of behavior, meaning that great importance is placed on using the right words, dressing appropriately, and acting in a prescribed way in a given situation. Business is always conducted via rituals even when these rituals do not affect decision-making.

The higher the uncertainty avoidance within a traditional society, the more individuals within that society will view God or the gods as difficult to please and threatening. They will also find it more acceptable for individuals to express their emotions openly, since they find themselves living in an uncertain and frightening world. Additionally, they will have little tolerance for those who fail to adhere to society's rituals and formal codes of behavior. Cultures with low uncertainty avoidance are much more able to tolerate divergent ideas and individuals, and are much more likely to see uncertainty as positive or neutral rather than threatening.

The five cultural patterns that Hofstede focuses on in his works are crucial to understanding intercultural communication, and have applications far beyond their relationship to work values and management theory. His work has had a significant impact on the researchers and theorists who have come after him. No understanding of intercultural communication can be developed without grasping the core dimension of Individualism versus Collectivism and how it relates to all other dimensions of culture.

Edward T. Hall's contexting cultural patterns

Edward T. Hall is an eminent cultural anthropologist whose work spans six decades; his early work at the Foreign Service Institute helped to shape the field of intercultural communication as we know it today (see Part II Introduction). Hall's study of diverse cultures led him to develop the idea of *contexting*, which is the notion that in some cultures, much of the meaning in any communication is derived from the context of the encounter, while in other cultures, communication is much more dependent on explicit verbal and non-verbal cues. Cultures that are high-context cultures are ones in which meaning is communicated implicitly through a shared understanding of a given situation; the environment or context provides clues as to how to interpret an encounter. In other words, information is a function of the context in which it occurs; most of the meaning communicated is in the context and little is in the actual message. An example of a high-context communication might be the communication between two members of the same family who have lived together for a long time. Because of their shared history, environment, and their intimacy, they may be able to communicate without a lot of explicit statements.

Low-context cultures, on the other hand, are ones in which meaning is dependent on overt verbal and non-verbal cues. Low-context communication is extremely explicit and can be compared to communication with a computer.

The exchanges between two lawyers in a courtroom would be another example of low-context communication.

Hall developed a "Context Square," which is a graphic representation of the relationship between context, information, and meaning in any given communication. For any communication to have meaning, both context and information are necessary. However, the more context surrounding a communication, the less explicit meaning is required to get the message across.

In today's society more than ever, we are bombarded by all types of information. Hall explains that one function of culture is to determine what we pay attention to and what we ignore. He states that culture helps structure our world and keeps us from experiencing information overload. The way we experience life is a direct result of what we choose to pay attention to, and what we pay attention to is determined unconsciously — largely as a result of our presuppositions and expectations about the way the world is. The culture that we are immersed in influences our beliefs about the world, and those beliefs influence the cues that we select from our environment. So, in a very real sense, culture determines how we perceive the world around us.

Members of high-context cultures derive most of the information in a given communication from a combination of their internalized context (their beliefs about the world) and the actual physical context of the communication encounter. High-context cultures tend to be very homogeneous, rooted in the past, and slow to change. In general, communication in high-context cultures is more indirect and ambiguous than it is in low-context cultures. People in high-context systems frequently talk around the point and expect others to know what they mean. They also tend to make a greater distinction between members of the culture and "outsiders." Although high-context communication can be found in any society, high-context cultures are more likely to be collectivistic cultures.

Low-context cultures are likely to be more diverse cultures. In low-context cultures, most information is communicated through explicit verbal and non-verbal cues. Individualistic societies usually use low-context communication, but may use high-context communication in intimate relationships. Low-context communication is generally precise, clear, and direct. Members of low-context cultures may be impatient with high-context communication because they perceive it as less efficient.

For effective intercultural communication, it is important that members of both high- and low-context cultures make an effort to understand one another. Neither method of communication is better than the other. However, when members of high- and low-context cultures attempt to communicate without any awareness of their different styles, they are very likely to experience misunderstandings and cultural clashes.

Limitations of cultural value frameworks

When studying intercultural communication from the perspective of taxonomies of cultural patterns, it is important to bear in mind that not all members of a particular culture will adhere to these value frameworks. While such frameworks are useful to help us understand the broad outline of cultural patterns, they do not account for individual differences. We should avoid stereotyping members of other cultures based on these categories. Not all members of a particular culture will share all of its values; for example, not all members of Asian cultures adhere to the Confucian values of thrift and modesty. Not all Americans are achievement-oriented and individualistic. Even those individuals who do ascribe to the values of their culture may not do so at all times and in all contexts.

Most people (including both the masses and the elite) experience some tension between their individual and group identities (see the section "The Interplay of Personal and Group Identity," p. 56); few people behave exactly the same way in all situations. For example, a member of a culture that values modesty and group harmony may behave more assertively and be more outspoken about accomplishments when charged with representing the interests of his nation as part of an international team than he would be when interacting at home with members of his own culture. Often individuals behave differently when interacting with members of their own group than they do with people from outside their group. When communicating with members of other cultures it is important to be sensitive to both the individual and his/her cultural background. Few of us would appreciate being told: "I assumed you were competitive because you are a member of that culture." As mindful communicators, we will pay attention to the individuals we are communicating with at the same time that we draw on our knowledge of cultural value frameworks.

Thinking about Reality and Perception

As we study the value frameworks of other cultures, we should also be aware of the way our own culture shapes our perception of the world. To quote diarist Anaïs Nin, "We see the world not as it is, but as we are."[17] Our own cultural values and beliefs influence our perception of reality. In a sense, culture is a lens through which we perceive the world around us. Perception can be defined as the process of constructing meaning out of external stimuli through our sensory receptors. None of us could possibly attend to all the external stimuli we are exposed to at any given time; therefore, the first part of the process is the selection of what to attend to from among all the competing stimuli available to us. Once we have selected the stimuli, we then assign meaning to them. Both the selection and the evaluation are an unconscious process and are influenced by many factors, including our cultural backgrounds, education, emotions, and beliefs.

Perception is culturally determined. We learn perceptual patterns that are based on our culture. The same behavior or event may be perceived differently by members of two different cultures. For example, a student in a classroom who frequently asked the teacher questions might be considered a good student for exhibiting an inquisitive mind in the United States. In Japan, a student who continually questioned the teacher would be perceived as behaving inappropriately because teachers in Japan are not to be questioned by their students; questioning a teacher demonstrates a lack of respect.[18] Just as the proper behavior for children is perceived differently by diverse cultures, so too are appropriate social roles for women and the elderly. In some cultures, women are expected to have contact only with men within their own families. In many Latin American and Middle Eastern cultures, an unmarried woman who spends time alone with a man who is not a relative could run the risk of ruining her reputation.[19] In many European cultures, relations between the sexes allow women the same freedom as men, and a young woman would not face dire social consequences for spending time alone with a man.

Perceptions of elders also vary greatly across cultures. In many cultures, the elderly are afforded great respect. For Asian, Arab, Latin American, and Native American cultures, elders are perceived as wise. Their advice is sought because they have lived a long time and have many varied experiences to drawn upon. Many African men who are under 25 years old will seek the advice of older family members before making decisions.[20] In African cultures, age is considered an asset and is revered. By contrast, the American culture values youth, and old people are seen as being unproductive and not of use to society; the youth-oriented culture in the US perceives the elderly as having less to offer than younger members of society. Further, while many cultures honor their ancestors, Asian cultures worship them and believe that their ancestors have a powerful influence over their lives. These differing perceptions are related to cultural patterns that assign different meanings to social roles and relationships.

Every person's experience of reality is subjective; there is no reality separate from our perception. Perception is a process of selection of stimuli from our environment and interpretation of that stimuli; cultural background strongly influences both what we select and the way we interpret it. Our cultural beliefs, values, and attitudes influence the cues we select from the information we receive and the way we categorize those cues to make sense of the world. Therefore, perception is culturally determined.

Identity and Communication

In addition to influencing our perception of the world, culture also influences our perception of ourselves. Our identity, or self-concept, is who we think we are and how we see ourselves. An individual's identity is created through communication with others and is influenced by society. We all have multiple identities that are related to group membership and to the different contexts we find ourselves in at different times. Our identities are dynamic. Also, they are developed differently in different cultures; in individualistic cultures there is more emphasis on personal identity, while in collectivistic cultures there is more emphasis on the familial identity. Although they may develop in different ways across cultures, we all have cultural, social, and personal identities.

Cultural identity

Our cultural identity is based on membership in a particular cultural group; it is developed as we grow up and learn the values, beliefs, and attitudes of our culture from our parents and other caregivers. We are also influenced by language usage, educational systems, mass media, social institutions, and peer groups within our culture. Our cultural identity is our sense of belonging to a particular culture; as members of a particular culture, we learn about and accept its traditions, heritage, religion, aesthetics, social structures, and perceptual patterns. A child growing up in New Zealand will develop an identity related to the cultural value patterns of the New Zealand culture.

Members of one's own culture are seen as members of one's in-group, those people with whom one has a shared identity. Individuals from other cultures are part of one's out-group; they are people with whom one does not share a common identity. In some cases, a natural ethnocentrism, a belief that one's own cultural group is superior to others, can lead to negative stereotyping of members of out-groups. This commonly occurs in IR among nations and states. Often, we believe that our own culture's way of perceiving the world is superior to the ways of other cultures. Unfortunately, the belief that one's cultural group is superior and that other groups have negative qualities can lead to many challenges for intercultural communication.

Even in situations where individuals do not stereotype members of their out-groups, differences in beliefs about appropriate behavior can lead to difficulties in communicating. For example, many challenges have occurred in healthcare communication between American doctors and members of other cultures because of different views of the appropriate way for doctors and patients to interact; Mexicans expect a healthcare professional to be formal and to establish confidence (*confianza*) before treating them. The doctor should use formal greetings and establish rapport by asking about the patient's family, offering a drink, or performing some other social nicety before discussing the patient's medical problem. From a US perspective, such behavior may be less important than the healthcare professional's ability to perform his/her job, but from a Mexican perspective, the healthcare provider's credibility is lessened when he/she does not establish rapport in a formal way.[21]

Social identity

An individual's social identity develops as a result of membership of various groups within his/her culture. The qualities and characteristics of the members of the social groups that individuals belong to influence the way individuals view themselves. There are many groups with which people may identify including those based on race, ethnicity, age, gender, religion, ideology, profession/occupation, and social class. We all identify with many different groups, and we may identify much more strongly with some groups than with others. We may also identify more strongly with some groups at particular times in our lives or in certain contexts than we do at other times and in other contexts. An individual may identify very strongly with her professional status as an engineer; a Chinese-American may identify strongly with his ethnic heritage; a Gen-Xer may identify strongly with membership in a group based on his/her age.

Personal identity

Personal identity is based on the unique characteristics that distinguish individuals from other members of their cultural and social groups. Your individual interests, abilities, and preferences set you apart from other members of the groups to which you belong. You may enjoy surfing, or disc golf, or playing the guitar. You may be gifted in math, good at web design, or talented in learning languages. You may be outgoing, a practical joker, studious, or witty. These qualities and interests set you apart from others and form your personal identity. We should bear in mind that an individual's cultural, social, and personal identities are often intertwined. They are related to and influence one another. For example, your personal preferences for certain types of music or sports may be partly influenced by your cultural background. Similarly, your gender identity may be influenced by the gender roles that are deemed appropriate within your culture. Often individuals experience tension between their personal and group identities.

The Interplay of Personal and Group Identity

Personal and social identities are developed in conjunction with one another, and both are acquired within the larger structure of culture. We all have multiple group identities; for example, in addition to your gender identity, ethnic identity, religious identity, and age identity, you may identify with the region of the country you are from, or with a political group of which you are a member, or with your college or university. You may describe yourself as a Republican Japanese-American woman from Arizona, or perhaps an American man of Greek ancestry who is a registered Democrat and an active participant in student government. Your identity as a non-traditional college student or as a member of a particular religious group may be of primary importance in how you see yourself and how you would like to be seen by others. Because we all have multiple identities, it is not uncommon for us to experience some tension between our personal and group identities.

Our membership in one particular group does not mean that we share all of the group's beliefs and values; this distinction is true for our cultural groups as well as for the many other social groups in which we have membership. While most members of our cultural group may be perceived as outgoing or modest, we may not necessarily share these qualities as individuals. In fact, while members of other cultures may perceive Americans as very individualistic and competitive, not all individuals who are American have these traits. Some Americans are very much oriented toward cooperation and group harmony within their families and communities.

There can be a dialectical tension between our personal identities and our group identities. A woman may experience a conflict between her religious identity and her personal identity if her religion teaches that women should be subservient to men, and she does not share that belief herself and wishes to be treated as equal to men. Similarly, a young Chinese-American man whose family has strong ties to his ethnic heritage may wish to separate himself from what he perceives as the old-fashioned ways of his ethnic group, and express himself in ways that would not be sanctioned by the more conservative members of his family and ethnic community. He may not reject all of the values and traditions of his ethnic identity, but may still wish to express his personality in ways that go beyond what his ethnic tradition says about how a good Chinese son must behave.

Differing Perspectives and Communication

Our cultures determine the way we perceive ourselves and the way we perceive the world around us. Culture determines our view of how the world works, our beliefs about God, human nature, good and evil, humanity's relationship to nature, and many other important issues. Each culture believes that its views about the world are the correct views, and that other cultures holding conflicting views are wrong. Just as a natural ethnocentrism leads us to believe that our culture's way of doing things is superior, we tend to believe that our culture's view of the world is the true picture of it. Of course, as mindful and actively engaged communicators, we can move beyond these beliefs to recognize and respect the validity of the world views of other cultures. For example, we do not have to agree with the views on the role of women or the relation of humans to nature in another culture, but we do have to understand and respect the world view that leads members of that culture to have the beliefs that they do. The only area where we would ever question and challenge the beliefs of another culture is when those beliefs lead to behavior that violates basic human rights (see "Considering Ethics" in this chapter and also Chapter 9), which is often a hotly debated and controversial subject in IR.

When cultures hold different world views, it can be difficult for members of those cultures to communicate with one another. Such differences may lead to miscommunication, and in some cases, to conflict. Historically, differences in ideology and religious belief have, unfortunately, led to many conflicts. All cultures have some form of religion.[22] In fact, in the history of the world there have been no peoples anywhere who have been without some type of religion. Religion serves to help human beings address challenging questions that otherwise could not be understood. Typically, these questions have to do with the nature of life and death, the creation of the universe, the relation of human beings to one another and to nature, and the structure of society.[23] Because religion provides answers that guide human life and give it meaning, religious beliefs are deeply held, and cultures are willing to sacrifice a great deal to preserve them.

Many wars have been fought over religious differences, and many people have died because of conflicts related to religious beliefs. Many longstanding conflicts in the world today have religious differences at their center, including conflicts in Northern Ireland, India/Pakistan, and in the Middle East. Often, the conflict has to do with attempts by one group to impose its religious beliefs on another group. In the United States, we believe in a separation of church and state. The founding fathers left England in order to have the right to worship as they pleased, and one of the beliefs the US is founded upon is the individual's right to freedom of religion. However, in many other nations, religion and the state are not separated.

In some cases, religious beliefs may be linked to other ideologies espoused by political leaders; in other cases, political ideology may not be linked with religion. However, much like religion, a particular ideology can dominate a nation, causing it to create certain foreign policies that can lead to conflicts between nations. While ideologies are much like religions, they in general tend to have a weaker hold on core values than religions do.[24] One example of an ideological conflict would be the Cold War between the Soviet Union and the United States, in which there was an ideological struggle between communism and capitalist democracy. Strong ideologies can lead to revolutions as in Iran's Islamic fundamentalism in 1979 or China's Maoist communism in 1949. The imposition of ideologies by a government on its people can cause much suffering. Thich Nhat Hanh, Vietnamese Buddhist monk and peace activist, has said, "You can transform your nation into a prison because you are committed to an ideology."[25] Both ideology and religion can lead to conflict among peoples who do not share one another's beliefs and wish to impose their own beliefs on other nations. As mindful communicators, we must understand the challenges that such deeply held beliefs can pose to intercultural communication. We should be actively engaged in understanding others and conduct mindful behavior in our own intercultural interactions.

Realities of a global community

In this book, we approach the study of intercultural communication from the perspective of issues of power and conflict/cooperation in our global community. In order to understand these issues, we draw upon concepts from the field of international relations. As mentioned previously, the field of international relations studies the relationships among the world's governments; it is concerned with international politics, that is, the decisions and actions of governments toward one another. Political relations between states encompass diplomacy, trade, alliances, war, cultural exchanges, and participation in international organizations.

Studying international relations can help us understand the role of power in intercultural communication. One of the most useful international relations themes is the dichotomy between the forces of "centralization of power" and "decentralization of power." In a *centralized* system, the power is concentrated in the hands of few. In contrast, a *decentralized* system is characterized by power being divided among many hands. For example, the demise of the Holy Roman Empire contributed to the decentralization of the power in the international system at the time. Henry VIII of England also contributed to forces of decentralization of power when he separated the Anglican Church from the Catholic Church. The American Revolution contributed to the forces of decentralization as it fractured the British Empire and gave independence to some of its subjects.

On the other hand, some individuals and events have contributed to the concentration of power. For example, the political role of most popes has been to concentrate the power base of the Catholic Church across international boundaries. The expansion of Islam in the Arabian Peninsula (during Mohammed's era), North Africa (during the Four Caliphs), and Eastern Europe (during the Ottoman period) helped the forces of centralization of power. The rise of individuals like Hitler and Mussolini also contributed to the forces of centralization of power, as they brought more territory under their control.

Some social scientists use other terms to refer to this dichotomy between the forces of centralization and decentralization of power. For example, some refer to centralization of power as creating universalism or a universal authority as opposed to regionalism or local authority. These factors have a variety of implications for intercultural communication. We will discuss the way centralization of power, whether it is in the hands of a government or a majority culture within a nation, tends to privilege certain types of communication and devalue or even suppress others. We will also examine the various ways disempowered groups seek to have their voices heard by the majority, through both peaceful and violent means.

Issues of power are inevitably related to issues of conflict and cooperation.

At the international level, the most accepted norm of behavior is respect for state sovereignty (or independence), just as North American and European nations respect the independence of individuals above 18 years of age. This respect for sovereignty means that states do not theoretically recognize any source of authority above their own decision-making process. Technically, a state is free to initiate aggressive behavior, which can even lead to war, just as individuals may initiate aggressive behavior that can lead to a conflict or a fight. That is why war is still considered a legitimate tool of foreign policy despite all the condemnations of war.

All in all, we can divide norms of behavior into two general categories: cooperative and conflictual. In fact, one major goal of this book is to help to increase the understanding of intercultural issues via improved communication skills, which promote cooperation and avoid unnecessary conflicts that often lead to a waste of precious human lives and natural resources. The first step in preventing conflict is to cultivate openness to other perspectives, so that we may be mindful in our encounters with members of other cultures.

Citizen diplomats

As you read this, you may feel that wars are initiated by governments, and that average citizens are powerless to prevent conflict despite having a mindful approach to cross-cultural communication. However, we propose the concept of the "citizen diplomat," whose actions as a mindful communicator can help contribute to a more peaceful world. Citizen diplomats are "ordinary citizens who open their homes, offices, or farms to emerging international leaders, entrepreneurs, and scholars."[26] They are also citizens who travel abroad either as students, teachers, or volunteers. They may travel through programs like the Fulbright Program, the Peace Corps, Sister Cities Programs, or a host of other exchange programs. These individuals believe that "in a democracy the individual citizen has the right — indeed, the responsibility — to help shape foreign relations."[27] Perhaps the earliest citizen diplomat from the United States was a Philadelphia Quaker named George Logan, who traveled to Europe in 1798 to try to prevent the United States and France from going to war. Upon his return, carrying a decree from France stating its willingness to free all captured US seamen and end its trade embargo, Logan was harshly criticized for interfering in US foreign policy. The Logan Act was passed to make direct intervention of US citizens in foreign affairs a crime. Despite this early attitude toward citizen diplomacy, the Logan Act has never been enforced, and today the US government is quite open to allowing its citizens to travel abroad.[28]

Citizen diplomacy is sometimes referred to as two-track diplomacy, with the first of the two tracks being official diplomatic relations between nations through official governmental representatives, and the second being the person-to-person relations of ordinary citizens. Citizen diplomacy serves many valuable purposes. It maintains international dialogue even when government-to-government relations are disrupted; it helps to dispel stereotypes and prejudices; it builds constructive relationships with emerging leaders around the world; and it paves the way for official diplomatic relations (first-track relations).

Citizen diplomacy serves an important function by "allowing human interaction to continue when formal negotiations are suspended or terminated. For example, before the fall of the Soviet Union, many American citizen diplomats established relationships with Soviets through cultural exchanges, joint scientific projects, and simply through personal contact. The work of these individuals helped to keep the lines of communication open and to lay the groundwork for peace and understanding between the two nations. Citizen diplomacy is particularly important between individual citizens in nations or regions where official relations are strained or non-existent.

Another valuable function of citizen diplomacy is to dispel stereotypes and present America in all its complexity to the outside world; of course, the same applies to citizen diplomats from other nations who wish to present a more accurate picture of their nations to the rest of the world. Richard Carlson, president and CEO of the Corporation for Public Broadcasting, has commented on the fact that many of the images of American culture that are exported via satellite to billions of people in other nations are not a realistic portrayal of American life. He cites the popularity of two American television programs in particular: *The Bold and the Beautiful* and *Baywatch*.[29] Through person-to-person contact, some of the stereotypical images of American life that are proliferated abroad can be dispelled.

When citizen diplomats welcome visitors from abroad, they are performing an important function that may have far-reaching implications on a large scale. For example, future world leaders are often hosted by citizen diplomats. In 1999 former French President Valerey Giscard D'Estaing, who was an exchange visitor to the US in 1956 while a young parliamentarian, observed: "The America that I experienced was vigorous, self-confident, and all the while welcoming us with generosity: an indelible image I always remember when our relations are involved."[30] Similarly, German Chancellor Gerhardt Schroeder, who was an international visitor in 1981, has said that "one of the most intelligent ways of giving young politicians a positive attitude about America" is through the International Visitors Program.[31]

Citizen diplomacy can create a climate of cultural understanding and, therefore, can shape the way that nations interact with one another. In addition to the International Visitors Program there are many other opportunities for citizen diplomacy, including the Fulbright Scholars Program, the Peace Corps, Sister Cities programs, and countless regional and community-based volunteer organizations, as indicated earlier. Finally, any time that you interact with anyone from another culture, you have the potential to increase understanding and promote cooperation.

POWER CHECK
The Coalition for Citizen Diplomacy Holds National Summit
In July 2006 the Coalition for Citizen Diplomacy held a national summit in Washington, DC. The Summit was held in conjunction with the Sister Cities International 50th Anniversary Conference. The purpose of the Summit was to increase the ability of Americans "to engage with the global community through people-to-people contacts that foster international dialogue and exchanges." The Coalition has started a national movement with three goals: Recruitment, Recognition, and Resources. In the area of Recruitment, the Coalition desires to exponentially increase the number of Americans who see themselves as citizen diplomats. The second goal, Recognition, has to do with increasing the visibility of citizen diplomacy, both its impact and its potential. Finally, the third goal, Resources, focuses on securing both public and private funding for the work of citizen diplomacy.

In addition to the National Summit, the Coalition collaborated with other groups across the United States to hold a series of Community Summits on Citizen Diplomacy. The Coalition was started when 32 leaders from the U.S. met at the Johnson Foundation's Wingspread Conference Center in Racine, Wisconsin in March 2004. These leaders, who came from corporations, local government, non-governmental organizations, and educational institutions, were concerned about "the vulnerability of national security, the growing anti-American sentiment around the world, and the lack of understanding among Americans regarding other countries and cultures." The Coalition seeks to gain increased support of international exchange and education initiatives from the federal government and "to raise the profile and strengthen the impact of the citizen diplomacy movement."

To find out if a Community Summit is planned for your area go to the U.S. Center for Citizen Diplomacy website: http://uscenterforcitizendiplomacy. org

Source: U.S. Center for Citizen Diplomacy website, http://uscenterforcitizendiplomacy. org, accessed November 5, 2010.

As technology increases our ability to communicate easily and rapidly with other people from all over the world, we should be aware of the opportunities that we have to make a positive impact on cooperation within the global community. Throughout this book, we will discuss the issues of power and conflict/cooperation and how we can address these challenging issues as mindful communicators.

Dynamics of intercultural encounters

Intercultural encounters, that is, any communication between members of different cultural groups, are complex interactions. Each intercultural encounter is unique and will be shaped by the context in which it occurs, the expectations of the communicators involved, and their perceptions of what is at stake in the encounter. Because societies are becoming increasingly diverse, we all have frequent opportunities to interact with members of other cultures. If you live in a large city or attend a university with a large number of international students and faculty, you probably experience intercultural encounters on a daily basis.

The context in which an intercultural communication encounter occurs can have a significant influence on whether or not the outcome of the encounter leads to the formation of positive attitudes toward members of other cultures. The classic work of Amir describes four conditions that typically lead to positive attitudes: (1) the encounter is arranged by a person in a position of authority; (2) the communicators have a personal stake in the outcome; (3) the encounter is pleasant; (4) all parties derive some benefit from the contact, that is, the communicators share a common goal or one that allows them to achieve their individual goals.[32]

When we interact with members of other cultures, we may experience some anxiety because we are challenged to move out of our comfort zone. In a sense, we are encountering the unknown; we may be unfamiliar with the non-verbal communication cues that members of other cultures use, and we may also experience difficultly due to language differences. Communication scholars Gudykunst and Kim use the concept of the "stranger" to describe intercultural encounters. By "strangers" they mean "people who are members of different groups and are unknown to us."[33] There is usually some anxiety associated with communication with strangers. Another way to think of intercultural communication encounters is in terms of communicating with individuals who are not members of one's in-group.

When we encounter people who are not part of our in-group, it is important that we communicate mindfully and respect each other's cultural norms. When in a situation where we feel some anxiety, there may be a temptation to rely on categorization to make sense of unfamiliar stimuli. However, to do so would put us at risk of falling into the trap of ethnocentrism, which tends to influence many aspects of IR. When confused and frustrated by the challenges of intercultural encounters, it may at first seem comforting to reassure ourselves that our way of communicating and viewing the world is the "best" one or the "correct" one. Yet, if we do so, we are likely to greatly decrease our chances of having a positive and meaningful intercultural encounter. Stephan and Stephan describe the situations in which we are least likely to experience anxiety about communicating with members of other cultural groups. When we are in a structured situation, when there are norms to guide our behavior, and when we are in a situation that requires cooperation rather than competition, we are more likely to feel at ease with members of out-groups. Further, in situations where our in-group is in the majority and/or is afforded higher status, we are also less likely to feel anxiety.[34]

As mindful communicators, we can recognize the situations where we are in the majority, that are least likely to cause us anxiety, as precisely those

Figure 2.2 This exchange student is being shown around campus by some of her fellow students. When we are members of the majority, we can help reduce the anxiety that others may be experiencing by understanding their feelings and acting in a way that will put them at ease in the situation. Mindful communicators will be aware of the ability they have to facilitate a communication encounter and will avoid ethnocentric thinking.

situations that are most likely to cause those individuals with whom we are communicating the most anxiety. In such a situation, we have the opportunity to act mindfully by understanding their anxiety and doing all that we can to put them at ease. When we are the ones experiencing high levels of anxiety, we can cope with it better if we perceive it as something positive, that is, anxiety about the encounter because we fear we may appear prejudiced in our interactions.[35] We should be aware that some level of anxiety is normal and healthy in an intercultural encounter; however, when our anxiety is above our maximum thresholds, we may begin to lose our ability to think critically and begin processing information in a simplistic manner.[36] This book will help you reduce your anxiety about intercultural encounters by increasing your knowledge of other cultures and of effective means of intercultural communication. The more mindful you become, the less anxiety you will experience in intercultural communication encounters.

Technology's Impact

Technology can be defined as the inventions or innovations of a culture that involve the creation of systems that solve problems and extend human capabilities. Technology often refers to tools that have been designed to modify the natural environment in such a way as to meet a human need or desire. The term "technology" can be used to refer to a wide range of innovations from the printing press to the microwave oven to the fax machine. Historically, technology has had an impact on cultures, often leading to dramatic changes in the way people live. Certainly, the invention of the automobile and the telephone dramatically changed the lives of people and lead to further innovations like superhighways and answering machines.

From the perspective of communication, the technologies that are particularly influential have been the computer and communication technologies. Rapid advances in telecommunications and computing have given many cultures the opportunity to communicate in ways that were once unimaginable. These changes have influenced nearly every aspect of our lives. They have opened up many new opportunities for communicating with members of other cultures via the internet and email, in virtual teams, and in virtual university courses, to name just a few. As we have more opportunities for intercultural communication, we also have the responsibility to develop as mindful communicators so that we serve as citizen diplomats in all our encounters with members of other cultural groups. Whether you chat with an international group of friends in an online chat room, work with a diverse group of people on a virtual team, or attend class with a multicultural group of students at your university, you are communicating interculturally. Sometimes, the challenges of communicating across cultures in virtual environments make the possibility of miscommunication much more likely. These challenges are due in part to the absence of many of the non-verbal cues that we rely on in face-to-face communication encounters (see Chapter 6). Throughout this book, we will discuss the ways that technology and culture interact with and influence one another.

The Media's Impact

Of all the technologies that influence culture, mass media has arguably had the most significant influence. When we refer to mass media, we are speaking specifically about the news media. Stereotypical portrayals of cultural groups in the media can be damaging; they are harmful both to the self-image of individuals who are members of the groups and to relationships between members of the groups and others in society. Both news media and entertainment media (film, television, and radio) have the ability to influence culture. By its portrayal of cultural groups, the media can influence the way they are perceived by others.

Another concern related to mass media is the proliferation of US media in other cultures. Some members of other cultures perceive the spread of American movies and television programs and other media as threatening to their traditional cultures. They do not want American values and beliefs to replace their own cultural values, and they fear the pervasive influence of American popular culture. The influence of American media and popular culture on the rest of the world is sometimes referred to as *cultural imperialism* (see Chapter 8). In each chapter of this text, we will discuss the impact of media on the topics being discussed and examine the effects of the spread of American popular culture around the world.

Considering Ethics

As mindful communicators, we respect the different world views of members of other cultures and realize that events can be seen from more than one perspective. We avoid ethnocentrism and do not assume that our culture's values and beliefs are superior to the values and beliefs of other cultures. Ethics are principles used to guide the behavior of people within society, and typically they emerge in response to a culture's judgments about what are good and bad behaviors. We should avoid making ethical judgments regarding the behavior of members of other cultures because we do not have one set of ethical guidelines that can be applied to all cultures: the issue of the universality of human rights often arises due to this issue. We cannot judge ethical behavior in a culture other than our own because there is no set of standards that is outside both cultures. While US law or the teachings of our religion may help us to determine good and bad behaviors in our own culture, these guidelines may not have meaning to members of other cultures.

From this relative perspective, we cannot state that the values or beliefs of any culture are wrong. In contrast to the relative approach, the universal approach, or *universalism*, would seek to find some behaviors that all societies would condemn as bad, such as murder or treason. This approach, if taken to an extreme, can lead to us back to ethnocentrism and to condemning practices because they differ from our own. On the other hand, extreme *cultural relativism* would deem that any cultural act can be justified within the context that it occurs, and that it can be judged as good or bad only by members of the culture in which it occurs. This extreme position would lead to accepting genocide, apartheid, slavery, and other such actions — actions that we clearly do not condone. Therefore, when dealing with ethical issues, there are some standards related to the rights of all human beings that are not culturally relative. Specifically, we may oppose human sacrifice, torture, suffering, and political oppression without being considered ethnocentric. Hatch states that "there are certain absolute standards against which all cultures may reasonably be judged."[37] The study of ethics is complex and challenging; we will discuss ethical issues as they relate to intercultural communication more fully in Chapter 9.

References

1. L. Robert Kohls, *Survival Kit for Overseas Living* (Chicago, IL: Intercultural Press, 1979), p. 17.
2. Edward T. Hall, *The Silent Language* (New York: Anchor/Doubleday, 1981), p. 29.
3. Paul DiMaggio, "Social Structure, Institutions, and Cultural Goods: The Case of the United States," in Pierre Bourdieu and James S. Coleman, eds., *Social Theory in a Changing Society* (Boulder, CO: Westview Press, 1991), pp. 133–55.
4. Joshua S. Goldstein, *International Relations*, 3rd ed. (New York: Longman, 1999), p. 11.
5. Gibson Campbell and Kay Jung, "Historical Census Statistics on Population Totals by Race, 1790 to 1990, and by Hispanic Origin, 1790 to 1990, for The United States, Regions, Divisions, and States," Working Paper Series no. 56, September 2002, www.census.gov/population/www/documentation/twps0056.html, accessed October 3, 2005.

6. Ibid.
7. U.S. Census Bureau, United States Census 2000 Questionnaires, www.census.gov/dmd/www/2000quest.html, accessed October 3, 2005.
8. Paul R. Spickard, "The Illogic of Racial Categories," www.pbs.org/wgbh/pages/frontline/shows/jefferson/mixed/spickard.html, accessed August 16, 2005.
9. Ibid.
10. Isabel Wilkerson, "The All-American Golfer Tiger Woods — The Many Ways of Looking at a Black Man," *Essence*, November 1997.
11. S. Cornell and D. Hartmann, *Ethnicity and Race: Making Identities in a Changing World* (Thousand Oaks, CA: Pine Forge Press, 1998).
12. Myron W. Lustig and Jolene Koester, *Intercultural Competence*, 4th ed. (Boston, MA: Allyn and Bacon, 2003), p. 33.
13. Margaret K. Nydell, *Understanding Arabs* (Yarmouth, ME: Intercultural Press, 1996), p. 61.
14. Florence Rockwood Kluckhohn and Fred L. Strodtbeck, *Variations in Value Orientations* (Evanston, IL: Row, Peterson and Company, 1961), p. 11.
15. Ibid.
16. Geert Hofstede, *Culture's Consequences: Comparing Values, Behaviors, Institutions and Organizations Across Nations* 2nd ed. (Thousand Oaks, CA: Sage, 2001), p. 374.
17. Stephen R. Covey, *The 7 Habits of Highly Effective People* (New York: Fireside, 1989), p. 28, also attributed to Anaïs Nin.
18. Norine Dresser, *Multicultural Manners* (New York: John Wiley & Sons, 1996), pp. 41–2.
19. Ibid., pp. 128–9.
20. Carley H. Dodd, *Dynamics of Intercultural Communication*, 5th ed. (Boston, MA: McGraw-Hill, 1998), p. 105.
21. Dresser, pp. 247–8.
22. Kluckhohn and Strodtbeck, p. 11.
23. Ibid., p. 11.
24. Goldstein, p. 223.
25. Thich Nhat Hahn, *No Death, No Fear: Comforting Wisdom for Life* (New York: Riverhead Books, 2002), p. 54.
26. Sherry Lee Mueller, "Citizen Diplomacy: What You Can Do to Prevent Terrorism," *Transitions Abroad Magazine*, 27: 1 (July/August 2003), www.transitionsabroad.com/publications/magazine/0307/citizen_diplomacy.shtml, accessed October 2, 2005.
27. Ibid.
28. Michael Shuman, Gale Warner, and Lila Forest, "Citizen Diplomacy: What It Is, How It Began, and Where It's Going," *In Context*, 15 (Winter 1987), 35, www.context.org/ICLIB/IC15/Shuman.htm, accessed October 2, 2005.
29. Alvin A. Snyder, "US Foreign Affairs in the New Information Age: Charting a Course for the 21st Century," 1994, www.annenberg.northwestern.edu/pubs/usfa/default.htm, accessed October 3, 2005.
30. Mueller.
31. Ibid.
32. Yehuda Amir, "Contact Hypothesis in Ethnic Relations," *Psychological Bulletin* 71 (1969), 319–43.
33. William B. Gudykunst and Young Yun Kim, *Communicating with Strangers*, 4th ed. (Boston, MA: McGraw-Hill, 2003), p. 24.
34. W. Stephan and C. Stephan, "Intergroup Anxiety," *Journal of Social Issues* 41 (1985), 157–66.
35. K. Greenland and R. Brown, "Categorization and Intergroup Anxiety in Intergroup Contact," in D. Capozza and R. Brown, eds., *Society Identity Processes* (London: Sage, 2000), pp. 167–83.
36. D. Wilder and P. Shapiro, "Effects of Anxiety on Impression Formation in a Group Context," *Journal of Experimental Social Psychology* 25 (1989), 481–99.
37. Elvin Hatch, "The Evaluation of Culture," in Larry A. Samovar and Richard E. Porter, eds., *International Communication: A Reader*, 7th ed. (Belmont, CA: Wadsworth Publishing, 1994).

APPROACHES TO THE STUDY OF INTERCULTURAL COMMUNICATION

II

Introduction: History of the Study of Intercultural Communication

There are four primary approaches to the study of intercultural communication. Knowing the history of the field will help you understand each of the different approaches: social science, interpretive, critical, and dialectical. Since its early development, intercultural communication has been an interdisciplinary field; an interdisciplinary field is one that draws on the scholarship of more than one discipline to present a more coherent and integrated understanding of commonly shared issues or topics. The various approaches to intercultural communication scholarship have their roots in the disciplines that helped shape the field. These disciplines are anthropology, linguistics, and psychology. The influence of each of these fields can be seen in the way we study communication across cultures today.

The Development of Intercultural Communication as a Discipline

The field of intercultural communication developed during the period of post–World War II expansion in the United States. The Foreign Service Institute (FSI) was created to prepare government workers for assignments abroad, and brought together many anthropologists and linguists to train Foreign Service personnel. The work of these theorists forms the basis for the contemporary study of intercultural communication.

An expanding US realizes need for a Foreign Service Institute

In the 1940s, more American diplomats and business people went to work overseas. In the period immediately following World War II, there was a re-evaluation of the preparation of diplomats; for the most part, they were not well prepared to work among people from other cultures. Although they were given some language training before going abroad, it was not adequate to prepare them for the intercultural communication challenges they faced. During the period from 1946 to 1956, the field of intercultural communication grew out of this need to prepare American diplomats to function effectively when serving abroad. The greatest area of concern was related to the preparation of Foreign Service Officers.

In 1945 the *American Foreign Service Journal* held a contest to get ideas for improving the training given to Foreign Service personnel. Common themes emerged in the essays related to the need for better language training and more education regarding the countries and regions to which the officers were sent.

The following year Congress passed the Foreign Service Act, which resulted in the reorganization of the Foreign Service and the creation of the Foreign Service Institute (FSI). The purpose of the Institute was to provide initial and continuing training to Foreign Service Officers throughout their careers.[1]

The language program at the FSI was based on the Intensive Language Program (ILP) used by the Army during World War II. The advantage of using this method was that it had already been proven effective. Unlike the traditional methods of teaching languages that focus on reading, writing, and learning grammar, the ILP emphasized the importance of spoken language; this method used native speakers of each foreign language as teachers. The native speakers were supervised by linguists to insure the consistency of the instruction. This innovative approach was quite successful and clearly demonstrated the possibility of language training on a large scale. Henry Lee Smith, who had run the Army program, was made the Director of Language Studies for the FSI. By adopting the Army's language training program, the new FSI was able to put in place a proven language program immediately.

In addition to learning languages, the Foreign Service Officers were given training in how to interact with members of other cultures. The FSI had a number of anthropologists on staff to instruct the Foreign Service personnel. However, the anthropologists soon learned that their students were not interested in learning abstract theories related to culture, but rather that they wanted practical advice regarding specific ways of interacting with members of other cultures. They wanted concrete information they could use in face-to-face intercultural encounters.

Early theorists (Trager, Hall, Birdwhistell)

The newly formed Foreign Service Institute hired many anthropologists and linguists; three of the most influential of these early theorists were George L. Trager, Edward T. Hall, and Ray L. Birdwhistell. George L. Trager was among the first group of linguists hired by the FSI. He described the approach of the language program as operating from the assumption that cultural systems (social organization, technology, religion, law) are dependent on language for their organization and existence.[2] He also emphasized the importance of "metalinguistics" in understanding communication across cultures; the metalinguistics of a culture are the meanings that derive from the relations between the language and the other cultural systems. For example, the meaning of the term X in culture A is dependent upon the linguistic meaning of the term and its meaning in the legal system of culture A. Both of these concepts were influential in shaping the field of intercultural communication.

Anthropologist Edward T. Hall joined the FSI later than Trager; Hall's job was to ensure that the students were given general anthropological training. He discovered that the students were not interested in learning about cultural patterns, but rather wanted to focus on what he termed "microcultural analysis." Microcultural analysis examines smaller units of a culture: tone of voice, gestures, and temporal and spatial orientations as they relate to interactions between members of different cultures. The students wanted what they perceived as practical information, rather than a discussion of the deeper aspects of cultures and their values, beliefs, and traditions. Hall recognized that unlike students of anthropology, his students at the FSI were unwilling to spend time observing interactions among members of other cultures; the diplomats studying at the FSI needed to have practical guidance for face-to-face intercultural encounters.

This emphasis on practical application of intercultural knowledge rather than on theory had a profound influence on the early development of the field. Hall's work has been criticized because it emphasized anecdotes rather than theory. However, his work serves as the basis for much of the study of intercultural communication even to this day. He established a new series of concepts including the study of space (proxemics) and time (chronemics). Further, Hall applied a linguistic model to the material studied in a microcultural analysis; in other words, he stated that the non-verbal aspects of communication (gestures, spatial orientation, eye contact) were learned in the same way that language is learned. He made explicit the connection between linguistic analysis and cultural analysis.[3]

Ray L. Birdwhistell only spent one summer working at the FSI; however, his work on the study of gestures (kinesics) made a major contribution to the field of intercultural communication. He became recognized as the expert in kinesics when he published *Introduction to Kinesics* through the FSI. His work was influenced by the emphasis on microcultural analysis at the FSI during his time there. Today, kinesics is an important part of the study of intercultural communication.

These three theorists together with many other linguists and anthropologists helped to shape the early development of the field of intercultural communication. Their work was driven by the needs of the Foreign Service personnel who were their students at the FSI. These students were interested in practical applications at the micro level that would help them interact with members of other cultures immediately rather than in understanding theories of culture and larger cultural patterns.

Emphasis on non-verbal communication and applied linguistics

The students' interest in practical applications led to the focus on non-verbal communication and applied linguistics. In order to function effectively in intercultural communication encounters, the Foreign Service personnel needed to be able to understand both the linguistic and the nonlinguistic aspects of intercultural communication. They needed guidance regarding important non-verbal aspects of communication including: gestures, voice, and orientations to space and time. Similarly, they needed a working knowledge of spoken languages more than they needed proficiency in the written language.

The needs of students led the FSI to focus on non-verbal communication; Hall's work led to the recognition that non-verbal communication is learned in much the same way language is acquired. Hall's approach to the study of culture and communication as described in *The Silent Language* and *The Hidden Dimension* had a major impact on the development of the new discipline of intercultural communication. Hall's work did not include exhaustive discussions of theory, but rather gave some general guidelines supported by numerous practical applications and anecdotal examples. Many intercultural communication textbooks to this day still discuss practical applications of theory and case study examples — including the one that you are reading.

Cross-Cultural and Diversity Training

The FSI's emphasis on practical guidelines for individuals interacting with members of other cultures has led to the development of two other approaches to the study of communication across cultures that are related to, but distinct from, the academic discipline of intercultural communication; they are *cross-cultural training* and *diversity training*. Cross-cultural training actually began with the FSI's training of government employees. In the 1960s, the field of cross-cultural training was expanded to encompass the training of business-persons and students preparing to go abroad. Like the early training given by the FSI and unlike the field of intercultural communication today, this type of training focuses primarily on practical guidelines with much less attention given to theories of culture.

The field of diversity training is closely aligned with the field of cross-cultural training. However, instead of preparing individuals for intercultural encounters abroad, it focuses on effective intercultural communication among members of the diverse workforce in corporate America. It is projected that by 2050 the US population will be 50.1 percent European American, 14.6 percent African American, 8.0 percent Asian, and 24.4 percent Hispanic.[4] As the workforce becomes increasingly diverse, the need for diversity training continues to grow.

The Interdisciplinary Nature of the Field

The field of intercultural communication is currently located within the communication discipline; however, in its early development the field was interdisciplinary because the scholars at the Foreign Service Institute who shaped its development represented many different disciplines, including anthropology, linguistics, and psychology. It was natural that these scholars would draw upon their respective disciplines in their work on intercultural communication. The field of linguistics helps us understand the relationship between language and other cultural systems. The field of anthropology helps us to recognize cultural patterns and realize the importance of non-verbal communication. The field of psychology brings to light the role of human cognition in understanding and categorizing the patterns of behavior of members of other cultures.

Many of the research techniques used in the field today derive from these disciplines. For example, the use of ethnography to study other cultures is taken from the field of anthropology. Ethnography is a branch of anthropology concerned with the description of ethnic groups. The term ethnography, derived from *ethno* meaning people and *graphy* meaning to describe, is literally the methodology of describing peoples. The influence of the field of linguistics can be seen in the use of *rhetorical analysis* to study culture; *rhetorical analysis* is based on the analysis of public speeches and other oral discourses studied in the context in which they occur. Researchers using the rhetorical approach analyze films, newspaper articles, and television programs to study public representations of a culture. These are just two examples; many more influences will be noted when we discuss contemporary approaches to the study of intercultural communication.

Today, many disciplines are recognizing the importance of addressing global issues and of improving communication among members of diverse cultures both internationally and domestically (as in the case of diversity training). Scholars and teachers in fields that include business, international studies, journalism, engineering, environmental studies, criminal justice, and technical communication are recognizing the need to address issues of intercultural communication. They often adapt intercultural communication theories and research to their own disciplines. In turn, the field of intercultural communication continues to be influenced by other disciplines such as cultural studies, international relations, political science, psychology, anthropology, and sociology. The approach in this textbook is an interdisciplinary one focusing on the relationship between the fields of intercultural communication and international relations. We believe that both fields share key issues related to communication and power and that understanding of these issues can be greatly enhanced by an interdisciplinary focus on them. The following discussion of the contemporary approaches to studying intercultural communication will show you even more clearly, we hope, the way an interdisciplinary focus has shaped the field and how such a focus can lead to a more comprehensive and effective approach to communicating across cultures.

Contemporary Approaches to Studying Intercultural Communication

Again, the four contemporary approaches to studying intercultural communication are the social science approach; the interpretive approach; the critical approach; and the dialectical approach. Each of these approaches is based on different basic beliefs about human nature and about the nature of knowledge. Each one is valuable for its unique contribution to our study of intercultural communication. However, each approach is also limited by the particular assumptions it makes about human behavior and by its methodologies.

In Chapter 3, we discuss the social science and interpretive approaches to studying intercultural communication. The social science approach is based on the assumptions that human behavior is predictable and that there is a describable external reality. This approach, also called the functionalist approach, is based on research in the fields of sociology and psychology. Scholars using the social science approach seek to describe and predict behavior, and they frequently rely on quantitative methods. The interpretive approach is based on the premise that human beings construct their reality and that communication is a subjective experience. Scholars using the interpretive approach see communication and culture as interrelated and believe that one influences the other.

Then in Chapter 4, we introduce both the critical and the dialectical approaches. The critical approach focuses on the historical context of communication and on understanding the role that power and power relationships play in communication. The dialectical approach is an attempt to move beyond the limitations of the first three approaches. Martin, Nakayama, and Flores put forward the dialectical approach as a way to reconcile the contradictions inherent in intercultural communication. This approach emphasizes the relational and processual nature of intercultural communication. The dialectical approach will provide a framework for reconciling the many different approaches and different types of knowledge that you may encounter when studying intercultural communication. This approach challenges us to move beyond thinking in dichotomies like "right and wrong" and "good and evil." It encourages us to reconcile seemingly contradictory information in order to view intercultural encounters from a larger perspective.

As you study the four contemporary approaches to the study of intercultural communication, be sure to bear in mind your understanding of the history of the field and its interdisciplinary nature. At the same time you may wish to reflect on the significance of the field to other disciplines that you are studying. Finally, we suggest that you keep in mind issues of power and the challenges of conflict and cooperation in our global community.

References

1. Wendy Leeds-Hurwitz, "Notes in the History of Intercultural Communication: The Foreign Service Institute and the Mandate for Intercultural Training," *Quarterly Journal of Speech* 76 (1990), 264–5.
2. George L. Trager, "The Field of Linguisitics," *Studies in Linguistics*, Occasional Paper 1, (1950), 7.
3. Edward T. Hall, "A Microcultural Analysis of Time," in A. F. C. Wallace, ed., *Selected Papers of the Fifth International Congress of Anthropological and Ethnological Sciences* (Philadephia, PA: University of Pennsylvania Press, 1956), p. 122.
4. U.S. Census Bureau, 2004, "U.S. Interim Projections by Age, Sex, Race, and Hispanic Origin: 2000–2050," www.census.gov/ipc/www/usinterimproj, March 18, 2004, accessed April 12 2004.

Social Science and Interpretive Approaches

3

Communication scholars Sue Ellen Christian and Maria Knight Lapinski conducted a study of high school students' knowledge, attitudes, and stereotypes about Muslims and Islam. Their findings revealed student attitudes toward and negative stereotypes of Muslims were directly linked to their interaction with Muslims. Those students who reported knowing and interacting with Muslims were significantly less likely to hold negative stereotypes and more likely to have positive attitudes toward Muslims. Additionally, the more students knew about Islam, the less likely they were to hold negative stereotypes. The study also discovered that students' attitudes were more strongly influenced by contact with Muslims than by the news media. In fact, they found that the students' "self-reported exposure to news alone was not related to endorsement of negative stereotypes."[1]

Tomoko Kanayama conducted a study of the experience of elderly people in Japan establishing virtual communities online. Her research was based on observations and on extensive interviews. Kanayama describes how the participants were able to develop supportive relationships online and how they created a sense of closeness by sharing old stories and memories.[2]

Christian and Lapinski's study is an example of the social science approach to intercultural communication research, which frequently examines causal relationships. In this particular study the relationship between contact with Muslims and attitudes toward Islam is examined, as is the relationship between media exposure and attitudes toward Islam. Kanayama's study is an example of the interpretive approach. The interpretive approach is based on the premise that human beings construct their reality and that communication is a subjective experience. Scholars using the interpretive approach see communication and culture as interrelated and believe that each influences the other. There are many differences between these two approaches to the study of intercultural communication, and their application within the field of IR. One of the most basic differences is that the social science approach is etic, meaning that culture is studied from the perspective of a researcher-imposed structure, and the interpretive approach is an emic approach, that is, it studies culture from the perspective of members of the culture being studied.

Both of these approaches have their roots in the disciplines that shaped the field of intercultural communication. These two approaches use elements from the following three disciplines: psychology, linguistics, and anthropology. The social science approach is influenced by the field of psychology and the research methods used in that discipline. The interpretive approach, on the other hand, has its foundations in the field of anthropology. In this chapter we discuss the nature of each approach and the research methods used. We demonstrate how an event might be studied from the two different approaches and examine the impact of technology on each of the approaches. We also discuss the benefits and limitations of each approach. We begin by discussing the social science approach and then move on to the interpretive approach.

The Social Science Approach

The social science approach is based on the assumptions that human behavior is predictable and that there is a describable external reality. This approach, also called the functionalist approach, is based on research in the fields of sociology and psychology. Scholars using the social science approach seek to describe and predict behavior, and they frequently rely on quantitative methods. Also, in political science, scholars and researchers compile their work based on the assumption that human behavior is predictable. A classic example of this is found during any election period, when political scientists often attempt to predict voter behavior. The relationship between sovereign states is also affected by this assumption, as states are generally believed to act rationally and towards their best interests. Scholars using the social science approach believe that culture is a measurable variable, and that culture influences communication in much the same way that personality traits do. The goal of the social science approach is to predict how culture influences communication. In a similar way, the goal of political scientists studying international relations is to predict how culture influences major decisions by those with power.

In social science research, communication and culture are seen as causal variables. In other words, researchers believe that an individual's culture will determine how he/she will behave in communication encounters. Behavior is predicted based upon hypotheses that are drawn from research studies. Data is gathered by breaking down communication and culture into discrete variables that can be measured. Once the variables are measured, a causal relationship is established, often with the use of statistical calculations. For example, a study by Merritt and Helmreich of the influence of national culture on the behavior of flight crews on commercial airliners used the Cockpit Management Attitudes Questionnaire, an instrument designed to assess attitudes toward performance on the flight deck. The results of the questionnaire were analyzed using Individual Differences Scaling (INDSCAL), a method that accounts for individual differences and allows for responses to be standardized. These findings were then interpreted statistically to yield a discussion of causal relationships; the findings suggested that Asian flight crews placed more emphasis on group loyalty and were less likely share their personal problems with other crew members than those of other global regions. Both of these attitudes are related to the collective nature of Asian societies and to the high power distance of these societies. The study led to the development of a new questionnaire, the Flight Management Attitudes Questionnaire, (FMAQ) designed to capture cross-cultural differences in flight management attitudes.[3] Social science researchers remain objective and removed from the participants in their research studies. They often use methods drawn from psychology and sociology, such as questionnaires, standardized tests, and observation.

Assumptions about culture and people

Scholars who use the social science approach to studying intercultural communication operate from the assumption that the behavior of people can be predicted by their cultural backgrounds. They believe that an individual's communication style is influenced by his/her cultural background as much as it is by his/her personality traits. Social science researchers view culture as an independent variable, and study value framework and theoretical notions that influence communication. For example, a study by Naomi Sugimoto examined different styles of apology used in the United States and Japan. She asked members of the American and Japanese cultures to construct the message they would use to apologize if they offended someone in their own culture. The messages were coded for the style of apology used and then differences between the two cultures were studied. Sugimoto discovered that the American participants were more likely to explain in their messages while the Japanese respondents were given to including remorse, reparation, offers of compensation, and requests for forgiveness in their messages.[4]

Scholars using the social science approach also believe that it is possible to understand communication patterns by studying isolated instances of communication behavior. They typically conduct cross-cultural comparisons of communication patterns from a researcher-imposed framework. This approach has helped identify broad cultural differences in linguistic and non-verbal behavior among cultural groups. Communication scholars such as Andersen have studied the influence of cultural variables (including individualism, gender, power distance, and uncertainty avoidance) on non-verbal behavior across cultures. They use these cultural variables to help explain cross-cultural differences in non-verbal communication. For example, members of individualist cultures tend to use facial expressions and gestures in communication encounters more than members of collective cultures do; this difference may be related to the need for members of collective cultures to maintain group harmony and to preserve the face, or social self-esteem, of all group members. In order to do so, they may refrain from expressing their own feelings too openly (see Chapter 6).[5]

The social science approach has also identified the influence of variables, such as national cultural, ethnicity, and gender, on intercultural communication and helped predict how these factors can lead to either successful or unsuccessful communication across cultures. The work of Ting-Toomey and Oetzel examines intercultural conflict management from a cultural variability perspective. Their work focuses on the influence of cultural value dimensions (individualism/collectivism, power distance) on "the way an individual experiences conflict, defines conflict, and attributes meaning to the micro-events that take place in the conflict."[6] Differences in the power distance value dimension may influence how individuals react in conflict situations. In cultures with a large power distance, that is, in cultures that emphasize the importance of rank, age, status, and seniority, individuals may need to rely on personal and social contacts within the power structure to manage conflict. While in cultures with a small power distance, that is cultures that emphasize the importance of democratic decision-making and equal rights based on accomplishment rather than status, individuals will need to assert themselves in order to handle conflict situations effectively.[7]

A mindful intercultural communicator will bear in mind the impact of differing cultural conflict management styles in communication encounters. Today, many international conflicts are handled by third-party mediators. Such mediators work to resolve conflicts peacefully. Often the mediator is an intergovernmental organization; the United Nations is the most well-known and significant intergovernmental mediator. However, regional organizations like the Organization of American States may also serve as mediators. Even individuals like former US president Jimmy Carter, and the former president of Costa Rica, Oscar Arias, may serve as mediators. Arias won the Nobel Peace Prize in 1987 for mediating a peace agreement among Central American presidents that ended warfare in the region.[8] These individuals demonstrate the parallel between "citizen diplomat" and mindfulness.

Social science researchers view communication as static, and they emphasize the present-oriented aspects of communication. The social science approach is a reductive one, in that it studies communication encounters by breaking them down into small measurable variables. For example, when comparing Finnish and American conflict management and "face maintenance," researchers Siira, Rogan, and Hall used the Organizational Communication Conflict Instrument to determine which of three conflict management approaches (nonconfrontation, solution-oriented, and control) participants would use in a hypothetical situation involving a class project. The researchers isolated particular conflict management approaches in order to compare the responses of the Finnish and American participants. They found that both Finns and Americans preferred a solution-oriented approach to conflict management.[9]

Quantitative methods

The social science approach to the study of communication is an etic approach, that is, it is an approach that seeks to understand communication across cultures from outside the cultures being studied by comparing cultures using predetermined variables. The structure of the research is imposed by the researcher, and the criteria being studied are viewed as universal. Etic approaches often study dimensions of cultural variability in order to explain differences or similarities in communication behavior across cultures.[9] Hofstede's dimensions of cultural variability are a much cited example of an etic approach to the study of intercultural communication. The primary dimension of cultural variability studied by theorists is the individualism/collectivism cultural value dimension.[11] The core cultural value dimension of individualism versus collectivism has to do with the individual's relationship to society. In an individualistic society, the individual is valued over the group and there is an emphasis on individual rights, freedoms, and needs. In an individualistic society, people are expected to take care of themselves and there is no strong social cohesion. In collective societies, on the other hand, the group is valued over the individual and there is an emphasis on the individual's responsibility to the group and on the rights and needs of the group. Put simply, individualistic societies are "I" societies (like the US) and collectivistic societies are "we" societies (like China). In cultures with a strong individual orientation, the autonomy and self-reliance of the individual is fostered. In cultures with a strong collective orientation values of loyalty and harmony are fostered.

For example, Gudykunst used the value framework of individualism/ collectivism to inform his research on anxiety and uncertainty management. The purpose of his research program was to determine whether cultural background influenced the strategies used by individuals to reduce their feelings of anxiety and uncertainty when communicating with "strangers."[12] He found that people from individualistic cultures were more likely to ask direct questions in a communication encounter with someone new, while people from collectivistic cultures were more likely to ask indirect questions in the same situation. Gudykunst states that understanding other cultures in terms of the various dimensions of cultural variability "has tremendous practical value in improving the quality of our communication."[13] A person from an individualistic culture will be able to communicate much more effectively with someone from a collectivistic culture if he/she has knowledge of collectivism. However, Gudykunst also points out the problem of trying to use dimensions of cultural variability to develop causal explanations since such explanations do not take into account the influence of individual-level factors such as personality, individual values, and self-construals (how we think about ourselves).[14]

The social science approach often relies on quantitative research to analyze its findings. Research studies typically have a large number of participants who supply information to the researchers; the information is then analyzed by statistical methods to yield findings that establish causal relationships. Most social science research uses experimental methods derived from the fields of psychology and sociology. These methods include the use of standardized measurements, pretested instruments, self-report attitude questionnaires, surveys, and interviews. As with psychological research, there are ethical concerns related to the protection of subjects. Most research of this kind comes under the scrutiny of universities' human subjects' review boards to make sure that scholars protect the welfare of research participants.

Communication Accommodation Theory

The Communication Accommodation Theory is the result of social science research. Communication researchers Gallois, Giles, Jones, Cargile, and Ota studied how and when individuals accommodate their speech and non-verbal communication to others during a communication encounter. In other words, communicators choose to use language in different ways to achieve "a desired level of social distance between [themselves] and [their] listeners."[15] In some situations, individuals will adapt their communication patterns to accommodate others. For example, in a classroom a student may speak using a standard American accent, while at home she may speak with the regional accent used by her extended family and ethnic group.

Some speakers will either converge or diverge their communication behaviors in relation to the individuals with whom they are communicating. *Convergence* is a strategy whereby individuals adapt their communication patterns to become more similar to the linguistic and non-verbal behaviors of their communication partners. *Divergence*, on the other hand, is a strategy whereby speakers emphasize linguistic and non-verbal communication differences between themselves and others. The purpose of divergence is to call attention to differences between oneself and others, usually on the basis of group membership.[16]

In some situations, speakers will adapt to other patterns of speech in order to create harmony, to identify with others, or to put others at ease. For example, a host may adapt to the communication patterns of his guests in order to make them feel comfortable. Individuals are most likely to adapt during low-threat interactions or during communication encounters with individuals that they see as much like themselves. The assumption being made is that individuals tend to accommodate in situations where they have positive feelings toward the other person.

In other cases, speakers may change their speech in order to conform to the speech of individuals in positions of power. For example, an African American male who speaks African American English Vernacular at home and with his close friends may choose to speak Standard American English at work in order to fit in with and be accepted by the dominant group within the corporation. In general, the greater the speaker's need to gain approval from another, the more likely it is that the speaker will converge with the speech of the other.[17]

Speakers may also adapt their speech in order to establish a stronger rapport and identification with their listeners in order to persuade them of something. Political leaders may use simpler and more direct language when addressing voters than they would use in situations of diplomacy with other world leaders.

Former President Bill Clinton is an example of a leader who adapted his speech to his listeners, frequently using colloquial expressions and emphasizing his "down home" origins to certain audiences.

On the other hand, speakers may choose to diverge from the speech of others to express solidarity with a non-dominant group within society. An example of this can be seen in the behavior of Rep. Maxine Waters, who describes "how Willie Brown and she would . . . begin speaking Black English to one another, in the midst of the legislative sessions in Sacramento. By speaking Black English, they were messing with their white colleagues' minds, reminding them that they still see themselves as being in kinship with the everyday Black folk who they also represent."[18] Divergence can be a means of empowerment for members of co-cultural groups.

Divergence is often a way for individuals to assert their social identity, that is the part of their identity and self-esteem that is based on group membership. When their social identity is strong, individuals will use divergence as a technique to assert that identity. An experiment by Bourhis and Giles found that Welsh people studying the Welsh language broadened their Welsh accents and began using Welsh words when responding to a survey conducted in English that challenged their reasons for studying "a dying language."[19]

The accommodation of one's speech to the speech of others is a type of code-switching, selecting one language or linguistic variation of a language over another for use in a given communication situation. For individuals who speak more than one language or more than one variation of a language, the decision to use one language over another is influenced by several factors. In a multilingual nation like Belgium, code-switching is part of everyday life; the decision to use one language or variation of the language may depend upon numerous factors, one of which may be the status of a particular language. For example, linguist Jean-Louis Sauvage states that "I never speak Walloon with my son, considering that it is more useful for him to know French correctly. To tell the truth, I cannot say this without feeling a pang of remorse."[20]

Another consideration may be the context of the communication, whether the individual is at home or at work. Bilingual children may speak one language at home and another in school. An individual's conversational partner, as in the example of Maxine Walters and Willie Brown, may also be a significant factor in the decision to code-switch. Finally, the topic being discussed, as in the case of the Welsh language learners, may also influence which language or linguistic variation an individual chooses to use.

Applying the social science approach

Scholars using the social science approach seek to study the way culture influences communication. For example, a social science researcher might wish to examine the way members of different cultural groups use email, the internet, and other electronic media to communicate with members of their in-groups to establish virtual communities. In such a study, they would be likely to isolate specific variables — like the topics covered on websites or the level of formality used in email messages.

MEDIA IMPACT
South African Students Reject Foreign Television

We frequently hear claims that traditional cultural values are being lost in an age of cultural imperialism where global media shapes our identities and world views. Many theorists bemoan the spread of global culture that is frequently American in origin due to the prevalence of American television, movies, music, and other media internationally. However, most studies have focused on the production, distribution, and content of global media, rather than on its reception. Few studies have tested the theory of the rise of a global culture empirically. When studying the influence of media, it is important that we examine the interplay between media consumption and other social factors, and recognize the uneven penetration of global media into local cultures.

Strelitz reported on a group of students at Rhodes University in South Africa who rejected foreign television and chose to view local programming in order to reinforce their identity as "traditional" Africans. These students were all local African males who came from rural peasant or working-class backgrounds. They created a shared television viewing space, referred to as the "homeland," where they isolated themselves from the rest of the student body. The homeland students rejected the dominant student culture at Rhodes University, a culture that included excessive drinking and prank-playing. They saw this behavior on the part of the middle-class African students as a betrayal of their cultural roots and an attempt to copy the behavior of white students.

The homeland students met regularly in their viewing space to watch local African-language news and other local television programming, including dramatic series and local soccer matches. The students were drawn to the local programming because it raised issues relevant to their lives and because they found it more realistic than American films and television series.

One student said: "When watching *Isidingo* [a local drama], it's quick for us to select a particular aspect of what is happening and talk about it. But when it comes to these white soapies, I find it very difficult. In *Isidingo*, there's this guy on the mine who doesn't want to go underground because he had this dream which said he shouldn't. Those are things that happen in our culture and they reflect the way we think."

Another student is quoted as saying: "When I watch American movies I get bored with these technological things. I like it to be more realistic. In most cases I don't believe these overseas things . . . that the main actor will survive the whole movie . . . but he shoots everyone and everyone dies."

For these students, the local television programming plays an important role in reinforcing their identities and in mediating their experience of social life at Rhodes University.

Questions:

1. Do you think that popular culture (movies, television, and music) influences your identity in any way? If it does, how does it influence you specifically? If it does not, why not?

2. Are there any programs/films/music that you feel reaffirm your identity in some way? What are they and why are they relevant to you?

3. Are there any representations in the media of a group to which you belong that you find particularly inaccurate or offensive? If yes, what are they specifically?

Source: Larry Nathan Strelitz, "Media consumption and identity formation: the case of the 'Homeland" viewers," *Media, Culture & Society* 24 (2002), 459–80.

The social science approach could be applied to the study of an event like the July 7, 2005, terrorist attacks in London. There are several ways that scholars might research the impact of culture on communication about such an event. They might study the attitudes of the British people toward Muslims, particularly in light of the revelation that approximately 3,000 British-born or British-based people have passed through Osama Bin Laden's training camps. One study conducted by the Pew Research Center between July 7 and July 17 surveyed attitudes of Americans toward Muslim-Americans and Islam. A majority of those surveyed (55 percent) reported that they hold favorable opinions of Muslim-Americans, and the number stating that they believed that Islam is more likely to encourage violence than other religions was actually lower than two years earlier — it fell to 36 percent from 44 percent in a 2003 survey.[20] Similar studies might survey the attitudes of various nations around the world toward Muslims in the wake of the London bombings, and could compare the results with an earlier study like the 17-nation Pew Global Attitudes Project survey.

Scholars might also study the attitudes of members of various cultures around the world toward the event and their view of what type of response to the attacks is appropriate. Another approach would be to study the use of communication technology, such as blogs, to share information and attitudes about the events among people around the world. Researchers might examine cultural differences in the way blogs and other media are used.

Technology, communication, and the social science approach

The social science approach focuses on culture and communication as two causal variables; research is conducted to determine the causal relationship between these two variables. For example, a research study might examine how national culture influences conflict management styles. In recent years, scholars have begun to study technology use as a variable interacting with culture and communication; studies have been conducted to determine the effect of national culture on the attitudes toward and use of various types of computer-mediated communication, including email, the internet, and the communication technologies used by virtual teams. Researchers O'Kane and Hargie conducted a study to determine the influence of national culture on attitudes toward communication technology in the United Kingdom and Norway. They used Hofstede's cultural value dimensions (power distance, individualism/collectivism, masculinity/femininity, and uncertainty avoidance) to examine the impact of the national cultures of the UK and Norway on attitudes toward communication technology in the workplace. They found that employees in the UK exhibited a more positive attitude overall towards communication technology, which they linked at least in part to a higher degree of individualism in the UK.[22]

In addition to influencing attitudes toward technology, national culture has also been found to influence the use of technology. A recent study of national web portals by Zahir, Dobing, and Hunter revealed that despite similarity in the layout of nearly all the portals and the influence of US portals like Yahoo! as models, there are significant differences among the web portals of various nations that reflect their cultural values.[23]

Nearly all the web portals used multiple columns and a rectangular arrangement, but the use of colors differed significantly among the portals. The difference in the use of color is to be expected given the highly charged cultural significance of colors (see Chapter 7). Many portals used the colors of a nation's flag and also tended to use colors that had religious significance within the nation — green for Islamic cultures, saffron-yellow for Hindu and Buddhist cultures. Because color carries so much weight as a visual symbol, it can be used repeatedly to provide redundant cues intended to reduce ambiguity for members of cultures with a high degree of uncertainty avoidance.[24]

These are just two examples of the many studies being conducted to examine technology as a factor when it interacts with the variables of culture and communication. Many studies also examine email use, the use of intranets, and the impact of national culture on communication within virtual teams. We are sure to see a great deal more research being conducted in these areas.

Benefits and limitations of the social science approach

The social science approach is valuable because it helps identify psychological and sociological variables in the communication process; it has also been useful in identifying how communication styles differ from group to group. This approach has given scholars an understanding of how cultural variables such as ethnicity and gender influence intercultural communication.

The social science approach is limited because it does not recognize that human communication is not always predictable and that reality is not just external but is also an internal construct. It is not possible to identify and measure all the variables that affect communication, and we cannot always predict why some intercultural communication encounters are successful while others are not. Further, the methods used in the social science approach are not always culturally sensitive. For example, Maori oppose traditional social science research because much of it has focused on identifying characteristics that contribute to the "dysfunctional behaviors" of Maori in the dominant majority culture of New Zealand. Maori and their history have been negatively affected by much of the research conducted by the non-Maori academic community. Today, the Maori people argue that Maori research should be done by Maori themselves or at least be initiated by them since they are the ones who best understand "what is necessary to promote their own improvement and empowerment."[25]

Often researchers are too distant from the cultural groups that they are studying, and therefore, do not recognize when there is not an equivalence of measures. To overcome this shortcoming of the social science approach, researchers have developed strategies for ensuring equivalence in cross-cultural research (research that compares cultures). Richard Brislin, a cross-cultural psychologist, has identified several kinds of equivalence that social science researchers should strive to establish; they include *translation equivalence* and *conceptual equivalence*.[26] Translation equivalence is achieved by having material translated several times by different translators; literal translations are not adequate for cross-cultural research. Once materials have gone through the process of multiple translations, they are considered to be translation equivalent. Conceptual equivalence has to do with finding concepts in one language that match those in another. Conceptual equivalence is important to ensure that the concepts being studied are similar across cultures. Concepts like "privacy" or "aggressiveness" might not have exactly the same meaning to members of Asian cultures as they do to members of North American cultures. When researchers establish equivalencies they are better able to isolate and identify precisely how cultures differ from one another.

The Interpretive Approach

Interpretive researchers are interested in describing human behavior, which they believe to be unpredictable and creative; they believe that culture is both created and perpetuated through the means of communication. The interpretive approach uses qualitative research methods that originated in the fields of anthropology and linguistics. These methods include field studies, ethnographies, observations, and participant observations. Interpretive researchers typically become directly involved with members of the communities they are studying and often form close friendships with them. Unlike the social science and critical approaches, which are etic, the interpretive approach is an emic approach, that is, it studies culture from the perspective of members of the cultures being studied.

Researchers using the interpretive approach are interested in describing culture, not in predicting behavior. They seek to find and describe patterns in communication and approach research in a holistic and subjective way. Interpretive researchers seek to answer questions related to what it means to

Figure 3.1 This researcher is conducting an ethnographic study. The ethnographic tradition in intercultural communication grows out of qualitative methods used by anthropologists. When conducting ethnographic studies, researchers seek to describe behavioral patterns, particularly patterns of verbal and non-verbal communication. Ethnography is based on the assumption that culture is always changing and that communication shapes culture and reflects it.

be a member of a particular community and how participants in communities achieve "membering."[27] For example, when conducting her study of elderly Japanese people forming virtual communities online, Kanayama was interested in describing the behaviors of the elderly people and understanding how they interacted with one another when forming virtual communities. She found that self-disclosure through sharing stories and memories was an important part of achieving membering in the virtual community.

Cultural interpretation is concerned with understanding the actions of a group from the inside. Interpretive studies examine patterns of verbal and non-verbal communication in groups, and they also examine the rhetoric of public discourse. Anthropologist Clifford Geertz refers to cultural interpretation as *thick description*, that is, description from the perspective of members of the culture. Thick description contrasts with *thin description*, which merely describes a behavioral pattern without stating what it means to participants.[28] The interpretive approach to the study of intercultural communication uses ethnographic studies to examine patterns of communication in cultures.

Ethnographic studies

The ethnographic tradition in intercultural communication borrows from the qualitative research methods used by anthropologists. Ethnographic research proceeds from the assumption that culture is dynamic and that there is a reciprocal relationship between culture and communication. In other words, communication serves both to shape culture and to reflect it.

Communication scholar Gerry Philipsen has isolated four assumptions of the ethnography of communication. The first is that the participants in a cultural community create shared meanings, that is, they use a commonly understood code for communicating. A *speech code* is a given culture's unwritten set of rules for how to communicate within that culture. The second assumption is that the participants' communication actions have some order or system to them. The third is that the meanings and actions differ from one culture to another. The fourth assumption is that while the patterns differ from one cultural group to another, each group has ways of understanding its own codes and actions.[29] Cultural groups communicate in different ways, and members of a given group share communication patterns. Communication may be non-verbal as well as verbal; for example, wearing certain clothing or other bodily adornment such as a tattoo may be a form of communication just as much as using a particular language or linguistic variation of a language. A particular orientation to time may also be a form of communication and part of the speech code of a particular culture.

Milburn's ethnographic study of two events at a Puerto Rican cultural center located in the northeast United States revealed two differing conceptions of time, "Puerto Rican" time and "American" time. Members of the cultural group themselves made a distinction between the two types of time, and were able to switch between the two depending on the demands of the situation. Milburn found that Puerto Rican time is flexible and is characterized by its "quality." Puerto Rican time flows and focuses on valuing relationships; in Puerto Rican time, relationships between people take precedence over schedules. In contrast, American time is oriented toward schedules, being "on time," and definite beginnings and endings of events. In American time, schedules take precedence over relationships between people (see Chapter 6 for a fuller discussion of different cultural orientations to time).[30]

Anthropologist Dell Hymes has suggested nine categories that can be used for comparative ethnography, that is, for ethnographic studies that seek to compare cultures with one another. These categories are:

1. Ways of speaking, or patterns of communication familiar to the members of the group
2. Ideal of the fluent speaker, or what constitutes an exemplary communicator
3. Speech community, or the group itself and its boundaries
4. Speech situation, or those times when communication is considered appropriate in the community
5. Speech event, or what episodes are considered to be communication for the members of the group
6. Speech act, or a specific set of behaviors taken as an instance of communication within a speech event
7. Components of speech acts, or what the group considers to be the elements of a communicative act
8. The rules of speaking in the community, or the guidelines or standards by which communicative behavior is judged

9. The functions of speech in the community, or what communication is believed to accomplish.[31]

These concepts can be used to compare cultures. For example, different cultural groups have different rules by which communicative behavior is judged and different ideas of what makes for an exemplary speaker. In the Arab culture, speakers are expected to use flowery language and exaggerated statements, but by contrast, Americans value direct speakers who get to the point and "say what they mean." Still other cultures, like the Japanese culture, place a value on silence and knowing when not to speak.

A study by Ojha examined the different uses of humor among Asian Indians and first-generation Asian Indian Americans. The Asian Indians are recent immigrants as opposed to the Asian Indian Americans who were born in the United States. He found that both Asian Indians and Asian Indian Americans used humor as a way of communicating and establishing cultural identity. To some extent the two groups are in fact part of the same speech community. However, there are differences between the two groups; specifically many Asian Indians look down on Asian Indian Americans because they were born in the US rather than in their parents' or grandparents' native country. Different jokes separate the two groups and serve to establish "membering" within one group or the other — either Asian Indian or Asian Indian American. The biggest difference has to do with the Asian Indian Americans not following the traditions of the native country that are important to the more recent immigrants; Asian Indians see the Americanized second and third generation immigrants as a threat to their cultural identity. At the same time, the Asian Indian Americans put down the recent immigrants for being "fresh off the boat." The kind of jokes that they tell separate these two groups and serve to establish individuals as members of in-groups and out-groups based on their humor.[32]

Gerry Philipsen's work with speech codes informs much current interpretive communication research. Philipsen conducted an ethnographic study of the communication patterns of men in a white, working-class neighborhood in Chicago called Teamsterville. He found that men in Teamsterville were more likely to speak to express solidarity with other men who shared a similar identity to their own. They were less likely to use speech in situations with authority figures, such as their bosses at work, and in situations with their children, wives, and girlfriends, and with outsiders. Men were more likely to produce a lot of speech in particular places in their neighborhood — on their own turf. They were less likely to speak or speak openly outside the boundaries of Teamsterville. Their neighborhood, the street corner, the bar, the porch were all scenes where speaking could appropriately occur for the men in Teamsterville.[33]

Based on his work, Philipsen suggests that speech codes are distinctive, that is they vary from one cultural group to another. Speech codes constitute a culture's sense of how to be a part of the social group and how to be a competent communicator within that group. Further, speech codes give interactions meanings. These codes are embedded in daily speech, that is, they are evident when communicators talk about how they are speaking and explain why they communicate the way they do. Finally, speech codes are very powerful, as they form criteria that members of a culture use to evaluate individuals' performance as communicators and to judge whether or not they are competent and effective communicators within a particular group.[34]

The goal of scholars conducting ethnographic studies is to describe the communication patterns that represent the subjective experience of various cultural groups; these scholars use qualitative research methods like participant observation and interviews. For example, Aoki's ethnographic study of Mexican Americans in Biola in California examined the role of family and religion as unifying forces in a small, agricultural community. Aoki's study was conducted over four summers of participant observations that entailed 43 formal interviews and also included additional informal discussions and observations taken at other times of the year. He found that both religion and the family help to hold the community together in the face of economic hardship and lives of hard physical labor as agricultural workers.

Aoki also spent time collecting observational field notes and engaging in informal talks with people in their homes. He used both his own observations and data from his interviews to understand what it meant to be a member of the community. Aoki found that the primary influences that bound together members of the community were the importance of family, the Catholic religion, and the value placed on hard work. Being a member of the Mexican American community in Biola meant recognizing the importance of *la familia*, faith, and a strong work ethic.[35]

Rhetorical analysis

Rhetorical analysis is one type of interpretive research based on the analysis of public speeches and other oral discourses; these discourses are studied in the context in which they occur. This type of analysis may in fact be the oldest type of communication scholarship since it dates to the ancient Greek rhetoricians. Researchers using the rhetorical approach analyze films, newspaper articles, and television programs to study public representations of a culture. In their analysis they would study the rhetorical strategies, such as metaphor and simile, used to reveal or hide culture. Although they are not directly involved with the subjects of their studies, rhetorical scholars do take a subjective approach to their analysis. Typically, the rhetorical approach is used to study one speech community in depth rather than to look for differences across cultures. The contexts in which communication occurs are very important to scholars using this approach. A study by Merskin examines the rhetoric of President George W. Bush's addresses to the nation in the weeks following the 9/11 tragedy. Her textual analysis revealed that the President's speeches reflected "an identifiable model of enemy image construction."[36] Merskin argues that the words, phrases,

and allusions used in the presidential rhetoric were "grounded in powerful connections to universal notions of enmity."[37] She notes specifically stereotyping,
identification with evil, and zero-sum thinking (what is good for the enemy
is bad for us), which is a major component of realism or power politics in the
international relations field. Merskin focuses on the number of times the word
"evil" is repeated in the speeches and the continued reference to a struggle of
"good versus evil." She notes the animalistic nature of the stereotyping when
the President states that "my administration is determined to find, to get 'em
running, to haunt [*sic*] 'em down, those who did this to America."[38] Merskin
goes on to argue that the political rhetoric used in the President's speeches
leads to "the construction of all Arabs as terrorists and all Muslims as Arab
terrorists."[39] An analysis of the speeches of other world leaders is likely to
yield similar attitudes toward their nation's enemies; certainly, some nations
such as North Korea view the US as the enemy and espouse anti-American
sentiments. The public rhetoric of leaders and others in positions of power in
many nations can reveal important aspects of both cooperation and conflict
among nations.

Methodologies of the interpretive approach

The interpretive approach is based on fieldwork, that is to say, that researchers
using this approach typically go to the place where the intercultural communication encounters they wish to study occur; they may go to business meetings,
hotels, family gatherings or classrooms or all of these settings depending on the
aspects of a cultural group that they are studying. Fieldwork in intercultural
communication involves the study of day-to-day interactions as they are
happening. For example, in his study of the Mexican American community
in Biola, Aoki spent many days observing and interviewing members of the
community over a period of four years.

One aspect of fieldwork is a process called *participant-observation*; as the
name suggests, in participant-observation the researcher studies a setting in
which he or she is a legitimate participant. In other words, a researcher may
study intercultural encounters within his own ethnic community or at the
office where she works. Researchers using participant-observation techniques
may study new situations where they have to spend a period of time learning
about the setting and establishing their legitimate right to be a participant; for
example, a researcher may take a position working with a company abroad
and may over time become a member of the corporate culture or may go and
live within a community in another culture and may gradually gain legitimacy as a member of the community. If researchers study groups of which
they are already members, like their own ethnic communities, then personal
involvement may detract from their objectivity. However, if researchers join
a community for a period of time to study it, their experiences may not
truly represent the lived experiences of actual group members.[40] One way to
overcome these shortcomings is the process of "strange making" where the

researcher adopts the dual stance of participant and observer and views daily activities as if she did not know what was going on in order to "make strange" what is normally taken for granted.

Ethnographic researchers rely on many different types of data including photographs, video, film, audio tapes, handwritten field notes, and the collection of artifacts. They typically participate in meetings, social events, and ritual ceremonies within the culture in addition to conducting interviews and focus groups. They also study materials produced within the culture, such as works of literature, film, television, and other media. Ethnographers gather data from generalizations made by members of the culture, from their own observations, from the experiences of members of the culture, and also from their own interactions with members of the culture.

An ethnographic study by Scrase analyzed the impact of a globalized television culture on the transformation of middle-class Bengali cultural identities. Scrase and his co-researcher Ruchira Ganguly-Scrase conducted semi-structured in-depth interviews with 120 people over several months. Among the respondents were 20 key informants, individuals that the researchers had known for over 10 years from earlier research studies. The researchers spent time watching television with the informants and making observations. Their findings were not clear cut, but suggested that television had a limited impact on middle-class cultural identity in West Bengal. For example, while many respondents were concerned about the portrayal of women on television, they were concerned for different reasons. Some felt that the portrayal of women was degrading to all Indian women, some felt that such portrayals had no significant influence on women, and still others thought that television could play a positive role in getting women to question their social position and become open to greater opportunities outside of the role of housewife and mother.[41]

We have discussed how social science researchers might study the London bombings of July 2005. Interpretive researchers would take still another approach to this event. They might examine the rhetoric used by world leaders when speaking about the bombings. For example, they might analyze speeches given by Prime Minister Tony Blair and other members of Parliament immediately after the event, just as Merskin did an analysis of President Bush's speeches after the 9/11 tragedy. Or they might examine the rhetoric of leaders in other nations about the bombings.

Another approach interpretive scholars might take would be to conduct in-depth interviews with individuals in London to get their reactions to the bombing; such interviews might focus specifically on individuals who use London's public transportation systems or, perhaps, on members of the British Muslim community to get their responses to the event. Another approach might be to study the messages posted on listservs and in other virtual communities shortly after the attacks. Several blogs and websites posted the responses of individuals who were in London at the sites of the bombs, some of whom were actually evacuated from the subway. For example, *Slashdot*, a blog focused on technology-related news that typically gets a few hundred comments on a discussion, had more than 2,300 postings related to the bombings. Some visitors to the site blamed Britain's foreign policy for the attacks, while others "railed against terrorists," and still others stated that "political squabbles were inappropriate."[42]

A phenomenon related to the bombings is the rise of citizen journalism as many ordinary citizens with camera phones and video phones snapped pictures of the immediate aftermath of the bomb blasts. Their chronicling of the event both through their pictures and their comments on blogs where many of the pictures were posted marks a significant advance in citizen journalism. Flickr. com had more than 300 photos from these citizen journalists posted within 8 hours of the bombings. Some of the photographs were graphic images of the most severely injured victims of the blast, and questions arose regarding the ethics of taking such photographs. Mark Glaser of the Annenberg School of Journalism questions whether citizen journalists are in some cases really citizen paparazzi.[43] In addition to studying the reactions of Londoners who were at the bombing sites, an interpretive scholar might also study the impact of new technological capabilities on communication about the event; such a study might well examine the need for standards to guide citizen journalists as well as the ethical issues involved (see Chapter 9).

Technology, communication, and the interpretive approach

In recent years, scholars using the interpretive approach have begun to conduct ethnographic studies of virtual communities, that is, communities of individuals who communicate with one another through internet chat rooms, websites, email listservs, and other methods of computer-mediated communication. The elderly Japanese people in Kanayama's study are one example of a virtual community. There are many different types of virtual communities, including students taking an online course together, immigrants using a website to share information, business professionals working as part of a virtual team, and fans of a particular sports team or musical performer who share their opinions online. These communities share many of the characteristics of cultural groups that are situated in the same physical/geographic location. For both traditional and virtual communities, there are certain guidelines that dictate who can be a member and who cannot, there are rules of conduct for what constitutes acceptable and unacceptable behavior within the community, and there are — in extreme cases — means for getting rid of someone who the community feels has forfeited his/her right to membership. Of course, these rules are rarely formal or written, yet they exist and dictate who may participate in a group as a member and who is considered an outsider.

Many immigrants use the internet to establish virtual communities of their ethnic peer groups. For example, Russian immigrants to the US have used the internet to establish websites to share information with one another. Similarly, women of South Asian origin living in the UK created a virtual community to re-establish relationships that were severed by their geographic move from India.[44] Immigrants are only one group that uses the internet to create virtual communities; there are many sites where fans of popular entertainers communicate with one another and share opinions and feelings. Pop stars like Lady Gaga and Katy Perry and sports teams like the Green Bay Packers, the New York Yankees, and the Orlando Magic all have fan websites devoted to them.

Websites are not the only technology used to create virtual communities wherein individuals can establish and reinforce their identities through connection with others who share their experiences and concerns. For example, Finnish teenagers use mobile communication to establish their own personal space and communities. Finland has one of the highest distribution and penetration rates of mobile phones in the world.[45] Oksman and Turtiainen conducted a *media ethnography* of the use of mobile communication by Finnish teenagers. A media ethnography is the ethnographic study of the everyday use of new media and technologies. Oksman and Turtiainen found that mobile communication plays a central role in the social identity of Finnish teens and in the creation of social communities; the use of mobile communication defines membering in social groups and defines the boundaries of social networks. They found that teenagers particularly favored text messaging because it allowed them a "quiet and simple way to maintain their social network without their parents' knowledge,"[46] and it gave them more control over the presentation of self than in face-to-face encounters. Further, the researchers discovered that many teens saw the mobile phone as "symbolically representing the community to which they belong, be it a group of friends or people united by a common hobby."[47]

Benefits and limitations of the interpretive approach

The interpretive approach is valuable because it studies communication in context and provides a detailed understanding of communication within specific communities. There are two drawbacks to this approach to studying intercultural communication. One is the fact that few interpretivist studies have actually examined intercultural communication; most studies focus on one particular group and do not examine the interaction between two groups across cultures. A second drawback is the fact that researchers are often outsiders to the communities that they study, and therefore, they are not able to represent the communication patterns within a community from the perspective of its members. Scholars using the interpretive approach have been criticized for making assumptions about the meaning of symbolic activity in cultures and about who can speak "for" or "as" a member of a cultural group.[48] Their unspoken biases related to their privileged standpoints are called into question.

Some ethical concerns arise in ethnographic studies, particularly in relation to researchers forming intimate relationships with their informants while at the same time maintaining the neutrality and distance necessary to describe cultural patterns.[49] Tanno and Jandt suggest that one way to handle this ethical dilemma is for researchers to view the members of the culture they are studying as co-producers of knowledge; they argue that ethnographic fieldwork can become a collaboration between the researcher and the researched.[50] Following along the same lines, Gonzalez states that researchers should allow the research subjects to show them how to function in their world.[51] These approaches to ethnographic study should help to overcome some of the limitations of traditional ethnography.

POWER CHECK
Participatory Action Research (PAR)

Scholars using the interpretive approach to the study of intercultural communication must address questions related to their privileged positions when they in essence speak "for" or "as" members of the cultural groups that they study. Issues of power enter in to interpretive scholarship because the researchers often inhabit positions of power when they enter communities that they wish to study. Interpretive scholars have long been concerned with ethical issues related to their studies, and they have codes of ethics from both the American Anthropological Association and the American Psychological Association to guide them in conducting fieldwork. However, there is still concern over the fact that in many cases there is an unequal power distribution between the researcher and the cultural groups being studied.[1]

It is important for researchers to consider the effects they may have on the cultural groups they study. Of particular concern is participant observation ethnographies wherein the researcher establishes close personal relationships with members of the group being studied. Jandt and Tanno stress the importance of treating members of the group being studied as "co-researchers" rather than as "subjects" of study. They have suggested a research paradigm in which members of the cultural groups studied are both co-producers and co-owners of the knowledge produced. They believe that instead of producing scholarship whose only audience is other scholars, researchers should communicate their findings back to the research participants.[2] Communication scholar William Foote Whyte has suggested the title Participatory Action Research (PAR) to describe research studies that include participants at all stages of the process from the initial design of the project, to the data-gathering stage, to the analysis and conclusion stage, and finally to the actions that arise out of the research.[3] Jandt and Tanno and Whyte and other researchers like them are concerned about addressing the unequal power differential that exists in some interpretive scholarship and empowering research participants by having them share in the production and ownership of knowledge.

Notes
1. Judith N. Martin and Ruth Leon W. Butler, "Toward an Ethic of Intercultural Communication Research," in Virginia H. Milhouse, Molefi Kete Asante, and Peter O. Nwosu, eds., *Transcultural Realities* (Thousand Oaks, CA: Sage, 2001), pp. 283–98.
2. Dolores V. Tanno and Fred E. Jandt, "Redefining the 'Other' in Multicultural

Research," in Judith N. Martin, Thomas K. Nakayama, and Lisa A. Flores, eds., *Readings in Intercultural Communication*, 2nd ed. (Boston, MA: McGraw-Hill, 2002), pp. 378–85.

3. William Foote Whyte, "Introduction," in William Foote Whyte, ed., *Participatory Action Research* (Newbury Park, CA: Sage, 1991), pp. 7–15.

References

1. Sue Ellen Christian and Maria Knight Lapinski, "Support for the Contact Hypothesis: High School Students' Attitudes Toward Muslims Post 9-11," *Journal of Intercultural Communication Research*, 32 (2003), 247–63.
2. Tomoko Kanayama, "Ethnographic Research on the Experience of Japanese Elderly People Online," *New Media & Society* 5 (2003), 267–88.
3. Ashleigh C. Merritt and Robert L. Helmreich, "Human Factors on the Flight Deck: The Influence of National Culture," in Fred E. Jandt, ed., *Intercultural Communication: A Global Reader* (Thousand Oaks, CA: Sage, 2004), pp. 13–27.
4. Naomi Sugimoto, "A Japan-U.S. Comparison of Apology Styles," *Communication Research* 24 (1997), 349–69.
5. Peter A. Andersen et al., "Nonverbal Communication Across Cultures," in William B. Gudykunst and Bella Mody, eds., *Handbook of International and Intercultural Communication* (Thousand Oaks, CA: Sage, 2002), pp. 239–52.
6. Stella Ting-Toomey and John G. Oetzel, *Managing Intercultural Conflict Effectively* (Thousand Oaks, CA: Sage, 2001), pp. 27–8.
7. Ibid., p. 176.
8. Joshua S. Goldstein, *International Relations*, 3rd ed. (New York: Longman, 1999), p. 234.
9. Kalle Siira, Randall G. Rogan, and Jeffrey A. Hall, "'A Spoken Word is an Arrow Shot': A Comparison of Finnish and U.S. Conflict Management and Face Maintenance," *Journal of Intercultural Communication Research* 33 (2004), 89–107.
10. William B. Gudykunst, "Cultural Variability in Communication," *Communication Research* 24 (1997), 331.
11. Geert Hofstede, *Culture's Consequences* (Beverly Hills, CA: Sage, 1980); Y. Ito, "Socio-Cultural Backgrounds of Japanese Interpersonal Communication Style," *Civilisations* 39 (1989), 101–37; H. C. Triandis, *Individualism and Collectivism* (Boulder, CO: Westview, 1995).
12. William B. Gudykunst, "Individualistic and Collectivistic Perspectives on Communication: An Introduction," *International Journal of Intercultural Relations* 22 (1998), 107–34.
13. William B. Gudykunst, *Bridging Differences: Effective Intergroup Communication*, 3rd ed. (Thousand Oaks, CA: Sage, 1998), p. 45.
14. Gudykunst, *Bridging Differences*, pp. 49–55.
15. Howard Giles and Kimberly A. Noels, "Communication Accommodation in Intercultural Encounters," in Judith N. Martin, Thomas K. Nakayama, and Lisa A. Flores, eds., *Readings in Intercultural Communication*, 2nd ed. (Boston, MA: McGraw-Hill, 2002), p. 119.
16. Ibid., p. 120.
17. Howard Giles, Nikolas Coupland, and Justine Coupland, "Accommodation Theory: Communication, Context, and Consequence," in Howard Giles, Justine Coupland, and Nikolas Coupland eds., *Contexts of Accommodation: Developments in Applied Sociolinguistics* (Cambridge: Cambridge University Press, 1991), p. 19.
18. Beverly Jean Smith, "Black English: Steppin Up? Lookin Back," in Theresa Perry and Lisa Delpit eds., *The Real Ebonics Debate* (Boston, MA: Beacon Press, 1998), p. 199.
19. Giles and Noels, p. 120.
20. Jean-Louis Sauvage, "Code-Switching: An Everyday Reality in Belgium," in Judith N. Martin, Thomas K. Nakayama, and Lisa A. Flores, eds., *Readings in Intercultural Communication*, 2nd ed. (Boston, MA: McGraw-Hill, 2002), p. 158.

21. The Pew Forum on Religion and Public Life, "Views of Muslim-Americans Hold Steady After London Bombings," July 26, 2005, http://pewforum.org/docs/index.php?DocID=89, accessed October 6, 2005.
22. Paula O'Kane and Owen Hargie, "Technology Travels: Can National Culture Impact Upon Attitudes Toward Communication-Technology?" *Journal of Intercultural Communication Research* 33 (2004), 49–62.
23. Sajjad Zahir, Brian Dobing, and M. Gordon Hunter, "Analysis of the Cross-Cultural Dimensions of National Web Portals," in Sherif Kamel, ed., *Managing Globally with Information Technology* (Hershey, PA: IRM Press, 2003), pp. 37–8.
24. Ibid., p. 41.
25. Dolores V. Tanno and Fred E. Jandt, "Redefining the 'Other' in Multicultural Research," in Judith N. Martin, Thomas K. Nakayama, and Lisa A. Flores, eds., *Readings in Intercultural Communication*, 2nd ed. (Boston, MA: McGraw-Hill, 2002), p. 381.
26. Richard Brislin, *Understanding Culture's Influence on Behavior*, 2nd ed. (Belmont, CA: Wadsworth, 1999).
27. Gerry Philipsen, *Speaking Culturally: Explorations in Social Communication* (Albany, NY: State University of New York Press, 1992), p. 14.
28. Clifford Geertz, *Local Knowledge: Further Essays in Interpretive Anthropology* (New York: Basic Books, 1983).
29. Gerry Philipsen, "An Ethnographic Approach to Communication Studies," in Brenda Dervin et al., eds., *Rethinking Communication: Paradigm Exemplars* (Newbury Park, CA: Sage, 1989), pp. 258–69.
30. Trudy Milburn, "Enacting 'Puerto Rican Time' in the United States," in Mary Jane Collier, ed., *Constituting Cultural Difference Through Discourse* (Thousand Oaks, CA: Sage, 2001), pp. 47–76.
31. Dell Hymes, *Foundations in Sociolinguistics: An Ethnographic Approach* (Philadelphia, PA: University of Pennsylvania Press, 1974).
32. Ajay K. Ojha, "Humor: A Distinctive Way of Speaking That Can Create Cultural Identity," *Journal of Intercultural Communication Research* 32:3 (2003), 161–74.
33. Gerry Philipsen, "Places for Speaking in Teamsterville," in Judith N. Martin, Thomas K. Nakayama, and Lisa A. Flores, eds., *Readings in Intercultural Communication*, 2nd ed. (Boston, MA: McGraw-Hill, 2002), pp. 192–201.
34. Gerry Philipsen, "A Theory of Speech Codes," in Gerry Philipsen and Terrance L. Albrecht, eds., *Developing Communication Theories* (Albany, NY: SUNY Press, 1997), pp. 119–56.
35. Eric Aoki, "Mexican American Ethnicity in Biola, CA: An Ethnographic Account of Hard Work, Family, and Religion," *The Howard Journal of Communications* 11 (2000), 207–27.
36. Debra Merskin, "The Construction of Arabs as Enemies: Post-September 11 Discourse of George W. Bush," *Mass Communication & Society* 7:2 (2004), 157.
37. Ibid., p. 172.
38. Ibid., p. 169.
39. Ibid., p. 172.
40. Ron Scollon and Suzanne Wong Scollon, *Intercultural Communication: A Discourse Approach*, 2nd ed. (Malden, MA: Blackwell, 2001), p. 18.
41. Timothy J. Scrase, "Television, The Middle Classes and the Transformation of Cultural Identities in West Bengal, India," *Gazette: The International Journal for Communication Studies* 64:4 (2002), 323–42.
42. Vauhini Vara, "Bloggers and Photographers Chronicle Chaos in London," *The Wall Street Journal Online*, July 7, 2005, http://online.wsj.com/public/article/0,,SB112074780386479568-Fnj6Lqv_Hf1RxCwVSpb8eG0T4pg_20050806,00.html?mod=blogs, accessed October 11 2005.
43. Mark Glaser, "Did London Bombings Turn Citizen Journalists into Citizen Paparazzi?" *Online Journalism Review*, July 12, 2005, www.ojr.org/ojr/stories/050712glaser, accessed October 11, 2005.
44. Kenneth Thompson, "Border Crossings and Diasporic Identities: Media Use and Leisure Practices of an Ethnic Minority," *Qualitative Sociology* 25 (2002), 409–18.
45. Virpi Oksman and Jussi Turtiainen, "Mobile Communication as a Social Stage," *New Media & Society* 6:3 (2004), 320.
46. Ibid., p. 336.

47. Ibid.
48. Mary Jane Collier, "Constituting Cultural Difference through Discourse: Current Research Themes of Politics, Perspectives, and Problematics," in Mary Jane Collier, ed., *Constituting Cultural Difference through Discourse* (Thousand Oaks, CA: Sage, 2000), p. 6.
49. Judith N. Martin and Ruth Leon W. Butler, "Toward an Ethic of Intercultural Communication Research," in Virginia H. Milhouse, Molefi Kete Asante, and Peter O. Nwosu, eds., *Transcultural Realities* (Thousand Oaks, CA: Sage, 2001), p. 287.
50. Tanno and Jandt, p. 378–85.
51. Maria Cristina Gonzalez, "The Four Seasons of Ethnography: A Creation-Centered Ontology for Ethnography," *International Journal of Intercultural Relations* 24 (2000), 623–50.

4 Critical and Dialectical Approaches

Communication scholars Mastro and Stern examined over 2,000 television commercials to study the portrayal of racial minorities in prime-time advertising. They found different patterns of portrayals when African American, Asian American, Latino, Native American, and white characters were depicted in the advertisement. Asian Americans, Latinos, and Native Americans were underrepresented, and were, at times, negatively depicted. Their study provided insights into the impact of such ads on audience members' self-images.[1]

Tae-Soon, a Korean student at UCLA, shares the communication patterns of his culture; he is careful to use formal language when addressing his seniors and to adhere to the formal social hierarchy observed in Korea. For example, he has a good sense of nunch'i, or tact and social savoir faire. He knows how to communicate using subtle non-verbal clues and also how to read those clues in social situations.[2] In many ways, Tae-Soon's patterns of communication reflect his culture; however, he also has a personal communication style, a way of gesturing and phrasing his words that is unique to him. Further, as a student in the Amercian culture he has adapted to American communication patterns, particularly those of Southern California. When he is in class, he still uses polite and formal language to show respect for his professors. However, when he is with his roommates and other friends, he uses American slang and speaks in a much less formal manner. Tae-Soon's experience demonstrates two dialectics that are characteristic of intercultural communication. They are the tension between the cultural and the individual, and the tension between the personal and the contextual. At times Tae-Soon's communication patterns are representative of his culture, but at other times they are unique to him as an individual. Similarly, his style of communication changes depending upon the context he finds himself in — more formal in the classroom and less formal with friends.

Mastro and Stern's study is an example of the critical approach to the study of intercultural communication. Researchers using the critical approach are particularly interested in the historical context of communication and in understanding the role that power and power relationships play in communication.

Figure 4.1 In class, this student uses formal language (both verbal language and body language) to present himself as a serious student. Outside of class, he is much more relaxed. He speaks much less formally and often uses slang. His behavior demonstrates the tension between the personal and the contextual. Often individuals change their style of interacting with others based on the social role that they are playing. For example, a physician may be very serious when interacting with patients, but may behave quite differently when in the company of friends and family in a social setting.

The critical approach is similar to the social science and interpretive approaches in that the scholars who use it are interested in studying human behavior; however, the critical approach is different from the two other approaches in that scholars who use it are also interested in bringing about social change.

The description of Tae-Soon's experience demonstrates two of the six dialectics characteristic of intercultural communication. The dialectical approach was developed by Martin, Nakayama, and Flores in order to address potential contradictions among the three main approaches to the study of intercultural communication. The social science, critical, and interpretive approaches are all valuable; however, each one has its limitations. The dialectical approach provides a framework for reconciling the different approaches and the diverse types of knowledge that you may encounter when studying intercultural communication. While it is not a specific theory like the other three approaches, the dialectical approach is a valuable perspective from which to study intercultural communication.

In this chapter we discuss the nature of the critical and the dialectical approaches and the research methods used in each. We demonstrate how an event might be studied from the two different approaches and examine the impact of technology on each one. We also discuss their benefits and limitations. We begin by discussing the critical approach and then move on to the dialectical approach.

The Critical Approach

The critical approach views reality as subjective and focuses on the importance of studying the context in which communication occurs. Critical scholars view culture in terms of power struggles and study cultural differences specifically as they relate to the unequal distribution of power within society. They are not only interested in studying human behavior across cultures, but also in effecting change in society; they believe that by their study and analysis of the role of power in cultural encounters, they can assist people in opposing the oppressive forces in society.

Scholars using the critical approach use textual analyses, that is, they study media, television, movies, journalism, and other cultural "texts" in order to analyze the forces that shape cultures. The study of television commercials mentioned at the beginning of the chapter is a critical study because the researchers analyzed media (in this case television commercials) and sought to determine how that media shaped culture (in this case the self-images of members of different racial groups). Typically, the texts studied by critical scholars are products of a culture's economy and its social and political structure. These scholars usually do not use face-to-face interaction with or observation of cultures to study them, but prefer to rely on studying products of a culture that reflect its political and social structures.

The critical approach sees communication within and among cultures in terms of power struggles. It operates from the assumption that cultural boundaries are negotiated by groups that compete for power within a culture. Rather than assuming that members of a given culture will all communicate in the same way, critical scholars believe that those groups who are in power are privileged to determine the meanings that are assigned to communication within the culture. For example, critical scholars would argue that the dominant groups within a culture dictate the type of communication that exists in movies, books, newspapers, and other media. In the United States, images of female beauty depicted in advertisements and other media reflect the dominant culture — that is, the ideal female is most frequently depicted as Caucasian, usually physically fit and slim with blonde or brown hair and striking eyes. While there are some images of beauty that reflect the diversity of US society, for the most part, the image of female perfection is one that reflects the most powerful group in society (white Americans) as the ideal.[3]

Majority and minority cultures

A *majority culture* is the dominant group within a society; while the majority culture may often be the largest group within a society, it is not defined in terms of size, but rather in terms of power. The majority culture sets the standard for what is valued in society, and *minority cultures*, that is, those individuals who are members of groups other than the majority group, are typically disadvantaged in terms of social, economic, and political power. In Rwanda, the majority culture is the Hutu, while the minority culture is the Tutsi. During the civil war in 1990, political and economic upheavals exacerbated ethnic tensions culminating in the April 1994 genocide of roughly 800,000 Tutsis by Hutus. Minority cultures are also referred to as co-cultural groups. In some situations, minority group members may face subtle prejudice from members of the majority who oppose immigration, as is the case in the United States. While in others places, they may experience direct oppression, as was the case between Sunni Arabs in high political power versus the marginalized Kurds in Iraq during Saddam Hussein's rule.

The Welsh are a minority culture in Britain; they have been disempowered since Wales was annexed by England in 1536. As a result of the annexation, English became Wales' official language and in 1870 English was made the exclusive language of instruction in Welsh schools. Students who spoke Welsh in school were punished, and it was not until the 1970s that bilingual education was introduced. The Welsh culture was suppressed by those in power, in this case, the English, and it has only been in the past four decades that there has been a resurgence of the Welsh language and culture. Many economic inequalities still exist for the Welsh people as part of a minority culture within a large nation. Another example of a minority culture is French Canadians, who represent about one-fifth of the population of Canada and are concentrated in the province of Quebec. Despite their minority status, French Canadians have fought strenuously to maintain their language and culture and have even sought independence from the rest of Canada.

Minority cultures are not only associated with entire provinces or conquered regions, however, they may also consist of ethnic groups, co-cultural groups within a society, and even groups based on gender, age, and sexual orientation. Within the United States, individuals may face prejudicial treatment based on their gender, race, or sexual orientation. The groups that face discrimination based on minority status may also change over time as society changes. In the early 1900s, there was a large influx of immigrants from Ireland and Italy to the United States. These immigrants were the targets of bigotry and prejudicial treatment; they were often turned down for jobs and were confined to living in ghettos because of their ethnic backgrounds. The majority of immigrants to the US today come from Asia and Latin America. Many of these recent immigrants experience discrimination today just as the Italian and Irish immigrants did in the 1900s.

How political and social structures influence communication

The majority culture in a society controls that society's political and social institutions; typically, members of the majority culture hold positions of authority in government, education, the media, and other social institutions. One example of how dominant groups can dictate communication within a culture has to do with language usage, and which languages are allowed or which are privileged (see Chapter 5 for a more detailed discussion of language and power). Another example of how dominant groups control communication within a culture would be the way that American television stereotypes co-cultural groups within society. In 2000, Dixon and Linz found that on television news and in reality-based programming, African Americans were portrayed as criminals and troublemakers;[4] similarly, Oliver (1994) found that reality-based programs like *Cops, America's Most Wanted, FBI,* and *The Untold Story* prevalently depicted a black criminal stereotype.[5] Many negative outcomes can result from such stereotyping both in terms of black self-esteem and also in terms of encounters between African-Americans and other groups in society.

Of course in some nations the influence of political structures is very restrictive; some regimes censor the communication media and do not allow for freedom of expression. Following the controversial 2009 Iran presidential election, when the government restricted the media and regular channels of communication, the masses of Iranian youth and opposition began to use the internet and Twitter for the dissemination of information. Despite the economic changes in China since its adoption of a market economy, the Communist political system still controls the press and has been more successful than any other nation in censoring the internet. Access to many Western websites is blocked, and censors monitor email, chat rooms, and blogs to identify any suspicious online activity; one 23-year-old student was arrested for posting a message stating his support for the Roman Catholic Church, which is banned in China.[6]

However, even in nations that grant freedom to the press, the views of the majority culture often shape what is communicated and the way members of various co-cultural groups are depicted in the media. In his classical work, *Orientalism,* Edward Said illustrates how television and films can serve to reinforce stereotypical views of members of some co-cultural groups and can render some groups, like Native Americans, virtually invisible. A study by Mastro and Robinson examined images of minorities on prime-time television; their study focused on television characterizations that related to crime and violence. They found that Asian Americans, Latinos, and Native Americans were underrepresented. They also found that when minorities were depicted as perpetrators of crimes they were at greater risk of experiencing excessive force at the hands of police officers than were Caucasian offenders. Mastro and Robinson suggest that such depictions may give viewers the impression that members of minority groups are highly dangerous and must be controlled by any possible means. They further suggest that portrayals of minorities in association with crime may arouse fear and apprehension in Caucasian viewers when they interact with minority group members.[7] Media stereotyping of members of co-cultural groups is not unique to American culture. The news media in Eastern Europe reflects the rise of ethnic conflicts and ethnocentrism in that region. The Roma are one of the most threatened ethnic minorities in the Eastern European states. Karmen Erjavec describes the situation in Slovenia, an ethnically homogeneous nation, which recognizes Italian and Hungarian ethnic minorities. Slovenia does not recognize the over 7,000 Roma who live there as an official ethnic minority group. Because they are not recognized, the Romani children are not entitled to formal education in their native language and are, therefore, denied many opportunities in society because they lack education. Erjavec describes the way the Slovenian press serves to legitimize the discrimination against the Roma people. Erjavec's study revealed that news reports focus on events that present the majority culture in a positive light and typically do not depict members of the minority group unless their actions are consistent with the dominant stereotype of them. For example, even in a story that describes the efforts of villagers to prevent a Romani family from moving into a house which they bought legally and have every right to inhabit, the press depicts the villagers as nobly protecting themselves and the Romani family as lazy, as behaving in a way that is not "normal," and as having an unusually large number of children.[8]

Critical theory scholars, like the IR constructionists, believe that knowledge within a culture is socially constructed, but only by those members of the culture in positions of power. In addition to seeing culture and communication as dynamic, they also see it as contested. In power struggles, some groups are empowered and others are disempowered. The zero-sum mentality is classically associated with the work of the IR realist school. Groups may be disempowered because of their minority status within a nation, as in the case of the Roma in Slovenia. Changes in the political regime may also lead to changes in which groups are in power and disempowered respectively; many changes have occurred as a result of the dissolution of the former Soviet Union. Historically, many groups within US society have been disempowered because of their status as co-cultural groups, and many groups still are disempowered.

The efforts of critical scholarship have helped and continue to help members of co-cultural groups gain recognition and equality in society. Researchers using the critical approach believe that by studying intercultural communication from the perspective of power, they will be able to effect changes in the social and political structure in order to improve conditions for those individuals and groups who are disadvantaged within the society. These researchers focus on macro-contexts, particularly the social, political, and historical contexts that influence intercultural communication.

Critical scholars believe that the goal of intercultural research is to identify and make explicit power differences in order to liberate those individuals who lack power in society. The first step in addressing inequalities is to bring them to light. By examining the role of communication in creating group identities, critical scholars wish to deconstruct assumptions about reality in order to challenge social realities that reinforce exploitation of some groups within society. In most nations, power is not distributed equally between the majority and minority cultures.

Cultural studies and social change

Cultural studies is an interdisciplinary field that combines literary theory, film studies, cultural anthropology, sociology, and political science. Cultural studies researchers, much like scholars using the critical approach to studying intercultural communication, are interested in examining the dynamic nature of cultures, particularly in terms of relationships between majority and minority cultures. They seek to use their scholarship to bring about social change. Such research often focuses on popular culture, including television programs, movies, magazines, and video games. Popular culture can play an important role in the understanding of intercultural communication.

We are all surrounded by popular culture, from television programs to sporting events to musical performances. In fact, in most of the developed world it is very difficult to get away from the pervasive influence of popular culture. We are bombarded by advertisements, magazines, films, and various other cultural products every day of our lives. In some ways, our knowledge and perception of members of cultural groups other than our own is shaped by popular culture. Because popular culture is so influential in determining our perceptions, we need to be concerned about the way cultural groups are portrayed in films, television programs, newspapers, and other media. For example, much damage can result when some ethnic groups are portrayed as more likely to commit crimes or as less intelligent than others. In the same way, when individuals are portrayed as weak, ineffectual, or of little value to society based on their age, gender, or sexual orientation negative consequences can result both for the groups so portrayed and for society as a whole.

MEDIA IMPACT
Stereotyping Still Exists in Images of Female Scientists and Engineers

The media portrays and reinforces cultural stereotypes about women's roles in society. In the U.S., popular films have conveyed stereotypical images of women in science, engineering, and technology. Although the portrayal of women has improved over time, many female characters are still depicted as being more concerned about their appearance and about romance than they are about their academic studies and their profession. Communication scholar Jocelyn Steinke analyzed images of female scientists and engineers in popular films from 1991 to 2001, and found that subtle forms of stereotyping still exist. She conducted an analysis of 74 films that featured scientists and engineers as primary characters. The films included *Jurassic Park*, *The Lost World: Jurassic Park*, *Contact*, *Sphere*, *Volcano*, *The Saint*, *Batman and Robin*, *Nutty Professor II: The Klumps*, and *The Mummy Returns*.

While most of these films depict the female scientists and engineers as competent professionals, they almost exclusively portrayed the women as single and without children. The films did not depict the reality of women seeking to balance a career with family life. Because our culture largely conceives of scientists as "wedded to their work," women are depicted as having to sacrifice marriage and motherhood to succeed professionally. Further, the characters in the films experienced both overt and subtle discrimination and were "questioned or challenged by male colleagues or peers, criticized for a lack of credentials and professional experience, experienced a loss of research funding or lab space when male supervisors failed to see value in their research, ridiculed and dismissed for taking unconventional approaches when doing science, pushed aside and silenced when providing explanations or justification for their actions, sexually harassed when perceived as a threat by male colleagues, and pushed away as male colleagues stepped forward to take credit for their discoveries and accomplishments."

Steinke argues that media of images of female scientists and engineers like the ones in the films she studied may be used to develop media literacy programs to change adolescent girls' perceptions of scientists and engineers and their attitudes toward careers in science and engineering. Such programs would teach girls to "recognize and evaluate critically the gender stereotypes that may be limiting" their career goals. As a critical scholar, Steinke seeks to use her analysis of cultural texts to bring about social change.

Source: Jocelyn Steinke, "Cultural Representations of Gender and Science," *Science Communication* 27:1 (2005), 27–63.

Critical scholars bring to light the way cultural groups are stereotyped in popular culture. We need to be concerned about the representation of cultural groups both within our country and outside of it. International news coverage of events like the September 11 terrorist attacks or of US involvement in Iraq has the potential to influence opinions about the United States in other cultures just as American views of other cultures may be shaped by the way those cultures are portrayed in the media. Similarly, the way minority cultures are portrayed within the United States influences relations among the members of these groups and the majority culture and also has an impact on the self-esteem and identity of members of the groups themselves.

US culture is very diverse and contains many minority cultures based on race, ethnicity, age, class, and sexual orientation. Popular culture plays a major role in shaping images of these different groups as well as in rendering some groups, like Native Americans, nearly invisible. Critical scholars challenge stereotypical and limiting representations of minority cultural groups within popular culture. Through analysis of popular culture texts, such as films, newspaper articles, and advertisements, they help us to see how we can use popular culture to understand significant issues in intercultural relations and, ideally, bring about change in situations where inequalities exist.

Methodologies of the critical approach

Scholars using the critical approach often conduct analyses of media and other aspects of popular culture. They are usually interested in studying the unequal distribution of power within groups and place a great deal of emphasis on the privilege–disadvantage dialectic.

Leda M. Cooks' analysis of a Native American gambling casino as a cultural space is an example of the critical approach; Cooks analyzed the Foxwoods Casino located in Leyard in Connecticut, which is run by the Pequots, who are known as "the fox people." She examined the complex identities related to gambling, survival, warriors, land, and *wampum*. She focused on issues of power and stated that the casino represents that cultural space where the "imperialist and colonized stories are in conflict *with* and determinate *of* . . . modern Pequot identities."[9] For example, she comments on the giant warrior statue that dominates the mall area of the casino. The statue serves to reinforce the Hollywood stereotype of Native Americans as "Indians-with-feathers-in-their-hair-who-live-in-tepees."[10] While the statue represents a part of the history of the Pequots, who were skilled warriors, it does not represent the modern-day Pequots at all — thereby both reinforcing an old stereotype and rendering the Pequots themselves invisible. Further, since the casino's success has made the Pequots wealthy, they are still stereotyped, but now they are seen as "a different kind of savage," the Indian who prospers because of the gambling addictions of others.[11] They are still seen through the lens of the dominant culture and still presented in a stereotypical way, even if the stereotype has been changed.

In Chapter 3, we discussed how social science and interpretive scholars might analyze the London bombings. Critical scholars would take a different approach to studying the same event. Scholars using the critical approach would view the bombings from the perspective of macro-contexts, that is, they would consider the historical and political context of the bombings. One perspective on the bombings might be to study how the response of the British government and the British people reflects their long history of dealing with terrorist attacks in Northern Ireland. The spirit of the British people and their determination to carry on with life as usual after the bombings reveals a long history of handling similar attacks, as in the case of the IRA attempt to kill Margaret Thatcher and her cabinet in the Brighton bomb of 1984. Another approach would examine the British government's tolerance of extremists who preach war against Britain, and the claims by some that such a tolerance

POWER CHECK
The Nigerian Press Aids the Ogoni's Struggle for Justice

While depictions of co-cultural groups in the media can serve to reinforce stereotypes, the media can also be a powerful tool to fight inequality and give members of marginal groups a voice. Such has been the case in Nigeria where the Nigerian press "set the tone and tenor" of the struggle for equality and justice by the Ogoni. The Ogoni are a minority ethnic group of approximately 500,000 people living in the Niger Delta. They have suffered from the environmental effects of having more than 100 oil wells, most owned by Shell Oil, in their territory, with almost 3,000 separate oil spills between 1976 and 1991. The Ogoni, like many smaller ethnic groups in Nigeria, have been excluded from positions of power by the three large ethnic groups that dominate the region — the Hausa-Fulani, the Yoruba, and the Ibo.

The struggle of the Ogoni came to national and international prominence in 1992 with the murder of four Ogoni leaders and the subsequent arrest, trial, and execution of nine Ogoni activists. Progressively, the pro-marginal press presented the narrative of the Ogoni's struggle and "successfully narrated the *marginality* of the Ogoni into the *centre*."[1] The pro-Ogoni press provided narratives to counter the establishment press' reporting of the events surrounding the trial of the nine Ogoni activists. The anti-establishment (pro-Ogoni press) included condemnation from Western capitals. While the opposition press questioned whether the trial followed the "due process of law," the establishment press, argued that the trial and sentencing upheld the laws of the land. Further, while the establishment press still supported the historical inequalities in the nation, just the fact that the voices of the Ogoni minority were heard through the anti-establishment press gave rise to a dialectic between the two views and served as a starting point for the possibility of social and political change. Today the Ogoni are still under threat from environmental devastation. November 10, 2005, marked ten years since the murder of Ken Saro Wiwa and 11 other prominent Ogoni citizens. Ken Saro Wiwa started the Movement for the Survival of the Ogoni People (MOSOP), which fights for the right for the Ogoni people to choose the use of their land and resources. MOSOP is a model of non-violent protest, and "strives for a future where all 'stakeholders' in Ogoni's human and natural wealth can experience peace and prosperity, as equal partners."[2]

Notes
1. Wale Adebanwi, "The Press and the Politics of Marginal Voices: Narratives of the Experiences of the Ogoni of Nigeria," *Media, Culture & Society* 26:6 (2004), 763–83.
2. MOSOP — Movement for the Survival of the Ogoni People website, www.mosop. org (accessed June 20, 2005).

made the attacks possible. Such an approach might consider the claims that the British need a Patriot Act and need to toughen antiterrorist laws. Scholars using this approach might also examine the criticism leveled against the British government's policy of multiculturalism and claims that while it was intended to bring different communities together it has only served to keep them apart.[12] Critical scholars might also look at the prejudice directed against British Muslims to determine what role, if any, it might have played in the creation of "home grown" extremists.

Finally, critical scholars might analyze how the media covered the event both in Britain and abroad. After 9/11, many studies examined the media coverage of the attacks and the different approaches to the coverage taken in various nations. For example, Winfield, Friedman, and Trisnadi did a comparison of the different historical perspectives on the terrorist attacks taken in British and American newspapers. They found that newspapers in both Britain and the United States used a historical perspective and compared the event to other well-known catastrophic events. However, while the British papers included lengthy historical discussions, the historical references in American papers tended to be "bits and pieces of evidence throughout the coverage."[13] Further, the researchers note that by "relying primarily on American history to explain the story, British newspapers may have contributed to a new, shared history. Though the attacks of September 11 occurred in the US, the event resonated with Great Britain . . . Such use did not explain what it meant to be a British national, but rather what it meant to be part of a shared society, a part of a global community."[14]

Technology, communication, and the critical approach

As computer technologies have become increasingly sophisticated, the gap between those individuals who have access to technology and those who do not has become increasingly apparent. Critical scholars examine the implications of this digital divide, which is clearly a power issue, separating members of society and empowering some while disempowering others. While governments around the world advocate the necessity of computer skills in the global marketplace, the reality of public policies often serves to reinforce rather than eliminate inequalities.[15] Critical scholars Nakamura and Sterne have argued that computer practices actually perpetuate racial/ethnic inequalities and reinforce stereotypes.[16] The digital divide can be studied from the perspective of larger social, economic, and political issues that drive public policy decisions regarding technology. Critical scholars seek to find ways to understand these issues in order to help close the digital divide and take advantage of the potential of technology to create greater social equity.

For example, Mehra, Merkel, and Bishop bring together the findings from three studies on the internet usage of minority groups. The studies examined the internet usage of low-income families, sexual minorities, and African American women. The researchers brought these studies together to understand how members of these marginalized groups incorporated the internet into their daily lives; their purpose was to find ways to close the digital divide that would converge with the "goals, meanings and practices of people living on society's margins."[17] The researchers stress the importance of studying internet usage in the context of the social realities of the marginalized communities. In all three studies, they found that the internet could be used as a tool for empowerment for the disadvantaged users. They argue that the most important aspect of such research is that it be "action-oriented, participative and democratic."[18] In other words, they believe in engaging the users in setting goals for their use of the internet and in carrying out the necessary activities to research those goals. SisterNet.org was a website that provided health information to African American women. In the course of the research project, the women themselves were given training so that they could become community action researchers and find relevant health resources to include on the website. The women were involved in the creation of the very information that they themselves would need — they were empowered.

Similarly members of the lesbian, gay, bisexual, and transgender (LGBT) community at the University of Illinois at Urbana-Champaign used an electronic mailing list to create a strong and active community of LGBT individuals. Through their mailing list this group established a political agenda for creating awareness about LGBT issues, created a social support system that leads to face-to-face interactions, created awareness within the larger community about LGBT issues, and also exchanged information about cultural activities.

Benefits and limitations of the critical approach

The critical approach is valuable because it brings awareness to the power relations that underlie all cultural encounters. It emphasizes the importance of considering the historical context as well as existing social and political structures when studying culture. This approach is beneficial because it can bring to light inequalities that are embedded in existing power structures and challenge individuals and societies to address these issues rather than to accept the status quo.

With its focus on the analysis of large political and social structures and on the cultural products of those structures, the critical approach does not examine face-to-face interactions. It also does not provide empirical data. Because of these limitations, the critical approach may not offer practical advice to improve communication among individuals.

The Dialectical Approach

The social science, critical, and interpretive approaches to studying intercultural communication are all valuable. However, these approaches may seem to contradict one another. In order to address the potential contradictions among these approaches, Martin, Nakayama, and Flores have developed the dialectical approach to studying intercultural communication.[19] There are many dialectics within our society that attempt to get at the truth through discussion; one example is the judicial model where the prosecution and the defense both present cases. The Socratic method is an example of a dialectical approach to seeking truth. Another example is the US presidential election debates, when candidates present their positions to the public in pursuit of votes.

Communication scholar Leslie A. Baxter has identified three important dialectics in interpersonal relationships. They are: autonomy/connection; novelty/predictability; and openness/closedness. These dialectics reflect basic dichotomies in relationships that are sources of tension. The autonomy/connection dialectic is probably the most central source of tension in interpersonal relationships. Individuals tend to have varying needs for connection to and separation from others; these interpersonal needs may seem contradictory and can occur simultaneously. The novelty/predictability dialectic has to do with conflicting needs for excitement and for stability in relationships. Relationships with no novelty will become stale, but relationships with too little predictability will be chaotic.[20] Finally, the openness/closedness dialectic has to do with the desire to share or to withhold information. Some self-disclosure is necessary to establish relational intimacy, but there is a conflicting desire for privacy and personal boundaries. Understanding these interpersonal relationship dialectics will help you to grasp the complexity of the dialectic approach to the study of intercultural communication.

The dialectical approach stresses the processual, relational, and contradictory nature of intercultural communication. Many different types of information about other cultures can be gathered using the social science, critical, and interpretive approaches. Some information will focus on the history behind cultural conflicts. Other information will detail the importance of face, which can be defined as social self-esteem, in Asian cultures. Yet other studies may reveal how visuals are interpreted differently across cultures. The dialectical approach will provide a framework for reconciling the many different approaches and diverse types of knowledge that you may encounter when studying intercultural communication.

It is important to keep in mind that our understanding of culture is processual, that is to say, that cultures are dynamic and ever-changing. For example, there have been dramatic changes in the cultures of many of the countries of the former Soviet Union since its dissolution. Even nations whose political situation is stable will experience major shifts in their cultures over time. Many factors influence cultural changes including immigration, international business, and global media to name just a few. When we study culture, we are not studying a static body of information, but rather an evolving, living entity. For example, American culture has certainly changed throughout its history. Sometimes it is hard to imagine, but modern American popular culture in the twenty-first century is quite different from that of the early twentieth century, and even more different from earlier periods. In fact, we don't even need to compare centuries to observe major changes in American culture. The speed of change in US society is so fast that major changes have occurred in just a few years. For example, not long ago, there was no text messaging with mobile phones and no iPod, both of which are now taken for granted as part of everyday life. It is also important to bear in mind that individuals change and that not all individuals possess all the characteristics attributed to members of the cultural group to which they belong.

The relational aspect of intercultural communication has to do with taking a holistic view of communication within and among cultures. We must recognize that when we study intercultural communication we are dealing with many interrelated issues that cannot be understood in isolation but only as they come together. We cannot study culture without also studying communication. We cannot understand intercultural conflicts without understanding the situations of individuals on all sides of the conflict. For example, to truly understand the conflict in Kashmir we need to understand the experience of both India and Pakistan in terms of their cultural and political rivalry since their independence in 1947. Furthermore, we cannot understand the current challenges of the post-apartheid regime in South Africa if we have no knowledge of the life of both blacks and whites separately and in relation to one another during the entire Apartheid era.

Finally, the dialectical approach challenges us to go beyond dichotomous thinking. In other words, it requires us to hold contradictory ideas simultaneously without attempting to reduce them to a dichotomy such as "good/evil" or "right/wrong." Because formal education in the United States emphasizes dichotomous thinking, it may be challenging to break out of this way of reconciling contradictions. The dualistic approach to description is found throughout Western thought; we categorize people as either introverts or extroverts, we make sharp distinctions between the body/mind, masculine/feminine, and thought/emotion.[21]

However, if we adopt the dialectical perspective we can transcend seeming contradictions and view them as interdependent and complementary aspects of a whole. The idea is that a whole can embody two contradictory aspects; for example, someone can be both strong and weak or wise and foolish. For example, a young man growing up in a traditional South Asian family may be considered wise in relation to his younger siblings, but the same young man may be considered very inexperienced in relation to his parents and other elders in his family and community. By adopting this philosophy, we can meet the challenge to go beyond cultural conditioning in order to study intercultural communication.

The dialectical approach acknowledges the value of the social science, critical, and interpretive approaches, while at the same time it requires that we do not limit ourselves to the perspective provided by one of these approaches. The dialectical approach calls for the simultaneous acceptance of all three perspectives. An acceptance of multiple perspectives expands our perception of the world and allows us to create new categories and to see the complex potential of the study of intercultural communication.

The six dialectics of intercultural communication

Martin, Nakayama, and Flores have identified six dialectic characteristics of intercultural communication. They are: cultural–individual, personal–contextual, differences–similarities, static–dynamic, history/past–present/future, and privilege–disadvantage. These dialectics all relate to four building blocks of intercultural communication: culture, communication, context, and power.[22]

Cultural–individual

This dialectic refers to the fact that communication is both cultural and individual. All people share some communication patterns with members of groups to which they belong. At the same time, all people also have unique individual communication patterns that are idiosyncratic. For example, an individual who is Japanese may use indirect speech like many members of Asian cultures; however, that person may also have certain ways of speaking that are unique to him. Further, people may belong to multiple groups and their communication patterns may be influenced to a greater or lesser extent by the various groups of which they are members. For example, like many Italian-Americans, Madelyn tends to gesture a lot when she speaks, and like many people from the northeast she tends to have a rapid pace of speech. She also has certain ways of communicating that she shares with other women, other North Americans, and even other college professors. Similarly, Houman speaks English with an accent comparable to most Iranian-Americans who immigrated to the US in their teenage years. He also uses a great deal of body language as he speaks, like many Middle Easterners. However, when he is involved in a conversation with someone, he holds the same physical distance that most Americans do, which is much larger than the distance held by most Middle Easterners, who like to stand quite close to their conversation partners. Thus Houman shares some characteristics in common with Middle Easterners and others in common with Americans. He also shares some aspects of his communication style with other men and other academicians.

Because we are all so complex, it is dangerous to reduce our communication patterns to certain group characteristics; over-reliance on categorizing individuals based on group membership can lead to stereotyping. By recognizing the dialectic between the cultural and the individual we can avoid stereotyping and appreciate each person as an individual while still acknowledging the shared communication patterns of groups.

Personal–contextual

This dialectic has to do with the relationship between the social roles that we play and how they interact with our communication patterns on the personal level. Social contexts often shape the behavior of individuals. Roles related to our social position and our professional standing may influence our communication behavior. Some social roles require that we behave in a very formal manner. The way a lawyer in a courtroom or a scientist in a laboratory communicates will be a result of the context in which he/she is operating. A mayor addressing a city council meeting or a diplomat addressing an audience in another country will be likely to communicate in a formal manner. This point can best be clarified by including an example of teaching in another culture. Houman's teaching style is interactive, which works well in the US where students are encouraged to ask questions in the classroom and where questioning authority is a fully accepted behavior. However, the same teaching style did not work well when he taught in Russia and in the Middle East region, where students are expected to listen carefully and take notes, but are not encouraged by their culture to get involved in discussions with their professors. Most students probably behave differently in the classroom than they do in their dormitories or at parties or at home with their families. You may have to be more formal in some settings even though your personal style might be more relaxed. In some settings, in order to fulfill the expected social role, we may behave in ways that do not accurately reflect our personal style of communicating.

Differences–similarities

This dialectic recognizes the fact that people are simultaneously both similar to and different from one another in many ways. These similarities and differences exist both within and across cultures. There are real differences between the ways members of various cultures communicate; members of Arab cultures communicate differently than members of Asian cultures. However, when we focus on differences among cultures we run the risk of stereotyping others.

Of course, we cannot focus only on similarities, because to do so would be to overlook many significant cultural variations. There are many significant differences among cultures in relation to beliefs, values, traditions, verbal and non-verbal communication, and visual communication, to name a few. For example, in relation to verbal communication there are significant differences among cultures in their approaches to conflict resolution.

Therefore, it is best to study cultures by simultaneously examining differences and similarities. For example, in business negotiations both Japanese and American businesspersons may wish to resolve a conflict; however, their styles of negotiating to achieve resolution are likely to be quite different from one another. If each group makes the effort to understand the other's style, they are much more likely to reach a resolution that is satisfactory to everyone in a timely manner. Similarly, both American and East Asian businesspeople are interested in making a profit, but typical American businesspeople aim to start negotiating and closing the deal from the moment they arrive at their destination, while East Asian business people generally care about the business bond and relationship more than they do about just one deal; they want to get to know their American business partners via a number of meetings and ceremonies, before they actually start negotiating the deal.

Static–dynamic

This dialectic examines the fact that culture and communication patterns are both static and dynamic. Some cultural and communication patterns are relatively stable, while at the same time cultures are evolving and changing. In Iran, the attitudes of the people toward foreign and great powers have not changed since the nineteenth century, although the great powers have themselves changed over time. Most Iranians often feel relatively powerless in relation to the great powers, which have historically found a way to influence Iranian politics and the life of ordinary Iranians. In the 1800s, the British and Russian Empires were fighting for political influence among the Iranian political elite and masses. When the American–Soviet rivalry replaced the British–Russian struggle, the attitude of the Iranian people toward the Great Powers remained the same. Now in the post–Cold War era, the Iranians still have similar attitudes toward the current great powers, including the United States, the European Union states, Japan, China, and the Russian Federation.

Also, while cultures are influenced by the proliferation of new technologies, they will adapt these technologies to their cultural patterns and values. For example, a study by Ook Lee found that email use in Korea was influenced by the Confucian Dynamism cultural value dimension, which emphasizes respect for elders and a strict adherence to social order. Most employees working in a virtual office environment in Korea did not use email to communicate with their superiors because they felt it did not convey the appropriate level of respect to one's boss.[23]

While many cultural patterns do remain fairly constant, we have a tendency to view culture — at least cultures other than our own — as unchanging and easily categorized. It is interesting that most American students have a preconceived notion of people in other parts of the world. For instance, in his Middle East Politics class, Houman has observed that most students believe that all Middle Eastern countries have a much lower standard of living than that in the US. To show the diversity among the Middle Eastern nations and to deal with stereotypes about people in the region, Houman talks about the quality of life by providing examples from the Persian Gulf states. Seven years ago in Kuwait and the UAE, even ordinary people were enjoying the benefits of such sophisticated technology as GSM mobile phones, which have only relatively recently become available in the United States.

History/past–present/future

This dialectic refers to the need to be aware of both present conditions and historical influences as they affect intercultural communication. For example, it is not enough to understand the current situation of North African Muslims in France, which has the highest percentage of Muslims of any European nation. The unassimilated French Muslims are a major source of recruitment for al-Qaeda, which always searches for supporters among the alienated and poor Muslim communities around the world. To fully appreciate the current situation of the European Muslims (especially those in France), we must also have an understanding of how North African Muslim communities have developed in Europe and the factors that have shaped the interactions among these groups and their host countries.

However, we should also bear in mind that history is always seen through "the lens of the present."[24] For example, Houman's interviews with some of the survivors of the CIA-engineered 1953 coup in Iran indicated that they initially had a negative image of American intervention in Iranian domestic affairs. However, this image changed into a more positive feeling in the aftermath of the coup, and it is now very positive years after that historic event. In fact, such images and different perspectives have been rather controversial among both the Iranian political elite and the masses ever since the coup, and especially after the success of the Iranian Islamic Revolution in 1979.

Privilege–disadvantage

This dialectic addresses the contradiction that individuals may be simultaneously privileged and disadvantaged. Individuals may have power because of their social, economic, or political status, and may be privileged because of their position, just as others may be disadvantaged because of their lack of social, economic, or political power.

However, an individual may have a privileged status in some contexts, but may also be disadvantaged in others. An international student in England may be privileged and disadvantaged at the same time. He/she may be privileged to have the opportunity to study abroad, but he/she may be simultaneously disadvantaged by prejudice in the UK.

These six dialectics are useful to help us appreciate the complex nature of intercultural encounters. As Martin, Nakayama, and Flores suggest, when we communicate across cultures, we are simultaneously communicating with an individual and with that individual's cultural identity. To some degree we are all shaped by our cultural identities. However, using a dialectical approach will help us to avoid dichotomous thinking that divides members of other cultures into rigid categories.

Applying the dialectical approach

We have already discussed how scholars might use the social science, interpretive, and critical approaches to study the July 7, 2005, terrorist attacks in London. We suggested that a scholar using the social science approach might survey the attitudes of the British people toward Muslims following the attacks or might study the attitudes of members of various cultures around the world toward the event and their view of what type of response they feel the British government should make to the attacks. We suggested that researchers using the interpretive approach might conduct in-depth interviews with individuals in London to get their reactions to the bombings and that they might also examine the rhetoric used by world leaders in speeches about the event. Finally, we stated that scholars using the critical approach would be likely to consider the historical and social context of the bombings and also that they might analyze media coverage of the event both in Britain and abroad.

Now let's consider how scholars might use the dialectical approach to study the July 7 bombings in London. A dialectical scholar might focus on the cultural/individual and the history/future dialectics to understand the situation of Muslim immigrants in Britain. Such a study would examine the tension between the cultural and personal identities of British Muslims and prejudice and discrimination against Muslims in Britain. It would examine reasons why the suicide bombers were not assimilated into British society. However, the study would also be informed by an understanding of the history of the Muslim people, particularly immigrant communities of Muslims around the world, and by the historical and political context of terrorist actions in Britain. Such a study would consider many of the same issues studied by the other three approaches separately — however, it would bring them all together and look at them from a more holistic perspective.

Benefits and limitations of the dialectical approach

The dialectical approach brings together the strengths of the social science, critical, and interpretive approaches to studying intercultural communication. It allows for a much broader perspective on the study of communication across national identities and prevents us from falling into dichotomies that tend to reduce rather than enlarge our view of other cultures. The dialectical approach makes it possible for us to address the many contradictory aspects of intercultural communication, and thereby, gives us a much richer experience of the study of culture and communication. It is a more challenging approach to take because it does not offer simple answers, but rather requires that we examine issues from multiple perspectives and hold contradictory ideas simultaneously. However, by doing so we will gain a holistic view of intercultural communication that fully recognizes its processual and relational nature.

Bear in mind that the dialectical approach is not a specific theory that can be applied to the study of intercultural communication in the way that the critical, interpretive, and social sciences approaches can be used individually; rather it is a perspective from which to view complex and contradictory intercultural communication encounters. By adopting a dialectical perspective we enable ourselves to see intercultural communication from various perspectives and to draw on the strengths of all of the other approaches to the study of intercultural communication.

References

1. Dana E. Mastro and Susannah R. Stern, "Representations of Race in Television Commercials: A Content Analysis of Prime-Time Advertising," *Journal of Broadcasting & Electronic Media*, 47 (2003), 638–47.

2. James H. Robinson, "Professional Communication in Korea: Playing Things by Eye," *IEEE Transactions on Professional Communication*, 39 (1996), 129.
3. Deborah Schooler et al., "Who's That Girl: Television's Role in the Body Image Development of Young White and Black Women," *Psychology of Women Quarterly*, 28 (2004), 38–47.
4. T. L. Dixon and D. Linz, "Overrepresentation and Underrepresentation of African Americans and Latinos as Criminals on Television News," *Journal of Communication*, 50 (2000), 1–25.
5. M. B. Oliver, "Portrayals of Crime, Race, and Aggression in 'Reality-Based' Police Shows: A Content Analysis," *Journal of Broadcasting & Electronic Media*, 38 (1994), 179–92.
6. Jehangir Pocha, "China's Press Crackdown," *In These Times*, September 12, 2005, www.inthesetimes.com/article/2304, accessed October 6, 2005.
7. Dana E. Mastro and Amanda L. Robinson, "Cops and Crooks: Images of Minorities on Primetime Television," *Journal of Criminal Justice*, 28 (2000), 385–96.
8. Karmen Erjavec, "Media Representation of the Discrimination Against the Roma in Eastern Europe: The Case of Slovenia," *Discourse & Society*, 12:6 (2001), 699–727.
9. Leda M. Cooks, "Foxwoods Casino and the (Re-)presentation of Native Identity," in Judith N. Martin, Thomas K. Nakayama, and Lisa A. Flores, eds., *Readings in Intercultural Communication*, 2nd ed. (Boston, MA: McGraw-Hill, 2002), p. 179.
10. Ibid., p. 176.
11. Ibid., p. 178.
12. Roger Hardy, "UK Multi-Culturalism Under Spotlight," *BBC News*, July 14, 2005, http://newsvote.bbc.co.uk/mpapps/pagetools/print/news.bbc.co.uk/1/hi/uk/4681615.stm, accessed October 9, 2005.
13. Betty Houchin Winfield, Barbara Friedman, and Vivara Trisnadi, "History as the Metaphor through Which the Current World Is Viewed: British and American Newspapers' Uses of History Following the 11 September 2001 Terrorist Attacks," *Journalism Studies*, 3:2 (2002), 297.
14. Ibid., p. 298.
15. Lynn Schofield Clark, Christof Demont-Heinrich, and Scott A. Webber, "Ethnographic Interviews on the Digital Divide," *New Media & Society*, 6 (2004), 529–47.
16. L. Nakamura, *Cybertypes: Race, Ethnicity and Identity on the Internet* (New York: Routledge, 2002); J. Sterne, "The Computer Race Goes to Class: How Computers in Schools Helped Shape the Racial Topography of the Internet," in L. Nakamura and G. B. Rodman, eds., *Race in Cyberspace* (New York: Routledge, 2000), pp. 191–212.
17. Bharat Mehra, Cecelia Merkel, and Ann Peterson Bishop, "The Internet for Empowerment of Minority and Marginalized Users," *New Media & Society*, 6 (2004), 781.
18. Ibid., p. 797.
19. Judith N. Martin, Thomas K. Nakayama, and Lisa A. Flores, "A Dialectical Approach to Intercultural Communication," in Judith N. Martin, Thomas K. Nakayama, and Lisa A. Flores, eds., *Readings in Intercultural Communication*, 2nd ed. (Boston, MA: McGraw-Hill, 2002), p. 6.
20. Myron W. Lustig and Jolene Koester, *Intercultural Competence* (Boston, MA: Allyn and Bacon, 2003), pp. 273–4.
21. Min-Sun Kim, *Non-Western Perspectives on Human Communication* (Thousand Oaks, CA: Sage, 2002), p. 160.
22. Martin, Nakayama, and Flores, pp. 4–6.
23. Ook Lee, "The Role of Cultural Protocol in Media Choice in a Confucian Virtual Workplace," *IEEE Transactions on Professional Communication*, 43 (2000), 198.
24. Martin, Nakayama, and Flores, p. 6.

INTERCULTURAL COMMUNICATION PROCESSES AND TECHNOLOGIES

Introduction: Models of the Communication Process

In Chapter 1, we defined communication as a symbolic process by which people create shared meanings.[1] Over time, communication scholars have developed increasingly sophisticated models of the communication process; these models evolved from linear to interactive and finally to the transactional models we use today.

Linear Models of the Communication Process

The earliest models of the communication process were linear. These models describe communication as a one-way process "in which one person acts on another person."[1] Linear models involve three elements: a *sender*, a *message*, and a *receiver*. The sender encodes a message and transmits it by means of a channel to the receiver who decodes the message. The communication channel is speech, writing, or any other means of conveying a message, such as Morse code.

Harold Laswell developed one of the early linear models. His model was based on five questions: Who? Says what? In what channel? To whom? With what effect?[2] Laswell was primarily interested in studying mass communication and propaganda. His questions were developed with the media in mind. The question "Who?" can be related to an area of research called control analysis wherein scholars examine the political leanings and other agendas that influence the way information is presented in the media. In the same way, Laswell's focus on the message relates to content research, which examines the way various co-cultural groups are represented in the media. Scholars conducting content research might ask questions about how women are represented in movies or how blacks are represented on television. Content research often involves counting the frequency of a particular image (black males portrayed as criminals in television programs) and then making a comparison against an objective measure (statistics on perpetrators of crime). Content research is sometimes used by scholars who take the critical approach to the study of intercultural communication (see Chapter 4).

Communication scholars Shannon and Weaver added the concept of *noise* to Laswell's model. Noise is defined as anything that interferes with effective communication of the intended meaning; noise may interfere at every stage in the process. There are three types of noise: *external*, *physiological*, and *psychological*.[3]

External noise, also called physical noise, consists of factors outside the receiver that disrupt communication either by making it difficult to hear the message or by distracting the receiver. Examples of external noise might include loud music playing when you are trying to have a conversation with someone or static breaking up the connection when you are speaking to someone on a cell phone. Physiological noise refers to the biological states of the sender and/or receiver, that interfere with efficient communication. Biological factors might include illness or fatigue. For example, when you are very tired, you might find it difficult to pay attention to a complex set of instructions being given to you by your professor. Finally, psychological noise refers to psychological states of the sender and/or receiver that detract from their ability to convey or to understand a message clearly and accurately. For example, an individual who wishes to impress others in order to boost his/her self-esteem may exaggerate when describing his/her skill in a particular area. An individual who differs with you on a sensitive political issue may be unable or unwilling to hear your logical arguments in favor of it.

Linear models served as a valuable starting point for the study of human communication. However, these models are too simplistic to convey the complexity of the communication process. Perhaps the greatest shortcoming of the linear models is that they depict communication as a one-way process moving from sender to receiver. Interactive models address this limitation.

Interactive Models of the Communication Process

Linear models of the communication process did not accurately represent the complexity of human communication because they suggested that in a communication encounter a person is either a sender or a receiver. Interactive models incorporate feedback; feedback is a receiver's response to a sender. Communication scholars Osgood and Schramm developed a circular model of communication that depicts ongoing interaction between the sender and the receiver; this model accounts for feedback and the fact that participants in a communication encounter are continually swapping roles from sender to receiver and back again.

Schramm also added fields of experience to the communication model. Fields of experience are the communicators' personal knowledge and backgrounds that inform the way they decode information. Schramm suggested that when communicators' fields of experience are similar they are more likely to communicate effectively and understand one another without misinterpretation.[4] The consideration of fields of experience is particularly relevant to the study of intercultural communication; we can see that miscommunication is more likely to occur when the individuals engaged in a communication encounter have vastly different fields of experience. Further, we can see the importance of studying other cultures to gain understanding and bridge differing fields of experience.

The development of interactive models by Osgood and Schramm and other communication scholars was an important step forward. These models portray communication as a process in which both senders and receivers are active participants. However, the interactive models still portray communication as a sequential process and do not account for changes in the process over time as a result of changing relationships between communicators.

Transactional Models of the Communication Process

Transactional models of communication, unlike linear and interactive models, recognize that in a communication encounter "we send and receive messages simultaneously." These models do not label individuals as either senders or receivers; rather, participants are defined as "communicators" who participate equally. At any time during the communication encounter, we may be receiving a message, decoding it, and responding to it while our communication partner is receiving, decoding, and responding to our message simultaneously.[5]

Wood's transactional model reflects the fact that communication occurs within contexts that influence what and how people communicate. These contexts include shared systems of communication related to geographical regions, co-cultural groups, nations, and cultures as well as personal systems of communication related to family, friends, and associates. This model shows how fields of experience may overlap when communicators have a shared context for communication. Wood's model also demonstrates that a communicator's field of experience may change over time. For example, as you study intercultural communication your field of experience will change to include your new knowledge and understanding of other cultures.

Wood's model emphasizes that communication is a process that is continually changing over time as people interact with one another and their relationships develop. This model depicts communication as a shared process that is "we-oriented." There is an emphasis on relationships, on seeking to understand one another, and on resolving conflict.[6] This model is particularly well suited to the study of intercultural communication.

Using the transactional model to understand intercultural communication

From the perspective of the transactional model, we can refine our definition of communication to state that communication is "a transactional process in which people interact with and through symbols over time to create meaning."[7] The "we-orientation" of the transactional model is particularly appropriate for the study of intercultural communication because it emphasizes seeking to understand others and resolve conflict. These goals are aligned with our mindful approach to intercultural communication. Mindful intercultural communicators strive to create a feeling of "being understood, supported, and respected" in the individuals with whom they are communicating.[8] Mindful intercultural communicators also seek to acquire skills for effective communication and conflict resolution (see Chapter 1).

The fields of experience depicted in the transactional model represent shared systems of communication, or contexts, which influence what and how individuals communicate. Clearly, culture is one such shared system of communication that affects how individuals communicate with members of their in-groups and out-groups. Our study of intercultural communication depends on understanding different contexts and creating bridges to share meaning across these cultural contexts. Our ability to expand our fields of experience over time is what makes possible our development as effective and mindful intercultural communicators.

In Part III, we will examine the various means by which we communicate using symbols. In Chapter 5, we discuss verbal communication and examine verbal communication styles, translation, multilingualism, the relationship between language and power, and the language of conflict management. In Chapter 6 we focus on non-verbal communication and the influence of cultural values on body language, gestures, and the conception and use of space and time. In Chapter 7 we examine visual communication and explain how culture influences perception and the use of graphic images. Finally, in Chapter 8 we discuss the effect of mass communication on intercultural communication with particular attention to the relationship between media and power and the global impact of American popular culture.

References

1. Julia T. Wood, *Communication Mosaics*, 4th ed. (Belmont, CA: Thomson Wadsworth, 2006), p. 14.
2. Ibid.
3. Ronald B. Adler and George Rodman, *Understanding Human Communication*, 8th ed. (New York: Oxford University Press, 2003), p. 11.
4. Wood, p. 15.
5. Adler and Rodman, p. 15.
6. Wood, p. 17.
7. Ibid.
8. Stella Ting-Toomey, *Communicating Across Cultures* (New York: The Guilford Press, 1999), pp. 46–54.

Verbal Communication 5

Michael Brooks is a senior manager for an international manufacturing company with several plants located in South America. One of the plants that manufactures metal products is located in Brazil, and this plant is not operating at peak efficiency. Michael is sent by his company to take charge of the plant, reorganize it, and introduce some new processes to the frontline workers. Michael is very hardworking and determined to get the plant reorganized and back on track as quickly as possible. He does not intend to waste any time while he is in Brazil because he wants to get back to his duties at the corporation's home office. On Michael's first day at the plant, he calls a meeting with the local plant manager and the plant supervisors. The local plant manager is a mature man. He is considerably older than Michael, who has advanced rapidly in his company due to his technical knowledge and education rather than on the basis of seniority. Several of the supervisors are late for the meeting Michael has called. Once they all arrive they spend some time talking about personal matters and asking Michael about his family. Michael is anxious to get down to business and cuts short the discussion of family relationships. However, he does spend a great deal of time asking the supervisors for their opinions about conditions on the factory floor; Michael has a democratic management style and he likes to get input from his team of employees. The supervisors, however, are not very forthcoming with information and continually defer to the plant manager. After the meeting Michael is frustrated and unsure why things did not go as he expected. He senses that the supervisors do not like him, and he is surprised since his democratic style works well with employees in the United States, where he is liked by all the people he manages.

Michael's initial meeting did not go well for at least two reasons having to do with verbal communication across cultures. First, he failed to establish a social rapport with his Brazilian colleagues before getting down to business. Second, he did not show the proper deference to the plant manager who is senior to him in years. Personal relationships are very important when doing business in Brazil, and Michael did not demonstrate even a minimal interest in getting to know the supervisors personally before beginning the meeting. Elders are afforded great respect in the hierarchical Brazilian society, and the supervisors wished to defer to the seniority of the plant manager. Despite his position at the home office, they perceived

Michael as subordinate to the plant manager, who in addition to being older than Michael was also a man of high social status within the Brazilian society. If Michael takes these aspects of verbal communication into consideration, his future meetings with the supervisors are likely to be more successful than the initial one.

Verbal communication encompasses both written and spoken use of a language. There are approximately 5,000 languages spoken in the world today.[1] The relationship between language and culture is a complex one; language and culture are inextricably bound together. From the perspective of intercultural communication we can examine how members of different language communities strive to understand one another and how language influences an individual's perception of the world. We can recognize the challenges of translation and interpretation from one language into another. We can appreciate how different cultures use different verbal communication styles and how these styles relate to their approaches to resolving conflicts.

We can see that language use and language choice is related to power issues for individuals, groups, and nations. Within a given language, certain dialects or accents are privileged over others, and the privileging has to do with the preferred speech of individuals who are in positions of authority and power, not with any intrinsic superiority of one language variation over another. Similarly, the privileging of certain languages within a nation is clearly related to issues of power within that nation. Belgium is an example of a nation with a long history of divisiveness directly related to language issues that are, in fact, political power issues. Further, the predominance of English as the language of globalization is an example of how language choice is related, at least in a significant part, to economic power.

This chapter begins with a discussion of linguistics and the basic structure of languages. Next we examine ideas about the relationship between thought, language, and culture. Then we introduce translation issues, multilingualism, and the various verbal communication styles. We go on to examine the relationship of language and power. Finally, we look at the relationship between communication styles and conflict.

Basics of Language: Phonology, Morphology, Syntactics, Semantics, Pragmatics

Linguistics is the scientific study of language. A study of linguistic differences among languages must begin with an understanding of the basic structure of languages. Every language has five basic components that govern its structure and use; these components are *phonology, morphology, semantics, syntactics,* and *pragmatics.*

Phonology refers to the most basic units of any language, the individual units of sound that account for all the words spoken in a given language. The individual units are called phonemes; the English language has 40-odd phonemes, the precise number depending on the accent. The number of phonemes varies across languages with the Pirahã language of Brazil having only 10 phonemes[2] and the !Xóõ language spoken in Botswana and Namibia having 141.[3]

When children learn a language they learn to form the phonemes that make up all the sounds in that language. When we learn another language as adults we sometimes have difficulty forming some of the sounds in languages that have phonemes that are not used in our native language. For example, speakers of English often have difficulty forming the rolling *rr* sound in Spanish because our language has no comparable sound unit. Similarly, speakers of languages that do not have *l* and *r* sounds, like Japanese, frequently have trouble distinguishing between them when speaking English. When we hear non-native speakers pronouncing words in a language that we are familiar with — whether that language is English or Farsi — what we perceive as an accent is frequently caused by difficulty pronouncing unfamiliar sound units not present in the speaker's native tongue.

Often accents reveal a speaker's status as an immigrant or as a member of a co-cultural group and, therefore, individuals may face prejudice and discrimination because they speak with a particular type of accent in a certain place and time. During the 2003 gubernatorial recall election in California, Gray Davis criticized the Austrian accent of the then candidate, now governor, Arnold Schwarzenegger. Davis went on to apologize for the comment after coming under censure by the State Senate. His remark drew attention to the prejudice directed towards individuals who speak with accents and the relationship between language and power in society.[4]

While phonology refers to the smallest units of sound in a language, morphology refers to the smallest units of meaning. A relatively small number of sounds in the English language can be used to generate millions of units of meaning (morphemes). The word *dog* would be an example of a morpheme as it cannot be broken down into smaller units that have meaning.

Semantics is the study of the meaning of words. In any language, words have both denotative meanings and connotative meanings. The denotative meaning of a word is the meaning found in the dictionary; it is the meaning that all speakers of a given language share. For example, in *The New Oxford American Dictionary* the word *dog* is defined as "a domesticated carnivorous mammal that typically has a long snout, an acute sense of smell, and a barking, howling, or whining voice."[5] However, not all English speakers have the same emotional reactions to or beliefs about dogs — they assign different connotative meanings to the word. Some individuals love their dogs as pets and treat them as well as they treat their own children. Others may perceive dogs as useful workers who can perform certain tasks, such as guarding a home or working in the canine unit of the police force. Still others may have had negative experiences that cause them to view dogs as dangerous creatures and to be fearful of dogs and

Figure 5.1 Gray Davis' criticism of Arnold Schwarzenegger's Austrian accent during the 2003 gubernatorial recall election in California called attention to the prejudice directed towards Americans who speak English with accents. Immigrants are often the victims of prejudicial treatment simply because of the way they speak. What we perceive as an accent may be caused by difficulty pronouncing sound units not present in the speaker's native language.

even dislike them. With such wide variations in the connotative meaning of a simple word, it is not surprising that abstract terms are subject to numerous interpretations by speakers of the same language and that the job of a translator or interpreter is complicated by the fact that the simple substitution of a word in one language for a similar word in another does not ensure equivalence of meaning.

Syntactics is the study of the ordering of words within a language. Students of foreign languages learn that not all languages order words in the same fashion to form meaningful sentences. Mistakes made by non-native speakers of English usually reflect the lexical and grammatical forms of their native languages. In English, a speaker would say "I have money," to express the possession of money. In Russian, a speaker would literally say "with me there is money." To express the same meaning, a Japanese speaker would say "to me there is money."[6]

Pragmatics has to do with the way language is actually used within a society. Languages are dynamic, and they evolve over time. Many historical and political factors influence how languages evolve and which form of a language is considered to be standard acceptable usage at any given point in time. Typically the language that is privileged within a society is the language of those in power in that society. In the United States, Standard American English reflects the language of white males of European heritage. The language of co-cultural groups has been looked down upon and inaccurately considered to represent a lack of education and/or intellect. One of the most notable examples of these attitudes can be seen in the controversy that arose in relation to Ebonics or

African American English Vernacular, believed to be a complex mixture of European and American languages born of the African slave trade. In 1996 when the Oakland, California school district passed a resolution to require that students be taught Ebonics rather than Standard American English there was an outcry. Proponents of Ebonics felt that the language of Americans of African descent should be honored and viewed the recognition of Ebonics with pride. Others felt that black students would be further disadvantaged in society if they were not taught Standard American English. Still other citizens, many of whom had ancestors who were required to learn Standard English upon arriving in America, felt that by teaching Ebonics our society would be treating Americans of African descent differently than other minority groups.

POWER CHECK
The Ebonics Debate

The term "Ebonics" was coined by Robert Williams in 1973. He defined Ebonics as "the linguistic and paralinguistic features which on a concentric continuum represent the communicative competence of the West African, Caribbean, and United States slave descendent of African origin. It includes the grammar, various idioms, patois, argots, ideolects, and social dialects of Black people." The term *Ebonics* comes from the combining of the words *ebony* and *phonics*, literally meaning black sounds.

Many questions have arisen as a result of the 1996 Resolution of the Oakland, CA School Board to teach Ebonics. These questions have to do with linguistics, with political power and racial prejudice, and with the U.S. educational system and its ability to meet the needs of students of African-American descent. Williams himself was concerned with the racial bias of standardized IQ tests. Clearly, tests like the SAT and GRE have an important impact on an individual's ability to excel academically and to succeed professionally. When such tests are racially biased, individuals may be held back from fulfilling their potential and be effectively kept down in society.

At the same time, some speakers of Ebonics cling to their language variation as a means of expressing solidarity with their heritage and as a refusal to conform to the larger society. Much discussion has also been devoted to the question of whether or not Ebonics is a language unto itself or merely a variation on Standard American English. The Ebonics debate is a dramatic example of the relationship between language and power within a society and the complex nature of such issues.

Source: John Baugh, *Beyond Ebonics* (New York: Oxford University Press, 2000), p. 15.

Without going any further into an analysis of the pros and cons of Ebonics, we can clearly see that issues of language are also issues of power. The language that is currently accepted as Standard American English is not inherently better in any concrete way than other variations of the English language — it is merely deemed to be better because those in power in society protect its privileged status. Linguistic science does not recognize any dialect or any language as innately superior to any other. Most of the earliest settlers in the 13 colonies were from England and Germany. Some of Benjamin Franklin's early publications appeared in German. It was the political clout of the Founding Fathers from England that led to the establishment of English as the language of the fledgling United States of America. Similar privileging of languages and dialects can be found in many nations. In mainland China, Mandarin is the dialect associated with those in positions of political and economic power and therefore it is privileged within the society.

The Relationship between Language, Thought, and Culture

Does our native language influence the way that we perceive the world? Does it influence our thinking and behavior? Does a native speaker of Swahili living in Kenya perceive and experience the world differently than a native speaker of Chuukese in Micronesia? Does a native speaker of English growing up in the United States perceive and experience the world differently than a native speaker of Swedish growing up in Sweden? What is the relationship between language and thought? We know that every language has unique linguistic features that distinguish it from all other languages. To what extent do these differences influence the way speakers of a given language perceive the world?

Language helps us to make sense of the world. It is a useful tool for categorizing our experience and perceptions. However, while language is a powerful tool, it does not define our experience and shape our mental activity. Language does influence how we mentally organize our world. The language we speak may make us more or less likely to notice particular features of the world around us; our native language may also make some things very easy for us to say and others difficult, or nearly impossible. We will begin our discussion by examining the researchers whose work has influenced our current ideas about the relationship between language, thought, and culture.

Early research on language and thought

Two of the most influential theorists regarding the relationship of thought and language are Edward Sapir and Benjamin Lee Whorf. Before the pioneering work of Sapir and Whorf, language was viewed as a means to express thoughts that existed independently of words. However, after studying the language of Native American and Mayan societies, Whorf hypothesized that the language an individual spoke actually shaped his/her world view and that "language produces an organization of experience. We are inclined to think of language simply as a technique of expression, and not to realize that language first of all is a classification and arrangement of the stream of sensory experience which results in a certain world-order, a certain segment of the world that is easily expressible by the type of symbolic means that language employs."[7]

Whorf argued that language created a world view and was inextricably bound up with culture. The assertion that language actually shapes an individual's reality is called the Sapir-Whorf Hypothesis. This relativist position calls into question the very possibility of intercultural communication. Because they share a language, members of a culture also share a way of viewing and interacting with the world. When they encounter members of cultures who speak different languages, they are encountering individuals with different world views and it is not possible for them to ever see the world from the same perspective because they are restricted by their linguistic differences.

It was Whorf's study of the language of the Hopi Indians that played a pivotal role in the development of his views on the relationship between language and thought. For example, the Hopi do not view time in the same way that North Americans do, as a continuum with concepts of past, present, and future that are reflected in verb tenses. A past tense allows a speaker of English or Spanish to indicate an action that is completed: he spoke; *el hablo*. In the Hopi language, verbs do not indicate different tenses, but rather indicate "what type of validity the speaker intends the statement to have."[8] There are three types of validity: (1) the statement is a report of an event; (2) the statement is an expectation of an event; and (3) the statement is a generalization or law about events.[9] The view that language determines our experience actually calls into question the possibility of effective communication among members of different cultures.

The Sapir-Whorf Hypothesis, while valuable for calling attention to the relationship among language, thought, and culture, has been replaced by a more moderate view of the influence of language on thought. The qualified relativist position states that language influences, but does not totally determine, our patterns of thinking. Language does influence the way we categorize our experience and the ease or difficulty with which we are able to communicate various types of experience to others. When we study the language of a culture different from our own we can learn a great deal about the way that culture views and orders the world.

Current research on the relationship between language and thought

The qualified relativist position is supported both by research with the language acquisition of children and by research on the cognition of children who are deaf.[10] The work of early theorists Piaget and Vygotsky with the language acquisition of children demonstrated that language and thought are so closely related that it is not really possible to determine that one has an initiating influence over the other.[11] More recent studies by Volterra and Iverson on child development demonstrate the primacy of non-verbal communication in children's early cognitive development.[12] Stokoe states that

> infants are attending to the world around them and making sense of it — and that they express their understanding through gestures. When children communicate using gestures, before they use what we call a language, they are using their uniquely human perceptual-action system to make sense of the physical and social world in which they find themselves.[13]

Similarly, in studies of children who are deaf, researchers Rhodda and Grove have found that these children had the same level of cognitive skill as children who could hear, and found no evidence that the children had a different world view.[14] Stokoe states that deaf children develop language and social sophistication at the same rate as hearing children if they are raised in a sign language environment.[15]

While research does not support the idea that language determines thought, we do recognize that language influences the way we organize our experience. Slobin has suggested that instead of focusing on the relationship of language and thought, we should more precisely focus on the relationship between speaking and thinking.[16] The thought process for speaking does differ from one language to another. Psychologists Imai and Mazuka have stated that the vocabularies and grammars of our respective languages influence the way that we categorize our experiences.[17] Further, as the work of Philipsen with speech communities and the ethnography of speaking has shown us, "whenever people speak, they organize their speech in ways not governed only by rules of grammar,"[18] but also by patterns that vary across cultures. While these patterns or rules for speaking are structured, they are also mutable, as is culture itself. Further, while they influence communication, they can be circumvented, challenged, and ultimately revised by members of the speech community. The speech patterns of any community reveal the culturally distinctive codes of that community, and demonstrate that community's response to the basic questions: What is a person? What is society? How are persons and societies linked through communication?[19] These questions bear some similarity to the questions posed in Kluckhohn and Strodtbeck's "cultural value orientations." We can see that languages do to some extent reflect the cultural values of their speakers.

Language and culture

Individuals often come to understand the grammar of their own language much more fully after studying the grammar of a foreign language. Differences in vocabulary and syntax can reveal different ways of ordering and interacting with the world and with other people.

For example, the fact that in the Hopi language verbs do not have tenses in the way they do in English and many other languages reflects the fact that the Hopi have a conception of time that is different from the one shared by speakers of languages where verb tenses are used to indicate the performance of an action within a particular frame of reference based on physics. The frame of reference used by the Hopi is a psychological time rather than the kind of time recognized by physicists. The challenge for speakers of English and other languages that view time similarly to the way Americans do is to realize that English reflects one world view and Hopi reflects another — and there is nothing inherently more logical or reasonable about one or the other of these views. Learning a foreign language is one of the best ways to gain sensitivity to the world views of members of other cultures. Bilingual and multilingual individuals have the opportunity to see the world through multiple lenses (see section on "Bilingualism and Multilingualism" this chapter).

Another way in which the verbs used in a language may serve to reveal underlying patterns of thinking is evident in the fact that some languages have verb forms that allow for both formal and informal modes of address. For example, in Mexico the second person pronoun *you* would be *usted* when speaking to someone who is to be afforded respect whether for reasons of age, status, or relationship to the speaker. Therefore, a young man addressing his elders, an employee addressing a boss, or a student addressing her teacher would be more likely to use *usted*. When addressing peers and intimates, the same speakers would be more likely to use the informal form of you, *tú*. In most instances, one brother addressing another, an employee addressing a co-worker, or a student addressing her classmate would probably use *tú*. This applies in French speaking countries with *vous* and *tu*, respectively.

Some Asian languages have elaborate rules for the proper way of addressing one's superiors. The structures of the Japanese and Korean languages emphasize relationships between individuals. It is not surprising that both the Japanese and Korean cultures are collectivistic and place a great value on harmony and conformity. Their languages both reflect and reinforce the emphasis placed on the group and on "facework" as a significant component of the cultures. There are clearly defined rules for how one is supposed to address a superior, a peer, and an inferior. The importance that the society places on conformity and the high degree of uncertainty avoidance within the culture are reflected in and shaped by a language in which many words take on different forms depending on the relationship between the speaker and the person being addressed.

For example, in Japanese there are levels of politeness, and words that have the same referential meaning may have different added meaning components that reflect a relationship between the speaker and listener that is humble, honorific, or neutral. There are three words for wife: *kanai* (humble), *okusan* (honorific), and *tuma* (neutral) in order to communicate different levels of politeness.[20] Language reflects different cultural values rather than different perceptions of the world. It is easy for speakers of Japanese to demonstrate respect for others. This aspect of the Japanese language reflects how the Japanese culture views differences between people, and the fact that the Japanese culture places a great deal of importance on showing proper respect for others based on age, relationship, and status.

Similarly, in north Queensland, Australia, the Dyirbal have a special form of speech used in the presence of relatives who are considered taboo; this form is called mother-in-law language. Every Dyirbal speaker knows when to use everyday speech and when to use mother-in-law language.[21]

Another aspect of language that both reflects and reinforces cultural differences is vocabulary. Most people are familiar with the fact that both the Eskimo language and the Sami language have many more words for snow than does the English language. Clearly there are differences in vocabulary in various languages that reflect how the speakers of these languages view reality. In Papua New Guinea, where pigs are an important part of the culture, words referring to pigs have positive connotations of food and wealth. In pastoral cultures, there is often one word that means "taking care of at night" because the activity of tending animals is an integral part of the life of that culture. For example, in the Quiché language of Guatemala the single word, *kwrax*, signifies both time (at night) and activity (taking care of).[22] Differences in vocabulary like differences in formality and grammar reflect different cultural patterns of relating to the world; many differences in vocabulary are related to words used to describe the environment. We can easily understand why it would be more important for someone living in a climate where there is snow throughout most of the year to have the ability to communicate with a great deal of specificity and precision about differences in the quality of the snow than it would be for someone living in the desert to have such a vocabulary. While members of both cultures see the same world, because of their different environments, they pay attention to different aspects of the world around them. Therefore, while the notion that language determines our reality is false, language does reveal a great deal about the values and beliefs of other cultures. In order to communicate mindfully with members of other cultures, we must strive to understand and appreciate those differences.

Translation and Interpretation

The fact that languages are inextricably bound up with cultural values and beliefs has obvious implications for the translation of documents and for interpreters. Interpretation is the process of conveying the meaning of a speaker's words from one language into another. Translation is the process of rendering the meaning of written text from one language into another. Translators refer to the original language as the source language and the new language as the target language. So if this book were to be translated into Russian, English would be the source language and Russian would be the target language.

However, neither translation nor interpretation is a matter of merely substituting words in one language for the corresponding terms in another; if it were possible to move from one language to another with such an exact correspondence, machine translation, the process whereby a computer program translates a text from one natural language into another, would have

Figure 5.2 In addition to being fluent in two languages, to be successful an interpreter must be familiar with both cultures. Interpreters may also need to know specialized terminology within the field or discipline being discussed.

replaced human translators. What has happened instead is the development of computer-aided translation, a process whereby human translators are assisted by computerized tools.

Computer programs can help with the substitution of comparable vocabulary words and supply *chien* in French when a speaker has said *dog* in English or provide *hond* in Dutch when a writer has written собака in Russian. Certainly, dictionaries are useful tools for translators, and they can use English/French and French/English and Dutch/Russian and Russian/Dutch dictionaries to arrive at lexical equivalents.

However, a good translator or interpreter must do much more than provide a word-for-word substitution of a business letter or a formal speech. Earlier we discussed the fact that the word *dog* may have the same denotative meaning for all speakers of English, but several different connotative meanings depending on the speaker's experience with dogs. When translating a text from one language into another, an interpreter must deal with the complexity of vocabulary, syntax, formal and informal means of address, and many other variables that differ widely from one culture to another. To be a successful interpreter or translator, one must know the culture very well and often a specialized field within the culture as well.

For example, Maria A. works as a translator for an international financial software company based in the United States; she translates documents for clients in both Latin America and South America. In addition to being fluent in both Spanish and English, she must be familiar with numerous Spanish-speaking cultures and the American culture, with computer-related terminology, and with the terminology of the fields of finance and banking. Rosie B. works as an interpreter for American emergency room doctors traveling to Italy and for

Italian emergency room doctors traveling to the United States. In addition to being fluent in Italian and English, she must be familiar with the Italian and American cultures, with medical terminology generally, and with the specialized medical terminology of emergency and trauma care.

Therefore, fluency in two or more languages alone is not a sufficient qualification to make someone an effective translator or interpreter. At a minimum translators and interpreters strive for equivalence between the original or source language and the target language. For example, if Maria is translating a computer manual from English into Spanish, English is the source language and Spanish is the target language. But many factors can intervene to make a word-to-word equivalence between the two languages very difficult to achieve. Maria recounted one example that she heard about from a fellow translator. The English word *time* has many meanings and in the field of banking it is used to specify certain types of accounts, such as *time deposit accounts*; however, in one manual the word was translated merely as the word for *time* in Spanish, *tiempo*. The Spanish-speaking users of the manual were confused by this use of the word and had no idea that it referred to a specific type of account.

There are several types of equivalence sought by a translator when rendering a text from one language into another. They include equivalence of vocabulary, idiomatic equivalence, grammatical-syntactical equivalence, experiential equivalence, and conceptual equivalence.

Modern translation theory places a greater emphasis on striving to translate a message so that it is understood by the intended audience as though it were the original rather than striving for a mathematical equivalence in which

---

SOME FREE TRANSLATION WEBSITES

Babel Fish Translation
www.babelfish.yahoo.com
Provides free translations for a number of languages.

Free Translation
www.freetranslation.com
Provides free translations for some European languages.

Mezzofanti
www.mezzofanti.org/translation
Provides free translations for some European languages. A fee is payable if further work is required.

Systran
www.systransoft.com
Provides free translations for a number of languages.

Translation Booth
www.translationbooth.com
Provides free and fee-paying services for a range of languages, including Chinese, Japanese, Korean and eastern European languages.

Translation Guide
www.translation-guide.com/free_online_translations.htm
Provides free translations for a number of languages.

words in the source language are substituted for their counterparts in the target language. An effective translation is one in which the translator discovers the meaning of the original and uses the linguistic structure of the target language to convey that meaning in a natural way.

Different Verbal Communication Styles

Another aspect of language that varies from one culture to another is the communication style favored by speakers of the language; put simply, communication styles are the ways speakers typically use the language in their normal discourse. There are four different types of verbal communication styles: direct/indirect, elaborate/exact/succinct, personal/contextual, and instrumental/affective.

Direct/indirect communication styles

The *direct* communication style is the one favored by Americans and to a greater or lesser extent by many Europeans as well. In this communication style, the speaker will state exactly what is on his or her mind in no uncertain terms. When using the direct style, an employee who wants to ask her boss for a raise will openly state her request. "I want a raise."

The direct style is valued by business people in the United States who see it as an efficient and time-saving method of interaction. Similarly, within the educational arena students are encouraged to use this communication style, and parents teach children to speak up and say what they mean. In a culture like the US that values the direct style, success is dependent, at least in part, upon one's ability to be verbally assertive, to get to the point, and to be confident in stating one's position openly. Individuals are expected to be straightforward in requesting what they want. For example, the employee who directly states her desire for a raise will also probably be direct in stating why she feels she deserves to be given one.

The direct communication style is related to low-context communication and is usually found in cultures where communication is dependent upon the explicit message and not upon the surrounding context for the communication. By contrast, the *indirect* communication style is one in which the speaker will avoid openly stating what he or she wants to communicate. The indirect style would be more likely to be found in cultures that practice high-context communication. In these cultures, the emphasis is placed on the group and not on the individual's desires. Indirect communication relies on the surrounding context and on the relationship between the speaker and the person being addressed to carry at least part of the message.

An employee who wishes to ask for a raise using an indirect verbal communication style would be much more likely to emphasize her commitment to the organization, her desire to fulfill the needs of her superiors, and so forth. She might say something like, "I am very committed to XYZ Corporation, and I want to perform my best work for the company. I have enjoyed working here for the past five years."

The example could continue, but however long the speaker went on, there would never be a direct statement like, "I want a raise in my salary." The indirect style relies on the listener to either pick up on the implied message or not; if the listener fails to do so, there is no loss of face or confrontation — which there could be if a direct request was made and then refused. The speaker using the indirect style would most likely assume that the boss was unable to give her a raise, if her indirect request was not met. Speakers who use the direct style often become frustrated with the indirect style and see it as inefficient at best and ineffective at worst. When discussing a scenario like the one given, they would be tempted to argue that the speaker would have gotten a raise if she had only come right out and asked for it. Certainly, this point is well taken if the speaker were communicating within a society that uses the direct style. However, they overlook the fact that within a society that uses the indirect method of communication, the message was conveyed clearly and in a way that allowed both parties to have a high level of social comfort and to save face. It is important to remember that communication always occurs within contexts, and what is effective in one context is not equally effective in another.

Instrumental/affective communication styles

The *instrumental* verbal communication style is one in which it is the responsibility of the sender to make the message clear. The sender is expected to convey a message that can easily be understood by the listener. Often in this communication style the sender is expected to persuade the listener and to assert his position. The instrumental style is goal-oriented. In other words, a speaker using this style of communication will strive to get a particular response from listeners. An example of the instrumental style would be a teacher who gives her students a set of instructions that tell the students very clearly what they should do and why they should do it. Most Americans use the instrumental communication style.

Rather than placing the responsibility for effective communication on the speaker, the *affective* communication style places the burden of making meaning from a message on the listener. The affective style requires the listener to anticipate what the speaker is trying to express even before the message is sent. Listeners are expected to be alert to non-verbal clues such as body language (see Chapter 6) and other contextual aspects of the communication situation. The affective style is more likely to be used by people who use the indirect style of communication. In a culture where the affective style is used, like Japan, students in a classroom would be expected to anticipate the teacher's wishes even before he began giving them a set of instructions for an assignment.

Figure 5.3 These Japanese students are expected to anticipate what the teacher wants them to do even before they are given instructions. The affective communication style is used in the Japanese culture and in many other high context cultures. When the affective style is used, listeners are required to anticipate what the speaker is trying to convey and to be alert for non-verbal cues such as body language.

It is easy to see why the indirect and affective styles are closely related, because both rely more on the context of the communication encounter and the relationship between the individuals who are speaking to one another. These styles are most likely to be found in cultures that are high context, ones in which much of the communication in any encounter lies not in the message but in the surrounding context. A parallel situation exists for the direct and instrumental styles as both are more likely to be found in low-context cultures where the message itself is expected to carry most, if not all, of the information being communicated.

Elaborate/exact/succinct communication styles

Another aspect of verbal communication that differs from one culture to another is the use of *elaborate*, *exact*, and *succinct* styles. The elaborate style is characterized by flowery phrases; frequent quotations from myth, fables, and sacred texts; frequent use of metaphorical language; and emphatic and exaggerated statements. Arab cultures use the elaborate verbal style and draw upon literary references, quotations from sacred texts and emphatic repetition in their everyday speech. In Egypt today, children are taught only in Arabic and learn to memorize and recite lengthy verses of the Koran. The linguistic style of Koranic writings is a model for speech throughout Islamic societies. Those individuals who have a descriptive and elegant style of speech have more credibility with members of Arab cultures.[23] Simple answers such as "yes" and "no" are rarely believed by members of cultures that use the elaborate style of speech. When offered more food by an Arab host, a speaker must repeat many times that he is full in the most emphatic and even exaggerated terms ("I swear to God that I cannot eat another bite") or his refusal will not be taken seriously.

By contrast speakers who use the succinct style value understatement and silence. They believe it is better to remain silent than to speak up in a situation that is in any way ambiguous or negative in character. They value simple assertions and would be likely to distrust the emphatic speech of individuals who use the elaborate verbal style. The Amish use this communication style.

The exact style falls somewhere between the elaborate and the succinct styles on a continuum of verbal communication styles. Speakers who use the exact style value using as many words as necessary to convey a message clearly, but no more words than necessary. They do not engage in flowery or exaggerated language use. The exact style is the one favored by most Americans, particularly in business and industry; this style emphasizes sincerity and cooperation. Speakers who engage in exaggeration may be viewed with distrust, just as speakers who are not emphatic enough in their speech may lack credibility within cultures that use the elaborate style.

Personal and contextual communication styles

The *personal* and *contextual* verbal communication styles have to do with how much emphasis the speaker places on himself/herself versus how much emphasis is placed on the relationship between the speaker and the listener. Speakers who use the personal style use the pronoun "I" and place more emphasis on themselves; on the other hand, speakers who use the contextual style tend to place more emphasis on their relationship to the listener and on the overall context of the communication.

People in the US use the personal style, as do most members of individual-istic cultures; this style reflects the cultural values of societies in which the individual's rights are placed above those of the group and in which self-expression and freedom are valued above group harmony and cooperation. Conversely, in collectivistic cultures, like the Korean and Japanese cultures, the use of the contextual style, which emphasizes relationships, is not surprising. The contextual style reflects the cultural values of societies where the good of the group is placed above an individual's rights and where group harmony and cooperation are deemed greater goods than freedom and individual self-expression. In Korean, and also in Japanese, there is little emphasis on indi-vidual identities in conversation and minimal use of the pronouns *you* and *I*. Usually, speakers who drop personal pronouns are members of collectivistic cultures, and speakers who do not drop them are members of individualistic cultures. Kashima and Kashima conducted a study of 39 languages spoken in 71 cultures and found that cultures with "pronoun-drop" languages were less individualistic than cultures with "non-pronoun-drop" languages."[24]

Bilingualism and Multilingualism

The American culture is one of the few cultures that does not value multilingualism. One reason for this fact may be that English is the primary language used in international business. In many other cultures children grow up learning several languages. A person who can speak several languages fluently is called *multilingual*; someone who speaks two languages fluently is called *bilingual*. Many Americans who are more recent immigrants or whose families still retain strong ties with their ethnic roots are bilingual. Further, despite the fact that few Americans seek out the opportunity to learn other languages, language diversity is a significant issue in the United States. According to the 2000 US Census, 18 percent of the 262.4 million people aged 5 and over spoke a language other than English at home. Spanish was the most frequently spoken language, and after Spanish, the top three languages spoken most frequently were Chinese, French, and German in that order.[25]

Individuals who are bilingual or multilingual have the opportunity to see the world from more than one perspective. This ability has the potential to make them much more competent and mindful as intercultural communicators. Of course, at times they may also find that their ability leads to conflict and confusion for them. The experience of Ruben Salazar is typical of the experience of many bilingual children:

> You know it almost from the beginning: speaking Spanish makes you different. Your mother, father, brothers, sisters, and friends all speak Spanish. But the bus driver, the teacher, the policeman, the store clerk, the man who comes to collect the rent — all the people who are doing important things — do not. Then the day comes when your teacher — who has taught you the importance of many things — tells you that speaking Spanish is wrong. You go home, kiss your mother, and say a few words to her in Spanish. You go to the window and look out and your mother asks you what's the matter?
>
> *Nada, mama*, you answer, because you don't know what is wrong.[26]

Bilingual individuals, particularly when they are the children of immigrants, are often urged to adopt the speech of the majority culture. Adapting to the speech patterns, dialect, or language of the majority culture is often a way to elevate oneself in society. For one of Madelyn's students, Jou-Ying Chen, the importance of proper speech was related to other cultural issues and beliefs within her family in Taiwan.

> I was born in Taiwan, a small island near the southeast coast of China. Though we call ourselves the Republic of China, the rest of the world seems to recognize us just as Taiwan. Living on a small island does not equal having a simple life. For one thing, there are people in Taiwan from just about every province in China, all crowded onto the island.
>
> After World War II, people from all parts of China came to Taiwan with different

attitudes and culture, all speaking different dialects. My parents were part of this great migration. They were both born in Zhejiang province, China. By the time of my arrival, they had been living in Taiwan for more than two decades.

I was the third child of the family, and like my siblings, a disappointment for both of my parents and for my grandparents. We were girls. No greater tragedy can happen than to have no sons in a Chinese family. In fact, people *know* that someone in your family, or your ancestors, must have done something wicked to have deserved this kind of "punishment" from God.

To create a counterpoint, my parents were determined to educate us as properly as they knew how. And the first thing they had in mind was language. How you speak is usually the first thing people notice, besides your appearance. My parents wanted all of their children to be able to speak a beautiful Mandarin Chinese, like the "proper" and "educated" people they saw on TV. Therefore, even though they spoke the Zhejuang dialect, they would use Mandarin Chinese when talking to us directly. And my parents were, and still are, very proud of our ability to speak Mandarin Chinese. This ability to master Mandarin proves their ability to bring us up the "right" way, despite the fact that there are all girls in the family.

(Personal communication, April 30, 2005)

For many bilingual individuals, one language is spoken at home while another is spoken at work or at school. Within the United States we have a large and growing number of Americans who speak Spanish, and many businesses and public facilities, particularly in cities with a high concentration of Spanish-speaking people, provide information in both Spanish and English. The growing number of Spanish speakers in the US has led some Americans to propose the establishment of English as the official language of the United States. Although English is the language used in government, business, and academia, it does not have an official or legal status as our nation's language.

Some individuals who are threatened by the increased use of Spanish have started the English Only Movement, which is a campaign to have English declared the official language of the US and to ban all other languages from being used in government, business, and the academic world. The English Only Movement began in the 1980s and advocated a return to monolingualism in the United States. In 1981, Senator S. I. Hayakawa, Rep. California, introduced a constitutional English Language Amendment proposing a declaration to make English the nation's official language. The bill died in Congress. Critics of the English Only Movement argue that many of its proponents are linked to anti-immigration groups.[27]

It is interesting to note that during the founding period of our nation from 1780 to 1820 there was no restraint on the number and kind of languages spoken, and, in fact, there was recognition of the plural nature of American society, even then. Members of the Continental Congress agreed that any and all languages could be used to spread communication needed to legitimate the political system of the new nation. Benjamin Rush, a member of the

Continental Congress and a signer of the Declaration of Independence, argued that German and French should be taught in America's "English Schools." The value of multilingualism both for practical reasons and to advance knowledge was clearly recognized by the Founders of the United States of America.[28]

Many proponents of the English Only Movement suggest that monolingualism is necessary for our nation to remain strong, that our common language is the glue that binds us together, and that we are in danger of becoming another nation torn apart by linguistic division like Canada. Those who oppose the English Only Movement point to the fact that pluralism has kept our country strong, and while immigrants should still be expected to learn English, allowing the use of other languages as well does no harm.

Language and Power

The English Only Movement in the United States is not a unique phenomenon. Many nations have dealt with multilingualism and the question of establishing one or more official languages. Belgium, India, and Canada are all examples of multilingual nations that have dealt with the question of establishing more than one official language. In Canada, both English and French are official languages. When establishing these two official languages Canadian policymakers hoped that national bilingualism would preserve and strengthen national unity. However, in reality most Canadians are monolingual and the province of Quebec has declared French as its sole official language. Similarly, Belgium is divided linguistically between its French-speaking and Dutch-speaking communities. In effect Belgium is like separate countries within one state. "To the extent that Belgium still exists, it's like a shell," says Bart Maddens, professor of political sciences at the Catholic University of Leuven, noting that only institutions such as the monarchy and the national football side command respect on both sides.[29]

The question of which language or languages become a nation's official language(s) is usually a political decision; the choice of an official language or languages generally has to do with the language spoken by those individuals and groups in positions of power. Often there are historical reasons for the preference of one language over another within a nation or a region of a nation. These reasons may be bound up in cultural conflicts and years of enmity between peoples of different nations or regions within a nation. At times language may be used as a tool of oppression, or at least may be perceived as such by individuals who do not speak the language associated with social mobility and success. Many of the conflicts can be traced to colonial times. For example, in postcolonial India and Africa many members of the ruling classes speak either English or French, while individuals of lower socioeconomic standing speak local tongues. In India, for example, the movement to replace English with Hindi and to establish Hindi as the sole language of the nation has been viewed as an attempt to block the social mobility of non-Hindis.[30] In many instances, a dominant language group has sought to use the establishment of an official language as a means to block the social mobility of individuals who do not speak the "right" language. For example, in Quebec there have been many documented incidences of discrimination against non-French-speaking Canadians.

Communication between co-cultural groups

Even individuals who share a language may speak it quite differently from one another. A *dialect* is a variation of a language peculiar to a social class, geographical region, or other co-cultural group within a society; dialects often include idioms and non-standard pronunciation and vocabulary. Dialects are an example of linguistic variations within languages. Dialects often reflect variations in the way a language is spoken within different geographic regions of a nation. Oftentimes dialects are also linked to particular socioeconomic classes. For example, in England an individual's speech reveals a great deal about his education and social status. Standard British English is derived from the speech of royalty, as is the standard of speech in many European and Asian societies.[31] In the film *The Princess Diaries* an American teenager learns that she is really a member of a royal family, and she is taught by her grandmother how to act as a princess; part of her education requires her to learn to speak in a more refined and polished way than she did formerly as a typical American teenager. Of course, in America, a supposedly classless society, we would argue that speech does not determine one's fate. However, prejudice does exist against non-standard speech and members of groups that do not speak Standard American English may, in fact, find themselves given fewer opportunities than those individuals who conform to the accepted way of speaking.

For these reasons, recent immigrants to the US often strive to learn Standard American English and do their best to eradicate their accents. However, for many immigrants a conflict exists between the desire to assimilate and the need to maintain one's roots and ethnic pride. Therefore, despite pressure to assimilate, many ethnic minorities and members of other non-dominant groups within society may actually cling to their way of speaking as a gesture of solidarity with one another and their roots.

These issues of power and conflict are not only related to the speech of immigrants, but can be seen within the US in regard to the privileging of certain accents and dialects over others and with prejudice directed to individuals who speak with these accents and dialects. In both cases, it is the question of power rather than an intrinsic value in one language or linguistic variation of a language over another that is at issue. In the US, the speech and communication style of white males has been privileged because of their dominance in government and in the business world. Members of co-cultural groups are often at a disadvantage in society when they do not conform to the communication styles of the dominant group. Communication scholar Mark Orbe posits the muted-group theory of communication, which is based on the work of anthropologists Shirley Ardener and Edwin Ardener. The work of Ardener and Ardener states that the groups in power within a society determine the dominant communication system of that society.[32] The communication system that dominates society supports the world view of the majority culture, and members of co-cultural groups are forced to function within a communication system that does not reflect their lived experiences.[33] The muted group theory suggests that many co-cultural groups within American society are made "inarticulate," that is, they are unable to express their unique experiences because they are forced to use a language that is based on the majority culture's perception of reality. For example, Kramarae's work demonstrates how women in American society have been muted by the male-dominated communication system that does not value women's speech.[34] Similarly, Orbe has researched the communication of African American men. He found that African American males use a variety of strategies to challenge their muted-group position. His work suggests that co-cultural groups that have been muted by the dominant communication styles of a society do not necessarily remain muted and may find ways to challenge the existing structure.[35]

The term *communication orientation* refers to the stance that members of co-cultural groups take when communicating with members of the majority culture. Generally, an approach to communication can be described as *non-assertive*, *assertive*, or *aggressive* behavior. Further, the likely outcome can be categorized as *assimilation*, *accommodation*, or *separation*. These two sets of three categories can yield nine different types of strategies (see Table 5.1).

The strategy used by a member of a co-cultural group will depend on the desired outcome, the perceived benefits or costs, and the context in which the communication encounter occurs. For example, an individual whose main goal is to be able to operate from within the existing communication system may choose non-assertive assimilation as the strategy most likely to achieve that goal. However, an individual whose primary goal is to change existing structures may adopt an aggressive accommodation strategy; this individual will not be concerned with fitting in but rather with having the opportunity to work with members of the majority culture to bring about social change. In contrast, individuals who adopt a stance of aggressive separation may resort to attacking the character and livelihood of members of the majority culture; such individuals perceive those who use assimilation and accommodation strategies as misguided and ineffective. They believe in using "whatever means necessary" to bring about change.[36]

Often members of co-cultural groups are stereotyped by others in society based on their speech and communication styles. Such stereotyping may cause them to be passed over for jobs or for scholarships merely because their communication style does not conform to the style used by the majority culture. There are significant differences between black and white communication styles in the US, and often these differences can cause obstacles to effective communication. The Communication Theory of Ethnic Identity (CTEI) states that inter-ethnic communication can only be understood in the context of a history of misunderstandings between races, and a history of

Table 5.1 Co-cultural communication orientations

	Separation	Accommodation	Assimilation
Nonassertive	Avoiding	Increasing visibility	Emphasizing commonalities
	Maintaining	Dispelling stereotypes	Developing positive face
	Interpersonal barriers		Censoring self
			Averting controversy
Assertive	Communicating self	Communicating self	Extensive preparation
	Intra-group networking	Intra-group networking	Overcompensating
	Exemplifying strengths	Using liaisons	Manipulating stereotypes
	Embracing stereotypes	Educating others	Bargaining
Aggressive	Attacking	Confronting	Dissociating
	Sabotaging others	Gaining advantage	Mirroring
			Strategic distancing
			Ridiculing self

The term "communication orientation" refers to the stance taken by members of co-cultural groups when communicating with the majority culture. Individuals will use different strategies depending on the desired outcome, the perceived benefits or costs, and the context in which the communication occurs. Source: Mark P. Orbe, *Constructing Co-Cultural Theory* (Thousand Oaks, CA: Sage, 1998).

oppression.[37] Communication scholars Hughes and Baldwin have conducted several studies of the communication predictors of stereotypical impressions in communication between black and white Americans. One of their findings is that frequently the use of "black slang" causes white communicators to negatively stereotype black communicators.[38] However, the CTEI suggests that ethnic groups use particular styles of English to enact their identities and that competent communication will not be possible if communicators ignore or fail to respect the identity others wish to claim in a communication encounter.[39]

For members of co-cultural groups there is often a tension between a desire to maintain their identities and the temptation to adapt to the communication styles of the majority culture in order to avoid being stereotyped and receiving prejudicial treatment. The Communication Accommodation Theory contends that speakers will often adapt their patterns of speech in order to identify with others.[40] Speakers may change their speech to converge with the speech of people in positions of power; for example, a woman may accommodate the speech patterns of her male boss in order to be perceived by him as a valuable employee. Similarly, an African American male may choose to use black slang when speaking to family and friends, but choose not to use it in the business world.

Generally, speakers will choose to converge with the speech of others when they wish to gain their approval and perceive that they will be rewarded for doing so. On the other hand, speakers may also deliberately diverge from the speech of those in power when they wish to maintain pride in their identities and when they want to demonstrate solidarity with other members of their co-cultural group.

In order to be mindful intercultural communicators, we need to avoid being influenced by the prejudices associated with speech and communication styles; be aware of the reasons for assimilation, accommodation, and divergence by members of co-cultural groups; and strive to avoid stereotyping others based on their accents and communication patterns. An understanding of the relationship between language and power can help us to resolve conflicts and enhance cooperation when we deal with others.

Conflict/Cooperation Approaches and Methods

When we consider the variations in communication styles and values from one culture to another, it is not surprising that misunderstandings occur among people from different cultures and that sometimes these misunderstandings, if not addressed, can lead to conflict. Members of cultures that value succinct speech may become impatient with individuals who use the elaborate verbal style. On the other hand, individuals using the succinct style may not be taken seriously by speakers who use the elaborate style. In cases like these two, there is great potential for misunderstandings to occur and for one or both parties to feel insulted.

The goal of the field of intercultural communication generally and of this book specifically is to provide individuals with the ability to communicate skillfully and mindfully in order to prevent conflict and enhance cooperation among the members of our global society. This goal is important first to prevent conflicts, but also beyond that to enable cooperation among nations so that we may address the key global issues that affect all of us today.

Certainly the first step in averting conflict and enhancing cooperation is to develop knowledge of the basics of intercultural communication and the different communication styles used by members of cultures other than one's own. Once that competence has been developed, the next step in becoming a skillful and mindful intercultural communicator is to learn specific conflict/cooperation methods that can be used in intercultural encounters. These methodologies are useful at both the individual and the group level.

Understanding the Relationship between Communication Styles and Conflict

Intercultural conflict can be defined as a situation in which two or more inter-dependent parties have incompatible goals, values, expectations, or outcomes;

the incompatibility between the parties may be real or perceived. Also, the parties must be interdependent; in other words, each party must have the ability to take action that would affect the other. If they do not have the ability to do so, then it will be easy for them to avert conflict. For conflict to occur, something must be at stake for both parties. Intercultural conflict involves four types of goals: *content* goals, *relational* goals, *identity* goals, and *process* goals.[41] Content goals refer to the issues being disputed. For example, an intercultural couple may experience conflict when deciding which religious tradition to raise their children in. Relational goals refer to the type of relationship being established. A conflict based on differing relational goals may occur between a manager from the US and a group of employees in another culture if the manager takes a very informal approach and the employees expect their boss to establish a much more formal relationship with them. Identity goals refer to the desired self-images of the parties involved. A conflict may occur between an employer and an employee who is an immigrant, if the employee perceives that the employer does not respect the customs or traditions of the employee's culture. Finally, process goals refer to the approaches taken to resolve conflicts (see "Differing Conflict Resolution Styles," this chapter).

Conflicts are often the result of long-standing enmity between people. For example, the roots of conflict in the Middle East have a lengthy history. Many times historical, political, and economic factors precipitate conflicts between nations, groups, and individuals. However, conflicts can also result from differences in communication styles, and even conflicts that have other initial causes can be fueled by incompatible styles of communication. Some differences are related to the cultural value dimensions of individualism/collectivism; to differences between high- and low-context communication; to different approaches to formality in communication; and to different verbal styles (direct/indirect, instrumental/affective, elaborate/exact/succinct, personal/contextual).

Cultural value dimensions and conflict

Most cultures of the world can be categorized as either individualistic or collectivistic in their value orientation. As we have already discussed, individualistic cultures value the rights of the individual above those of the group; in an individualistic culture freedom and self-expression are valued. By contrast, collectivistic cultures value the good of the group above individual rights; in a collectivistic culture conformity and group harmony are valued. Conflict may arise when members of individualistic cultures behave in ways that are perceived by their collective counterparts as not valuing group harmony; it may also occur when members of collective cultures behave in a way that does not value individual rights. Conflicts between individualists and collectivists are likely to occur in regard to relational and identity goals. For example, if a member of an individualistic culture behaves in a way that does not show concern for face-saving issues of importance to members of a collective culture, conflict may result. If a team leader publicly rejects the ideas put forward by a member of the team who is from a collective culture, that individual may feel that he/she has been publicly disgraced. Further, the disgraced individual and other members of collective cultures on the team may lose respect for the leader who they perceive as not valuing their face concerns. Such feelings may well lead to conflict among the team members and team leader.

These cultural value differences also have implications for addressing conflicts among individuals, groups, and nations. When engaging in problem-solving in a business setting, members of collective cultures may place a higher value on preserving a good working relationship and harmony with their colleagues, while members of individualistic cultures many be more concerned with arriving at a solution quickly. Members of collective cultures may feel that their individualistic counterparts do not value their relationship and may not choose to continue the business relationship in the future.

High- and low-context communication and conflict

Often conflict situations result from miscommunication. When individuals do not understand one another, one party may not even realize that the other party views the situation as one of conflict. As we have discussed, individuals who use high-context communication often do not make explicit statements, but rely on the surrounding context of the communication encounter to convey their meaning. Of course, when individuals from high-context cultures communicate with members of low-context cultures, those cultures where meaning is explicitly stated, there is great potential for misunderstanding. A low-context communicator may find communication with a member of a high-context culture somewhat ambiguous and may not be aware of sources of potential misunderstanding and conflict. For example, a member of a high-context culture may compliment his neighbor on his new sound system and his good fortune in not needing to get up early for work rather than directly tell him that he is angry because the neighbor is playing his music too loud and keeping him from getting sleep. If the low-context communicator takes his neighbor's meaning only from his literal message and does not read other cues, he may miss an opportunity to resolve a potential conflict.

Formality/informality and conflict

Some cultures have a highly structured social hierarchy that requires different forms of address for members of the society based on their age, social status, and relationship to the speaker. We have seen that many Asian societies place a great deal of emphasis on proper etiquette when communicating with others, and languages like Japanese and Korean have a grammatical structure that reinforces the hierarchical nature of the society. For example, different pronouns are used to communicate with peers than are used to address elders, teachers, and others whose social status affords them respect. Other cultures are much more informal and do not have pronouns to distinguish between addressing one's superiors and one's peers. In the United States, we typically use very informal modes of address. Often employees call their bosses by their first names. We may exhibit more formality in some situations than in others — addressing a professor versus addressing a classmate. However, in general, we are very informal in our speech and modes of address. When members of an informal culture like the United States or Australia interact with members of more formal cultures, we may find that it is challenging to adopt the appropriate level of formality. We may also find that a failure to show the proper respect for someone according to the social hierarchy of her culture may be a source of conflict. For example, in the African, Middle Eastern, and Asian cultures, elders are afforded great honor and respect. A businessperson negotiating with colleagues in these cultures who fails to demonstrate the appropriate level of respect for the senior member of the group would likely run the risk of creating a conflict situation, and perhaps, destroying any chance for a relationship in the future.

Verbal styles and conflict

Speakers who use different communication styles may have difficulty communicating effectively, and at times, such difficulty may lead to misunderstanding and conflict. Speakers using the direct communication style state whatever they wish to communicate very explicitly. This style is consistent with low-context communication, where the message is spelled out in great detail and little is left unstated. In contrast, speakers who use an indirect communication style frequently avoid openly stating their message, but rather rely on the surrounding context of the communication encounter to carry their message. Speakers who use a direct style may find it difficult to understand precisely what speakers using the indirect style want; they may also become impatient with speakers using the indirect style and perceive the style as inefficient. On the other hand, speakers using the indirect style may perceive the direct style as lacking in tact. They may criticize speakers who use this style for failing to be concerned with group harmony and with saving the face of those individuals involved in the communication encounter. For example, a group of German managers who speak very directly to their Japanese counterparts in an international business venture may cause negative feelings regarding their working relationship because of their use of a direct style of communication.

Like the indirect style, the affective communication style places much of the burden for understanding a message on the listener. The affective style requires the listener to try to anticipate the speaker's meaning and to pay attention to non-verbal clues to determine precisely what the speaker wishes to convey. In contrast, the instrumental style is very goal-oriented and explicit. Speakers using these two divergent styles are likely to experience misunderstandings and potentially conflicts as well. A teacher from Japan using an affective communication style with American students might become very frustrated by their inability to anticipate his wishes regarding their assignments. The students would also become frustrated by their perception of the teacher's inability to tell them precisely what he wants them to do.

Another divergence among cultures is in their use of elaborate, exact, or succinct communication styles. These three styles exist along a continuum where the elaborate style is the most flowery, emphatic, metaphorical, and exaggerated, the exact style is much more concise and plain, and the succinct style uses as few words as possible and values understatement and silence. It is not difficult to imagine how speakers using these three different styles might experience miscommunication and conflict. While speakers who use the elaborate style question the sincerity of individuals who do not, precisely the opposite is true of speakers using the exact and succinct styles, who distrust the exaggerated language of speakers using the elaborate style. When speakers do not grant credibility to the speech of individuals who use different verbal styles from their own, there is great potential for conflict, particularly when the sincerity of an individual's speech is questioned. Speakers of Arabic are prone to over-assertion in their speech, and they may find it difficult to understand that speakers who use a more direct style mean exactly what they say.

Speakers who use the personal style place more emphasis on themselves and frequently use the pronoun "I." In contrast, speakers who use the contextual style emphasize their relationship to the listener rather than themselves. Most members of individualistic cultures use the personal verbal style, just as most members of collective cultures use the contextual communication style. Speakers using the personal style when communicating with speakers who use the contextual style may well be perceived as self-centered and as not granting the proper importance to their relationship with their listeners. Once again, such a difference in verbal style could well lead to a situation of conflict.

Differing Conflict Resolution Styles

We know that different verbal communication styles can cause conflicts to occur; we should also be aware that differences in conflict resolution styles across cultures have the potential to escalate conflicts once they occur. Members of individualistic cultures generally want to approach conflict directly and in a conflict situation will be most concerned with trying to find a concrete solution. Individualists are also concerned about arriving at a resolution as quickly as possible and tend to believe that the conflict must be settled before they can give any attention to the relationships between the parties involved. They view getting to a solution as primary and seem to think that the interpersonal aspects of the negotiation are secondarily important and that they will work out once the issue at hand has been dealt with satisfactorily. Individualists will be much more concerned with self-face preservation, not with working to preserve the face of the entire group. They also are more likely to use dominating and competitive conflict-management styles than are their collectivistic colleagues.[42]

On the other hand, members of collectivistic cultures will want to take a more circular or spiral approach to conflict and will be more concerned with the relationships among the parties involved in the conflict than with arriving at a solution quickly. Collectivists, particularly Asian nations that are influenced by the Confucian dynamism value dimension, take a very long-term view of the relationship between the parties involved in the conflict. In fact, they see relationship-building and long-term maintenance of relationships as primary, and a solution to a particular issue at hand as secondary, in conflict situations. They tend to believe that once harmonious relationships are in place and trust has been established that then conflicts will be more easily settled. Collectivists are also more likely to take a holistic view of a situation and are less likely than individualists to be driven by a need for a concrete, action-oriented solution to an issue. They are also more likely to be concerned with mutual face-saving and to use compromising styles in conflict resolution.[43]

Because of their different orientations toward conflict resolution, it is not surprising that when members of collective cultures find themselves in conflict with members of individualistic cultures that their styles of addressing conflicts can actually escalate the conflict. Generally, individualists tend to be frustrated by the long-term approach taken by members of collective cultures and feel that time is wasted in circular approaches to the issue; collectivists are likely to find the individualists desire to move quickly to a concrete solution to be rash and may experience the emphasis on a solution rather than on relationships as disrespectful because there is no consideration of face-saving for all parties involved in the conflict.

There are five different styles of managing conflicts that are commonly used; these styles can be, and are, used by members of both individualistic and collectivistic cultures. However, different cultures do tend to favor certain styles over others, but the style that is favored may change based on the context and on the other parties involved in the conflict. The five styles are: *dominating, integrating, compromising, obliging,* and *avoiding.*

The dominating style emphasizes the existence of a winner and a loser in the conflict situation, which is called a "zero-sum game" in the IR literature and on a global scale. Individuals who use this style are concerned with their own self-esteem and their own interests. They use forceful behavior in order to get the other parties involved to comply with their wishes and show no concern for the rights or self-esteem of others. Moving from this individual level of analysis to the state level of analysis and system level of analysis, similar kinds of interactions occur among states and nations when they aim to change the behavior of the other. This is the essence of the notion of "power," which is fundamental to the study of politics and all social sciences.

Both the integrating and the compromising style emphasize gain for both parties and at least some concern for the self-esteem of both parties involved. The integrating style involves collaboration and open dialogue in order to find a solution acceptable to both parties. The self-esteem of both parties is highly valued in this style. The compromising style also involves finding a solution that both parties can accept, but requires both parties to give up something in order to arrive at such a solution. This style also values the self-esteem of both parties but to a lesser extent than the integrating style.

The obliging style requires that one party essentially give in to the other party in order to maintain the relationship. The person making concessions will generally downplay the incompatibilities that exist. This style is often found in relationships where there is a power or status differential between the two parties involved.

Finally, the avoiding style is used in an attempt to sidestep or deny conflict in order to withdraw from it. For the most part, from the perspective of American culture this style would be seen as ineffective and potentially leading to greater conflict in the future because things are not dealt with openly. However, in some cultures this style, particularly when it is used by both parties involved in the conflict, can actually serve to preserve harmony in relationships and to save face for all parties involved. For members of collective cultures, like the Chinese and Japanese cultures, the avoiding style may be an appropriate choice, particularly when stakes are low, because it will allow for both parties to save face and for the relationship to be preserved.[44]

Communication styles of co-cultural groups and conflict

Members of co-cultural groups have conflict management styles that may differ from the styles used by the majority culture. Communication researcher Mary Jane Collier conducted a study to examine the relationship between ethnic background and communication competencies in friendships in the United States.[45] As part of the study she questioned Mexican Americans, African Americans, and white Americans about the way they handle conflicts in close friendships. She also asked the participants if they thought that males and females handled conflict differently. Collier found that male and female ethnic friends differed in their ideas about the best way to resolve conflicts in a friendship. Mexican American males wanted to reach a mutual understanding while the Mexican American females focused on ways to reinforce the friendships. African American males emphasized the importance of stating convincing arguments, while African American females were more concerned with being assertive and avoiding criticism. The white American males focused on the value of being direct, while the females expressed concern for the other person and the relationship. Although Collier's study reveals ethnic- and gender-related differences in conflict resolution, much more research is needed to fully understand the impact of co-cultural status on approaches to managing conflict.

Technology and Verbal Communication

Throughout this chapter we have discussed the ways that language use is related to issues of power. Currently, English is recognized as the language of the global marketplace. A majority of e-commerce businesses use English as their official language and there are more websites in English than in any other language. There are over 499 million internet users who speak English — accounting for 27.7 percent of all internet users.[46] Of course there are historical reasons why English became the language of the internet. The internet was originally developed as a means for exchanging information between organizations in the US military-scientific complex and its early users were primarily American scientists and academics.

Today, however, the internet is a global marketplace, and the use of English as its language privileges certain cultural values over others. Typically, majority cultures and individuals and groups in positions of power dictate which language(s) and language variations are used, and in doing so, they can ensure that their message will have the best chance of being understood. As we saw in our discussion of co-cultural groups and muted-group theory, when the primary language used in a society does not reflect a group's experience, it becomes difficult for that group to express themselves. In our global society, speakers of some languages are at a greater disadvantage than others; some nations find themselves economically disadvantaged because they are on the "wrong side" of a "digital divide" that makes it difficult for them to participate in our global economy. For example, Ethiopia was recently labeled by its own infrastructure minister as one of the "least-connected" nations in the world. One language-related factor that has seriously inhibited wider internet use in Ethiopia is the fact that the Amharic language has 345 letters and letter variations; the number of letters and variations makes keyboarding very difficult.[47]

For many people around the world, being unable to communicate on the internet in their native language detracts from their ability to participate in the global economy, and in some cases, makes it impossible. But for the many non-American internet users who are fluent in English, there are still communication challenges related to the cultural imbalance on the internet. If we view the internet as a "virtual cultural region," we find that the American cultural values of low power distance and low uncertainty avoidance predominate. Because of the informal nature of communication in the virtual global community, members of hierarchical societies like Japan and Korea that value formality may be at a disadvantage when communicating on the internet. Many websites are still designed from the American cultural perspective. These sites may contain language and symbols that are offensive to members of other cultures, and may use figurative language that privileges an American world view. For example, computer terminology such as "abort" and "nuke" may be offensive to members of other cultures.[48]

MEDIA IMPACT
SiamWEB.org **Serves as a Forum for Young Thai Women**

SiamWEB.org (www.siamweb.org) is a Thai-managed, English-language website that serves as a forum for young, educated Thai women to respond to the dominant images of them as "happily subservient to western men." These images, which present Thai women as either prostitutes or mail-order brides, are prevalent in international film and television depictions of Thailand. SiamWEB.org encourages Thai women who have internet access to challenge the stereotypes of them proliferated by international media, and in doing so, to redefine their own identities and images of the Thai nation as well.

The creators of *SiamWEB.org* chose to use the English language. While doing so might initially seem to be merely an acknowledgement of the dominance of the English language, the creators argue that by using English "they hope to reduce its association with the U.S. and the U.K. and exploit the dynamic forces operating in this internationalized language." On the site they incorporate many "Thai-isms" into English that serve to bring the version of English used closer to Thai and to minimize the importance of standard English for communication.

Using English as the language of the site allows dominant English-language accounts of Thailand to be examined and challenged. Further, for many young Thais, the English language is associated with modernity and new ways of viewing sexuality and gender. By using English, the site has a wider potential audience than it would if the creators had used Thai. At the same time the creators repeatedly remind visitors to the site that fluency in English is not required for communication; a pattern of grammatical errors appear on the site in order to send the message that perfect language skills are not important and that visitors need not feel insecure about their English language skills. The site is a dynamic space that "contributes to the complex processes by which western culture and the English language are appropriated and reassembled in ways that challenge externally generated stereotypes."

Source: Jillana B. Enteen, "Siam remapped: Cyber-Interventions by Thai Women," *New Media & Society*, 7:4 (2005), 457–82.

Many steps are being taken to make the internet more accessible to speakers of other languages. While web translation tools make it easier for individuals around the world to access web content in their native languages, the use of a global English style can make content more easily understandable on English language websites. At the same time web designers are recognizing the need to take cultural differences into account when they create websites. As these changes go into effect, we should also bear in mind the changing demographics of internet usage. In 2005, there were only 125 million internet users who spoke Chinese — approximately 13 percent of the total number of internet users. More people speak Chinese than any other language, and recently there has been a dramatic increase in the percentage of internet users who are speakers of Chinese; currently, there are 407 million internet users who speak Chinese — approximately 22.6 percent of the total number of internet users.[49]

References

1. David Crystal, *The Cambridge Encyclopedia of Language* (Cambridge: Cambridge University Press, 1997).
2. Daniel L. Everett, "Cultural Constraints on Grammar and Cognition in Pirahã: Another Look at the *Design Features* of Human Language," *Current Anthropology*, 46:4 (August–October 2005), 621–34.
3. Anthony Traill, *Phonetic and Phonological Studies of Xoo Bushman* (Amsterdam: John Benhamins Publishing Company, 1986).
4. "Notebook: Senate Votes to Urge Davis to 'Class Up' His Campaign," *The Daily News of Los Angeles*, September 10, 2003, N15; Firoozeh Dumas, "Someday, We Won't Put an Accent on Accents," *Newsday*, September 2, 2003, A23; Lynda Gledhill, "State Demands Davis Apologize for Remark," *San Francisco Chronicle*, September 10, 2003, A13; Charlie LeDuff, "In California, Davis and Schwarzenegger Split the Pronunciation Vote," *The New York Times*, September 9, 2003, A26; "You Can Say That Again!: A Diabolical Wit," *The Nikkei Weekly*, October 6, 2003.
5. *The New Oxford American Dictionary* (Oxford: Oxford University Press, 2001), p. 502.
6. Mildred L. Larson, *Meaning-Based Translation: A Guide to Cross-Language Equivalence* (Lanham, MD: University Press of America, 1984), p. 5.
7. Benjamin Lee Whorf, "The Punctual and Segmentative Aspects of Verbs in Hopi," in John B. Carroll, ed., *Language, Thought, and Reality* (Cambridge, MA: The MIT Press, 1956), p. 55.
8. Benjamin Lee Whorf, "Science and Linguistics," in John B. Carroll, ed., *Language, Thought, and Reality* (Cambridge, MA: The MIT Press, 1956), p. 217.
9. Ibid.
10. Thomas M. Steinfatt, "Linguistic Relativity: Toward a Broader View," in Stella Ting-Toomey and F. Korzenny, eds., *Language, Communication, and Culture* (Newbury Park, CA: Sage, 1989), pp. 35–78.
11. Jean Piaget, *The Child's Conception of the World*, trans. Joan and Andrew Tomlinson, (Totowa, NJ: Littlefield, Adams, 1976); Lev Semenovich Vygotsky, *Thought and Language*, trans. Alex Kozulin (Cambridge, MA: MIT Press, 1986).
12. V. Volterra and J. Iverson, "When Do Modality Factors Affect the Course of Language Acquistion?" in K. Emmorey and J. S. Reilley, eds., *Language, Gesture, and Space* (Hillsdale, NJ: Lawrence Erlbaum, 1995), pp. 371–90.
13. William C. Stokoe, "Deafness, Cognition, and Language," in Diane M. Clark, Marc Marschark, and Michael A. Karchmer, eds., *Context, Cognition, and Deafness* (Washington, DC: Gallaudet University Press, 2001), p. 7.
14. M. Rhodda and C. Grove, *Language, Cognition, and Deafness* (Hillsdale, NJ: Lawrence Erlbaum, 1987).
15. Stokoe, p. 6.
16. D. Slobin, "From 'thought and language' to 'thinking for speaking,'" in J. J. Gumperz and S. C. Levinson, eds., *Rethinking Linguistic Relativity* (Cambridge: Cambridge University Press, 1996), pp. 70–96.
17. Mutsumi Imai and Reiko Mazuka, "Reevaluating Linguistic Relativity: Language-Specific Categories and the Role of Universal Ontological Knowledge in the Construal of Individuation," in Dedre Gentner and Susan Goldin-Meadow, eds., *Language in Mind: Advances in the Study of Language and Thought* (Cambridge, MA: MIT Press, 2003), pp. 429–64.
18. Gerry Philipsen, *Speaking Culturally: Explorations in Social Communication* (Albany, NY: Albany State University of New York Press, 1992), p. 10.
19. Ibid., p. 15.
20. Larson, p. 135.
21. Ibid., p. 134.

22. Ibid., p. 57.
23. Polly A. Begley, "Communication with Egyptians," in Larry A. Samovar and Richard E. Porter, eds., *Intercultural Communication: A Reader* (Belmont, CA: Wadsworth Publishing, 2003), p. 92.
24. Emiko S. Kashima and Yoshihisa Kashima, "Culture and Language: The Case of Cultural Dimensions and Personal Pronoun Use," *Journal of Cross-Cultural Psychology*, 29 (1998), 461–86.
25. U.S. Census Bureau, "Language Use and English-Speaking Ability: 2000," *Census 2000 Brief*, October 2003, 1–11.
26. Ruben Salazar, "Aqui No Se Habla Espanol," in James Crawford, ed., *Language Loyalties: A Sourcebook on the Official English Controversy* (Chicago, IL: University of Chicago Press, 1992), pp. 329–30.
27. Jamie B. Draper and Martha Jimenez, "A Chronology of the Official English Movement," in James Crawford, ed., *Language Loyalties: A Sourcebook on the Official English Controversy* (Chicago, IL: University of Chicago Press, 1992) pp. 89–94.
28. Shirley Brice Heath, "Why No Official Tongue?" in James Crawford, ed., *Language Loyalties: A Sourcebook on the Official English Controversy* (Chicago, IL: University of Chicago Press, 1992), pp. 20–31.
29. Leon Bruneau, "Belgium's Linguistic Divide as Strong as Ever," *Agence France Presse*, May 14, 2003.
30. John Baugh, *Beyond Ebonics: Linguistic Pride and Racial Prejudice* (New York: Oxford University Press, 2000), p. 29.
31. Ronald F. Inglehart and Margaret Woodward, "Language Conflicts and Political Community," in James Crawford, ed., *Language Loyalties: A Sourcebook of the Official English Controversy* (Chicago, IL: The University of Chicago Press, 1992), pp. 415–14.
32. Edwin Ardener, "Some Outstanding Problems in the Analysis of Events," in G. Schwinner, ed., *The Yearbook of Symbolic Anthropology* (London, C. Hurst & Co., 1978), pp. 103–21; Shirley Ardener, *Defining Females: The Nature of Women in Society* (New York: John Wiley, 1978).
33. Mark P. Orbe, *Constructing Co-Cultural Theory* (Thousand Oaks, CA: Sage, 1998), p. 20.
34. C. Kramarae, *Women and Men Speaking* (Rowley, MA: Newbury House, 1981).
35. Mark P. Orbe, "'Remember, It's Always Whites' Ball': Descriptions of African American Male Communication," *Communication Quarterly*, 42:3 (1994), 287–300.
36. Orbe, pp. 108–20.
37. M. L. Hecht, M. J. Collier, and S. Ribeau, *African-American Communication: Ethnic Identity and Cultural Interpretation* (Newbury Park, CA: Sage Publications, 1993).
38. Patrick C. Hughes and John R. Baldwin, "Black, White, and Shades of Gray: Communication Predictors of 'Stereotypic Impressions,'" *Southern Communication Journal*, 68:1 (2002), 51.
39. M. J. Collier and M. Thomas, "Cultural Identity: An Interpretive Perspective," in Young Yun Kim and William B. Gudykunst, eds., *Theories in Intercultural Communication* (Newbury Park, CA: Sage, 1988), pp. 99–120.
40. Howard Giles, Nikolas Coupland, and Justine Coupland, "Accommodation Theory: Communication, Context, and Consequence," in Howard Giles, Justine Coupland, and Nikolas Coupland, eds., *Contexts of Accommodation: Developments in Applied Sociolinguistics* (Cambridge: Cambridge University Press, 1991), p. 19.
41. W. Wilmot and J. Hocker, *Interpersonal Conflict*, 5th ed. (Boston, MA: McGraw-Hill, 1998).
42. Stella Ting-Toomey and John G. Oetzel, *Managing Intercultural Conflict Effectively* (Thousand Oaks, CA: Sage, 2001), pp. 48–9.
43. Ibid.
44. Ibid., p. 46.
45. Mary Jane Collier, "Communication Competence Problematics in Ethnic Friendships," *Communication Monographs*, 63 (1996), 314–36.
46. Internet World Stats, "Internet Users by Language," www.internetworldstats.com/stats7.htm, accessed June 10, 2010.
47. Andrew Heavens, "Progress in an Ancient Tongue," *Wired News*, November 5, 2004, http://wired.com/news/print/0,1294,65596,00.html, accessed November 20, 2004.
48. Carol Saunders and Madelyn Flammia, "Language as Power on the Internet," *Journal of the American Society for Information Science and Technology*, 58:12 (2007), 1–5.
49. Internet World Stats.

6 Non-Verbal Communication

An executive from McDonald's corporate headquarters in the United States goes to visit a newly opened McDonald's restaurant in Moscow. He is dismayed to see that the employees do not smile at customers when greeting them. All McDonald's employees are trained to be friendly and greet customers with a warm smile. However, none of the employees in the Moscow McDonald's are smiling. Weren't they given the usual training? Has something happened that day to make them all unhappy?

Two girls become friends in a California high school. Janice is Chinese and Yoki is Japanese. Janice is invited to Yoki's home for a celebration of Yoki's birthday with her family. During the meal, Yoki and her family make loud slurping sounds as they are eating. Janice does not make any sounds, and Yoki's family is insulted. Why is the family so insulted?

These examples demonstrate the importance of understanding the non-verbal aspects of intercultural communication. To become a mindful communicator, in addition to understanding cultural differences in verbal communication, one must also understand cultural differences in non-verbal communication. Communication scholars Burgoon, Buller, and Woodall tell us that between 60 and 65 percent of the information we receive is communicated non-verbally. Non-verbal communication is often beyond our conscious awareness and control. Despite the fact that non-verbal behaviors are often unconscious, when we receive conflicting verbal and non-verbal messages in a communication encounter, it is the non-verbal communication that we believe to be more trustworthy.[1]

Often when we feel uneasiness or discomfort in relation to a seemingly benign verbal exchange, it is the non-verbal aspects of the communication to which we are reacting. This dissonance may be especially pronounced in intercultural communication encounters when our non-verbal communication norms, many of which are unconscious, have been violated.

In our collective development as a species and in our individual development from infancy to adulthood, non-verbal communication precedes verbal communication. Babies' first experiences with their caregivers are based on touch. Touch is just one example of a non-verbal means of communication.

Non-verbal communication is comprised of various means of conveying information using one's body, physical adornments to the body, and one's environment. In this chapter, we will examine the role of body language (kinesics), gestures, eye contact (oculesics), and touch (haptics) in intercultural communication. We will also look at the use of clothing, adornments, facial expressions, and voice (vocalics) to convey information non-verbally. Finally, we will examine different cultural orientations to the use of space (proxemics) and to time (chronemics) and how they, too, are part of non-verbal communication.

Body Language

As we saw in the examples at the beginning of this chapter, a great deal of information is exchanged between people without the use of verbal language. Further, because there are cultural differences in non-verbal communication behaviors there is a great potential for misunderstanding among cultures.

When an individual enters a room and walks toward us, we may receive a great deal of information regarding that person and our interaction with him before a word is spoken. A significant part the communication is transmitted through the individual's gestures, posture, facial expression, and eye contact. Within our own culture we often read these signals unconsciously, and we can tell by downcast eyes and a serious expression that a person is unhappy. Conversely, we may observe a broad smile and expansive gestures as indications of elation and joy. However, we need to be cautious about interpreting non-verbal communication interculturally. The first step in mindful non-verbal interaction with individuals from other cultures is to raise our cultural norms for non-verbal communication to the level of conscious awareness. It is also helpful to learn about the range of behaviors that may be displayed and interpreted differently by members of cultures other than our own. Thus, since the same body language may mean different things to different people, one should be mindful of one's body language to avoid unintended negative signals, which may lead to a dispute or a conflict.

Movement and gestures (kinesics)

The study of the body's movement is called *kinesics*. Gestures are often used to communicate information non-verbally; in some cases they may serve to add to a verbal message while in others they may be substituted for verbal communication. Four different kinds of gestures are typically used; they are *emblems*, *illustrators*, *regulators*, and *adaptors*. Emblems are gestures that convey a specific verbal meaning, such as waving one's hand in place of saying "goodbye" or shrugging the shoulders and opening the palms upward to indicate "I don't know" in response to a question. Emblems may include greetings, insults, gestures of agreement, and beckoning gestures. In the American culture we use over a hundred emblems, whose meanings range from commonplace to obscene and insulting. There are no universal emblems that are used across all cultures, and it is important to be aware of cultural differences in the use of emblems to avoid miscommunication and offending others. Many intercultural misunderstandings and conflicts have resulted from the use of gestures whose meanings differ significantly from one culture to another.

For example, not all cultures use an up-and-down nodding of the head to indicate agreement and a side-to-side movement to indicate disagreement as we do in the United States. In many countries, including Bulgaria, Turkey, Iran, the former Yugoslavian republics, and parts of Greece, the exact opposite is true. Nodding the head up and down means "no" and shaking the head back and forth means "yes."[2]

The thumbs-up gesture is used to connote approval or to indicate that "everything is fine" in North America and much of Europe; it may also be used to signal that one is hitchhiking. However, this gesture has an insulting meaning in Nigeria. The gesture can be compared to gesturing with the middle finger in the United States. In fact, unsuspecting individuals trying to hitch-hike or "thumb a ride" using this gesture in Nigeria have been roughed up for insulting the passing motorists.[3]

Similarly, the "V for victory" gesture, signaled by holding two fingers upright with the palm outward, means "victory" or "peace" to a large number of people around the world. The gesture was probably first used to signal victory during World War II and, then, during the peace movement of the 1960s it was adopted to stand for "peace" as well. However, if the gesture is reversed so that the palm

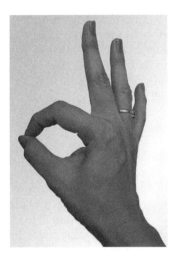 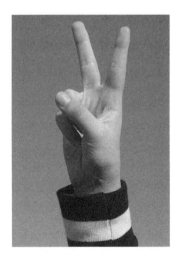

Figure 6.1 Because there are no universally understood gestures, there is great potential for misunderstanding when using them to communicate across cultures. These two gestures are commonly used in the United States. Beware of using them outside the U.S., as each has an obscene meaning in at least one other culture.

and fingers face inward rather than outward, it is a rude gesture in England. The origin of the gesture's meaning in England is said to derive from over 500 years ago, when English bowmen were deadly and greatly feared by their enemies. They were so feared, that if they were captured by the French, they would be disarmed by having their forefinger and middle finger cut off on the hand that drew the bowstring. After victories over the French at Agincourt and Crecy, the English taunted the survivors by holding up their fingers to demonstrate that they were intact.[4] Their gesture was extremely threatening. Today, for the English, this gesture is still considered highly offensive.

In the Arab world, the left hand is considered impure because it is tradition-ally used for bodily hygiene. During a visit to Kuwait, Houman observed an unnamed American diplomat try to pass food to his guests using the left hand. This action was extremely offensive, especially to the more traditional and religious guests. Innocently, the diplomat committed a serious error because he lacked sufficient knowledge of the local tribal Arab culture and the necessary skills to operate effectively.

Illustrators are gestures used to punctuate and add to speech rather than to substitute for verbal communication entirely. Illustrators are often used to add emphasis to spoken words. For example, a speaker who is angry may shake her fist or a parent who is scolding a child may shake his finger. Just as there are differences in the verbal communication styles among cultures, there are also differences in the use of illustrators. Cultures that are more verbally expressive and individualistic are more likely to use illustrators as additions to their communication; Mediterranean and Arab cultures use more illustra-tors. By contrast, cultures that are more concerned with social harmony and conformity are less likely to use illustrators, particularly very expansive ones, to enhance their verbal communication. Asian cultures tend to use relatively few illustrators.

Like illustrators, *regulators* are used in conjunction with verbal messages; they are in fact used to manage the flow of verbal communication. Regulators might include putting up a hand to stop conversation in order to inject a comment, shifting body position and eye contact to signal the end of a con-versational turn, or in fact the end of the entire conversation. Regulators allow participants in a conversation to manage the taking of turns among speakers. A difficulty arises in intercultural communication encounters when participants are not operating with the same set of regulators. It becomes difficult for some speakers to have an opportunity to take a turn in the conversation because they are waiting for cues that never occur. Members of some cultures will interrupt their conversational partners more frequently than others, and some will use silence to regulate the conversational flow. The Japanese frequently use silence to regulate conversations. Short pauses or breaks, referred to as *ma*, are used frequently in Japanese conversations. Silence may be employed to signal disagreement without a loss of face or it may be used in order to take time to formulate an appropriate response.[5]

Adaptors are gestures that are largely unconscious expressions of the emotional state of the individual. These gestures may include clenching fists, tapping feet, scratching, or rubbing the eyes. Once again, these gestures are not universal in their meaning — although all human beings may perform these actions. In most cultures, pounding one's fists signals anger. However, in the German culture, making two fists with the thumbs tucked inside and then gently thrusting them in a downward motion, is a way of saying, "good luck."[6]

It is also important to keep in mind that even gestures such as scratching, an action that may be performed by any person, may be governed by strict cultural rules regarding when and where such a behavior may be displayed. These rules, called cultural display rules, vary widely from one culture to another (see section on "Facial Expressions," this chapter). In some cultures it is considered rude to point or wink. Pointing with the index finger, a common gesture in the US, is considered rude in Japan and China, where they point using the whole open hand. In Taiwan and Hong Kong, repeatedly blinking at another person is considered impolite.[7] In general, collective cultures that value conformity and group cohesiveness are more likely to restrict expansive displays of emotions; individualistic cultures, on the other hand, value individuals' rights to express themselves freely, and, therefore, they are more likely to tolerate and even encourage a public display of emotional gestures.

Eye Contact (Oculesics)

Eye contact may serve as a regulating gesture and is typically related to issues of respect, attentiveness, and honesty in the American culture. We associate direct eye contact with forthrightness and trustworthiness. Have you ever heard someone say, "I just don't trust her because she won't look me in the eye"? Eye contact is a significant component of communication and may reveal a great deal of information to a mindful communicator. Houman recalls that in a Political Risk Analysis graduate seminar, his professor Allen Whiting, a former US diplomat in China, argued that he discovered that the Chinese had nuclear technology one year before it became generally known. Professor Whiting's hunch was based on the eye contact reaction of his Chinese counterpart following their one-to-one discussion.

The study of eye movement, called *oculesics*, examines the various functions of gazing; they are *regulatory*, *monitoring*, *cognitive*, and *expressive*.[8] The regulatory function is when eye contact is used to initiate communication, to signal turn-taking in conversations, and to end a communication encounter. Often when we establish eye contact we signal that we are open to communication. For example, we often seek to get a food server to come to our table in a restaurant by making eye contact with him or her. Similarly, individuals who wish to engage us in conversation begin by seeking to establish eye contact with us. Out-of-towners who go to a large city like New York for the first time are often cautioned not to make eye contact with the various people who try to accost them on the street. Eye contact is also used to regulate turn-taking in conversation. In general, speakers engage in less eye contact than listeners. Turn-taking occurs when the speaker comes to the end of a statement and shifts his gaze toward the listener, who then takes over the role of speaker. We usually break off eye contact when we wish to terminate a conversation.

The monitoring function of eye contact has to do with attentiveness and interest during a communication encounter. When engaged in a conversation, individuals may look at each other as a sign of attention and to monitor their partner's response to what they are saying. They also use their eye gaze as a way to encourage the speaker to continue, the non-verbal equivalent to saying, "That's interesting. Tell me more."

The cognitive function is the relationship of eye movement to the processing of information. During conversations, individuals may avert their eyes when processing complex information or when reflecting upon what has been said. According to Knapp and Hall, this movement represents a shifting of the attention to internal concerns.[9]

Finally, the expressive function is the relationship of the eyes and eye movement to the expression of emotions. Generally, the role of eye movements in expressing emotions is not examined separately, but as part of the overall facial expression (see section on "Facial Expressions," this chapter).

The use and meaning of these various functions differ widely among cultures and can lead to miscommunication with potentially serious consequences. Frequently, customs officers rely on non-verbal cues to evaluate the travelers that they deal with and to determine the truthfulness of their statements. As a consultant to a large seaport in Florida, Madelyn learned firsthand about the

Figure 6.2 Eye movement can be used to regulate turn-taking in conversation. Typically, speakers engage in less eye contact than listeners. When a speaker finishes speaking, she may shift her gaze toward a listener who then takes over as speaker.

frustrations and misunderstandings these officials encounter. The customs officers complained that it was difficult to deal with individuals from some countries who were unwilling to look them in the eye. They considered these travelers to be suspect and saw their behavior as secretive and uncooperative, sometimes even disrespectful. Of course, many of the travelers who averted their eyes from the officers were actually doing so out of respect for the authority that the officers represented.

Cultural norms for making and sustaining eye contact are far from universal. In many countries that have a high power distance, it is not uncommon for individuals to avert their gaze when interacting with someone who is of higher status, whether because of age, rank, or social position. In doing so, these individuals are showing respect; failing to do so would be unthinkable to them. Countries with a high power distance include the Philippines, Mexico, Venezuela, India, Singapore, Brazil, Hong Kong, Iran, and Colombia.[10] A US Peace Corps volunteer teaching in an African school greatly upset the tribal elders because she required her students to look her in the eye. The elders were upset because in their culture children were not permitted to look adults in the eye.[11]

By contrast the United States, Canada, Austria, Germany, Israel, Norway, Finland, and Switzerland are all low power distance countries. Individuals from low power distance cultures will not hesitate to make direct eye contact with authority figures like the customs officers. Often American children are taught to look people in the eye as a sign of honesty and forthrightness.

In the post-9/11 world, it is vitally important for security personnel to have a thorough understanding of cultural norms regarding non-verbal communication so that they may correctly interpret downcast eyes as a sign of respect rather than an indication that an individual is suspicious and potentially dangerous. The relationship between cultural differences in non-verbal communication patterns and security issues will be discussed more fully at the end of this chapter.

In addition to dictating different uses of eye contact to show respect, culture dictates who it is appropriate to gaze at and for how long. In some cultures, there are significant differences in what is deemed appropriate eye contact depending on the relationship, age, and gender of the parties involved. In the American culture, eye contact may be part of a flirting or courtship ritual. For many Native Americans and Africans, prolonged eye contact may be seen as threatening and even sexually aggressive. Arabs believe that a prolonged gaze between men signals interest and helps determine the trustworthiness of their conversational partner.[12] By contrast, the Japanese will avert their gaze or even sit quietly with closed eyes to indicate attention to and agreement with a speaker.[13]

Touch (Haptics)

Haptics, the study of the perception and meanings of touch as communication behavior, is very closely related to eye contact in the way it is used by different cultures. Edward T. Hall's work classified all cultures as either contact or non-contact cultures.[14] *Contact* cultures are those cultures that display interpersonal closeness and use touch freely as a means of expression. Members of contact cultures tend to stand closer to one another, to speak more loudly, and to prefer sensory stimulation in interpersonal encounters. In general, members of contact cultures would be described as warm and accessible as opposed to members of non-contact cultures, who tend to be colder and more distant.

Non-contact cultures are those cultures in which individuals tend to stand farther apart and touch less when interacting. Some of these cultures expressly restrict the use of touch or in some instances forbid it altogether. Japan is an example of a country in which the use of touch is strictly avoided in public.[15] More recently these categories have been expanded to include low-contact, moderate-contact, and high-contact cultures, which is likely to be a more accurate description of the differences among cultures regarding the use of touch as a means of communication.[16]

The US culture, together with other North Americans and Australians, is categorized as a moderate-contact culture. High-contact cultures tend to be found in countries located closer to the equator that have warm climates; they include Latin America, Mediterranean countries, and most Arab countries. Houman remembers that he was once surprised in Saudi Arabia when his male counterpart suddenly held his hand as they were crossing the street. While Houman was wondering about the true intention of his host, the real meaning of this Arab gesture (same-sex hand holding) was showing utmost respect, caring, and protection for a guest. Low-contact cultures are found in Northern Europe and Asia; the low-contact cultures are generally found in cooler, more northern climates.[17]

According to Peter A. Andersen in *The Handbook of International and Intercultural Communication*, the amount of interpersonal closeness, or immediacy, experienced in a given culture is related to the climate and geography of the culture. In colder climates that are farther from the equator, individuals generally need to focus on tasks required to survive the long winters, and a high degree of cooperation is necessary. These cultures emphasize structure, order, and constraint, including repression of emotional displays to enable them to take care of survival needs and planning for the harsh winters they face. In contrast, individuals in warm climates that are located closer to the equator experience fewer demands related to planning for winter and have more access to one another throughout the entire year.[18]

The one exception to the relationship between climate and immediacy is found in Asian cultures. However, researchers have suggested that the influence of Confucianism, which emphasizes restraint, modesty, and decorum, may account for the fact that Asian cultures are low contact. In general, Asian cultures discourage open displays of emotion, and, therefore, are likely to repress behaviors associated with immediacy.[19]

Within each culture there are also different rules regarding appropriate same-sex and opposite-sex touching. Although many Arab cultures tend to be high-contact cultures, those with strict Muslim heritages forbid opposite-sex touching. For example, when in Iran, Houman was unable to shake hands with a female colleague at a university because of the taboo surrounding opposite-sex touching.

Although same-sex touching between women is commonplace in the United States, same-sex touching between men is generally restricted to handshakes and playful punches or other sports-related rough-housing. In contrast, men in Italy, Spain, Portugal, Eastern Europe, and much of the Arab world will kiss one another as a greeting. In fact, in the Mediterranean, same-sex touching between men is more prevalent than same-sex touching between women. Similarly, a full embrace between males is more acceptable in Latin America than in Great Britain or the United States. At the opposite end of the spectrum co-workers in Japan and Korea are unlikely to touch each other at all either as a greeting or during the course of their interaction.[20]

Often interactions between members of high-contact and moderate- or low-contact cultures can become a dance with members of high-contact cultures moving closer during a conversation while their low-contact counterparts back away. This type of dance frequently occurs between Americans and Arabs, with the Americans feeling crowded and resenting having their space invaded, while the Arabs are feeling frustrated by the distance and their perception of rudeness on the part of the Americans. Most Americans travel within an invisible bubble of personal space that they do not like to have violated by others (see section on "Relationship to Space [Proxemics]," this chapter).

In addition to gender, other factors that influence haptics include the age and social status/role of the participants. For example, in many high power distance countries it would be more likely for employers or individuals in positions of authority to touch their subordinates than for the subordinates to touch them. In the same way, in countries such as China and Brazil, where respect for elders is an important social value, it would be more likely for elders to touch others than for the elders to be touched, as restrained non-verbal behaviors signal respect, which is directly related to the unequal power relationship between individuals.[21]

In general, the rules of who may touch who are more strictly adhered to in collective cultures and also in countries with high population density. They are more strictly followed in collective cultures because in these cultures a high priority is placed on maintaining social order and harmony. The larger a population becomes, particularly in societies like Japan and India where space is at a premium, the more important it becomes to have formal structures for managing interaction among people. When we discuss proxemics we will find that many of the same factors that affect the use of touch as a means of communication also apply to the use of space. Thus, distance, touch, and space share similar politics in relationships between individuals who have a power gap.

MEDIA IMPACT
Dressing in Barbie's Clothes
The clothing styles worn by celebrities, particularly film, television, and music stars, often set fashion trends that are copied by the general public. However, a recent trend may be set not by a person, but by a doll.

In June 2004, Mattel, the manufacturer of Barbie, announced its plan to launch a Barbie clothing line for women to be carried in department stores like Nordstroms; although the clothing is contemporary, it looks like clothing Barbie would wear. The line first debuted in Japan with "relative popularity." Mattel also launched lines of Barbie accessories, cosmetics, and girls' clothing.

Since premiering at the American Toy Fair in New York City in 1959, the Barbie doll has been adored by millions of children and adults around the world. A great deal of criticism has also been directed at the Barbie doll because of the image of the female body that the toy presents. If Barbie was a real woman, she would be 5 feet 6 inches tall, weigh 110 pounds and have a 39-inch bust, 18-inch waist, and 33-inch hips. Critics say that the doll presents an unrealistic image of the female body to young girls.

What do you think:
1. Do you think that Barbie clothing will be a quickly forgotten fad? Or do you think it will become as popular as the doll herself?
2. Why do you think the clothing line was launched in Japan before being sold in the United States?
3. Do you think that the clothing line and accessories will become popular in other cultures? Why or why not?

Source: Adrienne Breaux, "Barbie Not Just a Doll," *The Reveille* (Baton Rouge, LA: Louisiana State University, June 18, 2004).

Clothing and Physical Adornments

The old saying "You can't judge a book by its cover" has been around for a very long time, and yet, we do just that all the time; both within our own culture and across cultures, we tend to react to others, at least initially, based on their physical appearance. Would you find it odd if one of your classmates consistently showed up on campus dressed in a suit and tie? If your parents started dressing the same way your favorite rock star does? If your minister or rabbi dyed his/her hair green? Maybe you have experienced some of these occurrences and maybe you have even taken them in your stride. The point is, though, that generally we have ideas about the appropriate way for individuals to dress and look based on their age, gender, social role, and status in society. More than ever our society is concerned with being able to determine whether individuals traveling through airports are average citizens or suspicious persons (see section on "Cultural Diversity in Non-verbal Communication and National Security," this chapter).

As with any aspect of intercultural communication, mindful communication begins with understanding ourselves and our own culture — whether we come from Beijing, China; Tehran, Iran; London, England; or Chicago, Illinois. When discussing physical appearance as a form of non-verbal communication, we are speaking primarily of those aspects of an individual's appearance that are chosen by the individual, specifically clothing and other adornments put on the body. We are not talking about physical characteristics that we all have by virtue of being a member of a particular racial or ethnic group, such as the color of our skin or the shape of our eyes.

We make this distinction because for the most part what we choose to put on our body is a way for us to express ourselves just as the gestures we make and the words we say are also means of self-expression. By contrast, our racial and ethnic physical characteristics are not chosen by us but rather passed down to us by our parents and ancestors.

Clothing

The clothing that we put on is a statement about who we are or in some cases who we would like to be, whether it is a dress designed by a top Paris designer or the turban worn by a Sikh. Although the business suit and tie can be seen in cities all around the world, there are still many cultures that retain their traditional ethnic dress. As with any aspect of culture, it is important to realize that what we see on the surface, whether it be an African *dashiki*, the Hasidic Jew's *yarmulke*, or the *abaya*, the long black cloak worn by Arab women, is a reflection of a much deeper aspect of the wearer's culture.

In some cultures in the Middle East, a strong emphasis on modesty requires that women cover their bodies completely from head to toe. The Arab culture's emphasis on modesty for women is so great that young girls are not allowed to take swimming classes because they would have to expose their bodies to do so.[22] In some cultures formality and conservatism is valued to the extent that all businessmen are expected to wear the same "uniform" of a dark suit with dark shoes and socks and a plain shirt.[23] Similarly, in collective cultures, like Japan, the emphasis on social harmony leads to very conservative dress; this conservatism in dress is seen as a way to prevent nonconformist behavior. Most school children in Japan wear uniforms, and corporate executives in Japanese companies wear the same "company uniform" of a dark business suit.[24]

Of course, within cultures there may be variations in dress among different subcultures, socioeconomic groups, and age groups. However, the important point to remember is that seemingly superficial differences in attire may in fact be related to cultural values that are central to a particular group; these values may include conformity, modesty, social status, conservatism, or the right to free expression. The importance placed on the "right" brand of athletic shoes in many grade schools across the United States is a good example of the power of clothing to ensure "in-group" status and also of the price of nonconformity. Although the American culture is fiercely proud of the individual's freedoms, we tend to be surprisingly conformist in the matter of what is considered the "in" thing to wear. The same type of conformity can be seen in the "uniforms" of various professions within our society. Despite all our emphasis on individuality, most individuals who interview for jobs within the corporate world still wear a business suit. Another example is the similar dress code patterns that college students follow in different regions of the United States.

We need to be mindful of the reasons for the different clothing worn by individuals from other cultures. If we are, we will learn about much more than fashion. We will learn about deep levels of the culture. As we learn about the clothing worn by other cultures, we need to be careful to avoid stereotyping members of other cultures based on their dress. It is unfortunate that since 9/11 many individuals of Middle Eastern heritage have been attacked for nothing more than wearing the traditional clothing of their cultures (see section on "Cultural Diversity in Non-verbal Communication and National Security," this chapter). The recent hate crimes against Muslim-Americans are just one example of intercultural conflict; we can see similar instances of prejudice and stereotyping occurring in other cultures. They are an extreme response to lack of knowledge about other cultures. To fully understand such conflicts we must study them in context (see Chapters 3 and 4); however, developing an ability to see beyond the superficial aspects of cultures, such as clothing and adornments, is the first step toward mindful communication. Only through mindful communication can we hope to prevent similar occurrences in the future.[25]

Physical adornments

In addition to our clothing, there are many other physical adornments that we use as a means of non-verbal communication. These physical ornaments include tattoos, piercings, hairstyles, and makeup. In some cases, they may represent solidarity and conformity within one's culture. In other cases, these same adornments may be worn as a symbol of rebellion against the dominant culture and may represent membership in a co-cultural group.

In some native African and South American cultures, face painting is still practiced. In other societies, tattooing and piercing may be part of a rite of passage from childhood into adulthood. These rites are a way for the young person to become fully indoctrinated in the adult culture of his/her society. Yet, by contrast many young people in the American culture may use tattoos and piercings as a means to distinguish themselves from the adult culture of their parents' generation. As with clothing, there may be significant variations in the use and meaning of physical adornments among various co-cultures, age groups, and socioeconomic classes.

In general, the impetus towards conformity in one's physical appearance is much more likely to be found among members of collectivistic cultures. By contrast, individualistic cultures are much more likely to tolerate and even encourage nonconformist expressions of the self through clothing and other physical adornments. However, even within individualistic cultures, we find

Figure 6.3 Many traditional forms of adornment are still worn today; these adornments include face painting, hand painting, piercings, and various types of jewelry. These adornments are often related to particular cultural rites of passage such as weddings, funerals, and the passage from childhood to maturity. For example, many Indian brides have their hands painted with henna on the eve of their weddings; such painting is believed to make the bride more beautiful.

Figure 6.4 Tattoos are a popular means of self-expression within U.S. culture; tattoos may be a sign of belonging to a particular co-cultural group or they may merely be a form of personal adornment.

many instances of conformity in dress within the business world and as an expression of socioeconomic status.

Facial Expressions

A great deal of research has been devoted to the study of facial expressions as a powerful form of non-verbal communication. In the field of intercultural communication this research has centered on the question of whether or not there are facial expressions that are understood universally across all cultures. As early as 1872 in *The Expression of the Emotions in Man and Animals*, Charles Darwin studied similarities in emotional expression across species and across human cultures. Darwin argued that emotions "were evolutionarily adaptive, biologically innate, and universal across all human and even nonhuman primates."[26] Much of our current research is grounded in Darwin's work.[27]

Today, most researchers agree that facial expressions are simultaneously universal and culturally specific.[28] There are in fact six universally recognized facial expressions that have the same meaning within all cultures. The six universal facial expressions are: happiness, sadness, fear, anger, surprise, and disgust.[29]

A large body of cross-cultural research studies exists to document the universality of these six facial expressions.[30] In some studies participants were asked to show how their face would look if they were in a particular situation. Ekman and Friesen did a study with members of an isolated culture in New Guinea; they were asked to show how their face would look if they were in four specific situations: (1) your friend has come and you are happy; (2) your child has died; (3) you are angry and about to fight; and (4) you see a dead pig that has been lying there for a long time. The participants were videotaped, and the tapes were shown to American college students who had no previous knowledge of the culture. They were asked to identify the emotional contexts the expressions portrayed. The students had very little difficulty identifying the facial expressions for the emotions of happiness, sadness, anger, and disgust.[31]

Other studies have used hidden cameras to record the facial expressions of subjects in situations likely to elicit emotional responses. Ekman videotaped Japanese and American students watching both stressful and neutral films. There was an extremely high correlation between the facial behavior of the Japanese and American subjects when watching the stressful film.[32]

Further evidence for the innate nature of these universal facial expressions can be found by studying children. Eibl-Eibesfeldt found a universal pattern of the facial display of emotions in child development. Across all cultures children display the same maturation process in the expression of emotions. Lending even more support to the theory that facial expressions are inborn rather than learned from the surrounding culture is the fact that children who are born blind display the same facial expressions as sighted children.[33]

While research strongly supports the fact that human emotions are innate and that at least six facial expressions of emotion are universally understood across cultures, facial expressions are governed by culture-specific display rules. Because these rules are learned, cultural display rules for emotions may vary a great deal from one culture to another. For example, while the facial expression associated with sadness is universal across all cultures, the rules for when it is or is not appropriate to display that expression may differ greatly from one culture to another.

Paul Ekman and his colleagues developed the neurocultural theory of emotional expression, which states that emotional expressions are innate in the human brain, but the rules for their display are culture specific. A good example of this theory is found in the study done by Ekman (1972) with Japanese and American participants viewing stress-inducing and neutral films; the behavior of the Japanese participants varied depending upon whether they were alone in the room or in the company of another person. When they were alone viewing the stress-inducing films, the Japanese reacted exactly the same way that the American participants did. However, when they were with another person, the Japanese participants masked their negative emotions with smiles.[34]

Some differences in cultural display rules may be related to the individualism versus collectivism cultural dimension. Members of individualistic cultures are more likely to display their emotions freely and openly; by contrast, members of collective cultures are more likely to suppress emotions that could potentially disrupt group harmony. David A. Matsumoto conducted a study with Japanese and American college students and found that the American students were much more adept at identifying anger, disgust, fear, and sadness (all universally recognized emotions) than the Japanese students were. One possible explanation for this difference may be that such emotions are more likely to be suppressed in the collective Japanese society than they are in the individualistic American society, and, therefore, Japanese students did not have as much experience of them as did American students.[35] Ekman and Matsumoto also found a difference between Japanese and American participants' perceptions of emotions displayed. Japanese participants made less intense attributions of the emotions shown than did Americans, regardless of whether the emotion was displayed by a Japanese or an American person.[36]

In general, individualists will feel that it is their right to express their emotions freely whenever they choose to do so. Collectivists, on the other hand, will be much more likely to consider the reactions of others and how their behavior will reflect on and affect the larger group — whether that group is their family, community, or society. Members of collectivistic cultures are most concerned with other-focused emotions such as shame and embarrassment; members of individualistic cultures are more concerned about self-focused emotions such as frustration and anger.[37]

Another related cultural consideration that affects the display of emotions is the previously mentioned concept of face and saving face found in many Asian societies. Members of Asian cultures place a high value on the importance of maintaining the face or social self-esteem of all members of the group. In order to preserve face, it may often be necessary to refrain from expressing negative emotions that could lead to conflict. By contrast many Mediterranean cultures value exaggerated expressions of emotions and engage in public displays of grief and sadness. Despite the generally open display of emotions in the individualistic US society, most men in our culture suppress public displays of grief and sadness and refrain from crying in public. Houman's father, who was a consultant for the UN Food and Agricultural Organization, used to claim that any excessive body language, from smiling to frowning, is not helpful in effective negotiations.

Facial expressions of emotion are one significant way to communicate emotional states. Another equally powerful non-verbal indicator of emotion is through vocalics, or the use of vocal cues.

Voice (Vocalics)

Vocalics, or paralanguage, is the use of *voice qualifiers* and *vocalizations*; it is a way of expressing emotions and establishing one's identity as a member of a particular group. Voice qualifiers include the volume, pitch, rhythm, tempo, resonance, and tone of speech. Vocalizations include vocal sounds that are separate from speech such as vocal characterizers and vocal segregates. *Vocal characterizers* include laughing, crying, moaning, yelling, whining, yawning, and belching; *vocal segregates* include pauses, "um" for hesitation, "uh-huh" for agreement, and "sh" for silence.

In addition to conveying information about a speaker's emotional state, both voice qualifiers and vocalizations can reveal his/her group membership in terms of race, ethnicity, age, educational level, and socioeconomic status. Cultures differ in their use of vocalics and, in some cases, these differences may lead to misunderstandings and even to conflict.

One voice qualifier that differs markedly among cultures is the use of volume. Some cultures value and respect loud speech, and others emphasize the importance of speaking softly. Many Arab cultures believe that speaking loudly signifies confidence and strength. They also believe that loud volume connotes a speaker's sincerity.[38] In comparison with Arabic speakers, the volume of American speech would be seen as much calmer and less emotional. However, many other cultures that speak more softly than Americans often characterize Americans' speech as noisy and childlike.[39]

Volume of speech may also be related in part to the individualism versus collectivism value dimension and to the power distance value dimension. Members of individualistic cultures often speak more loudly than members of collectivistic cultures. In collective cultures, there is much greater concern for maintaining group harmony and social balance. In the Japanese culture, a very collectively oriented society, speaking softly is associated with good manners and the ability to fit into society without being disruptive.

Another factor that affects the volume of speech is whether a culture has a low or high power distance. Individuals in cultures with a low power distance tend to be less aware that loud volume of speech may be offensive to others.[40] Individuals in cultures with high power distances are much more likely to be mindful of the effect the volume of their speech may have on others. In Japan, where there is a great deal of emphasis on the social hierarchy, speakers often adjust their tone of voice and the pitch of their speech to fit the social status of the person they are addressing.[41]

While the use of voice qualifiers within cultures can serve to facilitate communication, their use is often misunderstood across cultures. Members of Arabic cultures speak with a much higher pitch than Americans, and often the pitch of their speech is interpreted as denoting much greater emotion than is actually intended by the speaker. During his first visit to Arabia, Houman originally thought that his hosts were shouting at each other until he learned more about how Arabs communicate with each other. Members of cultures that value speaking softly may interpret the relatively loud speech of Americans or Arabs as angry or emotional even when it is not. The tempo of speech may also be misinterpreted across cultures; when individuals speak relatively quickly, listeners from cultures that speak more slowly may feel that the speaker is angry or unfriendly. Such differences in the tempo of speech exist between the Northeastern and Southeastern regions of the United States. When Madelyn moved from teaching at a university in the Northeast to teach at one in the Southeast, she found that her students misinterpreted the tempo of her speech and considered her to be impatient with them just because she spoke so quickly.

Vocalizations, like voice qualifiers, are often culturally determined and can be misinterpreted across cultures. Vocalizations include vocal characterizers and vocal segregates. Vocal characterizers, such as laughing, yawning, and belching, are universally used, but the appropriateness and meaning of their use may vary among cultures. In some cultures, belching after a meal would be considered rude while in others it might be considered a compliment to the preparer of the meal. Laughing is generally associated with joy or amusement, but in the Japanese culture laughter may also be used to mask embarrassment or anger.[42]

Vocal segregates also differ across cultures. Americans frequently use sounds such as "uh-huh" to indicate that they are listening or to urge a speaker to continue. Similarly, the Maasai use the drawn out "eh" sound to mean "yes" or "I understand."[43] The Japanese have numerous vocal segregates, such as "hai," "soo," "un," and "ee," that they use to indicate that they are paying attention to a speaker.[44] The emphasis on attentiveness to a speaker in Japanese culture is consistent with their collectivistic orientation that values social harmony and respectfulness.

It is as important to understand the paralanguage of a given culture as it is to understand the particular language that is spoken in that culture. For some cultures, like the Japanese, an understanding of paralanguage is crucial for effective communication.

Relationship to Space (Proxemics)

The study of *proxemics* has to do with spatial relationships that human beings have with each other and with their environment. Without giving it any thought, we choose to stand closer to our intimate partners than we do to our friends; similarly, we maintain an even greater distance from strangers. Although our norms for proximity are unconscious, we react immediately when they are violated. If you have ever found yourself moving away from someone who you felt was standing too close to you, you were unconsciously seeking to maintain the appropriate spatial relationship to that person. According to anthropologist Edward T. Hall, who coined the term *proxemics*, most cultures recognize four types of spatial relationships: (1) intimate, (2) personal, (3) social, and (4) public.[45]

Although most cultures recognize the different types of spatial relationships, they do not all assign the same distances to the four types. In American culture we generally define intimate space as between 0 and 1½ feet and personal space as between 1½ and 4 feet. We consider social space to be between 4 and 12 feet and public space as anything 12 feet or more in distance.[46] Most Americans travel in an invisible bubble of personal space that they do not like to have violated. But as mindful intercultural communicators, we must remember that members of other cultures do not share our definitions of the appropriate distance for personal and social interactions.

As in our discussion of haptics, we can refer to Edward T. Hall's distinction between contact and non-contact cultures to better understand different cultural orientations toward space. In general, members of contact cultures, those cultures that display interpersonal closeness and touch more frequently, stand closer to one another than members of non-contact cultures. Members of Arab, Latin, and Mediterranean cultures all interact more closely than do members of Northern European and Northern Asian cultures. For example, the average conversation distance for European Americans is 20 inches, for Latin Americans is 14–15 inches, and for Arabs is 9–10 inches.[47] Based on these differences we can see that a European American having a conversation with an Arab is sure to feel that his/her personal space has been violated. Similarly, a Latin American communicating with a European American may feel that the latter is being stand-offish and even rude.

High-contact cultures are cultures that enjoy sensory exposure and require a high degree of tactile and olfactory stimulation as part of the communication encounter. The closer conversation distance makes it more likely that individuals will smell one another's breath and have a generally more intense sensory experience of one another. Nomadic Arab tribes will actually be offended if their conversation partner is unwilling to stand close enough so that they can smell one another's breath because they consider such a high level of contact a normal and necessary part of communication.[48]

When interacting with culturally diverse others it is important to remember that because our sense of appropriate personal and social space is largely unconscious we may react to people who violate our personal space as though they are being intentionally offensive rather than realizing that they are merely adhering to the sense of appropriate interpersonal distance that they have learned from their own cultures. Cultures also differ in terms of the formation of lines in public places and preferred seating arrangements. Some cultures like the English will queue up in orderly lines while other cultures see nothing wrong with pushing their way to front of the line.[49]

In the American culture, we tend to sit at right angles to one another when engaging in conversation and to prefer to speak with someone seated across from us more than someone seated next to us in a social or business setting. In fact, we usually reserve the seat at the head of the table for the leader of the group or the head of the family. In Chinese culture, individuals prefer to sit side by side and are uncomfortable when sitting directly across from someone at a desk or table.[50] In Asian cultures seating is usually determined by hierarchy with high status individuals being given the "best" seats.

In addition to our invisible bubbles of personal space, we also have territorial instincts. Territoriality, or the act of claiming certain spaces as our own, can be as simple as putting a jacket on a chair to reserve a seat in a classroom. It can also be much more complex and violent as in the many conflicts that have arisen over disputed ownership of various tracts of land (see Chapter 4). Approaches to territoriality also differ among cultures. Some cultures are much more territorial than others. In the American culture, as in many individual-istic cultures, there is a strong emphasis on personal property. We put up "No trespassing" signs and fence in our homes and put up walls to keep others out of our "gated" communities. As might be expected, members of collectivistic cultures are less territorial and more open to sharing — at least with members of their own cultural in-group.

One semester Madelyn taught a course that met in a workshop setting of a computer lab. There were 12 students in the course, and during each class meet-ing throughout the semester they all sat in exactly same seats around a large rectangular table. The course was the first one in a series of three sequenced core courses in the students' major. The following semester she had the same 12 students in the second course, which met in the same computer lab. On the first day of class the students all came in, and each student sat down in exactly the same seat he/she had occupied during the previous semester. They continued to occupy these seats throughout the semester with no variations.

In addition to differences in the degree of territoriality exhibited, cultures also differ in terms of the spaces about which they are territorial. Members of the German culture are as territorial about their automobiles as they would be about a violation of the personal space surrounding their bodies.[51] In some cultures, the workspace is much more individual and private while in others it is much more communal and shared. Office workers in the US are used to having private offices, or cubicles, or at the very least, an individual desk. In other cultures, it would be much more likely that the office space would be totally open with no cubicles or other separations of personal space.

In some cultures, including the American culture, middle-class homes are set apart on separate plots of land and are often surrounded by fences and security systems. Similarly, in Germany doors are very heavy and walls are soundproofed to insure the privacy of the individuals within.[52] Homes in collectivistic cultures are often organized around a central courtyard or other communal space. In Mexico, for example, homes are oriented around a central plaza that often contains a church and some type of community center. Such homes promote the interaction of the family with the larger group.[53]

In general, collectivists live in closer proximity to one another than do individualists.[54] For example, in many homes in Japan walls are made of paper, and Japanese mothers enter their children's rooms more often than mothers in the US do.[55] When interacting with members of other cultures we must be mindful of their different orientations to space and territoriality. Misunderstandings regarding these orientations can lead to ineffective communication and even to conflict.

Cultural space

A cultural space is a place that has a particular meaning constructed around it; a cultural space can be a home, a neighborhood, or a region of a nation, such as the Northwestern United States or a *kibbutz* in Israel. The cultural spaces that we grow up in influence our identities. One of the most powerful influences is, of course, our home, because it is the first cultural space we inhabit and where we begin to learn about our culture from our parents, extended families, and other caregivers. A home can be a place of safety and stability; it can also be a representation of our family's position and status in the community. Many of our ideas about who we are and where we fit in the larger community are developed in relationship to our childhood homes. In some cases, we may be happy to accept the identity of our childhood home and try to replicate it in our homes as adults. In other cases, we may wish to escape from what we perceived as a less-than-ideal home setting and make sure that our homes as adults are quite different from what we experienced as children.

Helen Norris has fond memories of growing up on a farm:

> I grew up on a 500-acre farm just east of Montgomery . . . In early spring, there were fields of wild dewberries and blackberries, which we loved to pick, then red and yellow plums, muscadines, and persimmons in the fall. Deep in the woods was a wide place in a stream where a sloe tree dropped its blush-tipped fruit to float in the water. I tell you this because it was extremely important to me . . . There is something about picking wild things to eat that makes you know that you are living in a world that likes you.[56]

Another writer, C. Eric Lincoln, describes how his consciousness was shaped by growing up in a small town in Alabama:

> Athens wasn't much of a town, but that's where I was born, and there is a part of me still there, left over from those tender years . . . In the South, where I was raised, the pervasive awareness of race was helped along by a series of "lessons" learned in the process of growing up . . . By the time I was in high school I had internalized all the learning I needed to cope with coming through the fire of race and place in Alabama. I knew the boundaries. There was a white world and a black world, and they were not the same.[57]

The poet Reginald Shepherd writes about feeling dislocated much of the time and about how important gay space is to him:

> Gay space has been crucial in my life: gay bars and clubs most especially, gay social and political groups, gay bookstores, gay boothstores and back rooms, gay baths . . . Such spaces have been central to my sense of how I related to a place, of what a place had to offer me, and what my place in that place could be.[58]

Closely aligned to our experiences in our family homes is our experience of the community immediately surrounding our homes, our neighborhoods. Historically, in the United States, power issues led to the development of neighborhoods that segregated people based on their ethnic or racial identity. Although such treatment of minorities is no longer legal, many large cities like Chicago, Los Angeles, and New York still have neighborhoods that are largely composed of one racial or ethnic group. When such groupings emerge by choice they may represent a desire, particularly among recent immigrants to the United States, to support one another and keep cultural traditions alive in their new home.

Regionalism is an identification with a particular geographical area within a nation or with an area that ignores or defies national boundaries. Many Americans identify themselves as Southerners or Yankees or Midwesterners. Similarly, some Canadians may identify themselves as Quebecois, and some Italians may refer to themselves as Neopolitans. Regionalism may be represented by wearing certain clothing, flying a regional flag, or celebrating a particular holiday. A popular T-shirt seen in Florida bears the capital letters "GRITS"; the initials do not stand for the corn meal product but rather are the initial letters of the phrase "Girls Raised in the South."

Many ongoing conflicts are related to regionalism, particularly in places like Eastern Europe, where wars have frequently redrawn national boundaries. In many instances the regions being fought over are not neatly defined on maps, but are related to historical identifications of a group of people with a particular cultural space, such as East Timor, Kosovo, or Chechnya. When studying regional conflicts we must understand the historical context as it relates to issues of power and identity (see Chapter 4).

POWER CHECK
Non-verbal Communication and Negotiation

In his book *Negotiating Across Cultures: Communication Obstacles in International Diplomacy*, author Raymond Cohen argues that there is no single international diplomatic culture. He states that seasoned diplomats report that cultural differences in non-verbal communication have a significant impact on negotiations. One difference that Cohen cites has to do with monochronic cultures and their desire to rush to the end phase of negotiations quickly.

Similarly, Professor John Graham reporting on his 15-year study of negotiation styles in 17 cultures concluded that variation across cultures is greater in relation to the structural aspects of language and non-verbal behaviors than to the verbal content of negotiations. He states that negotiators who rely heavily on a shared global language such as English may overlook critical differences in non-verbal communication styles such as the use of silence, interruptions, and touching.

Both Cohen and Graham emphasize the fact that it is dangerous to underestimate the importance of non-verbal communication in international negotiation.

Sources: William Briggs, "Next for Communicators: Global Negotiation," *Communication World* 16:1 (1998), 12; Raymond Cohen, *Negotiating Across Cultures: Communication Obstacles in International Diplomacy* (Washington, DC: United States Institute of Peace Press, 1991).

Relationship to Time (Chronemics)

Chronemics is the study of how cultures structure, use, and interpret the meaning of time. Cultures differ both in their orientations toward the past, present, and future and also in their ways of structuring and using time on a daily basis. The work of Kluckhohn and Strodtbeck on classical value orientations includes the temporal value orientation. Their research revealed that cultures differ in their beliefs about the importance of the past, present, and future. Those cultures that are oriented toward the past are described as *tradition-bound*; those that are oriented toward the present are *situation-bound*; and those that are future oriented are *goal-bound*.[59]

Many Asian cultures are strongly tradition-bound. They revere the past and base present-day decisions on historical precedents. Cultures like the Chinese and Vietnamese worship their ancestors and inform much of their life in the present with reference to those who have gone before them. The Mexican culture and many Latin cultures, by contrast, believe in living fully in the present. A high value is placed on sensory experience and on helping one's family and friends. Most Americans have a future, or goal-oriented, approach to life. They are not particularly concerned with past traditions and are eager to move forward into the immediate future. The glorification of youth in the American culture is related to the emphasis on "futurism."

Some cultures combine a past-present or past-future orientation. Many African cultures both revere their ancestors and place a high priority on living fully in the present moment; in fact, their concept of time is different from the North American and European conception of linear time. They focus strongly on the present as the only true experience of time.[60] Similarly, despite their strong orientation to the past, Asian cultures are also influenced by the Confucian dynamism dimension; the teachings of Confucius emphasize both a reverence for the past and a long-term orientation toward the future. The ability to plan far into the future and to work diligently toward distant future goals is one reason for the business success of many Asian cultures.[61]

The work of Edward T. Hall has had the most profound influence on our understanding of differing cultural orientations toward time.[62] Hall describes the distinction between *monochronic* (M-time) and *polychronic* (P-time) orientations to time. The monochronic orientation sees time as linear, organized, scheduled, and divided into neat segments. Cultures that are monochronic in their approach to time value punctuality and believe in doing one thing at a time. Time is seen as a commodity that can be spent, saved, and wasted. For monochronic individuals, the schedule takes precedence over everything else and dictates social and business interactions. Many individualisitic cultures, like the American culture, are monochronic in their orientation to time.

By contrast, polychronic cultures are much more fluid in their approach to time. Time is seen more holistically, and it is normal for many activities to occur at the same time. Polychronic cultures emphasize personal relationships over schedules. Members of polychronic cultures would be likely to choose personal obligations over the need to adhere to a time schedule. Many collectivistic cultures, like most Latin American cultures, are polychronic in their orientation to time.

One of Hall's classic examples of polychronic time is the trading post of Lorenzo Hubbell described in his book, *West of the Thirties*. Hubbell deals with many different demands and tasks in an informal setting and suits his schedule to the needs of the people involved rather than the clock:

> In Oraibi we stopped to meet the famous Indian trader Lorenzo Hubbell. His store stood in the middle of a bare, shadeless space in the center of New Oraibi (now called Kyakotsmovi). Parking in the intense sunlight, we entered his office via a porch through a side door. It was like entering a movie theater. Once our eyes had adjusted to the low light level, we could see several people sitting around in chairs and a heavyset man behind a desk who greeted us in a gravelly voice with "I'm Lorenzo Hubbell. Please sit down. Which way did you come?" We sat there for thirty minutes while Lorenzo conducted business with a variety of people, orchestrating perhaps a dozen transactions from behind his desk. Even during that short visit, I sensed the power of this man's magnetic presence.[63]

Hall claims that for many Europeans and Americans, the management of time is a kind of "fetish."[64] Certainly, the proliferation of appointment books, electronic schedulers, and books and seminars on time management in our society bear out Hall's assessment of our obsession with time management. Hall discusses the way in which scheduling dominates not just our organization of time but our entire experience of life: "In fact, social and business life, even one's sex life, is commonly schedule-dominated. By scheduling, we compartmentalize . . . [s]ince scheduling by its very nature selects what will and will not be perceived and attended . . . [it] constitutes a system for setting priorities for both people and functions."[65]

By contrast, many Latin American, Middle Eastern, and Mediterranean cultures are quite comfortable with unscheduled time and with many things occurring simultaneously with no clear-cut order. They are used to interacting with many other people at all times and being deeply involved in one another's lives. For most members of cultures that are oriented to P-time, relationships are the key to getting things done rather than schedules. People are always placed before schedules. Hall notes involvement with other people is at "the core of the existence" of most P-time people. He says that "[i]f you value people, you must hear them out and cannot cut them off simply because of a schedule."[66]

Many business people from monochronic cultures are greatly frustrated by the polychronic approach to time when they arrive for meetings only to find that their polychronic colleagues are "late" according to the schedule. Differences in time orientation can lead to misunderstandings. M-time colleagues may assume that their P-time colleagues do not consider the meeting important and may be offended; they may also form a negative impression of the professionalism of colleagues who arrive late. By contrast, P-time colleagues may not understand why the schedule is so important and may be more concerned about the quality of the relationship they have with their M-time colleagues; they may feel that their colleagues do not value personal relationships enough when they are so driven by an arbitrary time schedule.

Madelyn faced an interesting challenge regarding time orientation when taking a group of American teachers to study at a university in the Caribbean. The group was told to arrive at 9 a.m. for a lecture, and she duly got the group together to be in the classroom by 9 a.m. only to find that the scholar who was lecturing to the group did not arrive until 9:30 a.m. The teachers were frustrated, and Madelyn found it increasingly difficult to get the group to show up on time when the lecturers who were addressing them were late in arriving. For negotiations and diplomacy, the role of time in Asia and the Middle East is very different from that in the US and Europe. In Asia, and especially in the Middle East, no serious negotiations about substantial issues start before the opposing sides spend a good deal of time to get to know their opponents. Thus, it often takes a great deal more time than in the US and Europe to negotiate on an issue.

As with all aspects of non-verbal communication, we must remember that the differences in time orientation are more than superficial. Initially, what we see is that the lecturer shows up late or the administrator keeps us waiting, but there is much more to the different orientations to time than different approaches to scheduling. Differences in temporal orientation are differences in how cultures believe the world is organized and how people should conduct themselves in relation to others. They are essentially value differences in the sense that a culture's orientation to time reveals what it values. Monochronic cultures value accomplishment, schedules, and procedures; polychronic cultures value human relationships. As Hall points out, neither orientation is "right." Both approaches have positive and negative qualities associated with them. M-time is good for organizing and getting things done; most people like to be able to predict when their appointments will take place and about how long they will last. M-time can be criticized for not placing enough emphasis on the human element of temporal relations. Often, people are cut off because their time is up in a given situation when they still need more assistance. Because of its M-time orientation, American business has come under criticism for being cut off from human beings.

P-time strongly values the human element in any interaction. People are given the time they need and life moves at a much more natural pace rather than by a rigid adherence to a schedule. However, emphasis on the human element can sometimes lead to problems for outsiders as in many polychronic cultures small bureaucracies tend to require that one have a "friend" on the inside in order to get anything to happen.

As with all aspects of non-verbal communication behavior across cultures, it is important that we be mindful and have an understanding of cultural differences before entering a communication encounter. We must avoid evaluating other cultures means of communicating and strive instead to open our minds and adapt to other approaches in order to avoid misunderstandings and conflict.

Technology and Non-Verbal Communication

The widespread use of new communication technologies has created new challenges in intercultural communication. One of the most significant differences between face-to-face communication and computer-mediated communication is the fact that many of the non-verbal cues used in face-to-face communication are either diminished or totally absent in computer-mediated communication. A large percentage of what we communicate in any face-to-face encounter is communicated non-verbally. A businessperson may nod her head and smile to show agreement with a client. A teacher may demonstrate enthusiasm for his subject matter with his facial expression and gestures and may engage his students by making eye contact with them as he lectures.

A team working on a collaborative project may use eye contact and other non-verbal cues to regulate group discussion when tackling problems in team meetings. We not only rely on these types of non-verbal messages to convey information, but we also tend to trust them more than we do verbal messages when we are receiving conflicting information in a communication encounter.

When communicating via email, we do not have any of the non-verbal cues to rely upon. Similarly, when using collaborative technologies we do not have non-verbal cues to carry part of the message being conveyed. The only exception would be the use of videoconferencing, but even that medium provides limited cues in comparison to face-to-face communication encounters. Lack of non-verbal cues can lead to misunderstandings even among members of the same culture. An email message, for example, may convey statements intended to be ironic or humorous, but the recipient of the message may misinterpret the meaning and take the statements more seriously than they were intended because email cannot convey an ironic tone of voice or a humorous facial expression.

Global virtual teams

Global virtual teams are a relatively new phenomenon, and we still have much more to learn about their functioning. A global virtual team can be defined as a boundary-less work group composed of individuals from different countries that is assembled on an "as-needed basis for the duration of a task."[67] These teams rarely, if ever, have face-to-face meetings. Team members typically come from a number of different cultural backgrounds. Many factors have given rise to global virtual teams; these factors include the growth of international business, the loosening of boundaries between markets, the flattening of corporate structures, and the development of sophisticated technology for computer-mediated communication.

Because of the challenges related to non-verbal cues in virtual communication, it is important for team members to have the opportunity to communicate using technology that is designated "rich media." Rich media would be any technology that allows users to experience each other as being psychologically close.[68] Videoconferencing is a richer media than email according to this definition, since individuals participating in a videoconference can see one another and hear each other's voices. Email is a relatively lean media, relying solely on written messages; it is, at least in part, this lack of immediacy in email communication that led to the development of emoticons as a way to enrich the communication encounter and invest it with more interpersonal cues. As one Japanese-American global team member says, "Electronic messaging tends to strip off everything but the message and leave the rest to inference . . . It intensifies all the differences in work style and values among team members."[69] Of course, for individuals who know each other well, communication via email may have a much richer context.

Email communication, voicemail, and fax communication are all primarily linear means of communication. They do not allow for the rich context of face-to-face meetings. Lack of shared context is particularly challenging for members of high-context cultures, like the Japanese, but it is problematic for all team members at some level. Despite the useful technologies we have and the improved technologies that are now being developed, most research suggests that an initial face-to-face kick-off meeting is one of the best ways to ensure the success of global virtual teams. It is crucial that these meetings allow time for the development, or at least the inception of, interpersonal relationships. In *Globalwork: Bridging Distance, Culture, and Time*, O'Hara-Devereaux and Johansen state that "face-to-face meetings are usually essential to establish trust" and "[v]oicemail and videoconferencing can provide ongoing support for maintaining trust because they convey some of the emotional context and interaction impossible in a text-only technology like email."[70]

Cultural Diversity in Non-Verbal Communication and National Security

In the post-9/11 era, some aspects of non-verbal communication, especially if viewed without a mindful perspective, have the potential to lead to misinterpretation and misunderstanding of the behaviors of people from other cultures. One result of the terrorist attacks of September 11 has been fear and suspicion of people from the Middle East. It is unfortunate that following 9/11 many individuals became targets for hatred and harassment because of their physical appearance and clothing. Some of these cases did not even have a connection to the Muslim community. Just to name a few, soon after the 9/11 disaster, the media reported cases such as: airport security officials having concerns about a Hasidic Jew who was reading the Torah in the back row of a plane before takeoff; an American pilot refusing to fly because of a few African passengers (who looked like Middle Easterners); and an Indian of the Sikh ethnicity, who was wearing a turban, being killed in a hate crime. In addition to these instances related to non-Muslims, there are hundreds of cases of abuse and harassment of innocent Muslim Americans. There are numerous examples of Muslim women being harassed and even assaulted because they were wearing traditional Islamic headscarves. Similarly, Muslim men wearing turbans have also been targets of attacks. Some women have removed their head scarves in an effort to protect themselves. In one school in Wisconsin, when Muslim girls were teased for wearing headscarves, their non-Muslim friends put them on in a gesture of support.[71] However, in general hate crimes against Muslim Americans have risen dramatically since 9/11. Interestingly enough, none of the nineteen 9/11 hijackers were Muslim Americans. In fact during a trip to the Arabian Peninsula following 9/11, Houman's random interviews with the local elite indicated that many supporters of the al-Qaeda did not have high regard for most Muslim Americans at the time.

When studying the reactions to 9/11, we should keep in mind that such instances of prejudice and stereotyping have occurred throughout history both in the United States and in many other nations in our global community. After the bombing of Pearl Harbor by the Japanese in 1941, there was a similar reaction against Japanese Americans. In fact, many American citizens of Japanese descent were confined to internment camps during World War II. Similar instances of prejudice against a group because of misplaced national security concerns can be seen in many places around the world.

All states aim to protect their citizens from terrorism with security forces. In this global age, however, one long-term method to protect our nations and indeed our world is to foster a climate of mindful intercultural communication. Before we impose our value system on others and assume, as some US customs officers did, that the individual who will not make eye contact with us is a suspicious character up to no good, we need to determine if it is possible that he comes from a culture where individuals show respect to officials by averting their eyes. Before we determine that every woman who wears a headscarf is anti-American, we need to consider all the innocent Muslim American women who have been victims of hate crimes simply because of the way they dress. This is not to suggest that all of us Americans are guilty of ethnocentric mistakes, but those few who make such errors go against the American political culture of freedom and our tradition of tolerance even though we live in an age of "the end of the innocence," as some claim.

Of course, it is vital to have security measures in place, but one of our greatest long-term security measures is the ability to communicate mindfully and meaningfully with members of other cultures. Doing so may be much more demanding in terms of what we have to learn than merely targeting members of cultures that we may not yet understand. However, not doing so may also be interpreted as un-American. It is essential to note that this is a significant subject, not only in terms of dealing with cultures outside the US, but also for the sensitivity that is needed to address cultural diversity in our own immigrant society, which is concerned about issues like ethnic and racial profiling.

References

1. Judee K. Burgoon, David B. Buller, and W. Gill Woodall, *Nonverbal Communication: The Unspoken Dialogue* (New York: McGraw-Hill, 1996), pp. 136–7, 7–8.
2. Roger E. Axtell, *Gestures: The Do's and Taboos of Body Language Around the World*, rev. ed. (New York: John Wiley & Sons, 1998), p. 65.
3. Ibid., pp. 45–6.
4. Ibid., pp. 47–8.
5. Edwin R. McDaniel, "Japanese Nonverbal Communication: A Reflection of Cultural Themes," in Larry A. Samovar and Richard E. Porter, eds., *Intercultural Communication: A Reader* (Belmont, CA: Wadsworth, 2003), p. 257.
6. Axtell, p. 103.
7. Ibid., p. 68.

8. Mark L. Knapp and Judith A. Hall, *Non-verbal Communication in Human Interaction*, 3rd ed. (Fort Worth, TX: Harcourt Brace College Publishers, 1992), p. 298.
9. Ibid., p. 300.
10. Peter A. Andersen et al., "Nonverbal Communication Across Cultures," in William B. Gudykunst and Bella Mody, eds., *Handbook of International and Intercultural Communication*, 2nd ed. (Thousand Oaks, CA: Sage, 2002), p. 95.
11. Axtell, p. 67.
12. Ibid., p. 163.
13. McDaniel, p. 255.
14. Edward T. Hall, *The Hidden Dimension* (Garden City, NY: Doubleday/Anchor, 1966); Andersen, 2002, pp. 90–2.
15. McDaniel, p. 256.
16. Andersen, 2002, pp. 90–2.
17. Ibid.
18. Peter A. Andersen, "In Different Dimensions: Nonverbal Communication and Culture," in Larry A. Samovar and Richard E. Porter, eds., *Intercultural Communication: A Reader* (Belmont, CA: Wadsworth, 2003), pp. 247–8.
19. Andersen, 2002, p. 92.
20. William B. Gudykunst and Stella Ting-Toomey, "Nonverbal Dimensions and Context-Regulation," in William B. Gudykunst and Young Yun Kim, eds., *Readings on Communicating with Strangers* (Boston, MA: McGraw-Hill, 1992), pp. 278–9.
21. Axtell, p. 211.
22. Norine Dresser, *Multicultural Manners: New Rules of Etiquette for a Changing Society* (New York: Wiley & Sons, 1996), p. 58.
23. Edward T. Hall and Mildred R. Hall, *Understanding Cultural Differences: Germans, French, and Americans* (Yarmouth, ME: Intercultural Press, 1990), p. 53.
24. Alan S. Miller and Satoshi Kanazawa, *Order by Accident* (Boulder, CO: Westview Press, 2000), p. 27.
25. Ammar Askari, "Double Pain: Arab-Americans Still Suffering Since 9-11," *Milwaukee Journal Sentinel*, September 13, 2003, 13A; Hossam E. Fadel, "Muslim Americans Seek Respect and Tolerance as Citizens," *The Augusta Chronicle*, October 8, 2002, A05; Richard Lewis, "R.I. Muslims Fend Off Harassment, Spread Message Since Attacks," *The Associated Press State and Local Wire*, September 11, 2002; "Anti-Muslim Incidents in California, Michigan, and Illinois: Women Verbally Assaulted, Father and Son Refused Service, Mosque Threatened," *PR Newswire Association*, March 20, 2003.
26. Charles Darwin, *The Expression of the Emotions in Man and Animals* (New York: Oxford University Press, 1998 [1872]).
27. Knapp and Hall, p. 265.
28. David Matsumoto, "Cultural Influences on Facial Expressions of Emotion," *Southern Communication Journal* 56 (1990), 128.
29. Paul Ekman, E. R. Sorenson, and W. V. Friesen, "Pan-cultural Elements in Facial Displays of Emotions," *Science* 164 (1969), 86–8; Paul Ekman and W. V. Friesen, "Constants Across Cultures in the Face and Emotion," *Journal of Personality and Social Psychology* 17 (1971), 124–9; Paul Ekman and W. V. Friesen, *Unmasking the Face* (Englewood Cliffs, NJ: Prentice Hall, 1975), pp. 21–32.
30. David Matsumoto, Harald G. Wallbott, and Klaus R. Scherer, "Emotions in Intercultural Communication," in William B. Gudykunst and Young Yun Kim, eds., *Readings on Communicating with Strangers* (Boston, MA: McGraw-Hill, 1992), pp. 284–5.
31. Ekman and Friesen, pp. 124–9.
32. Ekman, pp. 216–17.
33. I. Eibl-Eibesfeldt, "Universals in Human Expressive Behavior," in Aaron Wolfgang, ed., *Nonverbal Behavior* (New York: Academic Press, 1992), pp. 19–20.
34. Ekman, pp. 217–20.
35. David Matsumoto, "Cultural Influences on the Perception of Emotion," *Journal of Cross-Cultural Psychology* 20 (1989), 92–105; David Matsumoto, "American and Japanese Cultural Differences in the Recognition of Universal Facial Expressions," *Journal of Cross-Cultural Psychology* 23 (1992), 72–84.

36. David Matsumoto and Paul Ekman, "American-Japanese Cultural Differences in Rating the Intensity of Facial Expressions of Emotion," *Motivation and Emotion* 13 (1989), 143–57.
37. Stella Ting-Toomey, *Communicating Across Cultures* (New York: The Guilford Press, 1999), p. 120.
38. Ibid., p. 122.
39. J. C. Condon and F. Yousef, *An Introduction to Intercultural Communication* (Indianapolis, IN: Bobbs-Merrill, 1983), p. 76.
40. Andersen, 2003, p. 246.
41. McDaniel, p. 257.
42. Ibid.
43. Larry A. Samovar and Richard E. Porter, *Communication Between Cultures* (Belmont, CA: Wadsworth Publishing, 2001), p. 183.
44. McDaniel, 2003, p. 257.
45. Hall, pp. 116–25.
46. Ibid.
47. Gary P. Ferraro, *The Cultural Dimension of International Business* (Upper Saddle River, NJ: Prentice Hall, 2002), p. 88.
48. A. Almaney and A. Alwan, *Communicating with Arabs* (Prospect Heights, IL: Waveland, 1982), p. 17.
49. Edward T. Hall, *The Silent Language* (New York: Anchor/Doubleday, 1981), pp. 172–3.
50. Samovar and Porter, p. 186.
51. Hall and Hall, p. 10.
52. Ibid., p. 180.
53. Ting-Toomey, p. 132.
54. William B. Gudykunst et al., "Influence of Cultural Individualism-Collectivism, Self-Construals, and Individual Values on Communication Styles Across Cultures," *Human Communication Research* 22 (1996), 510–43.
55. K. Omata, "Territoriality in the House and its Relationship to the Use of Rooms and the Psychological Well-being of Japanese Married Women," *Journal of Environmental Psychology* 15 (1995), 147–54.
56. Helen Norris, "Stalking an Early Life," in Jay Lamar and Jeanie Thompson, eds., *The Remembered Gate: Memoirs by Alabama Writers* (Tuscaloosa, AL: University of Alabama Press, 2002), pp. 81–2.
57. C. Eric Lincoln, "Coming Through the Fire," in Jay Lamar and Jeanie Thompson, eds., *The Remembered Gate: Memoirs by Alabama Writers* (Tuscaloosa, AL: University of Alabama Press, 2002), pp. 2–11.
58. Reginald Shepherd, "This Plac/Displace," in Mark Doty, ed., *Open House: Writers Redefine Home* (Saint Paul, MN: Graywolf Press, 2003), pp. 170–2.
59. F. Kluckhohn and F. Strodtbeck, *Variations in Value Orientations* (New York: Row, Peterson & Co., 1961).
60. D. Locke, *Increasing Multicultural Understanding: A Comprehensive Model*, (Newbury Park, CA: Sage, 1992), p. 35.
61. Ting-Toomey, p. 74.
62. Edward T. Hall, *The Dance of Life: The Other Dimension of Time* (New York: Doubleday, 1983).
63. Edward T. Hall, *West of the Thirties* (New York: Anchor/Doubleday, 1994), p. xxvii.
64. Hall, 1983, p. 43.
65. Ibid., p. 45.
66. Ibid., p. 50.
67. Sirkka L. Jarvenpaa, Kathleen Knoll, and Dorothy E. Leidner, "Is Anybody Out There? Antecedents of Trust in Global Virtual Teams," *Journal of Management Information Systems* 14 (1998), 29.
68. M. H. Zack, "Interactivity and Communication Mode Choice in Ongoing Management Groups," *Information Systems Research* 4 (1993), 207–38.
69. Mary O'Hara-Devereaux and Robert Johansen, *Globalwork: Bridging Distance, Culture, and Time* (San Francisco, CA: Jossey-Bass, 1994), p. 150.
70. Ibid., p. 163.
71. Askari, 13A.

7   Visual Communication

Web designer Steve Chu faced many challenges when developing an English/Chinese bilingual website; one very sensitive issue for his English development team was how to refer to Taiwan. Although Taiwan refers to itself as the Republic of China, its status is disputed. The development team had to determine how to refer to Taiwan and China and how to use their national flags appropriately. Their ultimate solution was to refer to China simply as "mainland China," and Taiwan as "Taiwan," and not to use either flag on the site. These choices allowed them to avoid appearing to take a political stance that would be sure to alienate some members of the audience for the website. The flag of a nation is a powerful visual symbol that is so closely aligned with the nation it represents that disrespecting or defacing a nation's flag is generally considered a symbolic assault on that nation. Including the national flag of Taiwan on the website would have been an affront to China since China does not recognize Taiwan's status as a separate nation; at the same time, including China's flag and not Taiwain's flag would have been an insult to Taiwan. The symbolic power of the nations' flags is so great that the designers feared alienating their audience members by using them, and they solved the problem by not using any flags on the website. They faced a similar challenge in relation to the use of the official names of China and Taiwan.[1]

At first it may seem that visual communication and non-verbal communication are really the same and that what needs to be understood about visual communication can be covered in a discussion of non-verbal communication; after all, both are forms of communication that rely on something other than verbal messages to convey information. However, while there are areas of similarity and overlap, visual communication is really quite distinct from non-verbal communication. Non-verbal communication is sometimes referred to as body language with good reason; for the most part, non-verbal communication has to do with the way human beings use their bodies, physical adornments to their bodies, and their environments to communication with one another. Much of non-verbal communication is unconscious, and often individuals send messages unintentionally by the way they move their eyes or by how close they stand to one another.

Visual communication, by contrast, actually has more in common with verbal communication than it does with non-verbal communication in that visual communication is much more likely to consist of intentionally crafted messages. Also, visual communication, like verbal communication, has a grammar and syntax for the structuring of messages using a system of signs. The main difference between verbal and visual communication is that for verbal communication the signs are the characters in alphabet systems, and for visual communication the signs are pictorial symbols. The roots of modern languages can be traced back to early Egyptian and Sumerian writing, which was *pictographic* and *ideographic*; pictographs are pictures that represent things, and ideographs are pictures that represent ideas. Early peoples began by making images to represent common objects; it was when images were created to represent sounds in their spoken language that pictographs became the precursors to modern alphabets. The traditional characters of the Chinese language still used today are pictographs and ideographs.[2] Individuals learn to speak the language(s) of the culture that they are born into; in a similar way they also learn to perceive the world visually in the way that their culture does.

In this chapter we will discuss how visual perception is influenced by culture and how *semiotics*, the study of signs, can inform our examination of visual communication. We will look at the ways visual images are used across cultures and at the various attempts to create a universal visual language. Finally, we will examine particularly challenging aspects of visual intercultural communication, such as the depiction of people and animals and the use of color.

Perception

While all sighted human beings use their eyes in the same way to take in visual images, culture does influence an individual's visual perception of the world in many ways. Our eyes register images, but it is our brains that process the incoming images and assign meanings to them. On a daily basis we are all exposed to a flood of visual images, and our brains must determine which ones to pay attention to and which ones to ignore. For the most part, our visual perception is unconscious and automatic. We do not think about it any more than we think about our breathing.[3]

Generally we interpret as significant those images that we have prior knowledge of or experience with; in other words, we "see" those images that we can fit into the frames of reference, or schema, within our brains.[4] A great deal of our ability to make sense of the world is culturally determined, and therefore, the way we order the world within our own minds will be influenced by our membership in a particular culture. By extension, then, the schema in our brains that largely determine what we "see" and do not "see" are also culturally influenced. In fact, researchers have found that "members of a culture will fail to see things that are completely outside their cultural experience or will interpret what they see in terms of their own cultural reference frames."[5]

One example of the cultural aspect of perception is the story of an African pygmy who lived his life in the forest; when he first stood on a high promontory where he could overlook a vast area of grassland where buffalo were grazing, he thought that the buffalo were insects. The reason for his inability to make an allowance for distance when judging the size of the buffalo had to do with the fact that in a dense forest he had not had the opportunity to learn how apparent size diminishes with distance.[6] His perceptual skills had not developed in this way because there was no survival need for them to do so and hence no cultural support for such a development. Similarly, research has shown a correlation between hunting activity within a culture and good visual discrimination and spatial skills. A culture will reinforce those perceptual skills that are linked to survival.[7]

The *carpentered-world theory* has been proposed to explain cultural differences in depth perception. The theory posits that individuals who live in more technologically advanced societies tend to perceive straight lines, corners, and angles as part of the "natural" environment. By contrast members of cultures that live in round huts in the jungle or grasslands do not perceive angles and corners as part of the "natural" environment. Individuals who are used to the straight lines, corners, and angles can use them as cues for depth perception in pictures because the angled lines suggest different corners of a three-dimensional box. However, individuals who have little or no experience with such cues can only see pictures in two dimensions.[8] Interestingly, individuals who are used to the carpentered environment are more prone to optical illusions since their experience living in houses with right angles makes them more likely to believe that the top horizontal line is longer than the bottom one when they are, in fact, the same length.

It seems clear that we do not view an objective reality outside of ourselves that appears exactly the same to all human beings. Rather, we make sense of all the sensory impressions we receive from the world around us through the filter of our culture. Differences in our perception and depiction of the world around us have obvious implications for our ability to be mindful intercultural communicators.

Semiotics

Just as culture influences how we perceive visual images, it also influences the way we create visual images. Visual communication is a language composed of signs. *Semiotics* is the study of signs. The Greek philosopher and linguist Augustine first proposed the study of signs and the word semiotics comes from *semeion*, the Greek word for sign. Our contemporary study of semiotics comes out of the work of two linguistic theorists just before World War I; Swiss linguist Ferdinand de Saussure and American philosopher Charles Sanders Peirce. Although the work of Saussure and Peirce focused more on traditional linguistics and the study of words as signs, the field of semiotics today focuses on visual signs and their use across a wide range of disciplines including graphic design, theatre, television, advertising, and tourism.[9]

A *sign* may be anything that stands for something else. The meaning behind the sign must be learned. The study of signs is based on the idea that our brain stores images symbolically so that it can recognize objects instantaneously and classify what we perceive as either helpful or harmful. Peirce posited that there were three types of signs: *iconic*, *indexical*, and *symbolic*. Iconic signs or icons are easiest to interpret because they closely resemble the thing they represent, such as drawings of men and women on restroom doors and photographs.

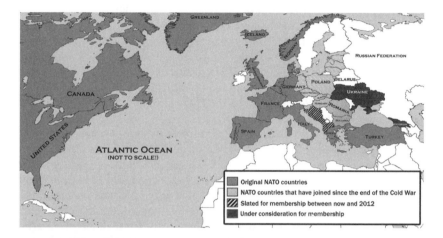

Figure 7.1 There are three types of signs: *iconic*, *indexic*, and *symbolic*. Iconic signs, like the generic figure on a men's room door, most closely resemble the thing they represent. Indexic signs have logical rather than a direct connection to the thing they represent; maps are indexic signs. Finally, symbolic signs are the most abstract of the three and have no representational or logical relationship with the thing they stand for. Flags and most corporate logos are symbolic signs. We must learn the meaning of symbolic signs just as we must learn the meaning of words.

Indexical signs have a logical rather than a direct connection to the thing or idea they represent, such as a map representing a particular geographic location.[10]

Symbolic signs are the most abstract of the three because they have no representational or logical relationship with the thing they represent. Symbols would include flags, most corporate logos, religious images, colors, and words. Symbols are deeply rooted in cultures and they usually have the potential to evoke a much stronger emotional response than iconic or indexical symbols do.[11] As a symbol of a nation, the flag may be invested with great emotional weight because of feelings of loyalty and national pride. Burning, taking down, or otherwise dishonoring a nation's flag is an action that carries tremendous symbolic meaning beyond the destruction of one particular piece of cloth. The meanings of symbols more than the other two types of signs must be taught. Just as we learn to speak a certain language(s) and to use certain gestures when we grow up within a given culture, so too, we learn to recognize and revere certain cultural symbols and, perhaps, to dislike or fear others. A symbol like the swastika cannot be viewed neutrally by individuals who are aware of its relationship with Nazi Germany and the Holocaust, and more recently, of its use in relation to hate crimes.

The meanings of symbols are as deeply rooted in the core values and beliefs of a culture as are the meanings of a culture's verbal and non-verbal communication. To understand the symbols that are central to a culture we must also understand that culture at a deep level. It is a good idea to keep in mind that symbols like words can have both denotative and connotative meanings. A symbol may have one common-sense meaning that is noticeable on the surface, but may also have different connotations to members of different cultures. For example, for many cultures a butterfly would be symbolic of beauty and fragility. However, in the Korean culture a butterfly is a symbol of masculinity because the butterfly goes from flower to flower collecting nectar. Traditional Korean culture is one in which women are expected to be more passive and men more aggressive and active.[12]

POWER CHECK
Controversy Over Flag-Draped Coffins
Both national flags and coffins are powerful visual symbols. In April 2004, a controversy was sparked by the release of unauthorized pictures of the flag-draped coffins of U.S. soldiers killed in Iraq. During the 1991 Persian Gulf War, George Bush Sr. put in place a ban that forbids the media access to photographs of coffins returning from the battlefield. The purpose of the ban is to protect mourners from seeing the coffins of their loved ones in the national news media. The National Military Family Association Inc. (NMFA) agrees with the ban. The NMFA argues that the grief of surviving families should be respected as should their right to privacy at a very difficult time.

However, political leaders and others who disagree with the ban argue that it serves to conceal from the American people the reality of the war in Iraq and the number of lives that are being lost. They believe that the ban serves political purposes as much as it serves the rights of the families of the fallen soldiers. During the Vietnam War, which was long before the ban was enacted, images of coffins and body bags went a long way to strengthening anti-war sentiment in America. Even some of the mourning families opposed the ban. They believe that the deaths of their loved ones should be recognized and remembered by the general public, despite the pain it might bring them personally.

What do you think:

1. Should the ban be kept in force? Why or why not?
2. Does the public have the right to see the flag-draped coffins of American soldiers? Why or why not?
3. What does this controversy reveal about the power of visual images in the media?

Sources: Paul Berton, "Ban on Photographs Comforts Some, Annoys Others," *London Free Press* (Ontario, April 24, 2004), A2; Anne E. Kornblut and Bryan Bender, "Pentagon to Review Photo Ban; More Debate Over Images of US Coffins," *The Boston Globe* (April 24, 2004), A1; Sheryl Gay Stolberg, "Senate Backs Ban on Photos of G.I. Coffins," *The New York Times* (June 22, 2004), 17.

Making assumptions about the meaning of signs, like the butterfly, without knowledge of the culture can lead to miscommunication and potentially even to conflict. We need to remember that the use of signs and other visual images varies widely across cultures and that what may seem intuitive to us is not necessarily a perception that will be shared by members of other cultures.

Co-cultural groups and semiotics

When we discussed verbal communication in Chapter 5 we examined the relationship between language and power. We discussed the way certain languages and linguistic variations of languages are privileged and the fact that co-cultural groups who do not conform to the communication styles of the dominant group within a society are often at a disadvantage within that society. A similar privileging often occurs in relation to signs. Semiotician David Chandler states that reality is a system of signs; he goes on to say that by studying signs we can determine whose reality is privileged within a society and whose reality in repressed. Chandler claims that "even the most realistic signs are not what they appear to be."[13] For example, images in the media may portray members of co-cultural groups in ways that are stereotypical. Frequently the media presents images of women that focus in a reductive way on their sexuality.

British sociologist Stuart Hall has proposed a model of mass communication that emphasizes both the *encoding* and *decoding* of signs. When we assign meaning to a sign we are encoding it; for example, an advertiser may use a picture of a woman in a seductive pose to help sell a product. When readers look at the advertisement, they decode, or determine the meaning of, the picture in the same way that they determine the meaning of the written words that accompany the picture. Hall's model suggests that there are three possible types of reading or decoding of a text: *dominant* reading, *negotiated* reading, and *oppositional* reading.[14]

A dominant reading of the text would be one where the reader accepts the "preferred reading" of the text. For example, the reader would agree with the implication of the advertisement that uses a seductive woman to sell a car. He would see the woman primarily in terms of her sexuality and link having a nice car with being attractive to the opposite sex. A negotiated reading would be one where the reader accepts the preferred reading up to a point, but also modifies or resists it in a way that reflects his own experiences. This position involves contradictions. In this instance, the reader might enjoy viewing the seductive woman, but based on his own experience, he might not believe that having such a car will equate with attractiveness to the opposite sex. An oppositional reading would be one where the reader is in a social situation that places him in direct opposition to the dominant code, and, therefore, while the reader understands the preferred reading, he rejects it and brings to bear an alternate frame of reference. For example, because of his alignment with feminism and his belief that it is degrading for women to be treated as sex objects, he will understand that the ad is meant to sell him a car based on the woman's attractiveness, but he will reject that interpretation and will view the advertisement as sexist and inappropriate. He will not find it persuasive, but rather offensive. The creators of the SiamWeb.org website (discussed in Chapter 5) sought to challenge the preferred reading of media images of Thai women as prostitutes and mail-order brides; SiamWeb.org offered an oppositional reading of those images of Thai women that dominate the media.

Figure 7.2 Woman in a seductive pose.

ANALYSIS OF A SIGN

Like most corporate logos, the McDonald's logo is an example of a symbol. Symbolic signs have no representational or logical relationship with the thing they represent. Corporate logos typically become associated with brands through advertising campaigns that may take years to build up brand recognition. The McDonald's logo is the golden arches. When American families go to a fast-food restaurant like McDonald's they are seeking affordable food, fast and friendly service, and a clean and congenial atmosphere. They are seeking convenience. In their analysis of the McDonald's logo, communication scholars Marcel Danesi and Paul Perron suggest that the golden arches "constitute a mythic symbol beckoning good people to march through them triumphantly into a paradise of law and order, cleanliness, friendliness, hospitality, hard work, self-discipline, and family values." They go on to point out that today many families have two working parents and rarely eat dinner together, and when they do it is often in front of the television. McDonald's is a place where families can eat together in a pleasant atmosphere with no distractions. They even go so far as to state that McDonald's has the same organization and standardization that many of the world's religions do, and therefore, the arches represent entry into a paradise. Even if we feel that the linking of the McDonald's logo with paradise is a bit of a stretch, we can see that for many harried and overworked parents it does offer a kind of respite, and it is affordable enough for most budgets.

However, if we look at McDonald's from the perspective of members of other cultures around the world we may find quite different meanings attached to the symbol of the golden arches. The fast-food lifestyle of America has been exported to over 100 countries on six continents with over 31,000 McDonald's restaurants worldwide. While some people may welcome the spread of American culture in the form of a fast-food restaurant, others see the proliferation of McDonald's around the world as part of the unwanted spread of American values, and even as a kind of cultural imperialism. In fact, political scientist Benjamin Barber, writing about the spread of consumerism and American values in our global society, entitled his book, *Jihad vs. McWorld*. In writing about the breakdown of national boundaries and the rise of the global marketplace, Barber both discusses the inevitability of these changes and the reaction against them by many individuals and nations. For individuals who view the spread of American culture in a negative light, the symbol of the golden arches would represent the encroachment of unwanted values, and perhaps, even a force breaking down traditions and disrupting family harmony.

While for American consumers the preferred reading of the golden arches is as a paradise of convenience, an oppositional reading might well exist for members of cultures who resent the spread of American values. Such individuals might view the golden arches as representing an outpost of an invading culture and as an attempt to pull young people away from family values and traditions. Still other negotiated readings might exist both for American consumers and for members of other cultures. For American consumers concerned about health, the fast food represented by the golden arches may not be perceived as a good choice. While such consumers may agree with the view of the golden arches as representing convenience and affordability, they may experience a contradiction in terms of their own ability to avail themselves of what the golden arches offer if they cannot eat the food without facing health concerns such as high cholesterol. Similarly, members of other cultures may experience contradictory feelings because while they may dislike the American values represented by the golden arches, they may also welcome the jobs and economic prosperity brought by the presence of McDonald's restaurants.

We can see that one symbol may be packed with several layers of meaning. The symbol may have different meanings for different viewers depending on their perspective, experiences, and interests. A symbol may also have contradictory meanings for the same viewer depending upon that individual's background, experiences, and viewpoint.

Source: Marcel Danesi and Paul Perron, *Analyzing Cultures: An Introduction and Handbook* (Bloomington, IN: Indiana University Press, 1999), pp. 281–2.

Cultural studies is aligned with the critical approach to the study of intercultural communication (see Chapter 4). Cultural studies scholars like Richard Dyer and Homi Bhabha examine the stereotypical portrayal of co-cultural groups in the media. Dyer states that "the most important function of the stereotype [is] to maintain sharp boundary definitions" and "to make fast, firm and separate what is in reality fluid and much closer to the norm than the dominant value system cares to admit."[15] In our discussion of language and power, we saw that language is frequently related to social mobility, and that individuals who do not speak the language of the majority culture are often disadvantaged in society. A similar type of prejudice is attached to the images of co-cultural groups that are depicted in films, on television, and in other media.

Writing on the discourse of colonialism, Bhabha argues that stereotypical representations of the colonized that depict them as incapable of self-government, independence, and Western modes of civility, serve to lend authority to the actions of the colonial power.[16] Images that stereotype members of co-cultural groups based on gender, sexual orientation, ethnicity, and skin color help to reinforce prejudicial treatment and discrimination of members of these groups and may deny them the opportunity to be seen as individuals. Such depictions can serve to help maintain the status quo in society — a status quo that favors the majority culture. Scholars using the critical approach to intercultural communication seek to challenge the preferred readings of such images and to offer oppositional readings for the purpose of enacting social change.

Use of Signs and Other Visual Images

For the most part iconic signs or icons closely resemble the things that they represent. However, common everyday objects do not look the same all across the world. For example, users of many computer programs encounter icons meant to represent two everyday objects, a mail box and a trash can. As icons, the signs look very much like mail boxes and trash cans — in the American culture where the software program was created. However, for many other individuals around the world, there is no recognition because for them mail boxes and trash cans look very different. While this difference may not interfere with their ability to use the software programs, it is an illustration of the way in which mindful visual communication across cultures presents the same kinds of challenges that verbal and non-verbal communication presents.

In fact, visual communication has the potential to create even greater challenges if we fall prey to the illusion that there is a totally objective world out there that we all perceive in exactly the same way. We all understand that individuals from other cultures may well speak languages and use gestures that are different from our own; however, we must also remember that they may also perceive the world in ways that are different from our own.

A San Francisco-based company had an image of the Golden Gate Bridge shrouded in fog on its English-language website. For individuals in San Francisco this image of the Bridge served as an indexical sign to represent the city. For an international audience, the sign would be very difficult to decode particularly because the image was partially obscured by fog. The company wanted to use the image on a website that was to be translated into 21 languages. Although the designer cautioned the client against using the image, the client refused to change it. The bridge obscured by fog is, perhaps, an apt symbol for the difficulty of bridging cultures using culture-specific visual images.[17]

Cultural value orientations play a role in the type of drawings and paintings that cultures produce. For example, as previously mentioned, the work of Kluckhohn and Strodtbeck with classical value orientations examined the temporal orientation of human life and noted that most cultures fall into one of three categories: past-oriented, present-oriented, or future-oriented. An analysis of artwork reveals a difference in the presentation of depth that is related to cultures' temporal orientations; in fact, time and space are related concepts for most cultures, and this relationship is evident in visual messages, such as paintings and drawings. Cultures that are past-oriented are more likely to place both close and distant objects on the same level. One example of this type of perspective can be found in murals in Belfast, Northern Ireland, a culture that has kept alive historic enmity between Catholics and Protestants for generations. By contrast, cultures that are more present-oriented are likely to exhibit a field of view that incorporates depth perception cues. Finally, Asian cultures that are typically future-oriented and that value long-range planning as part of their Confucian heritage typically exhibit images without any noticeable cues to depth perception. This lack of depth perspective is found in traditional Japanese and Chinese art.[18]

Cultural values also affect the way visual elements are incorporated into documents. Differences between high-context and low-context cultures are evident in the way these cultures use visuals in documents and the way they integrate text and visuals throughout documents. According to Hall, high-context cultures are those cultures in which the message being communicated is derived primarily from the surrounding context, that is, the larger culture and shared cultural values and beliefs; in contrast, low-context cultures are those cultures in which the message being communicated is derived primarily from the literal and explicitly spelled out information within the message itself. Often in low-context cultures, the burden is placed on the speaker or writer to make himself clear; conversely, in high-context cultures the burden is placed on the listener or reader to derive meaning from the communication.

A study of the use of visuals in corporate annual reports is an excellent illustration of the differences between the way high-context and low-context cultures use visuals to convey meaning in corporate documentation. Kaushiki Maitra and Dixie Goswami conducted a study of the responses of American readers to the use of visuals in a Japanese corporate annual report. They took the annual report of a medium-sized Japanese company and had it translated into English while retaining the layout and design of the original Japanese version. Normally, a Japanese corporation targeting a American audience would hire an American firm to redesign the document to make it more suitable for an American audience — but in this study the original graphics, layout, and other design features were retained. The American readers who participated in the study had a minimal knowledge of the Japanese culture.

All of the participants in the study found the visual elements of the annual report problematic. They had difficulty determining what the visuals were supposed to mean and were troubled by the fact that the visuals did not have captions that explained their significance. They were particularly confused by visuals that had no relationship to the content of the report; many visuals were added for purely aesthetic reasons, and this fact was confounding to the American readers.

The difficulty that the American readers had with the Japanese corporate annual report was due to different cultural expectations about the use of visuals in corporate documentation and due to the fact that the Japanese culture is a high-context culture and the American culture is a relatively low-context culture. The American readers expected the meaning of the visuals used in the annual report to be very explicit and clear cut; they did not expect any ambiguity about their meaning or their relationship to the text. Moreover, they had no expectation that visuals would be used for merely aesthetic purposes in professional documentation whose purpose is to persuade readers of a company's success and profitability. Although they initially found the visuals aesthetically pleasing, the American readers were annoyed by their lack of explicit meaning.

By contrast, Japanese readers, because they are members of a high-context culture, would not expect to have every piece of information in a document made explicit for them. Rather, they would take it for granted that it is the reader's job to extract information from a document. They would also value the fact that the visuals were ambiguous, as their culture values ambiguity. Rarely will members of the Japanese culture state facts bluntly; instead of making explicit statements, they will usually take a circular route to make their points. Therefore, for Japanese readers, the ambiguity of the visuals in the annual report was a positive attribute and not a source of frustration. Further, the Japanese readers would value the aesthetic quality of the visuals. They would believe that if readers were impressed by the visuals that they would then have a positive reaction to the company and be moved to learn more about it.

For Japanese readers aesthetics and ambiguity are very significant values. Because the American readers brought different values and expectations to their reading of the document, they were confused and frustrated rather than impressed and motivated to work to extract meaning from the document.[19] This example demonstrates that in addition to the need to select visuals carefully when communicating with members of other cultures, we also need to display the visuals and to integrate them with textual information in ways that are meaningful to members of other cultures.

A Universal Visual Language?

There have been several attempts to create a universally understood language of signs. In the 1920s Viennese philosopher and social scientist Otto Neurath worked with graphic artists to create a pictographic language that combined type and images into a single message. His language was called *isotype*, an international system of typographic picture education. Neurath had some success in getting his ideas accepted internationally, and the popular symbols that depict a silhouetted image with a thick diagonal "No" line are a reflection of the pictographic ideas of Neurath's work.[20]

Neurath dreamed that it would be possible to compress meaning into non-verbal forms in a way that would communicate across all cultures and eliminate language barriers.[21]

In 1949 the United Nations World Conference on Road and Motor Transport in Geneva met to address the need for greater consistency in road signs in the Western world. International leisure travel was increasing, and the system of road signs was meant to communicate visually by using stripped-down versions of existing European traffic signage. The resulting signs were very simplistic, and they introduced the use of silhouetted figures that included a "stooping workman" and "dashing school children."[22] Many signs seen in public facilities today derive from these early images. In the 1970s, the US Department of Transportation and the American Institute of Graphic Arts created 50 signs to be used around the world to guide passengers through transportation facilities.[23] Despite the fact that it is possible to create some compressed images that can communicate visually across cultures, these sign systems have limitations and are far from intuitive. We must remember that our interpretation of icons and symbols is heavily influenced by culture. While

Figure 7.3 The work of Otto Neurath led to the development of the popular "No" symbol. The "No" symbol is a visual image that is universally understood. Neurath hoped to create a pictographic language that could be used universally across cultures, but he had limited success because of the many challenges inherent in such an undertaking.

these signs are useful, they do not always work as effectively in the developing world as they do in Western countries.

In India, for example, a set of symbol-based signs was designed for use in hospitals. The need for effective visual communication is particularly critical in a country that has 14 major languages and over 1,600 dialects. Professor Ravi Poovaiah of the Indian Institute of Technology's Industrial Design Centre designed a new system of signage and used as his starting point the generic man from Neurath's isotypes. He created 21 symbols to direct people to the various hospital departments. The signage, although generic for the population of India, was still very clearly tied to the cultural context in which it was being used. For example, the generic figure of a woman used to indicate the women's bathroom is shown wearing a sari, not a Western mini-dress — the mini-dress figure comes from signage developed in the 1950s and 1960s. Another cultural difference has to do with the rigid class distinctions in Indian society. In addition to the signs for man and woman, there is an additional sign for "rural man."[24]

Despite the recognition that existing signage has a limited effectiveness and may not work well across all cultures of the world, there are still many projects in the works that seek to develop universally understood signs and icons to communicate across cultures. One example is the Kwikpoint system, a double-sided card with 600 pictures designed to help individuals communicate anywhere in the world by pointing to the relevant picture(s) on the card. The pictures cover a wide range of topics from buying food to requesting an ocean view in a hotel.[25] While examples like Kwikpoint are very useful for specific applications, we are still a long way from having a universally understood visual language. The worldwide prevalence of computer technology has revived the hope of communication through commonly understood symbols as more and more visual images are quickly and easily disseminated around the globe. But one only has to look at the challenges faced by designers preparing international documentation or advertising campaigns to see that we still have many cultural differences in our use of visual language. Depictions of people and animals and the use of color are especially challenging aspects of visual intercultural communication.

Depictions of Animals and Human Beings

Although most cultures use animals as symbols to represent a multitude of desirable and undesirable qualities, the various symbolic meanings attributed to animals vary widely across cultures. In some cultures certain animals are sacred, like the cow in India, or highly prized, like the pig in New Guinea. Some cultures respond positively to "cute" or "cartoon" images of animals, like frogs and cats in Japan. In Chinese culture animals have many symbolic meanings, including a fish representing prosperity; a crane representing longevity; and an ox representing fertility. In American culture we use images of rabbits to represent fertility and reproduction, but in other cultures rabbits may be perceived as vermin (Australia) or food (Germany).[26] The reasons for the qualities associated with various animals are usually deeply rooted within a culture's history and mythology.

As with the depiction of animals, the depiction of human beings can pose many problems in intercultural communication. One problem is related to non-verbal communication and the depiction of various bodily postures, gestures, or facial expressions that may be offensive or insulting to members of other cultures; even gestures that are not necessary offensive may be misinterpreted by or confusing to members of other cultures. For example, it would not be a good idea to depict someone making the thumbs up gesture if you knew that your visuals would be seen in Nigeria, and you would want to avoid showing someone using the "V" for Victory sign with palm and fingers facing inward if you knew your audience included England (see Chapter 6).

Often graphic artists and other individuals who are communicating visually across cultures seek to use very simplified representations of people, like stick figures and the "stooping workman" of the early international road signs, to avoid the pitfalls of representing individuals who are too obviously culture-specific in their physical characteristics and general appearance. One of the most common examples of this type of depiction of human beings is the kind of signage that grew out of Neurath's isotypes; it can be found in airports, hospitals, and other public buildings. We often see figures that are generic representations of men and women on the doors to restrooms; these figures are iconic signs that have a direct relationship to the thing they represent. However, as we have seen, they may still have some culture-specific qualities, like a woman in a sari versus a woman in a mini-dress. Writing about graphics in international documents, Charles Kostelnick describes the John Deere Company's use of "Flatman," a simplistic figure that represents a human being in a generic and culture-free manner.[27] Often such generic figures are created so that they do not indicate any particular age, race, ethnic group, or even gender.

By creating such generic figures, graphic designers and those individuals who use their designs are able to avoid any type of stereotyping based on race, ethnicity, age, or gender. There are many reasons to avoid depicting people that are recognizable as members of specific groups or subgroups. Even the depiction of a man's arm can lead to very different interpretations across cultures. A Harley-Davidson advertisement that contained a muscled arm with the Harley-Davidson logo tattooed on it worked well in the United States to depict the popular brand of motorcycle. In Europe, the ad was problematic because the image was associated with biker gangs, a problem in many European nations. In Asia, viewers assumed that the image represented gangsters and, therefore, saw it in a very negative light.[28]

Another aspect of the depiction of people that can lead to misinterpretation is related to the different roles of men and women across cultures. In many cultures around the world, women do not enjoy equality with men in the workplace. In some Islamic nations, women do not work outside of the home. Therefore, photographs of women at work or using women to illustrate examples within a technical manual might be inappropriate for certain audiences. The reverse is true in nations where men and women do enjoy equal status; in the United States we would find it strange and would be likely to consider the designer(s)/company biased if we encountered documents that showed only men in the workplace or all-male groups as users of various products.[29] The use of generic figures addresses both of these potential concerns.

A similar trend is occurring in the field of advertising where many advertisements geared toward an international market include models with mixed racial characteristics that do not clearly represent one particular ethnic group or subgroup. For example, many designers take the "Pan" approach; they select models that are Pan-Asian or Pan-Hispanic, meaning that they look universally Asian or Hispanic and their features do not identify them as being from any one particular nation.[30]

Even within the United States, symbolic figures used to represent products have been changed over time to more accurately reflect the multicultural nature of American society. The image of the "all-American" homemaker represented by the figure of Betty Crocker has been used for many years by the General Mills Corporation to sell various products, most notably those products related to baking and preparing food for the family. When Betty Crocker was first created in 1921, she was represented as a stern gray-haired woman who was

MEDIA IMPACT
Depiction of Female Beauty in the Media

The media's portrayal of women, particularly in advertisements, can have a powerful impact on women's self-images. One aspect of media representations of women that has received a great deal of attention is the proliferation of images of the ideal female body as extremely thin. Psychologists Sypeck, Gray, and Ahrens conducted a survey of the print media's depiction of the ideal of female beauty as presented to American women from 1959 through 1999. They found that over the period of 40 years, body size for fashion models decreased significantly. The media is often criticized for presenting an unrealistic image of female beauty which causes many young women to develop eating disorders in an attempt to attain the ideal. In addition to portraying what many consider an unrealistic idea of the perfect female body, the U.S. media still presents an image of female beauty that is predominantly white despite the changing demographics of the U.S. population.

As U.S. popular culture is exported to many other nations around the world, the effects of the predominant images of women are also being exported. For example, the development of many women's and teen magazines in Romania after the 1989 revolution has contributed to the transformation of female self-identity, and has in turn "had an impact on the collective conscience of Romanian national identity." The impact of such magazines is mixed. On the one hand, they are an expression of freedom of choice, and they create a feminine "public space" that would not have been possible prior to the revolution. At the same time, the magazines are promoting the U.S. ideal of beauty wherein the perfect woman is depicted as white, young, and slim. Such images are driven by the values of the majority culture within the U.S. — a cultural still dominated by white males — and by the advertising industry whose concern is for profit, not empowerment of women.

Sources: Mia Foley Sypeck, James J. Gray, and Anthony H. Ahrens, "No Longer Just a Pretty Face: Fashion Magazines' Depictions of Ideal Female Beauty from 1959 to 1999," *International Journal of Eating Disorders*, 36:3 (2004), 342–7; David Berry, "Is Popular Culture Subversive in Romania? An Assessment of Teenage Girls' and Women's Magazines," *Slovo*, 16:2 (2004), 131–42.

clearly a Caucasian. Over time Betty has had eight different looks. In the 1970s she was represented wearing a business suit to depict the growing number of American women taking on roles in the workforce. She is depicted as much younger than the grandmotherly image used when she was first created. Throughout the years her image has been changed to more accurately reflect the US population and a computer-generated image of Betty Crocker now presents her as someone who is multiracial in appearance; she does not look like she belongs to one particular racial or ethnic group.[31]

The designers of the new and improved Betty Crocker clearly did not want to exclude any members of the potential audience for their products. In a similar

Figure 7.4 Pan-ethnic models.

way, if we wish to communicate mindfully with members of cultures other than our own, we must challenge ourselves to go beyond our learned perceptions of the world and must seek to create new ways of seeing the world around us. One of the most emotionally charged and culturally divergent visual cues we experience is our perception and interpretation of color.

Use of Color

Imagine you are driving a car and are approaching a traffic light that is red; in most cases, you will stop your car. Conversely, if you drive up to a green traffic light you will keep going. Further, even though some of us do not always stop when we see an amber traffic light, we still know that it means "caution" and is a warning that soon the light will turn red. The American culture is not the only place where these colors signal the necessity for certain behaviors on the part of individuals driving automobiles. However, there is nothing intrinsic in the color red that means "stop." We have learned certain meanings for the colors used in the traffic signal. In some developing countries, citizens were unaware of the meanings of the colors in the traffic light; in 1984 in Botswana, after installing traffic lights, government officials learned that drivers did not know the significance of the red, amber, and green lights. They actually had to teach the citizens how to interpret the meanings of the colors in the traffic light.[32]

Our experience of color and the meanings we associate with various colors is learned just as our knowledge of a particular language is learned or the meanings we associate with certain hand gestures are learned. In intercultural communication, it is possible that we may use a word or make a gesture or take an action that a member of another culture finds offensive, even though offense is not at all what we intend. The same is true with the use of color. It is possible to use colors in ways that members of other cultures will find offensive and off-putting. In almost every culture, colors are invested with symbolic meanings. In some cultures, like the Navajo, there is actually a ranking system related to color that is very much like our ranking of precious metals with gold being superior to silver and so forth. When Americans working for the Indian Service sought a method of labeling political candidates so that illiterate Navajos could vote, they arbitrarily linked the candidates to colors and, thereby, labeled one of the candidates very negatively just because of the randomly selected color they used to represent him. They subsequently went to the method of using photographs of the candidates on the ballots.[33]

For the Navajo, blue is a good color and the candidate arbitrarily linked to the color blue got more votes than the others. Various cultures have colors that they prize and others that they associate with bad luck and even death. Perhaps some of the strongest color associations relate to ideas about death, purity, and good and bad fortune. In the American culture we have very clear ideas about the meanings of colors associated with marriage, death, and other rites of passage. Although our society is very pluralistic and allows latitude to those individuals who wish to deviate from the norm, we still see a great deal of conformity surrounding the association of the color black with mourning and funerals, and the color white with brides and babies being christened. But if we interact with members of other cultures, we would be mistaken to assume that they too consider white a color of purity and black a color of death. Similarly, our verbal associations with the meanings of colors will not translate well; for example, saying that "today is a black day" or that "someone is as pure as snow" (which is usually white). Our visual cues also fail to translate in the stereotypical cowboy movie, where the good guys wear the white hats and the villains wear the black ones. For Americans, the association of all things negative with black and all things positive with white serves to perpetuate negative racial stereotypes and may reinforce prejudice and discrimination.

In many Asian cultures, white is the color associated with death and funerals, particularly white flowers. Most Hindu brides wear red, although some Muslim brides wear green because it is considered a holy color.[34] Although colors carry a great deal of visual weight, there are not always clear-cut reasons why colors have the associations they do in various cultures.

Some associations, however, are logical. For example, many cultures associate the color green with the environment and by extension with practices that are safe for the environment. Of course, in the United States green is the color of money. For this reason, Americans often link the color to prosperity and to capitalism, but this meaning does not translate well across cultures.

Other associations for colors may be related to the natural world and to the geography of the country. In India some of the most popular colors are the colors of native foods, such as mangos, oranges, and tumeric.[35] Also, some researchers believe that there is a relationship between a country's weather and geography and its use of color. People in northern countries that are above the equator are found to wear more subdued colors, and people in countries that are near and below the equator, such as Malaysia and the Philippines, tend to prefer much brighter colors. This phenomenon is borne out within the United States as well where different colors are worn in California and Florida than are in Chicago, Illinois, or other northern locations.[36]

There may also be a correlation between the use of color and geography, the cultural dimension of immediacy, and the distinction between high- and low-contact cultures. The cultural dimension of immediacy has to do with how individuals express interpersonal closeness, that is, how likely they are to communicate warmth to others through non-verbal actions, such as smiling, standing close when interacting, making eye contact, and speaking in a more animated manner. High-contact cultures display a great deal of interpersonal warmth and closeness, while low-contact cultures tend to be much more distant and much less expressive. Most high-contact cultures are located in warmer nations that are close to the equator and most low-contact cultures are located in cooler nations that are farther away from the equator. It seems possible that the high-contact cultures' expressiveness and immediacy is evidenced in their choice of vibrant-colored clothing as much as it is evidenced in other aspects of their non-verbal communication. Similarly, the reserve and distance of low-contact cultures may be naturally expressed by their choice of subdued colors. Although there are likely to be some exceptions to this generalization, particularly in terms of co-cultural groups within a nation, geography clearly plays a role in non-verbal communication and in visual communication.

A great deal of importance is placed on the colors displayed in a nation's flag and other national symbols. Of course, in American culture, the colors red, white, and blue taken together carry great visual weight because they are the colors of the flag; taken separately the colors do not have the same significance. National colors must be considered with great care when selecting colors for international ventures. Designers working on documentation to establish the corporate identity of luxury hotels that were located in Hong Kong and Bangkok and owned by a British company faced many challenges related to the selection of color and other aspects of visual communication. They ultimately selected "Chinese Red" and a shade of orange taken from a swatch of fabric from the robes of Buddhist priests. Similarly, designers for the *UN Chronicle*, a magazine produced by the United Nations, face many challenges related to color choice and have in fact received formal protests from member nations because of the inappropriate use of their national colors.[37] As the members of the Indian Service attempting to help the Navajo vote learned, the choice of color is loaded with a great deal of significance across cultures and cannot be an arbitrary decision if one wishes to communicate mindfully with members of other cultures.

Technology and Visual Communication

Despite the shortcomings of the traditional IR literature about visual communication, most studies of intercultural communication to date have focused on the verbal and non-verbal aspects of communication, and rightly so. When communicating with members of other cultures we need to be mindful of the way we use language and of the non-verbal cues that we use in order to avoid misunderstandings that could lead to conflict. However, the significance of visual communication should not be overlooked. Over the last two decades, the primacy of visual communication has increased greatly; in many ways, societies are becoming much more visually oriented.[38] Much of the rise of visual communication can be attributed to the proliferation of technology, particularly computer technology, which allows users access to the World Wide Web and a dazzling array of visual images. Entertainment media, like MTV and VH1, have also served to reinforce the power of visual images in communication.

Further, the advent of computer technology like desktop publishing has given computer users the opportunity to produce and print their own visuals, a capability formerly held by a more restricted group of individuals who had access to printing presses. Digital photography also makes it possible for individuals to post pictures on websites and transmit them to millions of people around the world in a matter of seconds. Technology has given the average person a greater opportunity to contest stereotypical images that are put forward by the majority culture. Websites are a place where oppositional readings can be offered by co-cultural groups to counter media stereotypes. In Chapter 8 we will discuss the impact of the media, popular culture, and cultural imperialism.

We cannot escape the fact that visuals are taking on increasing importance as a means of communication. As we have discussed, visuals may range from the icons used in computer programs to the simplified road signs created for international motorists to the aesthetically pleasing visuals included in a Japanese company's annual report. In all cases, we must exercise the same care in selecting visuals as we would in selecting our words or our gestures. We must be aware of potential miscommunications that can result from inappropriate handling of visual images in intercultural communication. It is also important to remember the way the various cultural value dimensions affect the significance of visual images and circumscribe their use.

Clearly, the greatest danger in using visuals for intercultural communication is the mistaken perception that there is an external world that is seen in exactly the same way by members of all cultures around the world. Our culture does influence our perception of the world and our interpretation of what we perceive. Mindful intercultural communicators will be sensitive to the ways that members of other cultures perceive the world differently from the way that they do, and place different interpretations on what they perceive. Also, they will bear in mind that there are few truly universal visual images, despite many valiant attempts to create them. As mindful intercultural communicators, we must strive to use visual communication with the same level of awareness and sensitivity that we bring to our use of verbal and non-verbal communication.

References

1. Steve W. Chu, "Using Chopsticks and a Fork Together: Challenges and Strategies of Developing a Chinese/English Bilingual Website," *Technical Communication*, 46:2 (1999), 206–19.
2. Elizabeth S. Helfman, *Signs and Symbols Around the World* (New York: Lothrop, Lee & Shepard, 1967), pp. 23–54.
3. Paul Martin Lester, *Visual Communication* (Belmont, CA: Wadsworth Publishing, 1995), p. 70.
4. James Mangan, "Cultural Conventions of Pictorial Representation: Iconic Literacy and Education," *Educational Communication & Technology*, 26 (1978), 245–67.
5. Mangan, p. 246.
6. Colin M. Turnbull, *The Forest People* (New York: Simon & Schuster, 1961).
7. John W. Berry, "Ecological and Cultural Factors in Spatial Perceptual Development," *Canadian Journal of Behavioural Science*, 3 (1971), 324–36.
8. Christopher Miller, "Building Illusions: Culture Determines What We See," *Business Communication Quarterly*, 59 (1996), 87–90.
9. Lester, 1995, pp. 62–3.
10. Ibid., p. 63–4.
11. Ibid., p. 64.
12. Ronnie Lipton, *Designing Across Cultures* (Cincinnati, OH: HOW Design Books, 2002), p. 117.
13. David Chandler, *Semiotics: The Basics* (London: Routledge, 2002), p. 15.
14. Stuart Hall, "Encoding/decoding," in Centre for Contemporary Cultural Studies, ed., *Culture, Media, Language: Working Papers in Cultural Studies, 1972–79* (London: Hutchinson, 1980), pp. 128–38.
15. Richard Dyer, *The Matter of Images* (London: Routledge, 1993), p. 16.
16. Homi K. Bhabha, "The Other Question: The Stereotype and Colonial Discourse," in Jessica Evans and Stuart Hall, eds., *Visual Culture: The Reader* (London: Sage Publications, 1999), p. 378.
17. Lipton, p. 10.
18. Lester, p. 47.
19. Kaushiki Maitra and Dixie Goswami, "Responses of American Readers to Visual Aspects of a Mid-Sized Japanese Company's Annual Report: A Case Study," *IEEE Transactions on Professional Communication*, 38 (1995), 197–203.
20. Lester, pp. 159–60.
21. Michael Evamy, *World Without Words* (New York: Watson-Guptill, 2003), p. 14.
22. Ibid.
23. Ibid., p. 34.
24. Ibid., p. 76.
25. Ibid., p. 103.
26. William Horton, "The Almost Universal Language: Graphics for International Documents," *Technical Communication*, 40 (1993), 682–93.
27. Charles Kostelnick, "Cultural Adaptation and Information Design: Two Contrasting Views," *IEEE Transactions on Professional Communication*, 38 (1995), 182–96.
28. Lipton, p. 10.
29. Horton, p. 688.
30. Lipton, p. 11.
31. General Mills, *The Story of Betty Crocker*, informational pamphlet, July 2002; Advertising Age, "The Advertising Century: Top 10 Ad Icons – Betty Crocker" www.adage.com/century/icon04.html, accessed October 21, 2005.
32. Charlene R. Johnson, "Communicating Health Care Issues to Nonreaders in Developing Countries," master's thesis, University of Washington, 1991, quoted in Nancy L. Hoft, *International Technical Communication* (New York: John Wiley & Sons, 1995), p. 265.
33. Edward T. Hall, *The Silent Language* (New York: Anchor/Doubleday, 1981), p. 108.
34. Lipton, p. 161.
35. Ibid.

36. Ibid., p. 125.
37. Henry Steiner and Ken Haas, *Cross-Cultural Design* (New York: Thames and Hudson, 1995), pp. 143–7; 209.
38. William Gribbons, "Visual Literacy in Corporate Communication: Some Implications for Information Design," *IEEE Transactions on Professional Communication*, 34 (1991), 42–50.

8   Mass Communication

Views of Mass Communication

In September of 2005, Denmark's largest newspaper, the Jyllands-Posten, published twelve anti-Islamic cartoons many of which illustrated the Islam Prophet Muhammad and associated Islam with terrorism. Referring to the cartoons as "islamophobic," the majority of the Muslim community found the cartoons offensive, especially because they belonged to a group that already felt marginalized in the Danish society. As controversy escalated, Flemming Rose, the cultural editor of Jyllands-Posten, claimed that the publication of these cartoons treated Islam exactly as they treated Christianity, Buddhism, Hinduism, and other religions. Jyllands-Posten also stated that the publication was a contribution to a critical debate of the Muslim community and that, with the cartoon's publication, Danish Muslims could begin their integration into the "Danish tradition of satire." Nevertheless, Danish Muslim groups held public protests and spread knowledge of the Jyllands-Posten's cartoons in the Islamic World. The aftermath of the duplication of the Jyllands-Posten's cartoons included outbreaks of both peaceful and violent protests in many countries, especially those that are predominately Muslim. On March 23, 2006, an Egyptian newspaper titled Al Ahram published the article "Islam and Globalization," which argued that the perspective of the cartoons' critics was simply blasphemous for Muslims. Further, the publication of the cartoons was cited as evidence of Western ignorance about Islam, as well as the historical significance of Western imperialism in the region.[1]

To take a closer look at a contrasting view on the controversy, on February 9, 2006, an article in The Economist entitled "The Limits to Free Speech-Cartoon Wars" summarized the main arguments of the cartoons' supporters. The central argument of the cartoons' supporters claimed that the cartoons demonstrated the issue of Islamic terrorism and that such publications were based on a legitimate exercise of the freedom of speech in modern democracies. Finally, the authors noted that the intention was not to target the Muslim community since similar cartoons about other religions had also been published in the past.[2]

Although both sides of the controversy have developed strong arguments, Paul Reynolds' BBC article, "Cartoons: Divisions and Inconsistencies," discussed the gaps in perspectives of Muslim and Western cultures. Reynolds attempted to reconcile some of the inconsistencies within each of their arguments regarding the controversial Muhammad cartoons. The article briefly demonstrated that both sides of the argument were imperfect, inconsistent, and possibly hypocritical. Despite the inconsistencies on both sides of the argument, the long-lasting effects of the crisis will be remembered best by the words of the Danish Prime Minister, Anders Fogh Rasmussen, who referred to the aftermath of the Jyllands-Posten's cartoons as Denmark's worst international crisis since the Second World War.[3]

With the powerful presence of *mass-media* sources reaching large-scale audiences and the rapid growth of multimedia sources available online, mass-media industries have had a prevailing effect on culture and communication, as well as public political views, domestically and internationally. Mass-media industries are media businesses categorized into at least eight different forms: television, radio, newspapers, magazines, recordings, movies, books, and the internet.[4] The presence of media sources will multiply as the death of distance and improved local and global connections have an increased effect on the future of communication technology. Geographic distance will no longer be the determinant of electronic communication, and location will be a lesser influence within the business world since technological advances will allow companies to locate any screen-based activity globally. Technological improvements assist developing countries by increasing their ability to market products to developed countries through online services, while developed countries were once alone in domestically producing such services.[5] With the increase of electronic communication technologies, countries are becoming more interdependent, which spreads the ideas, aspirations, and lifestyles of different persons throughout the globe. With significant growth in the future of information technology, one can tell that the effects of intercultural communication on international relations will be more defined than ever. With the media serving as the key source of sensory stimulation, knowledge gain, and need satisfaction, the environmental nature of today's media technology will lead to cultural globalization and/or cultural imperialism. It is important to note that the widespread effects regarding the mass-circulation of information have both positive and negative dimensions. For instance, the way in which the professional media cover global information on an event, a foreign leader, a group of people, or a nation has a substantial impact in shaping public opinion and the world view of the political elite who construct foreign policy. Moreover, the dependence of society on various forms of media is more apparent than ever in our world of developing communications technology. This dependency on media illustrates the extensive soft power that the professional media holds and its impact on the knowledge of diverse audiences. The professional media plays an important role in connecting and transferring lifestyles and cultures between people from different nations worldwide. Because of this dependency on media, most citizens take the ideas and messages of the media's portrayal of other countries as factual. And since media is the primary distributor of cultural information to global audiences, most citizens gain their knowledge of other societies from the international media. For example, most US citizens develop their knowledge of other countries through new sources. According to a recent Pew poll, Americans still "heavily rely" on television as their main source for news.[6] According to industry estimates, the average American adult spends more than half of his/her waking hours using some source of media, thereby spending more time during the day interacting with the media than sleeping.[7] With their reliance on mass-media communications, the majority of Americans passively consume information produced about other nations as factual and inherit the mistakes and biases communicated by media sources.[8] To borrow the words of Stan Lee, the co-creator of the comic book character Spider-Man, with "great power must also come great responsibility."

Today, using the technological revolution, mass media instantly spreads influential information and news globally. The moment an editor approves an article for posting, a writer for a media service makes the article available globally in seconds.[9] Along with the technological growth in computers and telecommunication, both the power and responsibility of the media have greatly increased. Traditionally, modern media has adequately identified international conflicts, but has not necessarily suggested solutions.

Beyond any exceptional initiatives of conflict remedies, the media's main focus has been problem identification. For example, in 1938, the *Superman* creators Jerry Siegel and Joe Shuster, both children of Jewish immigrants, identified Hitler as a global problem and saw the need for a global solution. They used a form of media to identify the global problem by having their superhero fly over Hitler and Stalin to the League of Nations to highlight the dictators' crimes against humanity. A greater number of people throughout the world expect that the media goes beyond identifying problems by proposing solutions. In fact, many demand that the media should play a greater role in promoting different solutions, especially in the area of conflict resolution where it would educate and enlighten the public by highlighting the need for peace and welfare.[10] Others recognize the role of media as a tool for conducting foreign policy and public diplomacy.[11] On the whole, the professional media has a significant influence on the policy preferences of viewers. For example, a survey of North Carolina citizens revealed that the issues that citizens believed to be of greatest political importance were most likely the issues featured recently in newspapers and on television.[12] However, our analysis in this chapter recognizes that while mass media influences public opinion, it does not directly participate in policymaking or consider policymaking to be consistent within its commercial interests.

In the following sections, we explain the relevance of intercultural communication, and the plight of mass media in international relations, along with a discussion of the implications of the media's impact that may contribute to international conflicts. For this chapter, we define conflict as a state of disharmony between incompatible or antithetical persons, ideas, or interests: a clash, not necessarily involving violence. This definition allows us to better comprehend the significance of the mass media: to illustrate how their international production of information affects intercultural and international relations, to provide an opportunity for a critical analysis, and to consider appropriate suggestions for the socio-political problems that the media may identify.

Media and People

To better understand how media impacts people, it is necessary to see how the public is affected by media preferences. Numerous elements and strategies have been adopted by the mass media to gain an influential power position and impressive communication ability. Throughout this chapter, we illustrate and discuss these elements and strategies, and explain how they affect the public opinion in the United States and abroad.

The Elaboration Likelihood Model (ELM)

The media has many avenues to communicate its message to the public, as seen in the many new communications technologies available. It gains its vast power due to the way humans begin to process information and the routes to persuasion. The mass media recognizes how humans are persuaded through the processing of information, and uses this knowledge to its ability. For the purposes of this chapter, *persuasion* is defined as the process by which one's perspectives or behaviors are influenced by receiving a message. First described by Richard Petty and John Cacioppo in 1986, the Elaboration Likelihood Model (ELM) is considered a comprehensive model of persuasion. With the ELM having specific persuasion strategies that are outlined in relation to the source, message, channel, and receiver, this effective theory is used by public speakers and the professional media in order to captivate their audience worldwide.[13]

To note, humans have two memory banks, the working memory where information is processed and assessed, and the long-term memory, where information is stored to nodes in the brain to access them in the future. However, accessing nodes in the long-term memory takes time if they are not regularly accessed.[14] Accessing long-term memory nodes proves to be somewhat more time-consuming. As noted in the ELM model, there are two routes to persuasion: *central* and *peripheral*. In central route processing, which takes place in the long-term memory bank, persuasion is accomplished by the quality of the argument, therefore this type of processing is based on high message elaboration. In sum, in the central route processing, the receivers or viewers are motivated to engage in effortful information processing of the message or information provided by the information source, or medium. The other route of persuasion known is as peripheral route processing. In this route of persuasion, the receivers are influenced by other factors besides the quality of the message given. In these instances, the receivers are persuaded by the message or by the speaker's credentials or attractiveness."[15] With this route of persuasion, various sources of media, most notably television news networks, can capture their audience through the use of attractive anchors or state-of-the-art graphical presentations on screen, as well as three-dimensional images and logos for the beautification of network news programs and websites. In peripheral route processing, humans take cognitive shortcuts, which respond at a top-of-the-head level to relatively subtle cognitive cues, rather than storing gross amounts of information in the brain nodes.[16] Using this theoretical knowledge of communication, the media works creatively in constructing cue words and sound bites; displaying the message which in one or a few words immediately grabs the viewer's attention through an external cue. With external cues such as "9/11," viewers can immediately recall information in their long-term memory more quickly as they label the nodes. By adding additional words or headlines to "9/11," the media can construct a hard-hitting message as the viewer undergoes short-term persuasion. Obviously this system of storage, along with its routes of persuasion, can serve as a problem in some events. By creating interesting headlines by intertwining cue words such as "Osama Bin Laden" and "the Middle East," a viewer may take the peripheral route and begin to associate the two as one in the same, as the particular headline consistently appears in an attractive graphical format on-screen. The same theory applies to the use of "Saddam Hussein" and "Iraq" when the two cue words are constantly being meshed together in a single message. Now, in the eyes of many people, especially in the US, whenever the name Osama Bin Laden is mentioned, the human brain automatically associates "terrorist" with the Middle East and the symbol of "9/11," which may establish negative emotions. This is one place where the news media has the responsibility to clearly distinguish between nations and their menaces. Overall, the menaces and events tend to serve as the necessary symbols for faster recollection of the information.

Symbolic politics

The notion of *symbolic politics* is another important aspect of how media communicates with the public. Communication in itself is symbolic, for humans are naturally creatures of symbols and with our symbol-making nature we can participate in interaction with other cultures. However, in terms of intercultural communication, it is important to note that symbols are subjective. Gudykunst and Kim bring light to the subjectivity of symbols with their idea that "symbols are only symbols because a group of people agree to consider them as such." Therefore, fallacies and misassumptions may spark conflicts by the way they are introduced by the media. For example, in Europe and America, most citizens view communication as a way to interact in order to accomplish tasks. However, people in Japan, Taiwan, and China believe that information is "internalized by most members of culture." Moreover, in the cultural setting, the rules, values, and tradition of a culture all have a powerful impact on the communications system as a whole.[17] Therefore, political symbols often evoke and mobilize human emotions. These intense emotions historically energized some of the most devastating social, political, and religious conflicts. According to media coverage, virtually all wars that involved the US have been fought around rallying symbols. The Boston Tea Party symbolized the colonials' rebellion against the British rule in favor of American liberty and self-determination.[18] Pearl Harbor symbolized the beginning of American involvement in World War II for protection of peace and freedom, and ended the traditional policy of isolationism in favor of constructive engagement. Additionally, Japan's image was that of the military aggressor, which was made clear with their attack on Pearl Harbor, an attack that led to the United States declaring war on Tokyo. More recently, "9/11" symbolized the war against terrorism in Afghanistan. Political symbols, however, may cause serious problems if they are not presented fairly and properly.

Furthermore, visual symbols or figures play a large role in human emotions, and the same images elicit different emotions in different citizens.[19] For some individuals, images of religious figures (e.g. Buddha, Ayatollah Khomeini), or radical political leaders (e.g. Hitler, Stalin, Castro), or events (e.g. World War II, Vietnam War) are emotional experiences (see Chapter 7). Again turning to the symbol of "9/11" and the constant footage of the attacks in New York, various types of emotions had surfaced, from sadness to anger and fear to hate. These emotions, in combination with a lack of worldly knowledge, topped with distorted media coverage, complete a perfect a recipe for a range of problems, from local harassment of Muslims to national disputes between Washington and others. Thus, the media repeatedly displays images, which in turn transplants symbols, and eventually forms human perceptions.[20]

Political perceptions

The mass media also has the ability to contribute to the formation of one's political perceptions. A political perception refers to the process by which people develop impressions of the characteristics and positions of other nations and their foreign policies. This perception has implications for domestic public opinion as well as international opinion. These perceptions may also develop through culture and social experiences, personal understanding, and impact of institutions. These perceptions can be formed through sources of media that influence people during the crucial adolescence and adulthood periods.[21] The media's influence on perceptions is also supported by the fact that an overwhelming majority of people, for example in the United States, obtain their worldly information from television news, therefore the media unquestionably form some impressions. In addition, with the cultivation theory, the effect of mass communication is addressed in the theory's claim that television cultivates a world view that is inaccurate, but that viewers may assume reflects real life.[22] This theory can be applied when the media cover politics inaccurately or the way in which they slant news coverage to the best interests of a particular political party. In regards to the interpretation of political news by the media, in 1989 there was a sharp increase of 68 percent of the general public in the US who believed that the media tended to favor one side of the story.[23] However, political perceptions influenced by various sources of mass media also have a major international impact in addition to a domestic one. For example, the global governance position of the US has led to the international significance of American presidential campaigns in the mass media.

The perceptions can be derived through external stimuli or through the internal perceiver.[24] Since the global media often influences the political perception of the international public, it is necessary to identify two perception factors. To identify which set of factors have more influence, it is necessary to recognize whether the perceptions originate from the image of the candidate (*stimuli*), or judgment of the candidate through their own values, attitudes, and beliefs (*internal perceiver*). Most people's candidate selection process has grave implications, due to the fact that most research seems to indicate that political perceptions stem from external stimuli.[25] However, external stimuli may also be rooted in one's social group.

Group conflict

The media plays a critical role in determining cultural values and norms; and it also has impact on how we view other cultures internationally.[26] As individuals, we evolved into a particular social universe, or a specific category in which humans develop and form groups. For instance, some broad social classifications include: racial categories (e.g. "black" or "white"), ethnic or racial categories (e.g. "American" or "Japanese"), or religious categories (e.g. "Christian" or "Islamic"). The establishment of such categories is necessary for an individual to deal with the overwhelming complexity of the natural and social universes. The media assists people in choosing a social universe by associating their identity visually with a specific social universe category. The majority of such categories represent social groups, and individuals establish memberships in groups.[27]

With the establishment of specific social groups or categories, sub-categories of such broad classifications of groups include the previously mentioned *in-group* and *out-group*. For the purpose of this discussion, the in-group is defined as the existing social universe, which is considered socially acceptable by the majority. The out-group is the imported social universe and is predominantly considered not socially acceptable by the majority. Due to the divergent nature of having an in-group and out-group, one assumption of in-group/out-group conflict is that all people will strive to achieve a positive social identity. One of the methods that allow individuals to help manufacture a positive social identity is via the process of discriminatory comparison of the in-group with some relevant out-group.[28] This discriminatory process is visible in today's media, where misinterpretations, fallacies, and racial distortions are present.

The international media is not above and beyond "in-group polarization." In fact, the media is not a neutral monitor, as it follows discursive models in which conflicts are often framed according to Western conventional wisdom.[29]

The problem arises when the media products, along with their (hidden or obvious) social universe (e.g. Hollywood movies), are exported to other nations, which are in transition to accept the new foreign social universe. This process, also known as an *intercultural contact*, has major implications, including cultural imperialism.[30] The process of cultural change resulting from the contact between two groups is known as *acculturation*, which has many implications specifically regarding ethnic identity and the social universe.[31]

Ethnic identity refers to an individual's subjective feelings belonging to a particular group.[32] If the dominant social universe is contrary to an individual's ethnic identity, then one may defect from the old group and join another. As noted earlier, all members wish to belong to a positive social group. If a group is viewed negatively or is not socially acceptable, then it may wish to defect, practice social creativity, or establish social competition. The important aspect for this topic is the choice to establish a social competition against the out-group. The in-group may attempt to achieve positive distinctiveness by direct competition and confrontation with the high-status out-group. This confrontation may usually manifest itself over material assets or collective political action, such as insurgency.[33] A prime example of such clashes is found between the Westernization (or what some call Americanization) process and the resisting

Figure 8.1 Through an outreach program put together by Kevin LaChapelle's www.PowerMentor.org and Jose Villaescuza's Youth Group in San Diego, Califonia. They were able to donate soccer balls to be given to the children of Iraq by 1LT Sion Brannan's platoon. This photo is a clear illustration of two distinct groups both identifying with a congruent aspect in their cultural universe. Beyond their regular functions, the soldiers also act as American cultural ambassadors in the Iraqi community. Such images of the American soldiers are powerfully portrayed by the media.

local groups in the Middle East. This topic is discussed in more depth later in the section about cultural imperialism (see "Cultural Imperialism" later in this chapter). With a greater comprehension of how humans process information, it is now feasible to discuss where media gains its influential abilities.

Media and Power

Media and power (meaning soft power) go hand in hand. We generally define *power* as the ability of one to change the behavior of another without the use of violence. Our definition is general enough to bridge diverse definitions of power, while it is specific enough to distinguish between power (the ability to persuade) and the out-right usage of violence (or force). Moreover, this definition considers two important points. First of all, its main focus is behavior, a general term referring to action, speech, and thoughts of an individual, a group, or a nation. Furthermore, our definition takes a neutral position by using the term "change," as opposed to "improve" or "worsen."

Knowing that the media has no military capabilities or official political authority, one may ask: what sources of power do the media occupy? Here the distinction rests on tangible and intangible conceptions of power. Western media is an example of intangible power, that is, media influence is often attributed to cultural impact (soft power), as opposed to military advancement (hard power). There are many factors involved here, but in this chapter, it is important to discuss media's power through communication, and then address some of its influential capabilities.

POWER CHECK
Media and Soft Power

When a person thinks of power, they often think of large corporations and governments. Soft power is described as people power or the power to be heard. International relations expert Joseph Nye coined the term 'soft power' to describe the power of a country to attract and persuade. This source of influence is not explicitly tied to financial or military might. Soft power is derived from culture, ideas, and policies, none of which are the sole elements of a nation-state.

Soft power occurs when people collaborate and share to form a community. During the 1980s and 1990s, columnists and journalists were considered to be people with power. Both columnists and journalists had easy access to have their voices heard. Today, anyone with access to the internet can be heard. The age of the internet has made collaborating and sharing to form a community easier than ever before. The ability to link to the internet and download without concern for a nation-state's borders has resulted in a new pattern of circulating information, images, and spheres of influence. When people form together as a result of a commonality such as a message, belief, or idea, they are always stronger as a community than they could ever be as an individual.

In the 1980s and 1990s talk and radio show hosts were often the source for the general public to be heard. With the popularity of the internet more people are gaining a source of power. While the news media is structured so audience participation is at will, participatory media lets everyone be heard. Self-publishing tools on the internet now allow a meeting of the minds of the general public. As a result of the digital divide and continued censorship practices, a certain sector of the public continues to lack the power to be heard.

This new form of communication and exchange has reshaped the idea of power and who has the ability to obtain it. The new "citizen media" has caused the traditional news media to change the way news and information is presented to the public. The citizen media will continue to play a role in shaping and reshaping the way information is provided to the public.

Source: We Media website, http://wemedia.com; iFocus website: www.ifocus.org.

Intercultural communication

As we have discussed, the mass media determines who is communicated to and what is communicated.[34] Through the entertainment industry, popular culture is brought into the international arena where most democratic societies have relatively limited restrictions on reports and productions.[35] The free press can be detrimental to some traditional and social values, but it is also a critical factor in the establishment of contemporary democratic states, where individual rights have the highest priority. Problems occur when the media communicates controversial ideas or events to other nations.

In modern society, media is a major means of public communication, referred to as a symbolic process by which people create shared meanings.[36] More important, as stated in "A Comparative Study of Students' Attitude and Behavior in a Cross-National Setting," intercultural communication occurs when people creating shared meanings have different cultural perspectives and values.[37] Many of the distortions of transnational media may arise from misunderstandings.

To have a better understanding of the term, it is necessary to distinguish between *multicultural* and *intercultural*. The term multicultural refers to nations that have diverse cultural groups, usually as the result of immigration, while the term intercultural refers to the diversity among individual nations. It is essential to understand the difference between these notions. The separate cultural facets among people are significant for a society and allow one to distinguish one ethic group or nation from another one.

Another important notion for consideration is cultural assimilation, when people adopt the cultural values of another nation after they have moved to a new country. Many nations have dealt with immigrants by formally or informally requiring them to assimilate to the majority or dominant culture, sometimes referred to as monoculturalism.[38] Those states that accept immigrants have not all equally succeeded in treating them well. France currently faces ethnic and religious tensions because of the impact of strict secular French laws forbidding any religious symbols in schools. Also, until recently, the government of the Netherlands faced cultural criticism because of their notoriously difficult citizenship test and bureaucratic system.

As a result of the mass media and the advances in communication technology, however, cultural assimilation has gone global and it is not limited to the framework of one particular nation anymore.[39] In fact, the effects of the process of globalization are changing the very definition of the term "cultural assimilation," as it takes assimilation to the international level. Increasingly, the impact of mass media originating in the United States is streaming across the globe and causing effects similar to when diverse immigrant groups entered the US, as our history shows. Although this is not recognized as the contemporary US policy of "multiculturalism," it is still affecting our foreign policy abroad, and it is a major factor worth considering and studying.[40] Since media gains more power through contemporary modes of communication, we now turn to examine some of the influential powers of the mass media.

Media's influential powers

The media has the ability to influence people's behavior in the form of thoughts, speech, or action. Obviously, the media has no coercive might or political

Figure 8.2 Caption: Lt. Col. Patrick Thibodeau, serving with the Indiana National Guard's 76th Infantry Brigade Combat Team as project manager with the Iraqi-based Industrial Zone at Joint Base Balad, talks on October 19, 2008, with Hiadel Hassah, project manager for an Iraqi business that refurbishes shipping containers on base. I-BIZ is a designated secure area on a coalition base where a variety of Iraqi businesses can operate, and the Indiana National Guard spearheaded the I-BIZ effort at Joint Base Balad (U.S. Army photo by Staff Sgt. Jim Greenhill). Here the cross-cultural cooperation results in business development.

mandate, but this is not a source of weakness, since the power of the pen has increasingly out-maneuvered the ability of the sword, especially in the post–Cold War era. This is not to say that military might does not count anymore, but to suggest that military might is not necessarily the solution to all of the world problems. This situation is in contrast to that of the ancient times, when disputes were often resolved by military or physical campaigns; it was assumed that the winner enjoyed the divine blessing, and ordinary people accepted the result as the will of God or nature without a question. The power of media can also be depicted in what is called the Control Revolution. The Control Revolution is the ability of the media to influence the consumption of mass audiences with communication technologies. Furthermore, with the rapid growth in information technology, the control of government and major markets does not have to depend on face-to-face communication, now control is reinsured in bureaucratic organizations, telecommunications, and international communication with the new mass media. In addition, according to the "control function," information processing and communication are intertwined and, therefore, to be able to control a society — through interpersonal communication to international communication — will be "directly proportional to the development of its information technologies."[41]

Nevertheless, our contemporary world is very different, since people around the globe are increasingly questioning authority (even in the most religious societies), do not always follow blindly, and prefer justice over peace. The evidence for this is the increasing number of mass revolutions against the militarily strong dictators (e.g. in China, Cuba, Iran, Mexico, and Russia), since the start of the twentieth century. If military might was the answer to all present conflicts (as in the past), then there would not have been a Palestinian-Israeli conflict, considering that the military balance is overwhelmingly in favor of Israel. Today's underdogs do not accept forced solution. They value and pursue justice more than peace. People around the world want a more comfortable life, similar to the one in the West, mainly as the result of what they have seen, read, or heard, which were all produced and broadcast by the mass media.

The media has the ability to aim its message to whomever it wishes globally, and it has the ability to produce whatever information supports its interest.[42] The first aspect of media influence is the ability of *selective process*. The media has the capability to select whatever information it desires to produce. In addition, individuals use *selective perception*. When individuals face discordant content, they will choose what they find acceptable.[43] For example history showed that it was unlikely that pro-Vietnam interventionists would have chosen to watch media programs that had discussed the senselessness of the Vietnam War.

Priming is another influential power of the media. The media cannot control what the people think, but it can project what they should think about. The *priming theory* suggests that media images stimulate related thoughts in the minds of the audience. This is similar to and associated with another power of the media: agenda setting. *Agenda setting* is described as a process through which public figures and important events help to shape the content of the media. The audience's ranking of what they consider to be the most important issues tends to match the amount of coverage that the media gives to those particular issues.[44]

Similarly, media also has power associated with public diplomacy, which has traditionally been a power at the hands of governments. However, with the advances in communication technology and lesser legal restrictions, the news media can set their own agenda, and form international opinion through public diplomacy.[45] Public diplomacy is the idea of "direct communication with foreign peoples, with the aim of affecting their thinking, and ultimately, that of their governments."[46] It most often takes the form of cultural or academic exchange programs, public relations campaigns in foreign mass media, dissemination of print or video materials, or governmental or non-governmental sponsored radio or television broadcasting to foreign markets.[47] Pubic diplomacy is now empowered with the internet, so it is difficult, if not perhaps impossible, to censor its delivery system — media. This power, however, may have negative consequences, such as perception gap, or a perceptual screen, which will be discussed in detail later.

A fairly new power of the media is "digital delivery."[48] With the digital revolution, modern media may send information to people quickly, efficiently, and with any degree of accuracy. Advances in communication technology have made the online press a very powerful entity. These advances now allow the media to instantly deliver a message to millions of individuals via the internet. Additionally, many individuals use the internet as their main news source.

Furthermore, digital delivery provides the media with an "interactive" environment. The senders and receivers can exchange information back and forth simultaneously. With this method, opinion data can be collected much faster, making polls more accurate than ever before. This interactive environment or a two-way communication differs from traditional one-way communication and provides the media with even greater power and legitimacy.[49]

Last but certainly not least, another influential power of the media is the ability of political mobilization. The media has the capability to mobilize the public on a specific issue, whether it is to go to war, address economic problems, or influence an individual's opinion.[50] The media also has an educational role, which is an important factor in political mobilization.

Empowering Individuals

With the multimedia revolution and the growth of interactive media, the consumers and receivers of media now have power in terms of influencing the media as well as other members of society. Anyone with access to the internet can use the online world to create news-breaking stories of their own. The most dominant example of empowering the general public can be seen with the blogosphere. The blogosphere can be thought of as an interconnected social network on the internet in which various "bloggers," or members of the online community, post their own articles, commentaries, and suggestions. Another excellent example is empowerment of the Iranian protestors by Twitter technology following the 2009 Iranian elections. With this, individuals throughout diverse societies can post their thoughts, feelings, and criticisms freely for the whole world to see. This online interaction has many implications in terms of the media and those who are considered to be the professional media or "controllers." Not only can the professional media read firsthand what their mass audiences worldwide think of their news coverage and programs, marketing businesses can receive feedback about their products. Audiences can communicate feedback or reinforce demand for specific products and the professional media can receive their audience's preferences to better accommodate their viewers.[51]

However, on the flip side of the idea that new communications technologies are empowering individuals, it is important to consider what is called the "digital divide." For the purposes of this discussion, the digital divide is defined as those who have access to technology, such as the internet, versus those who do not have access. Government officials and academic researchers now agree that there is a digital divide; National Telecommunications and Information Administration's (NTIA) 2000 figures show that white and Asian American households with 46 and 57 percent access respectively have double the access of African American and Hispanic households. With a world increasingly dependent on electronic technologies, such as the personal computer, or communication technologies, such as the internet, it is obvious that anyone without access to these technologies is being left behind in the dust. To elaborate, because computers and the internet are used today by society as if it were second nature, relying on computer software, such as Microsoft Word, to complete school papers or reports for a professional job, the digital divide has more serious implications besides not being in the in-group. With our dependence on using technology, not only for personal reasons, but in academic and professional life, having technological skills and knowledge of basic computer software is key in acquiring professional, decent paying jobs.

Overall, the research studies describing and measuring the digital divide report two assumptions: that not introducing computers to various parts of the world worsens inequality and that access to cyberspace life gives freedom from certain social constraints to its users.[52]

MEDIA IMPACT
Blogs: The New Form of Media
The blogosphere has marked a new age for journalists and reporters. With the abundance of online social networks, the mighty blogosphere is alive and well in today's world and it is growing more powerful as the days pass. The professional media are not alone anymore in making and

breaking the news of the world; anyone who has something to say is able to bring their information, criticism, and commentary to the table. With the blogosphere's augmentation of information at a high-speed rate, it continues to intimidate journalists throughout the world, especially in America. Journalists and newsrooms throughout the country are now forced to gain their audience members' trust by articulating, "this is what we did, this is how we did it, and this is why you should trust us."

Anyone with a stable internet connection can play the role of a critical blogger. Bloggers can act not only as watchdogs of the professional media, but as newsmakers and newsbreakers. To display the power of the blogosphere, take into consideration the observation that was posted by "Buckhead," on Freerepublic.com. The unidentified person questioned the truthfulness of former CBS anchor Dan Rather's report about President Bush's service in the National Guard. His claim was that the font used in the memo was not even invented during the time the report was supposedly issued. The memo, purportedly written by Lt. Col. Jerry Killian, was evidently released in 1973 when only typewriters were used. Furthermore, the memo's font did not surface until the 1990s when word processing programs and personal computers were accessible. Buckhead's simple blog, posted within seconds of the release of Dan Rather's report, catalyzed further investigation of Rather's sources, breaking news media coverage, and caused millions of people to question Rather's credibility as a professional journalist. Although this example, illustrating the blogosphere's increasing power, is of greatest dominance in the recent past, other examples illustrating the power of the blogosphere are also apparent. For instances, Jessica Cutler's blog describing her "busy sex life" with references to the White House and Congress, as well as former Senate Majority Leader, Trent Lott's controversial comments at Strom Thurmond's 100th birthday. Both of these examples attracted attention in the national news: Cutler was fired and Lott lost his job as Senate Majority Leader at the same time many bloggers had argued for him to resign.

Overall, it is clear that the critical, watchful eyes of the blogosphere will be constantly watching during the present time and in the near future. As a well-known role of journalists has always included holding the powerful accountable, a subdivision of this role has been created. This new role includes the viewers holding the journalists accountable for the stories they produce, aggressively questioning the truthfulness of the news given to the public and examining the sources.

Source: Kelly McBride, "Journalism in the Age of Blogs," Poynter Online, www.poynter.org /latest-news/everyday-ethics/25545/journalism-in-the-age-of-blogs, posted September 16, 2004, accessed December 22, 2010.

The News Media

The news media both informs and educates our citizens as well as other nations.[53] Some even say that the news media is being used as a massive public diplomacy tool, while conspiracy theorists would argue that the media is politically motivated beyond its economic interest. Wars, revolutions, and political conflicts are often preceded by "info-attacks," disinformation, psychological warfare, and propaganda campaigns.[54] This is visible in almost all news media agencies. During the 1994 genocide in Rwanda, the international media failed to accurately report the events occurring in the country. In *The Media and the Rwanda Genocide*, several journalists discuss and provide details regarding the discrepancies between reports they provided to the news media and the stories eventually reported to the public. The international news media provided inaccurate information to the news audience. While the news media reported on the civil war, it failed to accurately report the events of the genocide occurring in the country. In early April 1994, many Western news organizations were reporting that the violence was waning. Instead, the violence was increasing at an alarming rate. During the same time, international news organizations grossly under-reported the numbers of Tutsi deaths in the country.[55] The disinformation and lack of accurate reporting played a crucial role in the public opinion and public diplomacy with regard to the genocide in Rwanda. The information or disinformation transmitted by the news media generates public opinion and collective action in both democratic and authoritarian societies alike.

The power of the media in real terms, however, lies in highlighting the situations, not solving them.[56] The news media becomes really dangerous when it solitarily initiates a public campaign to protect either its own interests or those of a particular interest group (also known as a pressure or private group). To defend such special and private interests, the news media can be represented in print or electronic forms, like radio, television, or the internet.[57] As discussed earlier the new "digital delivery" provides the news media with additional powers, which are protected by constitutional rights in the West. But the media must also feel the other side of this coin, which is responsibility and accountability.

Lately, the news media has undergone mass reconstruction in many parts of the world, beyond the Western democracies.[58] Until recently, the Middle East and Eastern Europe used to have a great deal of restrictions on their media. Fortunately, the process of democratization in Eastern Europe has led to the growth of free and independent media from Russia to Bulgaria, as well as from the Czech Republic to Romania. Nevertheless, there are still many challenges for free media, such as Moscow's trial of the NTV (Russian Independent TV) owner. Similarly, many Middle Eastern nations are enjoying freer and more independently minded media from Iran (especially during President Khatami's terms) to Qatar and from Morocco to Egypt. A fine example is Al Jazeera, which provides not only frank political critics of the many local regimes, but also represents indigenous cultural and political perspectives of the Middle East to the world. In his frequent trips to the Middle East, Houman observed that Al Jazeera's role has solidified in such a fashion that it also tactfully criticizes the Qatari regime without fear of persecution. Al Jazeera should also be given credit for extensive reports on the suffrage of the underdog individuals and groups in the region, especially before most international media began to cover such stories for a Western audience.

In today's world, with the rapid growth of communication technology, the mass media is very complex and includes diverse sources of interaction. However, it is important to focus on the three modern categories of press in current media revolution. The three modern categories of press are: the *mobilized* press, the *loyalists'* press, and the *diverse* press. The mobilized press is defined as absolute state-controlled press. The loyalists' press agencies are defined as privately owned, yet may be censored or self-censored and generally support the national governing elite. The diverse press are those who comprise the greatest degree of freedom. From the 1950s through the early 1990s, the mobilized and, to a lesser extent the loyalists' press, were the dominating paradigms within Eastern Europe. The change may be accredited to the end of the Cold War, limited economic and political liberalization within the regions, developments in broadcast technology, and increased globalization; all of which have led to a rise in a new and more competitive news paradigm. All of the above developments have set in motion a "liberal commercial television" style of press coverage, which contrasts sharply with the still somewhat dominant paradigm of "traditional government controlled" press. This new style can be characterized as a diverse press that is privately owned and predominantly transnational and that utilizes a "Western style" of journalistic practices, news content, and delivery model. With the knowledge of the three types of press comes the news media's greatest contribution.[59]

Public diplomacy

Among all powers of the media, public diplomacy has a special place. As stated earlier, public diplomacy is the idea of "direct communication with foreign peoples, with the aim of affecting their thinking, and ultimately, that of their governments."[60] The notion of public diplomacy is similar to that of public relations, which is defined as the art and science of establishing and promoting a favorable relationship with the public, just as public diplomacy is public relations among nation-states.[61]

Amid forms of media, television news that combines picture and sound in traditional culture-dominated societies typically comprises immense amounts of propaganda.[62] In the study of anti-Americanism, factors such as cultural, religious, and value divisions are viewed as the primary source of negative perceptions of the United States. In fact, some claim that nations dominated by traditional cultures typically have aggressive national news agencies, such as the Saudi Press Agency.

Oftentimes, the media uses public diplomacy as a power tool. A *perception gap* occurs when an inaccurate belief is partially created by the foreign news media. The media creates an inaccurate belief, many times intentional, for its own benefit and to lead to the success of its particular agenda.

The "Al Jazeera effect," as some call it, can serve as an example of the media's depiction of negative beliefs. The Al Jazeera effect is similar to the so-called "CNN effect" that was the focus of much speculation during the 1990s. The Al Jazeera effect refers to the network's comprehensive and graphic on-the-ground coverage of the US war in Afghanistan. Some argue that Al Jazeera raised the level of negative sentiment against the US in the Muslim world and created pressure on many Muslim governments to act against US policy in the region.[63]

The news media also characteristically differ from region to region.[64] In some areas, the media displays more power than others. The Middle East has a very complex social structure, and it differs culturally from Western society, as does its media.[65] One example of difference is in the media objectivity, in terms of the typical Western balanced reporting of conflicting perspectives. Media objectivity is viewed in another way in the Middle East, where certain sensitive topics are not subjected to such balanced scrutiny, such as Pan-Arabism and Islam.

Thus, from a Western perspective in the Middle East, one may not find "objectivity" when it comes to pan-Arab consensus. Moreover, it may also seem as though Middle Eastern news sources tend to have a "hyperpolitical" nature. Pan-Arab news coverage places the focus on security and political news, rather than its social or human interest topics, which are covered more by Western news agencies. With the constant subjectivity of news agencies, a "perceptual screen" is likely to develop, as individuals are expected to use their underlying predispositions as a screen, accepting only those considerations featured in the news that are congenial to their own preconceived attitudes, rejecting aspects of the news that are not.[66] It is also imperative to consider that most predispositions are developed as a result of previous experience with media products and preexisting beliefs that form in an individual's social universe.[67]

Cultural stereotypes in the news media

One negative aspect of any news media is how stereotypes are depicted. It is well established that the sociopolitical environment or social universe affects news media, and vice versa. Such an environment may mold people's perception of social and minority groups.[68] Like the rest of the world, American history illustrates that perhaps the most unfortunate aspect of news media is the misrepresentation of certain minority groups. Representing small out-groups, the minorities are often recognized by the news media on issues such as crime, violence, riots, and social unrest. As discussed earlier, the out-group may resort to social competition in pursuit of justice. As a result, members of minority groups may resort to disruptive events such as demonstrations and violent protests, and receive coverage only in a negative context by news media. The social universe significantly affects not only most interactions within any given society, but also behavioral patterns of individuals, organizations, and institutions. The media is influenced by the social universe, whose changes influence media in the way it covers issues, groups, and places.[69]

During the news production process, the perceived newsworthiness of different issues is invariably influenced by the perception of journalists and editors of the target audience, including their expectations and reactions. In the US, the media's target audience has traditionally been the white middle class.[70] Therefore, the media's target audience is the in-group or the majority. The target audience affects the reporting of out-groups, influences the choice of events covered, and the rhetoric or definitions used in the coverage of the event.[71] For example, this particular stereotype suggests the white middle class are typically viewed as law-abiding citizens, who are affected by problems created by minorities or out-groups.[72] The media not only portrays out-groups in a negative light, but due to the manner in which humans process information, the media actually shapes minority opinion. In the United States, the Hispanic minority is often viewed as "laid-back" due to their cultural history. In the Hispanic culture, it is not uncommon to take a break for several hours in the afternoon before returning to work. While many Americans believe they only work a few hours a day, in reality, they return to work until seven or eight o'clock in the evening. This notion is known as the "ultimate attribution error," since people tend to attribute undesirable behavior of out-group members to their "internal" or dispositional traits, but tend to attribute undesirable behavior of in-group members to characteristics of the situation. The news media is no exception to this rule, is not immune from such errors, and is exposed to the same internal or dispositional traits as typical citizens.[73]

The psychological notion of subconscious or "implicit" stereotyping rests on the idea that people hold a variety of beliefs and perceptions that influence their behavior but of which they are normally unaware.[74] So out-group observers may witness that newscasters and editors make racial misinterpretations regularly. These stereotypes are typically built upon one's social universe via development and education.[75] These subconscious stereotypes are not typically hostile, violent, or aggressive, but they still transmit fallacies into an editor's work. In Gilens' study, he recognized that the news media consistently portrays poor blacks more negatively than poor whites, and that these negative representations of poor blacks were also more distorted than the representations of non-blacks.[76] Moreover, among poor people pictured in newsmagazine poverty stories, only half as many blacks as non-blacks were identified as working (12 percent of blacks compared with 27 percent of non-blacks). With regard to employment, newsmagazines portrayed the image of poor blacks more negatively than that of poor whites. In reality, poor blacks are somewhat less likely employed than poor whites, but the difference is modestly 12 percent (42 percent for blacks compared to 54 percent for non-black poor).[77]

It is easy to determine the implications of this development on a global scale. Ultimately, subconscious stereotypes are the main focus of cultural, racial, and religious stereotypes by the media at the global level.[78] The social stereotypes are sometimes so strong that even when some media editors display the fallacies, they are labeled as very liberal or radical in their attitudes towards out-groups. In reality, the editors might have no deep understanding of their reported distortions. Subconscious stereotypes not only appear in professional news reporting, but also they unambiguously occur in the entertainment industry, to which we turn now.

The Entertainment Industry

Although the nature of news media is fairly self-explanatory, that of the entertainment industry is not as clear. As a result of the media's educating and informing tasks, it can easily distort the information or message presented to the audience. The entertainment industry's impact is more gradual, while the information or message is stronger in content and has a higher degree of legitimacy for many people. The entertainment industry creates popular culture, which is exported globally and invades the cultures of other nations. To fully understand its significant impact, the following section encompasses a discussion of the main elements of the entertainment industry: film and television, books and magazines, and recordings.[79]

Film and television

Film and television are intricate players in exporting American culture aboard.[80] Film and television industries have developed over the years, consistently improving their effectiveness and quality. From the *Three Stooges* to *Survivor*, the television industry has shown a wide variety of genres. The movies and television shows are mirror images of the society that creates them and project underlying political, religious, or social themes. Themes are topics of discourse or discussion, and are the most powerful aspect of the cinema.[81]

Contrary to the claim that the American film industry is a cultural threat to other nations, some nationalistically minded individuals argue that the dilemma with the film industry is its foreign ownership, like Sony Pictures Entertainment and 20th Century Fox.[82] These two companies represent 34 percent of the movie industry, which is more significant than other American media businesses. However, foreign ownership also means easier access to overseas markets. In fact, one of the strongest American exports is movie sales abroad. This accounts for about one-third of the movie industry profits.

In the West, it is imperative to recognize that media in general and the movies in particular are profit-driven businesses, with a "target audience." Typically, the media attempts to reach the target in-group through social competition against an out-group. Such social competitions bring visible distortions to television and film. These distortions are observed by the out-groups when American film and television programs are exported to foreign markets. This may force the out-group to defect from their group and join the in-group, accept the challenge of social competition, or rebel against the system.

The mega-movie *Titanic*, which portrayed a young love story in the Western cultural context, may easily represent the social rebellion of one class against the status quo and accepted social order in more traditional cultures. For instance, in the Persian Gulf region some believe the fiasco caused by one princess falling in love, escaping her native country, and eventually marrying an ordinary American GI as a local example of the anti-status quo social rebellion projected by typical American movies. With advanced technology, one does not need to go to a theater to see such movies since they are now available via the internet, video, or DVD.

Books and periodicals

Books have very limited censorship in Western democracies. They provide the most extensive social underlying themes, which in reality are not really hidden from the eyes of an observer. Political pamphlets were popular in the 1700s, such as Thomas Paine's *Common Sense*, which argued for independence from Great Britain. These writings were influential in demonizing Great Britain. Similarly, nowadays we observe the same behavior in the writings of militant and radical Islamic leaders who demonize America, and urge their readers to denounce and fight the US.

The magazine industry is commonly viewed as perhaps the main source of popular culture. Magazines may also comprise underlying themes, but usually gear their message to cultural aspects of the in-group reader. Magazines easily have the ability to reflect trends and culture. *Glamour* reaches more than 2 million readers every month. This socio-political movement displays the massive power of the magazine industry. In comparison to other print media, magazines are targeted more towards a particular audience. Many magazines are geared towards women, who are the majority population in most countries. As a result, print media fuels social competition in the US and abroad.[83]

Radio and recordings

Among many types of media, the producers, distributors, and exporters of music generally have the most freedom in spreading their messages via songs. Music is considered an art, and is not restricted by most governments, even the authoritarian ones. Music can comprise strong political messages, such as the music of bands like Rage Against the Machine, songs such as "American Idiot" by Green Day, or strong cultural messages such as those contained in country music. With the internet and MP3 files, music can be downloaded and listened to across the globe within seconds.

Nevertheless, there are differences in this regard around the world. Downloading music is a larger phenomenon in Europe than in the United States. In the 2003–2004 period, there were about 8 million users of the popular music file-sharing service Kazaa in the US, compared to about 9 million in Europe.[84] In Africa, radio (which is often considered to be the poor man's tool) is the main information source for both entertainment and news.[85] In many parts of the globe, radio is also the most commonly used form of communication to spread propaganda and public diplomacy. Returning to our example of the 1994 Rwanda genocide, the local radio station was the main tool used in order to spread propaganda throughout the country, propaganda that promoted violence and the killing of the Tutsi population. The Hutu government used the popular local radio station (which usually played "pop" music) to broadcast a message of hate and violence against the Tutsi population. The Hutu government went so far as to use the local radio station to direct the Hutu population to kill their Tutsi relatives and neighbors. The radio can also access global listeners in addition to the national audience. Furthermore, radio programs are able to impact children as well as the illiterate population, since the radio can easily reach them and reading is not required in order to understand the message.[86]

Political mobilization

With an understanding of the entertainment industry, now we turn to discuss its powers, one of which is the ability to mobilize. Political mobilization is essential to the health of any society, including the democratic ones. In larger democracies, however, political mobilization may be difficult to achieve. In order for individuals to mobilize politically, they must become emotionally involved.[87] As explained earlier, symbolic politics have implications for human emotional involvement. Symbols such as the 9/11 attacks on the World Trade Center and the Pentagon are clear motivational factors. Through film, television, books, and magazines these symbols are displayed by visuals. Visual information (e.g. pictures, images) presented in magazines, films or other aspects of the entertainment industry constitute an important underused and underestimated information resource.

Since the human brain processes information by the use of shortcuts, the media and entertainment industries utilize audiovisuals that have proved to be exceptional impact tools. The human brain extracts valuable information from audiovisuals more quickly and easily than from verbal sources. Visuals provide a less complicated and error-free grasp of information, and better emotional involvement. The use of audiovisuals in some forms of media falls short of the medium's potential to serve as a vicarious political experience and to offer benefit from the intimacy of the involvement.

The distortions through visuals may certainly impact the foreign-policymaking process by the elite in addition to ordinary citizens' opinions about international issues. In this regard, the notion of "audiovisual stimuli" plays a significant role when it comes to media distortions. The human brain is far more adept at extracting information from audiovisual stimuli than from verbal stimuli. Verbal stimuli are processed serially, one verbal unit at a time, whereas visual stimuli are processed simultaneously. This provides the reader or viewer with a more sufficient approach to information processing. Unlike the ability to process verbal messages, the ability to process visual information develops early in life. Therefore, youth and illiterate adults can learn from visual information with ease.[88]

This gives the leaders in less developed countries, where there is higher illiteracy, more power and the ability to take advantage of the segment of the population that cannot read but is easily influenced by visuals. This is currently the case in Venezuela where the authoritarian regime of Hugo Chávez focuses on the poor population to win their support. However, visuals are often used effectively by both authoritarian leaders in the developing world or elected officials in the developed countries attempting to sway public opinion. With greater emotional involvement comes greater political mobilization.

The film industries everywhere, especially in Hollywood, have expertise in dramatizing events, as practice makes perfect. Recently, visual imagery and advances in special effects have brought the entertainment industry to the same level of projecting reality as the news media clips of current events, especially in terms of the power of persuasion.[89] Our emphasis on the power of visuals, however, does not mean to discredit audio information, such as radio. Poorer nations with little access to television and cinema still use radio as the dominant tool to spread their message.[90] Moreover, it is not fair to give credit only to the entertainment industry for their ability for political mobilization, since popular culture also has such a capability. Now, we turn to a discussion of the popular culture.

What is Popular Culture?

Popular culture, or pop culture, is the vernacular culture that prevails in a modern society. The content of popular culture is determined in large part by industries that disseminate cultural material, especially in capitalist systems where commercialism prevails. All aspects of both the entertainment industry and news media (e.g. film, television, and publishing industries) are carriers of pop culture. Nevertheless, popular culture cannot be limited to a description of the aggregate product of industries; instead, it is the result of continuing inter- actions between the industries and ordinary people who use their products or services. There is "primary" and "secondary" popular culture: the first is related to mass products; and the second is associated with local reproductions.[91]

Popular culture is constantly changing, and aspects of it are specific to place and time. Pop culture often acts like social currents and eddies, in the sense that a small group of people may have strong interests in an area where the mainstream popular culture is partially aware.[92] It is important to note that items of popular culture typically appeal to a broad spectrum of the public and because of the cultural phenomenon they produce, items of popular culture usually spread from one society to another. Some argue that broad-appeal items dominate popular culture, simply because profit-oriented companies plan and sell pop culture goods and services to maximize their own profits, as they initiate or add to the broad appeal of such items.[93] We must emphasize that the capital-intensive entertainment industry and news media, especially in the West, are profit-centered businesses, and by directing popular culture, they maximize profits. That is not necessarily the case in the developing countries, where most capital investments are in public hands.

Traditionally, critics argue that popular culture tends to be superficial. Cultural items that necessitate lavish experience or educational value rarely become items of popular culture.[94] Moreover, items that have a business value, such as mobile phones, can become an integral part of the pop culture beyond their original purpose. For instance, many young mobile phone users developed their own social value of instant and constant communication with the family and friend circles even in the absence of an emergency. The perceived need to be constantly connected leads many youth to keep their creatively decorated mobile phones on, even when they are in a classroom environment that requires full attention and concentration. To avoid distractions in classrooms, it is not uncommon that many instructors request that students turn off their mobile phones before the lecture begins. On the negative side of this need for constant communication, there is evidence that frequent mobile phone usage, a fine example of a pop culture item, is often a major source of driving distraction for youth who are involved in car accidents.

Origins

Popular culture has multiple origins, of which a principal source is the entertainment industry, which makes a significant profit by inventing, broadcasting, and selling cultural materials. Such products include music CDs, movie DVDs, television shows, radio programs, video games, books, and so on. In recent years, the growth of movie merchandizing and product placement has significantly contributed to the commercialization of pop culture. In fact, movie merchandise is often a big business, especially after mega-movies like *Star Wars*, *Titanic*, *Harry Potter*, or *Spiderman*. In recent years, product placement, especially in movies and TV shows, has gained an important commercial and pop culture position. Many look forward to seeing which make and model of car is used in the next James Bond episode.

Another source of popular culture is the socialistic elements, which replace the traditional notion of folklore with the newer understanding of the social universe. The socialistic aspects are very common in any language. Jokes and slang have momentous involvement in popular culture. As stated earlier, the internet provides a new channel of social universe transmission, and thus has given renewed strength to this element of popular culture. The socialistic element of popular culture is heavily engaged with the commercial aspects.[95] The suppliers of commercial culture are fully aware that the public has its own preferences. It is not easy to predict which cultural items would be successful in sales, but the suppliers always try to prepare for the next ingredient of popular culture.[96] The beliefs and opinions about the products of commercial culture are often spread by word of mouth, social universe, and the media, all of which are interrelated. Meanwhile such beliefs and ideas are modified in the transmission process, as they move from in-group to out-group.

A more critical source of popular culture is the set of specialized communities that provide the public with facts and information about the world. The facts and information provided by these specialized communities are frequently accompanied by their own opinions and interpretations.[97] The news media and experts are unofficial agents of the distribution of pop culture globally. The work of experts and scholars is extracted by the media, which in turn process it, and then promulgate it to the general public. This is done by emphasizing "factoids" that have the power to astound the audience or marketing items with an intrinsic appeal.

Both scholarly facts and news stories are modified through social universe transmission, sometimes to the point of being transformed to outright distortions, known as fallacies.[98] For example, just before the Iraqi invasion of Kuwait in August 1990, Houman recalls the distorted news analyses by the major American national TV networks which were emphasizing the lessons of the Vietnam paradigm, that the US should not get directly involved in another regional conflict in a far land, which could become a graveyard for thousands of American soldiers. Moreover, they were mistakenly highlighting the notion that Saddam Hussein was only projecting his power, and was not really interested in capturing Kuwait. This was highlighted because his army had not established formal lines of supply near their common border, as European and American historical military experience suggested. The media's distorted analysis was based on a simple but fundamental error: Kuwait's geographic vulnerability toward Iraq did not require major lines of supply for an invasion. Such superficial analysis is only the result of a clear and comprehensive lack of understanding of regional politics by the news media, which is reliable in reporting events but is deficient in causal analysis of a crisis. Thus, one may argue that such distorted and shallow pop culture analysis is as superficial as any typical popular culture items sold for a profit. In other words, pop culture entails superficial products as well as ideas. This leads into the discussion of how popular culture affects individuals.

How does Popular Culture Affect Individuals?

Now that the nature, role, and impact of news and the entertainment industry is more clear, we turn to how media affects individuals and examine some of the major implications of popular culture. The media delivers popular culture to the doorsteps of ordinary citizens throughout the world. Thus, this discussion provides us with the opportunity to understand how popular culture personally affects individuals in reality.

International trust

Popular culture is a direct reflection of the norms and values of a society. People often build beliefs and knowledge about other countries on their own social values.[99] Citizens also base opinions about world affairs in part on generalized ideas about how much they can trust other nations.[100] This is referred to as *international trust*, and it influences how they perceive a specific nation, whether they endorse internationalism or isolationism, and if they favor specific foreign interventions. International trust is often evolved via personal experience and, more importantly, the contributions of mass media, which serves as people's prime international information resource. International trust is associated with the notion to give other nations the benefit of the doubt with an assumption that most countries are of good will and benign intentions. Popular culture regularly defines and describes such intentions.[101]

Social and political trusts and rationality

The idea of international trust is based on two other types of trust, *political* and *social* trust. Political trust is one's overall trust in government, whereas social trust represents general trust in other people as a whole. Ordinary people use these two forms of trust to shape heuristics, and materialize shortcuts in information processing, and political judgments. Citizens also use these types of trust as shortcuts to their knowledge of international environment, which was used to form their opinions about international issues and foreign policy.[102]

Traditionally, the *mood theory* would portray mass opinion about world affairs not only as uninformed but also as fundamentally irrational, and lacking any foundation in abstract reasoning.[103] Recent studies, however, lead us to believe that there is no reason to fear public opinion in the realm of foreign policy.[104] It is now understood that citizens behave according to the principles of "low information rationality," as they use information shortcuts to form political judgments, rather than engaging in more effortful information gathering and processing.[105] By doing so, the public is able to form "perfectly reasonable and even rational opinions of world affairs."[106] Since popular culture is a direct reflection of the social values of one nation, other nations may use it as a shortcut to form opinions, which can eventually impact the people around the globe.

The Global Impact of U.S. Popular Culture

Power and pop culture

For any nation, it is an enormous show of power to be able to define and determine what the most recent pop culture development is all about, in other words, "what is cool now." Without a doubt, the United States has the power to specify the components of popular culture and its timing.[107] This is not to say that all components of pop culture are 100 percent American made. In her study about cultural imperialism, Galeota argued that "America essentially samples the world's cultures, repackages them with the American trademark of materialism, and resells them to the world."[108] The concentration of media ownership during the 1990s enabled both American and British media organizations to gain control of many global news services and even enabled Hollywood to overshadow any rival industry around the world.[109]

For smaller and more vulnerable nations, this may be perceived as a national security threat, particularly if their culture does not share many values with that of the Anglo-Saxon world. In the current international arena, political rivals of the United States, including China, Cuba, India, and Iran are monitoring their citizens' access to the internet, and attempting to limit access to certain popular culture aspects of the West.[110] They fear that American pop culture will firmly establish American cultural values, such as individualism and capitalism, over their indigenous cultural and social values.

The internet is a superior tool of public diplomacy for the United States, since complete internet restrictions are impossible to impose on American supremacy over the World Wide Web. Some fear that the American capability to set the cultural values and use an effective delivery system may lead to cultural imperialism, which is targeted toward the international environment in order to control the behavior of others, and gain more even power.

Cultural imperialism

The idea of cultural imperialism is not a new idea, and both scholars and policymakers have talked about it since the end of World War II. In 1976, Herbert Schiller described cultural imperialism as "the sum of the processes by which a society is brought into the modern world system, and how its dominating stratum is attracted, pressured, forced, and sometimes bribed into shaping social institutions to correspond to, or even to promote, the values and structures of the dominant center of the system."[111] Cultural imperialism does not exist in a vacuum, but is a by-product of mass media, as it is usually mixed with economic, political, and security factors. For instance, with capitalism comes access to international markets, where US multinational corporations (MNCs) operate and they often care little for indigenous cultural values within such markets, since they do not traditionally support a materialistic world view that promotes and supports MNC profits.

In her essay, Galeota examined two reasons behind the hegemonic nature of cultural imperialism. The first reason is the desire to access foreign markets and the belief in the superiority of American culture. McDonald's has over 31,000 restaurants in over one hundred countries. Ironically, the largest McDonald's restaurant in the world is not even in the US, but in Moscow, Russia — the heritor to the Soviet socialist legacy and America's current main global political rival. For curiosity's sake, Houman visited the McDonald's restaurant in Moscow and noticed how the newfound capitalism and imported American commercialized culture changed the Russians in less than one generation. Nowadays, they do not wait in long lines for their ration of bread and vodka, but they order more food than they can eat and waste the leftovers, just like a typical American family at McDonald's would. Of course, the manner in which the "corporations" sell the alleged superiority of American culture is through excellent marketing. Marketers have always been able to successfully associate American products with modernity and quality in the minds of consumers throughout the world.[112]

The second reason for the US hegemonic nature is due to the modern business model for the stronger multinational corporations. Weak MNCs operate differently in different countries, adapting to the local cultures.[113] However, this takes time and eats up profits. The stronger MNCs will not respect local cultures and will force them to adopt the same agenda internationally. Modern corporations "pitch diversity" and this method allows them to exhibit citizens accepting American cultural trends internationally. Modern marketers attempt to portray their goods as products capable of transcending political, social, and economic differences to unite the world.[114] However, the marketers do not bend to local tastes; they merely insert indigenous celebrities or trends to present a façade of customization.[115] An example of marketers using celebrities to promote their products can be seen with the wireless service provider named T-Mobile™. T-Mobile™ marketed their T-Mobile Sidekick 3™ with the NBA basketball star Dwayne Wade or "D-Wade." Wade had a hand in designing the Sidekick™ and promoted the newer mobile phone in various advertisements. Other celebrities endorse the BlackBerry, which is particularly "in" right now (as of December 2010). However, Rothkoft argues, "the removal of cultural barriers through US cultural imperialism will promote a more stable world," one in which American culture reigns supreme as the most just, the most tolerant, the most willing to improve itself, and the best model for the future.[116] However, in a world of more than six billion people, this notion would be virtually impossible, even with the advances in communication technology. There will always be an out-group and an in-group, and there will always be differences in our social universes.

With the knowledge of how humans process information, how diverse cultures communicate, and how media has its own interests beyond its occasional incompetence, it is apparent how the mass media may contribute to negative opinions of other nations or groups. For the implications of this situation, the in-group/out-group theory is relatively inclusive. It is evident that group conflict is natural in human discourse. Whether consciously or unconsciously, the dominant social universe may attempt to overrun or dominate the lesser out-group in a society. The social universe of a dominant culture, like America's, may be transplanted into other social universes through the powers of the mass media. The news media plays a major role in the process of transplanting social universes via public diplomacy among its other powers.

Our discussion clarified how the media may contribute to international and domestic stereotypes, fallacies, and conflicts.

With a greater understanding of the entertainment industry, we analyzed its powers of political mobilization and popular culture. The former occurs in all societies, and it often requires the emotional involvement of the targeted audience. The latter contributes to formation of international public opinions, since people use popular culture as a cognitive shortcut to understanding the cultural values and norms of other nations. However, some nations may view popular culture formed by foreign values as a threat to their own national security and survival.

Our observations in this study lead us to better comprehend the conflict within and among nations. We discussed the role and impact that mass media and the entertainment industry have on other societies. On a lighter note, it is also possible for the media to play a more positive role in intercultural communication. In fact, the media can certainly be an influential actor in enlightening and informing the public opinion and helping people to understand the need for peace, justice, and overall social welfare.

The media can contribute to reaching a fair and an effective solution to many socio-political challenges by playing a proactive role in reporting national and international events. In fact, it can help the public and policymakers through an active discourse, constructive public debate, and open deliberation.[117] However, it is also important to emphasize that the nature of the mass media in the West is profit-centered, and constructing positive solutions to domestic and foreign conflicts are not necessarily profitable. After all, it is often the bad news that captures the headlines, not the good news.

References

1. "Islam and Globalization," *Al Abram*, March 23, 2006.
2. "The Limits to Free Speech: Cartoon Wars," *The Economist*, February 9, 2006.
3. Paul Reynolds, "Cartoons: Divisions and Inconsistencies," *BBC News*, February 13, 2006, www.simonbaker.me/2/hi/asia-pacific/4708216.stm, accessed November, 12, 2010.
4. Shirley Biagi, *Media/Impact: An Introduction to Mass Media*, 7th ed. (Australia: Wadsworth/Thompson, 2005), p. 9.
5. Erik P. Bucy, *Living in the Information Age: A New Media Reader*, 2nd ed. (Australia: Wadsworth/Thompson, 2005), p. 7.
6. "Survey Shows TV is Still Main News Source," *Wall Street Journal*, August 18, 2008, http://online.wsj.com/article/SB121902509874048617.html, accessed November 12, 2010.
7. Biagi, p. 3.
8. Martin Gilens, *Why Americans Hate Welfare* (Chicago: University of Chicago Press, 1999).
9. Robert LaRose and Joseph Straubhaar, *Media Now: Understanding Media, Culture, and Technology*, 5th ed. (Belmont, CA: Wadsworth/Thompson, 2008), p. 405.
10. S. Malik, "American Media and the War in the Balkans, A Pakistani Perspective," *Alternatives: Turkist Journal of International Relations*, 2:1 (2003), Spring, 140–57.
11. Erik C. Nisbet, Matthew C. Nisbet, Dietram A. Scheufele, and James E. Shanahan, "Public Diplomacy, Television News, and Muslim Opinion," *The Harvard International Journal of Press/Politics*, 9:2 (2004), Spring, 11–37.
12. James Wilson and John DiIulio, *American Government: Institutions and Policies*, 9th ed. (Boston, MA: Houghton Mifflin Company, 2004), p. 265.

13. Steven R. Brydon and Michael D. Scott, *Between One and Many: The Art and Science of Public Speaking* (Boston, MA: McGraw-Hill, 2006), pp. 31 and 351.
14. Shanto Iyengar and William J. McGuire, *Explorations in Political Psychology* (London: Duke University Press, 1993).
15. Brydon and Scott, pp. 31 and 351.
16. Iyengar and McGuire.
17. Larry A. Samovar and Richard E. Porter, *Communication Between Cultures* (Australia: Wadsworth/Thompson, 2001), pp. 24–7.
18. Iyengar and McGuire.
19. Doris A. Graber, "Say it With Pictures," *The Annals*, 546:1 (1996), 85–96.
20. Gilens.
21. Iyengar and McGuire.
22. LaRose and Straubhaar, p. 375.
23. Wilson and DiIulio, p. 267.
24. Gilens.
25. Iyengar and McGuire.
26. Jan Nederveen Pieterse, "Sociology of Humanitarian Intervention: Bosnia, Rwanda and Somalia Compared," *International Political Science Review*, 18:1 (1997), 77–93.
27. Iyengar and McGuire.
28. Ibid.
29. Pieterse, pp. 71–93.
30. Ibid.
31. Richard Clement, Susan Baker, Gorden Josephson, and Kimberly Noels, "Media Affects on Ethnic Identity Among Linguistic Majority and Minorities A longitudinal Study of a Bilingual Setting," *Human Communication Research,* 31:3 (2005).
32. Ibid.
33. Iyengar and McGuire.
34. Clement, Baker, Josephson, and Noels.
35. Nisbet, Nisbet, Scheufele, and Shanahan, pp. 11–37.
36. S. Littlejohn, *Theories of Human Communication*, 7th ed. (Belmont, CA: Wadsworth/Thompson, 2002).
37. H. Sadri, "A Comparative Study of Students' Attitude and Behavior in a Cross-National Setting," Poster Session, International Studies Association 2010 Annual Conference, New Orleans, February 17–20, 2010.
38. Ibid.
39. Clement, Baker, Josephson, and Noels.
40. H. Sadri, "Teaching and Learning about International Relations: Analysis of Cross-Cultural Issues," Poster Session, International Studies Association 2009 Annual Conference, New York, February 15–18, 2009.
41. James R. Beniger, "Technological and Economic Origins of the Information Society," in Erik P. Bucy, ed., *Living in the Information Age: A New Media Reader*, 2nd ed. (Australia: Wadsworth/Thompson, 2005), pp. 11–20.
42. Clement, Baker, Josephson, and Noels.
43. LaRose and Straubhaar, p. 450.
44. Ibid.
45. Nisbet, Nisbet, Scheufele, and Shanahan, pp. 11–37.
46. E. Gilboa, "Mass Communication and Diplomacy: A Theoretical Framework," *Communication Theory*, 10 (2000), 275–309.
47. Nisbet, Nisbet, Scheufele, and Shanahan, pp. 11–37.
48. Biagi.
49. Ibid.
50. Pieterse, pp. 71–93.
51. Beniger, pp. 11–20.
52. Jennifer S. Light, "Rethinking the Digital Divide," in Erik P. Bucy, ed., *Living in the Information Age: A New Media Reader*, 2nd ed. (Australia: Wadsworth/Thompson, 2005), pp. 255–63.
53. Gilens.
54. Malik, pp. 140–57.

55. Allan Thompson, *The Media and the Rwanda Genocide* (London/Kampala: Pluto Press/ Fountain Publishers, 2007), pp. 145–59.
56. Malik, pp. 140–57.
57. Biagi.
58. Nisbet, Nisbet, Scheufele, and Shanahan, pp. 11–37.
59. Ibid.
60. Gilboa, pp. 275–309.
61. H. Sadri, "Teaching and Learning about Globalization and Localization: Comparative Analysis of Cross Cultural Communication Issues," Poster Session, International Studies Association 2008 Annual Conference, San Francisco, March 26–29, 2008.
62. Nisbet, Nisbet, Scheufele, and Shanahan, pp. 11–37.
63. Ibid.
64. LaRose And Straubhaar, p. 405.
65. Ibid.
66. Nisbet, Nisbet, Scheufele, and Shanahan, pp. 11–37.
67. Gilens.
68. Ibid.
69. Eli Avraham, "Press, Politics, and the Coverage of Minorities in Divided Societies: The Case of Arab Citizens in Israel," *The Harvard International Journal of Press/Politics*, 8:4 (2003), Fall, 7–26.
70. Ibid.
71. Tuan A. Van Dijk, *News Analysis* (Hillsdale, NJ: Lawrence Erlbaum, 1988).
72. Gilens.
73. Ibid.
74. Ibid.
75. Iyengar and McGuire.
76. Gilens.
77. Ibid.
78. Ibid.
79. Biagi.
80. Ibid.
81. LaRose and Straubhaar, p. 405.
82. Biagi.
83. Ibid.
84. Ibid.
85. Elaine Windrich, "The Laboratory of Hate: The Role of Clandestine Radio in the Angolan War," *International Journal of Cultural Studies*, 3:2 (2000), 13 and 203.
86. Ibid.
87. Graber, pp. 85–96.
88. Ibid.
89. LaRose and Straubhaar, p. 405.
90. Windrich, 13 and 203.
91. W. L. Bennett, "The Uncivic Culture: Communication, Identity and the Rise of Lifestyle Politics," *Political Science & Politics*, 31 (1998), 741–61.
92. David Jackson, *Entertainment and Politics: The Influence of Pop Culture on Young Adult Political Socialization.* (New York: Peter Lang, 2002), p. 167.
93. Julia Galeota, "Cultural Imperialism: An American Tradition," *The Humanist*, May/June (2004), 22–4, 46.
94. Ibid.
95. Bennett, pp. 741–61.
96. Ibid.
97. Gilboa, pp. 275–309.
98. Iyengar and McGuire.
99. Galeota.
100. Paul R. Brewer, Kimberly Gross, Sean Aday, and Lars Willnat, "International Trust and Public Opinion about World Affairs," *American Journal of Political Science*, 48:1 (2004), 93–109.
101. Ibid.

102. Ibid.
103. Y. Robert Shapiro and Benjamin I. Page. "Foreign Policy and the Rational Public," *Journal of Conflict Resolution*, 32 (1988), 211–47.
104. Ibid.
105. Gilens.
106. Brewer, Gross, Aday, and Willnat, pp. 93–109.
107. Jackson, p. 167.
108. Galeota
109. Ibid.
110. Pashupati, Sun, and McDowell, "Guardians of Culture, Development Communicators, or State Capitalists? A Comparative Analysis of Indian and Chinese Policy Responses to Broadcast, Cable and Satellite Television," *Gazette*, 65:3 (2003), 251–71.
111. Galeota.
112. Ibid.
113. Levitt, Theordore, "The Globalization of Markets," *The McKinsey Quarterly*, Summer 1984, 2–20, www.vuw.ac.nz/~caplabtb/m302w07/levitt.pdf, accessed November 12, 2010.
114. Ibid.
115. Galeota.
116. D. Rothkopf, "In Praise of Globalization?" *Foreign Policy*, 107 (1997), 38–52.
117. Malik, pp. 140–57.

ISSUES IN INTERCULTURAL COMMUNICATION IV

Introduction: Opportunities for Ethical Global Engagement

Throughout the first three parts of this book we include many examples of opportunities for engagement in our global community. In this final part, we will offer more concrete guidelines for ethical global engagement because mindful intercultural communicators can make significant contributions to our global community. There are many organizations at the local, national, and international level that are designed to foster intercultural understanding and to promote peaceful coexistence among all the peoples of the world. Some of these organizations focus on offering medical aid and disaster relief; others are oriented around cultural and educational exchange; some focus primarily on justice and human rights; some address issues that are primary global concerns such as world health and the environment; still others are concerned with improving communication and understanding across national boundaries. Some of these organizations are intergovernmental organizations, while others are non-governmental organizations (NGOs) whose members span many nations. Some of the organizations are non-sectarian while others are under the aegis of religious organizations.

It is beyond the scope of this book to list and discuss all the many organizations that exist to foster global cooperation and understanding; it is truly heartening to realize so many organizations exist for humanitarian purposes that they could fill an entire book. Instead of attempting to offer exhaustive coverage of the many types of organizations that exist, we will discuss three types of organizations and offer some examples of each with the understanding that many more such organizations exist. Further, we will focus on those organizations most directly relevant to you, a college student in the United States. Again, we do so with the understanding that we are not attempting to discuss all the many organizations that exist around the world.

The three types of organizations and programs are: (1) medical and relief organizations; (2) cultural and education organizations and programs; and (3) human rights organizations. All the various types of organizations and programs are concerned with improving understanding among cultures. While there is clearly overlap among the various types of organizations and programs discussed, we believe that our categorization, although somewhat rudimentary, will help you get an overview of the myriad opportunities for global engagement available.

Medical and Relief Organizations

Médecins Sans Frontières (MSF) (Doctors Without Borders) is a well-known medical relief organization. It was founded in 1971 as a non-governmental organization "to both provide emergency medical assistance and bear witness publicly to the plight of the people it assists."[1] In addition to providing relief to individuals affected by armed conflict, epidemics, and natural disasters, MSF is committed to speaking out against "the causes of suffering and the obstacles to providing effective assistance."[2] MSF volunteers seek to raise public awareness of the plight of individuals who are at risk and to bring their concerns to the attention of governments, the United Nations, and other international organizations.

MSF is just one of many humanitarian relief organizations; these organizations are examples of international cooperation to address global challenges. Often these organizations are centered on one particular type of aid; for example, there are many organizations specifically concerned with helping children, like Save the Children, World Vision, and UNICEF. Save the Children was founded in 1932 by a group of concerned citizens who wanted to provide relief to the people of Appalachia during the Great Depression. The founders were inspired by the work of Eglantyne Jebb, a leader of the international children's right movement begun in England in 1919, who created the British Save the Children Fund. Today, the Save the Children Alliance is comprised of 27 national Save the Children organizations working in more than 100 countries to help change the lives of children and ensure their well-being.

Many humanitarian relief organizations strive to provide relief to those individuals affected by war or by natural disasters. Perhaps the leading intergovernmental organization offering humanitarian aid and long-term assistance is the United Nations (UN). The UN is a major provider of emergency relief, and also plays an important role in mobilizing action by governments and other relief agencies. The Organization for the Coordination of Humanitarian Affairs (OCHA), within the UN, "coordinates United Nations assistance in humanitarian crises that go beyond the capacity and mandate of any single agency."[3] Four UN entities play a role in providing relief; they are UNHCR, the United Nations Refugee Organization; the World Food Program; UNICEF; and the United Nations Development Program (UNDP).

Some organizations like Architects Without Borders, Architecture for Humanity, Relief International, Habitat for Humanity International, and Shelter for Life provide technical skills and construction materials to help build homes, medical facilities, and schools in areas devastated by hurricanes, floods, earthquakes, and other natural disasters. Other organizations are dedicated to relieving the suffering of individuals living in areas of armed conflict. One such organization is the well-known International Committee of the Red Cross. The Red Cross was founded in 1863 to reach out to those individuals affected by armed conflicts around the world.

Still other organizations focus on alleviating hunger and improving basic living conditions for individuals around the world. In addition to the UN's World Food Program, many other organizations are dedicated to ending world hunger. These organizations include Heifer International, an NGO whose mission is "[t]o work with communities to end hunger and poverty and to care for the earth."[4] Heifer International began as Heifers for Relief when Dan West, a farmer from the Midwestern United States, had the idea of providing families with livestock and training so that they would have the ability to feed their own children. Based on a philosophy of providing long-term resources and education rather short-term relief, Heifer International has assisted millions of families in more than 128 countries.

Cultural and Educational Exchange

Many governmental, intergovernmental, and non-governmental organizations provide opportunities for individuals and groups to participate in cultural and educational exchange programs. Some well-known programs include the Fulbright Program and Sister Cities International.

The Bureau of Educational and Cultural Affairs of the US Department of State has a Cultural Programs Division that carries out activities designed to share US cultural accomplishments with the peoples of other countries and to demonstrate the respect that the United States has for the achievements of other national cultures. American artists, musicians, filmmakers, and other specialists participate in these cultural programs and create presentations that seek to showcase American achievement in the arts at the same time that they promote intercultural understanding; such programs also promote greater awareness of global issues including human rights, the role of women in society, and environmental protection.

The Fulbright Program is sponsored by the US Department of State; its purpose is "to increase mutual understanding between the peoples of the United States and other countries, through the exchange of persons, know-ledge, and skills."[5] The Fulbright Program, established by the US Congress in 1946, is the largest international exchange program in the United States. The program offers US students, scholars, and professionals the opportunity to study, teach, and conduct research in more than 150 countries around the world, and provides "their foreign counterparts the opportunity to engage in similar activities in the United States."[6]

In addition to the prestigious Fulbright Program, there are numerous other opportunities for study abroad available to college students. The Council on International Educational Exchange offers study abroad programs for US university students as well as opportunities to teach abroad. The Council also provides practical training, internship programs, and seasonal work for international students in the United States. NAFSA, originally known as the National Association of Foreign Student Advisors, is currently known as the Association of International Educators. It is the leading professional association promoting the exchange of students and scholars to and from the United States. NAFSA is composed of approximately 9,000 members, most of whom are working on college and university campuses as study abroad advisors and as directors of international programs. There are a large number of opportunities for US students to study abroad; students who are interested in pursuing them can begin by consulting the office devoted to international education within their college or university.

As we mention in Chapter 1, Sister Cities International (SCI) is an example of international cooperation at the level of local government. The program was developed in 1956 by President Dwight D. Eisenhower during a White House summit on citizen diplomacy. The program pairs a city in one nation with a city of comparable size in another nation; the paired cities then decide together what type of activities they want to pursue. These activities may include humanitarian assistance, economic development, and youth exchanges. The purpose of the partnerships is to "increase global cooperation at the community/ municipal level, promote cultural and educational exchanges, and foster community and economic development."[7]

Human Rights Organizations

While most of the organizations discussed so far are concerned with human rights, some organizations are focused solely on issues of human rights and justice. Two well-known organizations devoted to human rights are Amnesty International and the Human Rights Watch. Amnesty International is a non-governmental organization that campaigns for internationally recognized human rights. Amnesty has a vision of "a world in which every person enjoys all of the human rights enshrined in the Universal Declaration of Human Rights and other international human rights standards."[8] (See Chapter 9 for a discussion of the Universal Declaration of Human Rights.) In order to make this vision a reality, Amnesty conducts research and takes action to prevent and end abuses of human rights including "the rights to physical and mental integrity, freedom of conscience and expression, and freedom from discrimination, within the context of its work to promote all human rights."[9] Amnesty International has over 1.8 million members and supporters in over 150 countries and territories in every region of the world, all united by commitment to ensuring human rights worldwide.

Human Rights Watch, like Amnesty International, is a non-governmental organization dedicated to protecting the human rights of people around the world. Human Rights Watch comprises more than 150 lawyers, journalists, academics, and country experts who investigate and expose human rights abuses around the world. HRW challenges governments and others in positions of power to end abusive practices and to respect international human rights laws.

Among those organizations who campaign for human rights there are some that focus specifically on the rights of women and children. These organizations include MADRE, the Global Fund for Women, the UN's Association for Women's Rights in Development, World Vision, and CARE. MADRE is an international women's human rights organization whose mission is "to address issues of health and reproductive rights, economic development, education, and other human rights."[10] Working together with community-based women's rights organizations, MADRE provides resources and training to promote long-term development and social justice for women and families. MADRE was founded as a result of the experiences of a group of women activists, poets, teachers, artists, and health professionals who traveled to Nicaragua in 1983 and witnessed the devastation wrought by the contra war. These women returned to the US determined to bring the plight of Nicaraguan women and children to the awareness of the US public. Their experiences led to the founding of MADRE, a women-led, women-run international human rights organization dedicated to finding alternatives to war and violence.

Other rights organizations strive to protect our environment and all life on planet earth. These organizations include Greenpeace, Friends of the Earth International, and the Sierra Club. Greenpeace International is a non-governmental organization devoted to protecting the earth from "the most crucial worldwide threats to biodiversity and the environment."[11] Since 1971 Greenpeace has campaigned against environmental degradation and has exposed environmental criminals and challenged government and corporations "when they fail to live up to their mandate to safeguard our environment and our future."[12] These organizations and others like them seek to protect our environment for future generations and ensure the sustainability of life on earth.

Ethical Global Engagement

We have given just a very brief overview of organizations dedicated to international cooperation for humanitarian ends in order to give you a glimpse of the many opportunities that exist for citizen diplomats to make contributions to our global community. We do so in order to challenge you to think about the roles you will choose to play as mindful intercultural communicators. You may wish to donate your skills and expertise to organizations like Doctors Without Borders or Architects Without Borders. You may decide to study abroad or to teach English in another country. You may support one or more organizations by volunteering your time or by helping raise funds. You may choose to participate at the local level in a program like Sister Cities International or by being part of a Global Summit on Citizen Diplomacy in your community. You may even join the ranks of the visionary individuals responsible for founding the humanitarian organizations we have discussed and countless others like them. We urge you to consider the ways that you can contribute to our global community.

However, even if you do not engage in international cooperation via a formal organization, you will still encounter many opportunities for ethical global engagement throughout your lifetime, both in the workplace and in your personal life. In every intercultural communication encounter that you experience, you have the opportunity to behave in a mindful and ethical manner. Global ethics present many challenges. When dealing with ethical issues on a global scale, we must go beyond the ethical code of our own culture to consider and respect the different values and beliefs of cultures other than our own. This final section of the book will help you prepare to meet the challenges of global citizenship. In Chapter 9, we discuss global ethics and offer guidelines for you to apply in intercultural encounters. Then, in Chapter 10, the concluding chapter of this book, we address the global issues that citizen diplomats must face today and offer guidance for practicing global citizenship with mindfulness.

References

1. Médecins Sans Frontières website, www.doctorswithoutborders.org/aboutus/index.cfm, accessed June 1, 2006.
2. Ibid.
3. United Nations website, www.un.org, accessed June 7, 2006.
4. Heifer International website, http://heifered.org, accessed June 7, 2006.
5. Institute of International Education website, www.iie.org, accessed June 7, 2006.
6. Ibid.
7. Sister Cities International website, www.sister-cities.org, accessed September 7, 2005.
8. Amnesty International website, www.amnesty.org.
9. Ibid.
10. MADRE website, www.madre.org, accessed June 9, 2006.
11. Greenpeace website, www.greenpeace.org, accessed June 9, 2006.
12. Ibid.

Ethical Issues in Intercultural Communication

9

In 2002 major chocolate companies, labor unions, and non-governmental organizations together with the UN International Labor Organization, established the "International Cocoa Initiative" to address child labor in West Africa, where much of the world's cocoa is grown. This initiative sought to eliminate abusive and forced child labor practices in the growing of cocoa.[1] However, despite this initiative and others like it, the UN International Labor Organization estimates that worldwide, some 179 million children are exposed to the worst forms of child labor, which endanger their physical, mental, or moral well-being.[2]

The World Health Organization (WHO) estimates that between 100 and 140 million girls and women have undergone ritual clitoral excision.[3] Efua Dorkenoo, a consultant on women's issues to the WHO, argues that the practice violates the fundamental human rights of girls and women and therefore should be banned globally.[4] Scholar Eric Winkel argues that if the practice is to be changed the change should be determined within Islam and not as the result of the imposition of external cultural values.[5]

As global citizens, perhaps one of the greatest challenges we face is how to develop a code of ethical behavior that can address the many diverse issues we are likely to encounter when communicating across cultures. Many ethical dilemmas face our global community; these include child labor, women's rights, corporate responsibility for the environment, political oppression, and many other issues that affect both our professional and personal lives. As mindful communicators, how do we know when to act to address global issues? How can we be sure that our actions are not motivated by ethnocentric values? How can we respect the beliefs and values of other cultures while still retaining the right to speak up for what we believe is right? Can we develop a code of ethics that can be applied to all intercultural encounters?

To maintain international ethical standards, there is fortunately a significant development in the international relations field, especially in the practice of the IR subfield of international law (IL). Up to World War II, a gap in the literature of IR and the shortcoming of IL application would allow individuals who had committed crimes against humanity to hide behind their governments' policies due to the responsibility toward their state. The approval of the Genocide Treaty and the Universal Declaration of Human Rights changed the playing field. Nowadays, individuals are subjects to IL application for their human rights crimes, as their governments have been. Thus, there is no room to hide behind government policy or military order for those who commit crimes against humanity. The establishment of the International Criminal Court and regional human rights courts are important moves in the direction of making individuals responsible for international ethical standards. The efforts to bring former Chilean strongman General Augusto Pinochet and the former Serbian President Slobodan Milosevic to justice are among other important steps in the right direction.

Ethical Issues and Culture

Ethics is a system of principles and rules used to guide the behavior of individuals and groups; these principles and rules are based on beliefs about what is "good" and "bad" in human behavior. Ethics are based on values, and since values are determined by culture, ideas about what constitutes ethical behavior differ across cultures.[6] Each culture has a unique set of standards for ethical behavior. These standards grow out of deeply held cultural values regarding what is "right" and "wrong," what constitutes virtuous behavior, and what is considered unacceptable within a particular society. For example, in some societies, the practice of ritual clitoral excision has been an important rite of passage; individuals who view the practice from outside those societies may find it problematic. However, it is equally problematic for any outside group to dictate their ethical values to members of another culture. It should be emphasized that in IR literature, a major point of international contention is formulating an expanded definition of "human rights" beyond the UN Charter and 1948 Declaration of Human Rights.

We have already discussed how different cultural values and beliefs can cause challenges for individuals wishing to engage in intercultural communication. In the realm of ethical issues, cultural differences have the potential to create many obstacles to competent communication among members of different cultural groups, both within and among nations. The topic of ethics in intercultural communication is a stressful one for people of all cultures.[7] The topic is stressful because individuals feel threatened when their beliefs about "good" and "evil" and about "right" and "wrong" behavior are challenged in any way. Most cultures believe that their ethical code sets a standard that is the "right" way for all people — in all cultures — to behave. Further, most cultural groups believe that their in-group is superior and behaviors of other cultures that differ from their own are "wrong," "inferior," or "immoral."

Ethnocentrism

Ethnocentrism is the belief that one's own culture or co-cultural group is superior to all others; that one's own nation (or co-cultural group) is at the center of the universe. The word ethnocentrism is taken from the Greek *ethnos* meaning "nation" and *kentron* meaning "center."[8] From this perspective, ethnocentric individuals will judge all other cultures in relation to their own. Ethnocentrism is a universal phenomenon. To some extent, all cultures believe in their own superiority.

Perhaps one reason for the incidence of ethnocentric thinking in all cultures has to do with its relationship to group survival. Within a given culture or group, ethnocentrism can increase group solidarity, cooperation, loyalty, and effectiveness. When a group is threatened, one way for it to maintain its identity is by differentiating itself from out-groups. Often, this bolstering of the in-group's identity is done through ethnocentric thinking — that is, by comparing the group favorably with out-groups and emphasizing the superiority of the in-group. Members of out-groups are stereotyped and judged harshly in order to strengthen the in-group's identity and self-esteem.[9] In times of war, soldiers may find it easier to kill the enemy if they perceive enemy soldiers as inferior to themselves and "less human." Such a dehumanizing attitude is revealed when animal names like "dogs" or "pigs" are applied to the enemy. During the Iran–Iraq War, a military commander referred to the enemy's defeat as "the annihilation of thousands of harmful . . . insects."[10]

However, while ethnocentrism may serve to help cultural groups survive, the survival of our global community as a whole is likely to be better served when we move beyond ethnocentric perspectives in our approach to intercultural communication. This is where "mindful communication" with people outside of one's own culture becomes a matter of survival. Being an appropriately active and mindful communicator has its benefits. There are several ethical issues that must be addressed whenever we encounter members of other cultures. These issues will be significant whether we are working or studying internationally or we are interacting with members of diverse cultures domestically. In our global community, we are all likely to encounter members of other cultures both in face-to-face and virtual encounters, in our professional and personal lives, in our families, in our communities, and in our travels. In any and all of these situations, ethical issues come into play at some level.

For mindful communicators, several ethical questions must be addressed when engaging in intercultural communication. When living in another culture, should an individual adapt to that culture's ethical beliefs or retain his/her own? What if the ethical standards of another culture clash significantly with one's own culture? In international business dealings, how do the parties involved decide whose code of ethics to follow? Should nations force members of diverse cultures living within their boundaries to give up their beliefs of "right" and "wrong" if they conflict with those of the majority culture in the nation? Should developed nations make their aid to developing nations contingent upon the developing nation's adhering to the developed nation's ethical standards? Most of these questions can be subsumed under the broad question: Should one set of ethical standards be applied universally across all cultures?

Ethical Issues and Power

Ethical questions are inherently questions of power, that is to say, ethical questions involve deciding whose standards will apply in addressing a given situation. For example, within a nation the majority culture's values are most likely to dominate that nation's ethical standards. In US history, there was a time when the white majority's code of ethics dominated society to the detriment of African Americans, who were not afforded the same treatment as white Americans. Because of its position of power, the majority culture is able to enforce its beliefs about "right" and "wrong" and about what is acceptable behavior and what is not. In some cases, the majority culture within a nation has used its position of power to exclude certain groups from the protection of the ethical code that applies to all other members of the culture. Extreme examples of such behavior can be seen in political oppression, slavery, and genocide. South Africa, Rwanda, and Darfur are all examples of societies that have excluded certain groups from protection under the majority culture's ethical code.

Moral exclusion

Morality is the conformity to a standard of "right" behavior within a particular society or group; morality relates to conformity to the values that underlie a culture's ethical code. *Moral exclusion* occurs when a society applies ethical standards of justice and fairness to members of dominant communities, but denies the same treatment to out-groups, who are seen as "nonentities, expendable, or undeserving."[11] In essence, moral exclusion relates to the question of "who is and who is not entitled to fair outcomes and fair treatment" in a society.[12] Moral exclusion allows members of some groups to be treated in ways that would be considered immoral if they were applied to members of the dominant culture or group. *Moral inclusion*, in contrast, is a stance that applies standards of fair treatment to all individuals across all boundaries, whether they are members of one's in-group or one's out-group. Such an approach can be extended beyond human beings to apply to all creatures on the planet. Some Buddhists, for example, would include not only human beings but all of nature in their moral community.[13]

Often political and social upheavals can lead to acts of moral exclusionism. For example, before the dissolution of the former Yugoslavia, Serbs, Muslims, and Croats in Bosnia were essentially part of one moral community. However, once the political upheaval began, with its vilification of ethnic groups, the members of the various groups began to exclude others from their moral community. As a result of this moral exclusion, members of the various ethnic groups began committing atrocities against one another — the very groups with which they had once peacefully co-existed. Moral exclusion also occurred in Rwanda between the Hutu and Tutsi tribes and led to the slaughter of 500,000 men, women, and children — mostly by machete. The extermination of the Jews in Nazi Germany and the Turkish genocide of the Armenians were the result of moral exclusionism. Other instances include the treatment of natives by colonizers, the treatment of slaves by slave traders and masters, and the politically motivated oppression of many peoples. Moral exclusion is based on a belief that the out-group members are somehow "less human" than members of one's own in-group, and therefore, are not deserving of the same treatment.

MEDIA'S IMPACT
Stereotyping of Arabs in the Media

Moral exclusionism occurs when a society applies ethical standards of justice and fairness to members of dominant communities, but denies the same treatment to members of out-groups who are seen as somehow less deserving and less human than members of the dominant culture. The media can play a powerful role in perpetuating stereotypes that fuel moral exclusionism within a culture. The American-Arab Anti-Discrimination Committee has expressed concern about the negative portrayals of Arabs in the media. Frequently, Arab women are portrayed as harem girls and belly dancers, and Arab men are portrayed as terrorists, oil sheiks, and marauding tribesmen.[1] In many popular films, like *Patriot Games*, *Death Before Dishonor*, *Navy SEALS*, and *Delta Force 3*, Arabs are portrayed as the villains.[2] Comic books, Saturday morning cartoons, and computer games also feature a great many Arab villains.[3]

Such depictions are particularly harmful when there is an absence of positive images of Arabs in the media. In "100 Years of Anti-Arab and Anti-Muslim Stereotyping," Mazin B. Qumsiyeh states that "[t]he Arab community in North America is vibrant and thriving . . . We are doctors, business people, engineers, scientists, judges, humanitarians, advocates for human rights, and in short a productive segment of the fabric of this great society."[4] However, the media rarely portrays Arabs and Arab Americans as average citizens — rather it continues to portray them as villains, as the enemy. In an article in the *Journal of Media Psychology*, El-Farra argues that the media has the power to change perceptions of Arabs and that "it is their responsibility to allow their audiences to form opinions that are free from the influence of bias and negative stereotypes."[5] A fair media portrayal of Arabs and Arab Americans will prevent the kind of stereotyping and prejudice that fuels moral exclusionism.

Notes

1. Marvin Wingfield and Bushra Karaman, "Arab Stereotypes and American Educators," March 1995, American-Arab Anti-Discrimination Committee website, www.adc.org/index.php?id=283, accessed November 5, 2005.

2. Mazin B. Qumsiyeh, "100 Years of Anti-Arab and Anti-Muslim Stereotyping," The Prism website, www.ibiblio.org/prism/jan98/anti_arab.html, accessed October 26, 2005.
3. Narmeen El-Farra, "Arabs and the Media," *Journal of Media Psychology*, 1 (1996).
4. Qumsiyeh.
5. El-Farra.

We can see the role that ethnocentrism plays in moral exclusionism in that if we perceive others as inferior it may become easier to exclude them from the same standards we apply to our own in-group. Further, if we believe that our own group is threatened we may be more likely to turn to ethnocentrism as a way to create social identity and solidarity. Of course, it is possible to protect one's own group without denying the essential humanity of others. However, ethical questions are complex because while on the one hand, we wish to treat all others with fairness, on the other hand, we must recognize and address significant differences among cultures in their beliefs about what is good and what is right.

Absolutism

Absolutism, often referred to as *universalism*, is an approach to ethics in which the importance of cultural differences is minimized, and the same standards are applied to all cultures. Such an approach may sound fair because everyone in the global community is judged by the same set of standards. Certainly it is a consistent approach to ethical questions across cultures. This approach is based on the belief that there are some ethical standards that apply universally to all cultures. This approach to ethics is espoused by the philosopher Immanuel Kant in his categorical imperative, which states "Act only on that maxim whereby you can at the same time will that it should become a universal law."[14] Kant believed that a code of ethical behavior should be based on principles that apply universally to all people.

The challenge of developing a universal code of ethics is a task that philosophers have struggled with for years. As with any set of rules or laws, there is the concern as to who decides what the universal ethical code should be. Who decides what behavior is acceptable and what is unacceptable? Historically, dominant cultures have the power to enforce their ethics on other groups. Today, most universally applied codes of ethics are "imposed ethics that rely heavily on Eurocentric moral philosophies to the exclusion of other cultural groups' voices."[15] An absolutist approach to ethics does not consider the fact that ethical principles are the result of cultural values, and that they differ widely from one culture to another. In contrast, the relative approach to ethical issues is based on the belief that it is not possible for any culture to judge the behavior of members of another culture.

Relativism

Cultural relativism states that evaluations of "right" and "wrong" behavior can only be determined within the context of an individual's culture and that an individual or group's actions cannot be judged by any outside criteria. Only members of a given culture can evaluate the behavior of individuals in that culture. Cultural relativism recognizes the importance of cultural values in shaping ethics. It also prevents ethnocentrism from interfering with ethical standards since it does not allow members of one cultural group to judge the actions of another. There is a problem with the relativist position, however, because when it is taken to an extreme it requires that we accept instances of persecution like the treatment of Jews in Nazi Germany and apartheid in South Africa. In both cases, and in many other examples of persecution, the cultural community in which these actions occurred accepted the behavior. Ultimately, the global community condemned the behavior; however, such actions would be accepted from a strictly relative view of ethics since they were not condemned by the cultural community in which they occurred.

Scope of the Issues

A mindful approach to intercultural communication is particularly valuable when wrestling with ethical questions. Both the universal and the relative approach to ethics have value, but neither one alone is sufficient to guide us in all of the many intercultural encounters we are likely to have throughout our lives; neither one is sufficient to address the many ethical issues facing our global community today.

Relative

As we have discussed throughout this text, when we study other cultures we should do so in order to understand, not to evaluate or stereotype them. As we appreciate the different values, beliefs, norms, and communication patterns of cultures around the world, we learn to appreciate each in the context in which it occurs. Just as we understand that the way our culture greets strangers or celebrates weddings or disciplines children is one way among many — not the "right" way, we also come to understand that different cultural values give rise to different beliefs about what is good and bad or acceptable and unacceptable behavior in society. Cultural relativism is based on the belief that each culture develops values that are most appropriate for its people in a particular place and time. The conduct of members of a given culture can only be judged by members of that culture. For this very good reason, from the standpoint of cultural relativism, we refrain from judging the behavior of members of another culture.

An important part of respecting another culture is to strive to understand its beliefs and values within the context of that culture rather than from the perspective of our own cultural values. When we communicate across cultures we may encounter behavior by members of other cultures that comes into conflict with our own deeply held code of ethics. We may feel uncomfortable with practices that we perceive as harmful to other human beings and as depriving them of their most basic rights. From our own cultural perspective, we may find it difficult to accept child labor, female genital mutilation, or persecution of various ethnic groups. Contextual relativism requires that we seek to understand the reasons that give rise to such practices. We will need to have an in-depth understanding of the social, historical, economic, political, and religious factors that have led to the development of such practices. However, once we have developed a full understanding of the context in which these practices occur, we may then determine that despite our respect for the uniqueness of cultures there are some practices that we still cannot accept. Further, we may feel that as engaged citizens of our global community we need to seek an ethical code that can be applied to all members of our global community.

Universal

David W. Kale has written extensively on ethical issues in intercultural communication and has suggested a basis for developing some ethical universals. Kale argues that the human spirit is the most basic commonality shared by people of all cultures. He states that we can find some universal values based on the human spirit and human dignity. The human spirit is that from which all cultures derive their ability to make decisions about what is "right" and "wrong." The guiding principle for Kale's universal code of ethics is "to protect the worth and dignity of the human spirit."[16] The dignity of the human spirit is ensured when all people are treated with respect and are given the opportunity to express themselves in their own unique ways. Further, Kale believes that all people wish to live in peace. He states that peace is a fundamental human value and that "a world where all cultures are living at peace with one another"[17] is an achievable goal.

Kale distinguishes between three levels of peace: *minimal peace*, *moderate peace*, and *optimal peace*. Minimal peace is "the absence of conflict."[18] This type of peace may only exist on the surface; for example, two nations may have hostility toward one another but may be refraining from conflict due to the intervention of a third party such as United Nations peacekeeping forces. Moderate peace is a situation where two parties involved in a conflict agree to compromise to achieve their goals. In this situation, both parties still feel irritation toward their opponents and believe that only their own goals are worthy. Finally, optimal peace is when two parties consider "each other's goals as seriously as they do their own."[19] In this situation, conflict may still arise, but during negotiation the parties involved will consider each other's goals as "worthy and deserving of serious consideration." Kale's universal code of ethics in intercultural communication is based on treating other people with

Figure 9.1 The absence of conflict may be the result of the intervention of a third party, like the UN peacekeeping forces shown in this photo. David Kale would describe this condition, in which peace exists only on the surface, as a minimal peace.

the same respect that we would like to receive ourselves and seeking points of commonality with them while at the same time respecting their uniqueness.

The United Nations Universal Declaration of Human Rights

In 1948 the United Nations proclaimed the Universal Declaration of Human Rights. The Declaration was preceded by the United Nations Charter, which defines the UN's procedures and operations. The United Nations was created after World War II, in 1945, by the victorious world powers. One of the primary purposes for the creation of the UN was to prevent conflict between nations and also to prevent the recurrence of the horrors of the Holocaust. In fact, a new category of legal offenses was created to address the war crimes committed by the Nazis — crimes against humanity. This new legal categorization came in response to the fact that that the genocide committed by the Nazis, although one of the most horrific crimes ever committed, was not a violation of any international or German law.[20]

The Declaration of Human Rights is based on the "inherent dignity" of all people and gives human rights precedence over the power of individual nations. It emphasizes the equal rights of all men and women to freedom, justice, and peace. The Declaration, which consists of 30 articles, is not legally binding but sets "a common standard of achievement for all nations"[21] to strive for. Although it is not a legal document, the Declaration has provided a standard of behavior for the global community and has been a valuable instrument for applying diplomatic pressure on nations that violate its principles. The Declaration has also served as the basis for non-governmental humanitarian organizations like Amnesty International.

However, despite the laudable goals of preventing conflict and protecting human dignity, the Declaration has still been criticized for taking a universalist approach to human rights. Before the Declaration was officially adopted by the UN in 1948 the American Anthropological Society warned that it would be perceived as presenting a notion of human rights based on Western European and American values. They expressed concern that the Declaration failed to account for cultural differences.[22] Since that time, the UN's Universal Declaration has been challenged on similar grounds. For example, in the 1980s Iran's UN ambassador repudiated the universality of human rights, saying that "conventions, declarations, and resolutions of the UN that are contrary to Islam have no validity in Iran."[23] Similarly, before the 1993 Vienna Conference on Human Rights, many Asian and Pacific states called into question the emphasis on individuality in the Western perspective, which shaped the Declaration.

While any attempt to set up a universally applicable code of ethics seems fraught with complexities, we do need to develop some guidelines from which to operate as ethical citizens of our global community. The impetus of the UN's Declaration was to prevent conflict and to preserve freedom for the peoples of the world. As engaged citizen diplomats we are likely to share those goals, and we seek guidance to ensure that our interactions with members of other cultures are ethical.

Reconciling Relativism and Universalism

As mindful communicators we must strive to reconcile the relative and universal approaches to intercultural ethics. As we have discussed, a position of extreme relativism could lead to the tacit acceptance of genocide, slavery, and oppression. On the other hand, as mindful communicators who respect cultural differences we are understandably hesitant to espouse a fixed universal code of ethics, particularly one based on our own culture's ethical values. We seek to avoid ethnocentrism, but also wish to be engaged in a meaningful way with other cultures. Bradford Hall has suggested viewing the tension between universal and relative ethical positions as the norm; that is to say, that rather than be torn between the two extremes, we seek to adopt an approach to ethical issues that is a compound of the two.[24]

Key aspects of relativism

We do not want to forget to respect the differences among cultural groups. Nor do we wish to dictate our own culture's values to other cultures — particularly when we do so through some form of coercion. However noble our ends, we cannot truly consider ourselves ethical communicators if we do not respect the uniqueness of other cultures and allow them to express that uniqueness. For example, despite our personal feelings we should respect the fact that in some cultures women are not permitted to work outside the home and may not be granted equal status with men in society; this disparity may be seen in the marriage and divorce laws in some cultures. Such laws may allow for a husband to dissolve a marriage, but not a wife, and may allow men to practice polygamy. We must strive to understand the cultural beliefs, often strongly grounded in religion, that give rise to value systems other than our own. It would be ethnocentric for us to assume that the way our culture deals with issues related to marriage and divorce, for example, is the only correct way for such issues to be handled. However, an ethical dilemma clearly exists in relation to the issue of women's rights as it comes into conflict with cultural and religious values if we feel that laws regarding marriage and divorce violate the basic human rights of women in some cultures.

Figure 9.2 In some cultures, women are not granted equal status with men, and these differences may be reflected in the marriage and divorce laws. It would be ethnocentric for us to judge other cultures' handling of marriage and divorce from the perspective of our own cultural values and beliefs. However, an ethical dilemma may arise if we believe that these laws violate the basic human rights of women.

Key aspects of universalism

While we may feel it is ethnocentric for us to impose our values on other cultures, we may be moved to act in extreme cases where acts of violent oppression and genocide are occurring. Innocent victims of horrific acts of genocide and oppression have the right to receive assistance. We do not want to turn our backs on suffering and intolerable actions against peoples simply because members of the culture in which they are occurring do not question them. Although ideally we would rely on each nation to protect the human rights of its citizens, there have been instances where government officials themselves have instituted policies that violated basic human rights. One obvious case is found in the actions of Hitler in Nazi Germany. More recent examples include the genocide in Rwanda, the situation in Darfur, and genocide in former Yugoslavian republics. Although there may be much debate about when and how it is appropriate for other nations to use military force to intervene in such situations, the need to stop such gross violations of human rights is not likely to be debated. Patricia Derian, who served as Assistant Secretary of State for Human Rights and Humanitarian Affairs during the Carter administration, puts it very clearly: "Electrodes applied to the gums shatter teeth in the same way in Manila as in Moscow. Cruelty knows no [distinctions] . . . the pain is universal, the demeaning and degrading of individuals is as hateful to those in the Peoples Republic of China, as it is in South Korea."[25]

Contextual Relativism

Because of the complexity of intercultural ethics, we cannot rely on a fixed set of guidelines that will address all the challenges we may encounter when communicating across cultures. There will always be tension between universalism and relativism. One way to approach ethical dilemmas is to treat each case as unique and to adopt a stance of *contextual relativism*. Such an approach differs from cultural relativism in that communicators who take this approach do not believe that it is impossible for them to take an ethical stance in relation to the behavior of members of other cultures, but strive to avoid doing so from an ethnocentric perspective.

Communication scholar Stella Ting-Toomey describes contextual relativism as an approach that emphasizes the importance of understanding the context surrounding any behavior. She states: "A contextual perspective means that the application of ethics can only be understood on a case-by-case basis and context-by-context basis. Each ethical case is a unique case, and each context is a unique ethical context that stands alone. With clarity of understanding of the context that frames the behavior in question (on socio-cultural, historical, and situational levels), intercultural learners can make a mindful choice concerning their own degree of engagement or disengagement in approaching the context."[26] As ethical communicators we must learn a great deal about the background and the surrounding economic, political, and social climate in which any behavior occurs.

For example, we may view the practice of child labor as problematic. The term "child labor" is used to describe "work which is likely to damage children's health, physical and psychological development as well as their chances of fulfilling other rights, mainly the right to education."[27] Our cultural perspective may dictate that children should be given an opportunity to gain an education and to enjoy freedom from harsh working conditions. We may deem that the actions of large corporations that use child labor in developing nations are guilty of exploitation, particularly when in some instances the working conditions are little better than those of slavery and have severely detrimental effects on the health of the children.

The world's attention was focused on Nike in 1996 when the June issue of *Life* magazine had an article about child labor in Pakistan. The article featured a photograph of a 12-year-old boy surrounded by the pieces of a Nike soccer ball, which he would spend the day assembling for a daily wage of 60 cents. Since that time Nike has developed a "comprehensive system of monitoring and remediation"[28] and has issued a Code of Conduct to its suppliers, binding them to a standard for wages, benefits, health, and a safe working environment. Other corporations have followed suit; however, much child labor still exists in the world and at least some of it is the result of unscrupulous corporate practices more concerned about profit than about human rights.

POWER CHECK
Four Moral Norms for Multinational Corporations
When doing business in other cultures multinational corporations (MNCs) must strive both to protect human rights and to respect the ethical standards of the surrounding community. Local communities in situations of extreme poverty may accept "sweatshop" working conditions because they are desperate for economic opportunities of any kind. However, as the Nike example demonstrates, public outcry by global citizens and socially responsible behavior by MNCs can prevent the violation of workers' rights. Ethicist Richard DeGeorge has put forward four moral norms for multinational corporations:

1. MNCs should do no direct international harm.
2. MNCs should contribute by their activities to the host country's development.
3. MNCs should respect the human rights of their employees.
4. To the extent that local culture does not violate moral norms, MNCs should respect the local culture and work with it, not against it.[1]

In some cases, an MNC can make a significant contribution to the host country's development of national standards. For example, Dow Chemical has developed Responsible Care, an international, voluntary program in the chemical industry for the safe handling of chemicals. Dow Chemical's operations in Thailand have served to help local government authorities develop an emergency response plan for environmental incidents and have offered valuable knowledge and equipment that would not have been otherwise available in the community.[2] Although the financial benefits of such actions are not easily measured, one could also argue that such responsible corporate behavior prevents costly accidents and other negative outcomes.

Notes

1. Richard T. DeGeorge, *Business Ethics*, 4th ed. (Englewood Cliffs, NJ: Prentice-Hall, 1995).
2. Laura P. Hartman, Denis G. Arnold, and Richard E. Wokutch, *Rising Above Sweatshops: Innovative Approaches to Global Labor Challenges* (Westport, CT: Praeger, 2003).

Of course, the actions of the corporations who use child labor are only one aspect of the situation. We may feel that the real problem lies with cultures like Pakistan that condone child labor. However, before we condemn the culture that allows children to work under such conditions, we should become informed of the social, political, and economic contexts in which such child labor occurs. In Pakistan, for example, children must earn money to supplement the family income in order for the family to have food to eat. Child labor in Pakistan is linked with other socioeconomic problems including "poor access to resources and production, gender inequality, inequitable distribution of land, [and] environmental degradation."[29] With the high incidence of poverty and the growing rate of inflation it is difficult for the low-income

Figure 9.3 In 1996, an article in *Life* magazine exposed Nike's child labor practices. Since that time, Nike has developed a Code of Conduct that requires its suppliers to ensure fair wages, benefits, and a safe working environment for its employees. While many other corporations have followed Nike's lead, much child labor still exists in the world.

population to survive. Pakistan has a per-capita income of $2,200 a year, and 32 percent of the population is below the poverty line.[30] In Pakistan and many other nations, extreme poverty is one of the primary causes of child labor. Families send their children out to work because they are in a desperate situation. Programs to enhance income and employment opportunities for adult workers are one important step toward alleviating child labor. Another important step is making education compulsory.[31] We may continue to be strongly opposed to child labor, even after we study the context in which it occurs, but we may wish to take a different kind of action to address it once we thoroughly understand the context. We may decide that it is not enough to refuse to buy goods that are the product of child labor. By supporting monetary aid for nations and for individuals in nations where many face conditions of extreme poverty, we may be able to help to alleviate practices that we find problematic.

Often ethical dilemmas can be most effectively addressed by a dialogue between the parties involved rather than by reference to a fixed set of standards. Rather than condemning behavior that we find problematic based on our own ethical code, we should seek to understand the context of the behavior and then to address the underlying issues that have given rise to the behavior. Once we have a thorough understanding of a particular situation, we will need to determine whether we wish to accept the practice, seek a compromise, withdraw from the situation, or take action to change the situation that gave rise to the practice.

For example, in an international business situation, a supplier in a conservative Arab state objected to a US corporation sending a female engineer to head a work group. Should the US corporation refrain from doing business with this supplier? Should they send a male engineer and say nothing about the situation?[32] What is the most ethical course of action in this situation? First, we must strive to understand the cultural differences that give rise to this situation. In some Arabic cultures men and women have strictly defined spheres of activity and influence, and women are not highly visible in public life. The status of women and their role in society grows out of traditions designed to protect; the intention of many "restrictions" is to provide women security and respect and to keep them from being subjected to "the stress, competition . . . and possible indignities found in outside society."[33] From our own cultural perspective, we may see the treatment of women as repressive rather than protective. However, while we do not have to share the values and beliefs involved, we must grant respect to the deeply held beliefs of members of other cultures.

This situation may well call for a compromise. Offering the female engineer another comparable position and sending a male engineer in her place may be the best solution — and not merely from a business standpoint. Sending the female engineer would be likely to put both her and the work group in the Arabic culture in a difficult and embarrassing position. Sending her despite the concerns of their business partner would demonstrate a lack of respect for the values of the host culture. At the same time, the corporation can let their Arabic counterpart know what their position is on nondiscriminatory treatment of employees and the importance of treating all employees equally. By doing so, they can open a dialogue regarding the role of women in the corporation.

As we have stressed throughout this book, the best starting point for engaging members of other cultures or any diverse others is to begin with an understanding of ourselves and our own cultural values, beliefs, norms, and ethical standards. The next step is to learn as much as we can about other cultures. Finally, if we are to interact mindfully with members of other cultures, we must seek to reconcile the universal and relative approaches to global ethics and to develop a set of ethical guidelines to inform our behavior.

Guidelines for Ethical Behavior in Intercultural Encounters

As mindful communicators we need to be aware that any and all of our actions in relation to individuals and groups in other cultures will have consequences. In this book we suggest basic guidelines for ethical behavior in intercultural encounters. As ethical communicators we should respect diverse others and seek common ground with them, while also respecting the significance of cultural differences.

Respecting diverse others

The most basic tenet of any code of behavior is to afford all other people the same respect that we would like to be granted ourselves. Virtually all the world's religions teach the importance of treating others as we would like to be treated. One of the most simple and straightforward statements of this tenet is the "Golden Rule" that exhorts us to recognize the value of all members of our global community; this tenet can be found in the teachings of Buddhism, Christianity, Islam, Judaism, the Native American cultures, and many others. It is also found in the first principle of David Kale's universal code of ethics, which states, "Ethical communicators address people of other cultures with the same respect that they would like to receive themselves."[34] This tenet applies to all peoples. Affording respect to all the diverse others with whom we interact both domestically and internationally is one of the benefits of mindful intercultural communication. In Chapter 1 we introduced the concept of mindfulness and stated that mindful communicators create a feeling of "being understood, respected, and supported"[35] in the individuals with whom they are communicating.

Seeking common ground with diverse others

Ethical communicators seek to establish common ground with members of other cultures and co-cultural groups. In intercultural encounters, they focus on the similarity of cultural beliefs and values rather than emphasizing cultural differences. Throughout this book it may seem that we have devoted a great deal of attention to the differences among cultural groups. We have done so in order to develop and expand your understanding of other cultures and of the differences among cultural groups that have the potential to lead to misunderstanding and conflict if we do not approach them from a mindful perspective. However, once we have developed self-awareness and knowledge of the values and beliefs of other cultures, we can move on to seeking commonalities in order to establish meaningful connections with members of other cultures. As human beings we share many basic concerns and values; we are all social beings, we all wish to be understood by others and to express ourselves, we all love our children and families, we all enjoy recreation (although it may take different forms in different cultures), and we all face the limitations of the human condition (health concerns, old age, and death).

Ethnocentric perspectives emphasize differences between in-groups and out-groups and often use such differences to justify discrimination, oppression, and violent conflict. By focusing on those things that we all share as human beings we are more likely to make possible meaningful dialogue regarding the many challenges we face as global citizens in the twenty-first century. We may disagree, but if we truly value each other's goals, we will have the opportunity to establish what Kale refers to as "optimal peace."

Respecting the significance of cultural differences

While we wish to find and emphasize the commonalities among all people, we also want to grant all people the right to their individual perspectives and opinions. We must grant that members of all cultural groups should be free to express their views even when those views oppose our own. In order for a genuine dialogue to occur we must allow culturally-diverse others to express their uniqueness. Kale stresses the fact that "ethical communicators place a high value on the right of cultures to be full partners in the international dialogue regardless of how popular or unpopular their political ideas may be."[36] Ethical communicators will recognize the need for a dialogic approach to ethical issues across cultures.

Global Ethics and Peace

As citizen diplomats, we seek to increase intercultural cooperation and resolve conflicts. Our ability to play a meaningful role in the global community depends on our ability to address the challenging ethical questions that arise across cultures. We must strive to avoid ethnocentric thinking and recognize that our own views of "right" and "wrong" behavior may not serve us well in a global context. The more we learn about other cultures, the better we will be able to appreciate and respect the different cultural values and beliefs that give rise to different codes of ethics. Through our understanding of and our respect for diverse others, we will be able to establish common ground with them so that we may all work together to establish optimal peace.

References

1. International Cocoa Initiative, www.sourcewatch.org/index.php?title= International_Cocoa_Initiative, accessed November 4, 2010.
2. Organisation for Economic Cooperation and Development (OECD), *Combating Child Labour* (Paris: OECD, 2003), p. 9.
3. World Health Organization, "Female Genital Mutilation," Fact Sheet 241, www.who.int/mediacentre/factsheets/fs241/en, accessed November 3, 2005.
4. Efua Dorkenoo, "Combating Female Genital Mutilation: An Agenda for the Next Decade," *World Health Statistics Quarterly*, 49 (1996), 142–7.
5. Eric Winkel, "A Muslim Perspective on Female Circumcision," *Women and Health*, 23 (1995), 1–7.
6. David W. Kale, "Peace as an Ethic for Intercultural Communication," in Larry A. Samovar and Richard E. Porter, eds., *Intercultural Communication: A Reader*, 10th ed. (Belmont, CA: Wadsworth/Thomson, 2003), p. 467.
7. Ibid., p. 466.
8. D. W. Klopf, *Intercultural Encounters: The Fundamentals of Intercultural Communication* (Englewood, CO: Morton, 1995).
9. R. A. Levine and D. T. Campbell, *Ethnocentrism: Theories of Conflict, Ethnic Attitudes, and Group Behavior* (New York: John Wiley & Sons, 1972).
10. Susan Opotow, "Deterring Moral Exclusion," *Journal of Social Issues*, 46 (1990), 174.
11. Ibid., 1–20.
12. Morton Deutsch, "Forms of Oppression?" Beyond Intractability.org, March 2005, www.beyondintractability.org/m/Forms_of_oppression, accessed October 19, 2005.
13. Ibid.
14. Immanuel Kant, *Foundations of the Metaphysics of Morals, and What is Enlightenment*, 2nd ed., trans. Lewis White Beck (New York: Macmillan, 1990).
15. Stella Ting-Toomey, *Communicating Across Cultures* (New York: The Guilford Press, 1999), p. 273.
16. Kale, p. 468.
17. Ibid.
18. Ibid.
19. Ibid., p. 469.
20. Joshua S. Goldstein, *International Relations*, 3rd ed. (New York: Longman, 1999), p. 330.
21. United Nations, The Universal Declaration of Human Rights, Preamble, December 1948.
22. David Little, "The Universality of Human Rights," United States Institute of Peace, 1996.
23. Ibid.
24. Bradford J. Hall, "Culture, Ethics, and Communication," in F. L. Casmir, ed., *Ethics in Intercultural and International Communication* (Mahwah, NJ: Lawrence Erlbaum, 1997), pp. 11–41.
25. Little.
26. Ting-Toomey, p. 274.
27. OECD, p. 15.
28. Laura P. Hartman, Denis G. Arnold, and Richard E. Wokutch, *Rising Above Sweatshops: Innovative Approaches to Global Labor Challenges* (Westport, CT: Praeger, 2003).
29. Pirzada Imtiaz Syed, Speech to All Pakistan Federation of United Trade Unions (APFUTU), cited on Labournet, www.labournet.net/world/0505/pakist1.html, date of speech September 12–14, 2005, posted on website October 5, 2005, accessed October 20, 2005.
30. CIA World Factbook, www.cia.gov/library/publications/the-world-factbook, accessed November 5, 2005.
31. Syed.

32. Dan Voss and Madelyn Flammia, "The Extreme Ethical Makeover: Getting Rid of Stereotypes, Tokens, and Ethnocentric Perspectives in Intercultural Technical Communication," paper presented at the Society for Technical Communication Conference, Las Vegas, May 2006.
33. Margaret K. Nydell, *Understanding Arabs: A Guide for Westerners*, rev. ed. (Yarmouth, ME: Intercultural Press, 1996), p. 63.
34. Kale, p. 469.
35. Ting-Toomey, p. 46.
36. Kale, p. 470.

10 Practicing Global Citizenship

Views about Global Issues and Citizenship

In this final chapter, we will closely examine the elements of global citizenship, as well as concrete examples of mindfulness in our global village. In Chapter 1, we stated that "often we do not set out with the intention of learning about other cultures, but our life experiences give us the opportunity to do so." Now, we highlight and evaluate this learning process at different levels of human interactions. This process causally and often occurs among the masses or between ordinary citizens and the elite. It also happens at the level of the elite, generally defined as individuals who exert a great deal of power or influence in their own field. Such individuals might include corporate CEOs, famous musicians, global financiers, Hollywood actors, national politicians, or world leaders. With their influence over society, the elite operate at a political level way above the reach of ordinary people. Like the masses, however, the elite should also become more mindful of their behavior in order to make decisions that will enable them to move forward in the direction of real global citizenship.

In Chapter 1, we used Langer's definition to describe a mindful individual as someone who is open to new information, fresh perspectives, and different environments. The experience of mindfulness may happen to anyone at any level of society and is a key to understanding and interacting with diverse cultures. The authors suggest that all individuals (from elite to masses) should interact with others in a state of mindfulness if one wishes to be tactful and considerate, or to prevent unintended conflicts initiated by cultural unawareness. Langer declared, "The consequences of trying out different perspectives [is that] we gain more choice in how to respond."[1] Having more choice is essential for people in any open and democratic society that values diversity.

Throughout this book, we discussed the foundation and intricacies of intercultural communication in the global society from the perspective of IR.

Moreover, we examined the relevant approaches, processes, and technologies of cross-cultural relations. Also, we explained the ethical issues in the cross-cultural communication. Primarily, we focused on the behavior of individuals and the group experience of various types of intercultural communication. Finally, the types, methods, and techniques of intercultural communication were presented in order to show the intricacies and dynamics of this field of study, which has a great deal of practical application. Now, it is time to shed some light on how the aggregated behavior of individuals works at the level of society, state, or international system. These levels are the foundation of studies in the IR literature, which often tends to seem abstract, impractical, and challenging to comprehend for the general public. We have shown, however, that adopting our new perspective allows anyone to understand the realities of modern communication age and to use them to ones benefits.

In the next sections, we begin by discussing the realities of how different international actors interact in our world. Next, we discuss how anyone from all levels of society may aim to be a global citizen. Our main point is that global citizenship is not reserved for the rich and powerful, even though they may receive more attention due to their social elite status. Finally, we address the basic question: Why should we care? In response, we address the four main global challenges of our time, and observe how we can make a difference using our new perspective.

POWER CHECK
Becoming a Global Citizen

What is a global citizen? In today's interdependent global society, our lives are affected by people from around the world. Whether it is the clothes you are wearing, the technology you are using, or the telephone call you make to a customer service center, our daily lives are affected by what people on the other side of the planet are doing. While global citizenship seems like a daunting term, it merely means a citizen of the world or anyone who works to make the world a better place. A global citizen is someone who is aware of the wider world; has a sense of his/her own role as a world citizen; respects and values diversity; has an understanding of how the world works, economically, politically, socially, culturally, technologically, and environmentally; is outraged by social injustice; participates in and contributes to the community at any level from locally to globally; is willing to take action in order to make the world a more sustainable and better place; and takes responsibility for his/her actions (Oxfam). If taking on the world seems too difficult, start at the local level. Even by changes made at the local level can impact the world in many ways.

According to TakingITGlobal, there are six simple steps to effectively make change and become a global citizen in your own right. The first step is to reflect on the changes would you like to see happen in your local community or in the world. The second step is to identify the interests or skills that you have? The third step is to get informed and inspired; gather as much information and sources as you can about your interests. The fourth step is to plan; create your own plan of action to address the changes you would like to make. The fifth step is to implement; get started, and stay focused and positive. You may hit obstacles in the road, but if you persevere you will eventually reach your goals. The sixth and final step is to evaluate; review the progress you made, reflect on the goals you were able to accomplish, and address what changes you would make if you did it again. By following these six simple steps, anyone can become a global citizen and change their own local community or the world.

Sources: Oxfam website, www.oxfam.org.uk/coolplanet/teachers/globciti/whatis.htm accessed March 10, 2009; TakingITGlobal website, www.takingitglobal.org/action/guide/Guide_to_Action.pdf, accessed November 12, 2009.

State-Centric and Complex Interdependence Models

In contemporary international relations, it is increasingly evident that the art of diplomacy, communication, and negotiation is no longer limited to the behavior of state diplomats. In fact, in our global village, even states no longer have the same monopolistic status in international affairs that they used to enjoy in previous centuries. Traditionally, political scientists, whose task is to study the behavior of governments, have explained the role of states in international relations and their interactions by employing the state-centric model. This model suggests that states, representing their own nations or people, behave as the primary actor while dominating the channels of international communication. In the international scene, the states are represented by presidents, monarchs, prime ministers, ambassadors, diplomats, or other political elite who are decision-makers and negotiators. Nevertheless, since the start of the twentieth century there have been new actors at the global level. The behavior of the new actors is beyond the explanatory power of the state-centric model. The new actors are related to the growth of multinational corporations (MNCs), international organizations, and non-governmental organizations (NGOs), which have gradually intruded and interfered in the state-exclusive sphere of international communication.

In addition to the new actors, the technological revolution shifted the nature of international communication by empowering ordinary citizens. Nowadays, the empowerment of masses is a fact of life in our global community. The individuals have the ability to travel with ease; they are capable of communicating with the furthest corners of the globe in mere seconds; and they can effectively share information with others.

With the exception of national security matters, in which states still possess the power of coercion and remain omnipotent, new international developments and events are challenging and eroding the authority of statesmen. In

1977, two scholars of international relations, Joseph Nye and Robert Keohane, reassessed the validity of the state-centric model and advocated the emergence of a fresh model that more accurately represents the realities of modern international interactions and communication.[2] The new model, known as the complex interdependence model, showed a different picture of the interactions among the actors in the state-centric model. The difference between the two models is best illustrated by the following figures, which simplify our complex global communications by focusing on its building block: the relations between two states.

Figure 10.1 illustrates that in the state-centric model, both states (as defined in Chapter 1) A and B represent their own nations (as defined in Chapter 1), as the arrows indicate. Moreover, international interactions are shown by a two-way communication arrow between states A and B. In fact, since the exchange occurs at the state level (among government officials), one may even identify it as an "interstate relation," not "international relation."

The complex interdependence model inherits the state-to-state channel of communication, but it is superior to the previous model due to its additional paths of communication. The complex interdependence model shows the interaction between state A and nation B (and state B and nation A), since modern states use public diplomacy to persuade citizens of other states to agree with their policy choices, goals, and means. Such campaigns used to be called propaganda, a term that has negative connotations these days and thus is rarely used. Finally, the direct channels of communication between nations A and B are free from their governmental channels, as individuals from MNCs (like IBM, Sony, and Volvo) and NGOs (such as Amnesty International, Greenpeace, and Red Cross), and even ordinary citizens directly interact with their counterparts in other states. Non-governmental channels of communication are a relatively new phenomenon in our increasingly global society, as both non-profit and profit-oriented organizations directly negotiate, sign agreements, and conduct

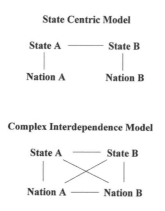

Figure 10.1 State-centric and Complex Interdependence models.

programs together. In fact, such behaviors have become so ordinary that we take them for granted these days.

Security has always been a crucial preoccupation for states, but the post 9/11 era has taken on a different scope. With the dynamic changes of globalization in the twenty-first century, one primary preoccupation of states is national security, whose scope has expanded into issues dealing with international environment, health, business, drug trafficking, arms trades, as well as international terrorism networks. Hence, the complex interdependence model seems more suitable for today's world, as organizations and individuals increasingly exercise their own abilities to influence the decisions of states and global issues. Many cross-border issues and NGOs are deeply involved with key global topics, from health to the environment and business to culture. Sometimes the resources of various NGOs are even greater than those of some state(s) that attempt to regulate them. It would be naïve to allude to a "borderless world" or even a centrally controlled global governing body. The latter does not exist, as there is much dispute to determine what particular model and philosophy would be globally acceptable or enforceable.[2] Still, the complex interdependence model is viable and to a large extent measurable. It is particularly useful for our purposes of examining intercultural communication, citizen diplomacy, and global citizenship.

We have examined many facets of communication as a whole, but one may ask: What about the results? Now, we will turn to observe some examples of mindfulness in action, along with the power that some NGOs have developed. These examples will provide us with the opportunity to take a glimpse into how interdependent our world has become. Moreover, we will address questions like: What happens when people face new information, expand their understanding, or are receptive to new perspectives? Who has actually done this and applied it? Is it simply a theory or an idea? Why should we make efforts to "put ourselves in another's shoes?" To start, as established in Chapter 1, we will observe that mindfulness is primarily a question of awareness.

Global Citizens at all Social Levels

Global citizens among the rich and powerful

In December 2005, *Time* magazine chose Bill and Melinda Gates, along with rock star Bono, lead singer of U2, as the "Person(s) of the Year," placed their picture on the cover, and wrote extensive articles about their journey into philanthropy. This prestigious honor was given based on the three recipients' outstanding philanthropic service. The award winners' international concern and community service was sparked by a new state of openness in thinking about the world. Thus, *Time* also credits 2005 as the year that "turned the corner" in the world of philanthropy.[3] In the same edition, they declared 2005 the year that the US public "demanded real accountability." They talked about the US public demand throughout 2005 for accountability from the Bush administration regarding the Iraq crisis, corruption in politics, and the government's unsuccessful response to the hurricane Katrina disaster. They stated that the success of the democratic process would bring disclosure of actions taken towards victory in Iraq, justice for corruption, accountability of government appointees, and prevention of bureaucratic stagnation.[4]

This issue of *Time* also had several articles about the efforts of individuals in managing some of the world's worst problems. Let's see how mindfulness and global citizenship in practice can lead to actions that spark interest in others all over our global community. Of particular interest is the effort of the Bono, a famous musician, who turned into a leading philanthropist for poverty eradication and health in Africa.

Based on *Time*'s report, Bono met with Bill Gates (founder and the then CEO of Microsoft and richest man in the world) and Melinda Gates (Bill's wife and co-founder of the Gates Foundation). *Time* quotes Gates saying, "World health is immensely complicated. It doesn't really boil down to a 'Let's be nice' analysis. So I thought a meeting wouldn't be all that valuable."[5] Originally, this was Bill Gates' feeling towards the issue of world poverty and health, that is, until he met Bono: *Time* said it took about three minutes with Bono for Bill and Melinda Gates to change their minds. Whether the time frame was an exaggeration or not, the fact remains that the Gates Foundation is now the largest charitable foundation in the world, with a $23.9 billion endowment (as of September 2010), which yearly matches that of the World Health Organization. Moreover, the foundation's investments have helped vaccinate 700,000 people.[6] The Foundation contributions reflect its commitment to bringing health innovations and education to the global community.

Many may expect Bill and Melinda Gates to have a charitable society. If they did not, they would certainly face some kind of public scrutiny. In fact, Bill Gates had been scrutinized on various occasions as to whether or not their corporation was contributing enough to society. However, once the Gates' decided to take action, they did not simply create a charitable organization. Instead, they created a business whose profits are measured in results, not dollars. They have created an approach to HIV problems that cross multiple state and cultural borders. Their approaches are geared to accommodate whatever cultural challenges may be faced. Since some African cultures do not allow certain approaches (like sex education), the Gates recognize there is not a "one size fits all approach," so they prepared a model that works with the different cultural traditions of the areas under focus.[7] The Gates Foundation specifically concentrates on money management, results, and accountability. They stop the funding process if a program does not meet an agreed upon target. They evaluate all the financial aspects of the programs, as one would expect from an engineer and financial guru. They know exactly where their money is going and they also follow up with visits. They visit both potential and current recipients, examine the potentials and results of the program, and gain inspiration from direct involvement and interactions with people in the field.[8] With their direct and personal interaction with the recipients, the Gates maintain a high level of optimism. On the website of the Bill & Melinda Gates Foundation, they explain why they are so committed:

> We're optimistic because, while the statistics are daunting, we know these problems can be solved . . . but they require that public and private sectors step up their investments dramatically to reduce the inequities that divide our world. It isn't enough simply to be aware of the problems; to make a difference, every one of us must take action . . . Whenever possible; the foundation acts as a catalyst. We work with a diverse mix of partners — governments, other foundations, the private sector, and nonprofits — to increase the momentum, scale, and sustainability of change . . . aiming always to create long-term, systemic change and develop models that can be replicated.[9]

The Gates have been so dedicated to their global goals that in June 2006, Bill Gates announced his intention to retire as CEO of the Microsoft Corporation and dedicate his full attention to the work of the Gates Foundation. This is an example of world citizen mindfulness in action.

In this regard, Bono is another global citizen that requires some explanation. If world health and poverty issues were a state, Bono would be its statesman. He has become the credible representative of the issue. He has learned how to bring groups of the least interested individuals (like the Gates) together to recognize that they all have a common interest and responsibility in global issues. Bono knows that he must communicate with different individuals based on their own "cultural" context. Cultures develop within societies, but they also develop within industries. Business, music, movies, politics and even philanthropy have their own cultures. Bono masterfully bridges the gaps between industry and society to create sustainable efforts in addressing global challenges. Consequently, Bono's charitable efforts exemplify the primary hope for anyone who develops mindfulness in intercultural relations, to create understanding across cultural divides. Why did it take him only three minutes to change the minds of the Gates to engage in a deeper level of commitment to global problems? According to Patty Stonesifer, CEO of Gates Foundation, Bono spoke their language and they saw him as one of them by talking the language of numbers, facts and results. "He was every bit the geek that we are," said Stonesifer.[10]

Bono observer Josh Tyrangiel chronicles his countless achievements and the testaments of his converts and contributors to his cause. All examples show Bono's ability to relate to people on their own terms from one side of the ideological spectrum to the other. By quoting scripture for the religiously faithful, like former Senator Jessie Helms and President George W. Bush, he brought them to his cause and secured the most US funding for Africa to date. By focusing on the bottom-line data for the business financier or results-oriented politicians, Bono learned over time to relate his cause to them as well. Beyond such "people skills," Bono adds common sense to his own bright ideas and personal credibility. Tyrangiel also charted the rock-star's life journey and evolution of mindfulness over twenty years, during which he developed from a musician donating money to a talented concert organizer for foreign aid, and from briefly engaging people for a cause to personally transforming their lives. Bono's own personal development was a function of a number of factors, from travel and observation, to encounters and real experiences with the cultural realities of poor societies in need.[11]

Despite his current superhero status, Bono was born in a middle-class Irish family, and received only a high school education. On his own, however, Bono educated himself about a variety of global humanitarian challenges and teamed up with organizations already working in the philanthropy field. Many talented artists and musicians can identify with social and cultural problems, or "feel the pain" of a society. However, in relation to Africa, Bono gradually developed his openness, mindfulness, and understanding of the regional problems and ultimately combined his thoughts with speech and action.

Following the motto of "actions speak louder than words," Bono has appeared in, participated in, or managed benefit concerts: 1984 Band Aid, Live Aid 1985, 2004 Band Aid 20, and Live 8 in 2005. Since 1999, he has been seriously involved in assisting with the debt crisis of developing countries and the African poverty calamity. In 2002, Bono took US Treasury Secretary Paul O'Neill on a four-country tour of Africa and established an organization called DATA, which we discuss later in this chapter.

In 2005, Bono shifted the focus to fair trade by developing a line of designer outfits produced in fair wage factories in Africa, South America, and India. In summer 2005, Bono played a major role in organizing a series of concerts around the globe aimed at encouraging the representatives of the G-8 Summit to write off Africa's massive debt, reform trade policy, and grant more foreign aid for problems such as the AIDS epidemic. At the 2006 Annual National Prayer Breakfast and ever since, Bono has encouraged the care of socially and economically depressed people by a speech documented with many biblical references. His Christian views are brought into harmony with other faiths as he noted that Christian, Jewish and Muslim writings universally call for the care of the widow, orphan, and stranger. All and all, these philanthropic efforts make Bono an excellent representative of what mindfulness and citizen diplomacy can achieve.

Some people may argue that individuals like Bill Gates are better equipped than everyday citizens to make a positive impact on the global community. After all, he is one of the wealthiest people in the world, so very little restrains him from a material standpoint from "making a difference." Bono is a world famous musician whose success allowed him to spread the word about the AIDS crisis. One may ask: How could ordinary citizens convince others to help? Despite some people's claims about their lack of means to "make a difference," there are numerous instances of ordinary people acting as global citizens by investing their time, energy, and efforts for the benefit of others or a cause.

The global impact of doing so much with so little

A well-known example of self-sacrifice and global impact is found in the life work of the nun Mother Teresa. Born to a very modest Albanian family on August 27, 1910, Mother Teresa (named Agnes Gonxha Bojaxhiu) felt that her life's calling was to be a world missionary, spreading the gospel. But what started out as a religious fervor turned into a life of charity. After a few months training in an Irish convent in Dublin, Mother Teresa was sent to work at a Catholic school in India where she took her initial vows to dedicate her life to God as a nun. As she continued to work at the Catholic school, her eyes were opened to the horrific poverty that surrounded the school. She began working with the poorest of the poor, feeding them, tending to them, and caring for them. Although she lacked material wealth, resources poured in from outside sources, allowing her to continue her work.

As her vision expanded from helping a few too many, Mother Teresa sought permission from the Church and began the order the Missionaries of Charity in 1950. It focused on loving the poor and caring for their physical, as well as spiritual, needs. In her own words, Teresa described the organization by saying that the Missionaries of Charity existed to help "the hungry, the naked, the homeless, the crippled, the blind, the lepers, all those people who feel unwanted, unloved, uncared for throughout society, people that have become a burden to society and are shunned by everyone." Her desire to help the impoverished sparked a rapid growth in the ministry. By 1965, the order was recognized as an International Religious Family by Pope Paul VI and became an International Association on March 29, 1969. Her organization spread worldwide, helping the poor and undertaking relief work in Asian, African, and Latin American. Currently, there are over a million organization members spread throughout over 40 countries. One of her well-known projects was the Hindu temple that she converted into a home for the dying, and the Shanti Nagar (City of Peace).

Her example inspired numerous other individuals to go beyond the level of mindfulness and be a world citizen. Affiliations to Mother Teresa's work arose in organizations like the Missionaries of Charity Brothers in 1963, the Missionaries of Charity Sisters in 1976, the Corpus Christi Movement for Priests in 1981, and the Lay Missionaries of Charity in 1984. Mother Teresa strongly believed in her mission, which had both a spiritual and physical focus. Her fervor for the spiritual well-being of the poor transformed into an incredible organization that ministered to the lives of thousands of the poorest of the poor all over the world. She acted as a global citizen, refusing to wait for someone else to solve the world's problems. "Do not wait for leaders; do it alone, person to person," she said. A global citizen bears mindfulness not only of the community needs, but also acts for a better life of others. Awareness of needs is the starting point for a global citizen; however, actions make a far greater impression. Mother Teresa's words embody how a global citizen should think.

"There should be less talk; a preaching point is not a meeting point. What do you do then? Take a broom and clean someone's house. That says enough."

Mother Teresa's influence had a global impact, stirring the hearts, minds, and actions of numerous individuals. She began at an early age with an attitude of mindfulness toward others. Her awareness that suffering existed in the world and that people could be instrumental in changing such conditions strengthened. Her mindfulness grew as she worked in a Catholic school in India. By engaging the Indian society, Mother Teresa learned to understand their culture and the people began to appreciate her heart. Her life's work brought physical, emotional, and spiritual life to thousands of the poorest, along with orphaned people. Furthermore, her work impacted the lives of those who joined her cause. Changing lives and cultural mindsets required the physical involvement of others as well. "Let us not be satisfied with just giving money," she said, "I would like more people to give their hands to serve and their hearts to love — to recognize the poor . . . to reach out to them in love and compassion." Service was of paramount importance in being able to understand the sufferings of the underprivileged. Mother Teresa welcomed the service and dedication of individuals. Her one criterion for new nuns was a disposition of cheerfulness. A charity showing compassion and love must be shown through the joyful countenance of a giving servant. "Let no one ever come to you without leaving better and happier," she said.[12]

Mother Teresa's example possesses similarities to that of Bill Gates and Bono. All saw a need that affected the lives of more than their immediate family or circles. Each understood that the problems they saw bore consequences that affected the global society.

The professional classes and NGOs

Ordinary people, like most college students, can also become involved as citizen diplomats and global citizens. Three college friends became aware of the human rights crisis in Africa. They discovered that in Uganda nearly 70 percent of the nearly two million internally displaced victims had no way of supporting themselves. The country had become incredibly dependent on outside aid. Eighty-four percent of Ugandan households relied on the deliveries from the World Food Program (WFP). The AIDS epidemic spread through the country, leaving 27 percent of the children as either partial or complete orphans. Two hundred fifty thousand northern Ugandan children had no education whatsoever. But, the students were most enraged by child abductions by the Lord's Resistance Army (LRA), who used the children as soldiers. The United States government labeled the LRA as a terrorist organization under the United States Patriot Act; however, Ugandan President Yoweri Museveni was slow to act against the LRA. So, the students started the Invisible Children organization. Its goal is to change "culture, policy, and lives through collisions of poverty and power." It seeks to provide resources, skills, and funds to provide for necessary healthcare and education needs of the displaced families and children. They created a system that gave numerous people jobs and also started a micro-economic program called the Invisible Children Bracelet Campaign, which employed Ugandans living in displacement camps to make bracelets out of reeds. These bracelets, accompanied by a video, which tell a Ugandan child's story, are sold in the United States to raise funds for the Invisible Children Education fund.

Moreover, they convinced Democratic Senator Russ Feingold and Republican Senator Lamar Alexander to sponsor the bipartisan Northern Uganda Crisis Response Act S.2262, which passed in February 2005. Their grass-roots efforts made a noteworthy impact both domestically and abroad. In the United States, it resolved the nation to support "a peaceful resolution of the conflict in northern Uganda, work with the Ugandan government and the international community to make available sufficient resources to meet the relief and development needs of northern Uganda and to assume greater responsibility for the protection of civilians and economic development in regions in Uganda affected by the conflict."[13] Beyond a sense of mindfulness and beyond acting as a citizen diplomat toward visitors who set foot on our soil, there is another level of global mindfulness that requires the person to step outside of his/her comfort zone to make an impact. It is the role of a world citizen. Among ordinary people, professionals are often better equipped to impact the globe and become global citizens, as the story of Doctors Without Borders suggests. This independent humanitarian organization offers emergency aid to victims of man-made and natural disasters. Found in over 70 countries to date, Doctors Without Borders sends teams out for more than 3,800 field assignments. Working alongside local staff and residents, doctors, administrators, health experts, non-medical professionals, and volunteers from around the world provide numerous services such as running hospitals, health clinics, and rehabilitation centers, perform surgeries, offer vaccinations, feed the starving, and provide basic necessities such as food, water, and shelter to the poor.

The organization was founded in 1971 as a non-governmental organization with the goal to provide medical assistance throughout the world to countries in need. Their programs have embarked to accomplish ambitious goals such as eliminating or at least reducing death counts due to malnutrition, tuberculosis, and HIV/AIDS. Members of the organization also provide psychological care for children who have been orphaned or been subject to the atrocities of war and blight. Over the years, Doctors Without Borders has been able to improve the efficiency of its services. Equipped with special medical kits designed for different field situations and geographic conditions, the organization is among the first of the humanitarian organizations able to arrive at the site of an emergency. And, unlike many other independent organizations, Doctors Without Borders takes action during a crisis solely based on the analysis of the needs of the people in the situation. The organization relies on the general public for around 80 percent of its funding. More than 3.1 million donations came from individuals, foundations, corporations, and non-profits in 2004. That same year, the United States, through the generosity of 380,000 private donors, contributed more than US$91 million. Political, economic, and religious interests are not important in the decision-making process. This allows the organization to remain neutral during conflicts and reduces the chances of governmental intervention on the part of the host nation. Volunteers and staff members have taken these grave issues to the general public, media venues, national governments, and the United Nations. Because of the nature of their work, the staff of Doctors Without Borders has seen numerous atrocities and human rights violations and spread mindfulness to adults and children alike through conferences and speaking events at businesses and schools.

Doctors Without Borders has reached numerous countries in Latin America, where the Chagas disease is responsible for the deaths of more than 50,000 people yearly. Bolivia suffers severely from the disease because it affects more than half of its inhabitants, the majority of whom live in rural areas. Using resources and programs, the organization also provides screenings for newborns and children up to the age of fourteen. As children are tested and the disease is detected earlier, treatment plans are set up. While prevention is the preferred method to win the battle, Doctors Without Borders has worked with the Bolivian government to set up a national Chagas program to fight the disease. The fight is difficult because very little research is being conducted for a treatment because no profit will be gained. The poor cannot afford to purchase a cure or medicine, so Doctors Without Borders must rely on its lobbying efforts and other resources to find donors who, as world citizens, will fund research to expedite the process of treating and curing the disease.[14] The organization also works with the newly established Drugs for Neglected Diseases Initiative (DNDi) and other similar programs in the hope of finding aid and relief to bring to the poor and needy. To note, the organization does not require its workers and volunteers to carry medical degrees. But, there are numerous fields of study that are required in order for Doctors Without Borders to operate. That is what enables the organization to have such strong international emergency medical relief. Doctors Without Borders has been able to improve communities by offering primary healthcare clinics to the populace. While the organization works with 25,000 national staff and 3,500 international volunteers, only half are actually some form of medic. The remaining half is composed of non-medical personnel or logisticians, ranging in fields from administration to finances to engineering.[15]

Another great example related to that of a joint venture in our global community is that of contemporary singer Steven Curtis Chapman — who created a global partnership as well. Known throughout religious circles for his positive music and his family values, Chapman emerged from being a domestic influence to a global influence when he traveled to China to adopt a Chinese orphan named Shaohannah. Chapman returned to China twice more to adopt two more abandoned girls. In China, the cultural influence pressures families with a one-child policy and traditionally, the preference has always been for males. Therefore, numerous cases of female infanticide have occurred as well as female child abandonment. Unregistered female children do not receive a legal recognition of existence, and thus have a very difficult time attaining an education. Chapman recognized this abuse and neglect of children and set out to make a change. His adoption of three Chinese girls heralded positive media from China and the United States. Internationally, he has a positive reputation. From this experience, he and his wife Mary Beth founded Shaohannah's Hope, named after his first Chinese daughter. Shaohannah's Hope is dedicated to assisting prospective adoptive parents through the process, both emotionally and financially. They award financial grants to families in order to make the success of this process attainable for loving, qualified families.

While states continue to negotiate and communicate with one another, the global scene increases in complexities. Governments no longer bear a monopoly in international deals. Multinational corporations, international organizations, and non-governmental organizations bear great influence on the world political stage. Amnesty International presents a prime example of an organization that influences the dealings of national governments. Amnesty is an organization centered on the mission to research, prevent, and eliminate human rights abuses around the world. The organization is supported by members in over 150 countries and boasts a membership of over 1.8 million people. In order to remain independent from governmental pressures, it receives no funding from national governments, which allows it certain freedoms in investigations and campaigns against human right violations. This independence has given Amnesty strong influence in world opinion. The organization brought and continues to bring attention to the serious human rights abuses in places such as the People's Republic of China and Vietnam.

China is ripe for change and Amnesty encourages that change. China shows increasing interest in expanding its international links and trade. Amnesty is taking advantage of the country's desire to apply increasing pressure for certain standards to be implemented in order for China to enter further into the global scene. There are numerous instances of ill treatment of detainees, political dissidents and common citizens. The denial of food, use of torture, and multiple occurrences of executions as a response to social problems reflect the corruption and mass-disconnection that the Chinese government currently possesses. Amnesty fights to change that. Specifically, Amnesty has offered ten recommendations to the Chinese government in which human rights violations can be prevented or stopped. It also offers recommendations to promote better human rights ideals in the culture. Global awareness, for which Amnesty bears a great responsibility, is causing increasing pressure on China to implement changes in its human rights policy. China still prohibits many freedoms, prohibiting free assembly and repressing certain schools of thought. However, since Amnesty stepped into the situation, China has signed some of the United Nations' international human rights conventions. As Beijing's international prestige grows, other democracies are beginning to insist that China adheres to internationally recognized human rights standards. The ethnic conflict between Muslim and Han Chinese in July 2009, during which

Chinese authorities intervened and limited information was disseminated to the foreign press, continues to present a problem.

Besides China, Amnesty continues campaigning on numerous fronts: stopping violence against women, controlling arms, halting torture, ending the death penalty, eradicating poverty, defending human rights, protecting refugees and migrants, participating in economic globalization, promoting international justice, ending the use of children soldiers, and supporting the United Nations.

Vietnam follows closely behind China in human rights concerns. Groups like Amnesty attempt to work independently of any government, political, or religious ideology. In a recent statement by the Advocacy Director for Asia and the Pacific of Amnesty International, the organization expressed its key concerns for Vietnam: restrictions on freedom of expression, assembly and association; the use of national security legislation and the criminal code to suppress criticism of the government; the continuing imprisonment of political prisoners; the use of severely repressive practices in some ethnic minority areas — notably the Central Highlands; independence of judiciary; restrictions on religious freedoms and continued intolerance of non-state sanctioned religions and denominations; and the application of the death penalty. Amnesty bears a local influence by applying pressure on the Socialist Republic of Vietnam's government. They have brought attention to corruption and scandal within Vietnam's government, especially in the state-controlled, censored, and propaganda-oriented media. The organization also cited censorship instances such as that concerning Dr. Pham Hong Son, a 37-year-old medical doctor and businessman who had translated the article entitled "What is Democracy?" from the United States' embassy's website. After sharing the article with officials and friends and the publication of subsequent articles calling for a peaceful political reform, Dr. Pham was arrested and had remained in detention since March 27, 2002, sentenced to 13 years' imprisonment and three years under house arrest.

At the hearing, Amnesty offered numerous recommendations to Vietnam's government: lift all the restrictions on using the internet for peaceful purposes and to repeal restrictive laws; end the use of national security legislation to stifle freedom of expression and association; immediately and unconditionally release all prisoners of conscience; allow independent and impartial agencies (e.g. the UN Special Rapporteur on Torture and the UN Working Group) unfettered access to the Central Highlands and other areas to investigate allegations of human rights violations; initiate full and independent investigations into allegations of human rights violations against the Montagnard minority and bring perpetrators to justice in accordance with international standards; take steps to allow freedom of religious practice to members of all churches, regardless of whether they are state-sanctioned, without conditions; take steps to reduce the number of capital offences and ensure that prisoners of non-violent crimes remaining on death row who have been convicted of non-violent economic crimes are not executed and that their sentences help move towards abolition of the death penalty. Members expose the human rights violations around the world, not just in China and Vietnam. They spread awareness of the negative aspects that need change and act as world citizens fighting for positive change.[16]

As Amnesty International impacts the lives of people around the globe, the Grameen Bank assists the needy in a different venue. The Grameen Bank began by offering small loans to the poorest of the poor in order to give them a hand-up economically. In 1976, Professor Muhammad Yunus, head of the Rural Economic Program at the University of Chittagong, founded the bank in the hope of making a positive impact among the poor community. The Grameen Bank works independently of the United Nations. It had multiple objectives: "extend banking facilities to poor men and women; eliminate the exploitation of the poor by money lenders; create opportunities for self-employment for the vast multitude of unemployed people in rural Bangladesh; bring the disadvantaged, mostly women from the poorest households, within the fold of an organizational format that they can understand and manage by themselves; and reverse the age-old vicious circle of 'low income, low saving and low investment,' into the virtuous circle of 'low income, injection of credit, investment, more income, more savings, more investment, more income.'"[17] By providing employment to the unemployed, the Grameen Bank empowers the poorest to accumulate their own capital. Because the loan system is based on a group liability (meaning that the village community is held responsible for the loan, not just the borrower), the loan return rate has reached 98 percent. The Grameen Bank credit system is based on the Baker-Hopkin formula model: $CE/E = [(D/E)(r - i) + r] (1 - c)$, where E = the amount of equity; D = the amount of loan; r = the rate of return on assets; i = the rate of interest paid on loans; c = the rate of consumption out of the income earned from assets; and C = the discrete change. Normally, it would be impossible for an impoverished borrower to pay back a loan, however, the formula allows for the recovery of the loan in small installments over a longer period of time. This enables the borrower to save money while returning the loan. Corporations like the Grameen Bank may have begun locally, but they have reached across borders to improve the lives of millions. A survey conducted by the Institute of Food and Nutrition of Dhaka University found that while a non-Grameen Bank member consumed, on average, 789 grams of food per day, a Grameen Bank member consumed, on average, 857 grams per day in 1986. And as of May 2006, 6.61 million people received loans from the Grameen Bank.[18] In Yunus' book *Creating a World Without Poverty*, he mentions a partnership with French-based food company Danone (c. 2006–2007): this is an example of his influence beyond the Grameen Bank.

Micro-credit loans offer that hand-up. Numerous NGOs have picked up on Dr. Yunus' idea of micro-credit loans and have maximized the abilities of deserving people to be given an opportunity to succeed and thrive where they are. Former Pakistani prime minister, Shaukat Aziz, applauds the efforts of the NGOs and feels that the United Nations should look at such efforts as examples for UN recommendations. Micro-credit loans have opened a door of communication among member states in the UN. Micro-credit has been used in numerous underdeveloped nations and appears to have a profound effect on the lives of countless impoverished people. Governments then take the idea and can implement it into their own programs. Pakistan has done so with such programs as the Rozgar Scheme, Zakat Fund, Baitulmaal, Khushhali Bank, and the Poverty Alleviation Fund.[19] Since these programs have been implemented, Shaukat Aziz claims a reduction of poverty due to the micro-credit projects' ability to empower his people.

The empowerment of people, especially women is a major goal of micro-credit projects. The UN reports that about 80 percent of the world's poorest people are women and children. Thus, women are the main clients of micro-credit loans. Seventy-four percent of the poorest clients of the 40 largest micro-credit programs are women. In Grameen Bank's case, 2.4 million borrowers are among the poorest, and from that group, 2.28 million or 95 percent are women. Moreover, 1.5 billion people, two-thirds being women, live on less than a dollar a day. Women are reportedly more dependable to repay the loans, upon which the well-being of their children relies. Noeleen Heyzer, executive director of the UN Development Fund for Women (UNIFEM), explained that experience has shown that when "women gain economic autonomy, the health, nutrition and education of members of the household, especially children, improve at the same time."[20] A key to eradicating poverty could very well be through the women.

In short, Amnesty International, Doctors Without Borders, Grameen Bank, and Shaohannah's Hope are all examples of successful organizations at the service of humanity. It is essential to recall that these institutions consist of dedicated, hard-working, self-sacrificing, and visionary individuals who "think globally but act locally." Starting with their founders, such organizations became successful because of the work of global citizens such as Muhammad Yunus and Steven Curtis Chapman. We emphasize the role of ordinary individuals, because the IR literature traditionally concentrates on the behavior at international system or state level, where the actions of individuals tend to be marginalized. When IR experts examine the behavior of individuals, they focus on powerful individuals, like political, business, or even religious leaders. Nevertheless, our new approach to IR suggests that one should not ignore the soft power of ordinary mindful people who can make a difference anywhere under any condition.

Why Should We Care?

As students of citizen diplomacy and global citizenship, why should we learn about Bono, the Gates, Yunus, Mother Teresa, or others? The answer is that they are examples and representatives of this work's theme that citizens of all types (and all levels) can make a difference, and that mindfulness can be the beginning as well as the foundation for a sustainable, peaceful, and balanced interdependent world. To measure the progress, however, we must examine the result of the programs established by the initiatives of such global citizens.

For an effective and sustainable program, Gates and Bono have created a partnership like none other to date; DATA is the organization through which Bono facilitates his work and is also where the Gates Foundation initially financed him. DATA is a double acronym for "debt, AIDS, trade, Africa" and "democracy, accountability, transparency in Africa." *Time* described the organization as strategically positioned as a nexus between the non-profit and development organizational world and the results-oriented political spheres.[21] The DATA website describes its aim as raising awareness and stimulating response to the crises swamping Africa, including unpayable debts, uncontrolled spread of AIDS, and unfair trade rules that keep Africans poor and discourage African leaders to strengthen democracy, accountability and transparency toward their own citizens.

One of the most successful programs championed by DATA is their micro-finance program — an idea attributed to Yunus. Loan can be as little as US$50–$100 to start, or help is offered to expand tiny businesses that offer sustenance for a family and/or community. Along with business investment, micro-credit programs offer a combination of services and resources to their clients, including savings facilities, training, networking, and peer support.[22] The 95 percent loans repayment rate makes the program extremely successful due to manageable interest rates that are eventually re-funneled back into communities to distribute further loans.

Studies are repeatedly showing the trickle-down effect of these programs. While most of the loans are given to women, empowering them to avoid the desperate choices of early marriage or the sale of young girls, it is also showing that the recipient's standards of living are improving in everything including nutrition, shelter, education, and healthcare. These improvements further lead into business expansion, which benefits communities at large. Plus, many of the recipients are affiliated with local health education programs for AIDS prevention. Microfinance is considered an integral part of HIV/AIDS prevention efforts. DATA also reports that there are over 2,500 microfinance institutions servicing over 8 million clients worldwide, most of whom are women. This is important, since 80 percent of world's poor consist of women and children, as indicated earlier. Thus, the extraordinary DATA program is a dynamic example of how small steps of mindful individuals and the efforts of culturally sensitive organizations can assist in empowering individuals in less fortunate societies by allowing them to achieve self-sufficiency — a social value which can easily be communicated over cross-cultural barriers.

We can see that mindfulness, citizen diplomacy, and world citizenship efforts produce measurable results and interactions that may have originally seemed unreachable, although many global problems can be insurmountable. The examples of Gates and Bono are extraordinary, so some people may be daunted by the sheer magnitude of the tasks at hand and the average person may feel overwhelmed. These examples are demonstrations of what political scientists refer to as initiations "from above," that is, elite organizations, or governments implanting change in a society, not necessarily demanded by the public. Yet, there are theories that speculate on the ability to facilitate change "from below," on which the industrialized democratic societies are founded.

In a world where the focus is often on the elite's behavior and their initiatives "from above" to bring a change, one message of this book for ordinary people is that the globalization process provides them with the opportunity to bring change "from below." By employing the notions of mindfulness and citizen diplomacy with their own natural talents and efforts, anyone can make a difference in the global village. The initiatives "from below" are the result of grass-roots behavior by masses and citizen or community organizations, but this does not make them less important. Mass revolutions, like the Chinese, French, and Iranian revolutions, are considered Great Revolutions, which are social movements from below. In fact, many dynamic American social movements have brought changes from below, like the abolition movement in the 1800s, the women's movement of the 1920s, and the civil rights campaign of the 1960s.

DATA is an example of change from below, because ordinary people are key in making the project work. The DATA website acknowledges its role in this regard, by saying, "Again and again, politicians tell us they want to do more for Africa. Then they don't. Why? Because they don't hear from YOU — citizens, voters and taxpayers — that you care and want to see something done. We're here to get the word out that you do care and to give YOU the best ways to get the word out for yourself."[23]

As explained earlier, the elite usually receive more attention than the masses as the agent of social change and communication in any society. Similarly, as the state-centric model suggested, the states and government agencies have traditionally received more attention as the means for change and communication. Nevertheless, we emphasized the important role that NGOs (both pro-profit and non-profit) play in terms of international communication and change. Thus, their impact should not be underestimated in a global village, as the complex interdependence model implies. In the same lines, one must recognize that initiatives "from below" are not any less effective or important than those "from above" in society, as the earlier examples indicated.

In practice, one may wonder where to start the journey for change. The answer rests in three major and overlapping steps. The first step is self-awareness of our environmental realities. Next is behaving as a citizen diplomat — one who is mindful in his/her behavior toward others. And finally, is the recognition that we are all parts of a larger game in life, as global citizens who aim to resolve international challenges beyond our individual abilities. As we repeated in different parts of this work, these steps can be taken only by effective communication, commitment, and cooperation toward common goals. These four "C"s are relevant at the micro level (e.g. improving our ties with someone special) as they are at the macro level (e.g. bringing peace to a community).

Time after time, this book has shifted focus from macro to micro issues and vice versa, while trying to show a connection between the two. This was consciously done because the macro and micro levels of behavior are not as isolated from one another as some assume. This point can be illustrated by a real example of how awareness, citizen diplomacy, and world citizenship work in our everyday life. The following example also illustrates that the macro and micro levels of issues and goals are actually interconnected.

International exchange programs

The Mutual Educational and Cultural Exchange of the US Congress Act of 1961 (better known as the Fulbright-Hays Act) is one of the best examples of connecting international and domestic issues as well as macro and micro levels. This Act is also the foundation of the International Visitor Leadership Program, which is administered by the US Department of State Bureau of Educational and Cultural Affairs and the Office of International Visitors. The goal of the program is to increase mutual understanding through communication at the personal and professional levels between American citizens and foreign nationals. Overseas participants are often among the established or potential foreign leaders in government, business, media, education, science, labor organizations, or other fields. They are selected by American embassies overseas to visit the United States to meet and confer with their professional counterparts, and to experience the country firsthand.

At the local level, this program is facilitated through community organizations such as the World Affairs Council of Central Florida (the former International Council of Central Florida or ICCF) located in Orlando, Florida, which hosts foreign visitors designated by the program leaders in Washington and introduces them to residents in the Central Florida region, local cultural amenities, and recreational activities. Appropriately enough, members of this NGO are referred to as citizen diplomats, who serve as American cultural ambassadors. The World Affairs Council of Central Florida members are ordinary people who converse with the visitors, organize their cultural activities, and escort them to local governmental and non-governmental agencies in addition to performing functions that one may usually expect from a diplomat accommodating a dignitary in the US.[24]

This example of how average citizens bring intercultural awareness and involvement to the local level is not limited to Orlando. In fact, there are a number of NGOs similar to the World Affairs Council of Central Florida with similar programs all around the US, from Los Angeles to New York and from Chicago to Houston. They all accommodate local individuals and businesses facing intercultural challenges and interactions. In fact, with more than 5,000 NGOs throughout the globe, there are many opportunities for cultural exchanges. In our "shrinking world," ordinary locals and professionals are empowered by engaging in intercultural relations and citizen diplomacy all over the country and around the world. They even provide informal training to people and businesses involved in intercultural relations, much like the knowledge presented in this book. Thus, all over the country, citizens have the opportunity to engage in citizen diplomacy, raise the level of mindfulness, and recognize themselves as global citizens.

The above case illustrates the interconnections between the micro and macro levels. Now, we will turn to a discussion of a few macro-level issues, since previous chapters have mainly concentrated on the individual and personal levels in IR. The macro-level issues include a diverse group of topics that a global citizen can either directly or indirectly address. Whether it is ending a war, dealing with the roots of terrorism, reducing poverty, helping to eradicate AIDS and other health hazards, or management of an environmental menace, we believe that an individual can make a difference.

Politics of war and peace

War and conflict are issues that have plagued mankind since the beginning of civilization. Throughout history, as humans have evolved and become more technologically advanced, their thirst for war and destruction has dramatically increased. There have been an estimated 350 wars since the battle of Waterloo, whereby Napoleon's defeat was thought to be the precursor of a period of peace. Nearly 100 years later, the war to end all wars (World War I) was fought on a global scale; only to have the destruction repeated (in the form of World War II) twenty years later.[25] War is an integral part of human history and is vital in the foundation of politics, international relations, and intercultural exchanges. More important, there is a remarkable correlation between war and power, usually the presence of one will bring on another.

In an international conflict, the various actors usually have different sets of socio-cultural values and norms. Just a few of their many differences can cause tension and eventually a full-scale clash of ideologies. Historically, it was the expansion of geographic power that motivated many powerful civilizations to act in aggression. Peace only came after one party dutifully pledged allegiance or subordination to the dominating power. In modern times, we observe many cases whereby the enemy is not constricted to a specific geographic boundary. We now have wars based upon ideologies, for example, the American "war against terror." There is a definite factor (9/11) that ignited the war on terror, however, we know that the differences in religions, power, distance, and culture have all contributed to the tragic situation and the late Samuel Huntington reiterated this point when he stated that American civilization is in a clash with others.[26] Huntington even argued that the American culture is on a collision course with the Islamic culture, prompting misunderstandings on both sides.[27] For some, this type of thinking is an important determining factor of the animosity that the populations of opposing sides may hold against each other. However, the themes of this work contradict with such reasoning.

A well-known conflict that has lasted since 1948 is the Israeli–Palestinian conflict. While the conflict has grown so complex that general labels cannot be used to pinpoint the main causes of the war, ideological and geographical interests play a vital role in the perpetuation of the clash. The two groups both claim the same territory as being rightfully their own. Amidst those claims are various groups that advocate everything from a peaceful co-existence to territorial transfer to complete territorial removal. Unfortunately, the religious ideology differs greatly, and causes an immense tension between the two nations. The future of important geographical and historical landmarks continues to be in question. The West Bank, the Gaza Strip, and East Jerusalem, which carries immense religious significance for both groups, are geographical points of conflict. In fact, over the centuries, Jerusalem has been completely destroyed and rebuilt 17 times. In addition to geographical factors, the security and recognition of the state of Israel has been challenged many times and the fate of Palestinian refugees is constantly called into question. Both civilizations understand the generalities of the other culture; however, many times there is an intentional rejection of each other on the political level. This animosity has become so entrenched that new generations grow up and are educated to despise the other. As the international community has grown, support for both sides has increased and awareness has spread globally. Some supporters of the Palestinian resistance feel that the violence is necessary and justifiable due to what appears to be an illegitimate occupation of Palestinian territory. However, friends of the Israeli front believe that the Israelis are acting in self-defense and have the right to demand the removal of Palestinians who are not Israeli citizens.[28] The U.N. has stepped in numerous times in an attempt mediate the situation, with mixed results. The United Nations Security Council has offered numerous resolutions, although many solutions have been vetoed due to the sympathy of Council members whenever certain resolutions harshly criticize one party.

The Israeli-Palestinian conflict continues to present itself as a perpetuating case study of international conflict. Numerous peace treaties have been signed throughout the years, such as the Egypt-Israel treaty (1979) and the Jordan-Israel treaty (1994). Furthermore, nations have attempted to aid in peace talks (e.g. the Hebron Agreement) that discussed the redeployment of Israeli military forces in Hebron or the Camp David Accords of 2000, which proposed temporary control of 10 percent of the West Bank to Israel, an area mostly inhabited by Jewish settlements. At the time, the late Palestinian President Arafat felt that such configurations would give Israelis the ability to block Palestinian travel in the area, thus the offer was rejected. Negotiations continued, but no agreements were made.

Globalization has increased the complexity of this conflict because more international parties are now involved. Arab nations offer their support to the Palestinians, while the Western states tend to favor the plight of Israel. Whether for geographical, religious, ideological, or political reasons, nation-states are clamoring to bear some authority over a Middle East resolution. These alliances tend to cause tension among other countries. For example, the United

States, an outspoken supporter of Israel, serves as a permanent member of the Security Council in the United Nations. China feels that the UN is hindered in the Israeli-Palestinian peace process because of the United States' influence. The United States has openly offered support of Israel's military attacks against Lebanon's Hezbollah, because the US government has labeled Hezbollah a "terrorist organization." Meanwhile, parties in Lebanon argue that numerous civilians are suffering because of Israel's military actions. Unfortunately, no military conflict will ever be waged without the loss of numerous civilian casualties, especially a conflict rooted as deeply as the Israeli-Palestinian conflict. The failure of the UN to bring peace to the region damages the authority and status of the United Nations, according to the former UN Secretary General Kofi Annan. When the globe is filled with sovereign nation-states, they may pledge global integration and peace, but they will ultimately work in a self-preservation mode. In a self-help world, according to Alexander Wendt, "anarchy is what states make of it." The US demonstrated this when it attacked Iraq without the formal "approval" of the U.N. This incident served as a reminder to all that countries are still ultimately sovereign over their own actions and affairs.[29] Powerful states still retain sovereignty to do as they will — assertion that realism remains relevant in explaining states' behavior in the international arena.

From this perspective, the Palestinian-Israeli conflict merely exemplifies the heightened intensity and strain between two different cultures. Perhaps no other conflict is as passionately and emotionally fueled by those so geographically removed from the situation than in this conflict.[30] Ultimately, even countries that are not the main parties in the conflict are still affected indirectly. The United States' support of Israel has cost it its reputation in the Middle East. Most of the Arab people are now diametrically opposed to US Middle East policy because it is viewed as tainted and imperialistic. Great Britain, a long-time US ally, has also suffered a damaged image. British opinion polls found that a large part of the British populace felt that Prime Minister Tony Blair's relationship with the Bush administration was too close and needed more autonomy.[31] In fact, many believe that Tony Blair's closeness with the Bush administration ultimately led to his and the Labor Party's downfall. This indicates that the British global role impacted its internal affairs. Public suspicion of Blair's policy led to his downfall.

In the Palestinian-Israeli conflict, negative stereotypes, misunderstandings, and long-lasting suspicions appear to dominate the political environment. Currently, communication from either side fails to bear any substantial weight, because each side views the other with a great deal of suspicion. The rift among them continues to grow, as both civilizations continuously feel threatened. As long as the Palestinians live under occupation, exposed to daily humiliation, and as long as Israelis are blown up in buses and in dance halls, the passions of both sides will rule and will be inflamed.[32] Moreover, resentment grows among these communities due to the lack of successful reforms. This in turn fuels extremism and violent action. Therefore, political leaders should utilize their resources to increase the mindfulness and communication among their people in order to encourage positive actions towards the peace process.

In the international arena, nations essentially have two general methods of securing their interests and reaching goals. They could use either hard or soft power. When a state utilizes soft power, it is using channels of diplomatic negotiations to obtain its goals. On the contrary, the use of hard power indicates the ability of a state to use aggression and brute force to achieve its interests.[33] An example of the successful implementation of soft power and diplomacy is the Cold War. Despite massive military armament and strategies on both sides, the superpowers rivalry never turned "hot" or into a battle of annihilation. Even during the Cuban Missile Crisis, the channel of communication between the American and Russian leaders remained open. After this crisis, the superpowers even upgraded the direct communication line between their capitals, with the establishment of the Red Line connecting Washington with Moscow. Furthermore, hard and soft power can be the reflection of war and peace. When leaders use diplomacy, they are essentially agreeing to a peaceful settlement of dispute, avoiding the escalation of the situation.

Communication can intricately weave states and nations together or it can tear them apart. Seemingly simple phrases and actions can have a profound impact across cultures. Neutral or well-intended words, spoken thoughtlessly, can destroy relations among nations. In 2006, Pope Benedict XVI gave a lecture at the University of Regensburg in Germany, where he used to preside as a professor of theology. His lecture, entitled "Faith, Reason and the University — Memories and Reflections," focused mainly on Christianity and the tendency to "exclude the question of God." However, amidst his lecture, the Pope mentioned Islam and quoted the Byzantine Emperor Manuel II Paleologos who stated, "Show me just what Muhammad brought that was new and there you will find things only bad and inhuman, such as his command to spread by the sword the faith he preached."[34]

While the Pope stated that the words were not his own and he had used the quote to compare the idea that there is "no compulsion in religion" as opposed to the mode of thought that is acceptable to "spread the faith through violence," his desire to explain backfired.[35] Pope Benedict's intentions were to spread awareness of the importance of reason when dealing with religion. However, his words spurred negative thoughts and actions from the Islamic world. Some Muslims staged marches in Jerusalem (Israel), the West Bank, Gaza, and Khartoum (Sudan). Palestinian protesters were seen waving Hamas' banners and accusing the Pope of being a "coward" and an "agent of the Americans."[36] Since then, the pontiff has opened his home to invite the Italian Muslim Consulates in the hope of alleviating the tension caused by his words, and reopen the dialogue between the Catholic and Islamic community.[37] Pope Benedict's statements may have been innocent and well intended toward improving relations between the West and Islam, but to many in the Islamic community, the perception of the statement's origin was negative. It portrayed the West as being "Islamophobic" and drew attention away from the Pope's interfaith initiatives. The lack of mindfulness of Islamic sensitivities and culture essentially confirmed the suspicious perception of Muslims toward Western thought. Moreover, the West was not given a strong perception of a peaceful Islam when the reaction of numerous extremist Muslims showed their disapproval through violent demonstrations. An Iraq branch of al-Qaeda promised to "break the Cross and spill the wine," thus leaving Christians the only option of "Islam or death." Later, in Mogadishu, a Muslim Somali was reported to have been shot in the back; he then murdered a Roman Catholic nun who ministered to the poor. These events led both cultures and religions to be painted in a negative light.

Since cultures are irretrievably different, they are likely to clash with each other, especially when there is a lack of mutual understanding. Thus, some claim "violent conflicts between groups in different civilizations are the most likely and most dangerous source of escalation that could lead to global wars."[38] Just as mindfulness at micro- or personal-level intercultural communication avoids unwanted conflicts, at the macro level where stakes are high due to war and peace issues, world leaders should also be mindful when dealing with leaders from diverse cultures in order to steer clear of unintended conflicts.

A closer look at terrorism

Ever since the 9/11 attacks on the World Trade Center and the Pentagon, the term "terrorism" has become a household word throughout America. We are constantly bombarded by the media and politicians spreading information about the "war on terror," even going as far as implementing a terror alert scale, which ranks the level of national security on a color-coded scale. Beyond clear-cut situations like 9/11, however, it is not always obvious who terrorists are, especially since our perception of terrorism is a function of the cultural values and political consideration of the day, as reported by the mass media and advocated by politicians.

Generally speaking, terrorism refers to an illegal use of violence against non-combatants to generate fear and bring about compliance with specific political, religious, or personal demands.[39] As a type of unconventional war, the influence of terrorism is usually attributed to the vivid attention of mass media in magnifying feelings of deep fear and anger. This is how cultural values change our perceptions of terrorism, which can be initiated by an individual, a group, or even a state. Terrorism is not confined to a single group, nation, or region, thus anyone who acts in the defined manner can be labeled as a terrorist, although some groups tend to get more attention than others.

Moreover, it is a cliché that one man's terrorist is another man's freedom fighter. Since "terrorism" has a negative connotation, many potential terrorists may identify themselves with a variety of other labels, such as freedom fighter, rebel, separatist, liberator, revolutionary, or guerrilla. Even terrorists believe that there are moral and immoral forms of terrorism. The use of violence in instances of defeating slavery and genocide can be seen as moral usages of terrorism. Contrarily, the use of terror tactics to oppress a group of people can be seen as immoral. Terrorists who are in the minority group often justify their actions as retributive, in that they believe their enemy deserves punishment, either under national law or religious law. There is also a thin line between traditional wars and terrorism, in that traditional wars are usually "legal" and terrorism is "illegal."[40] It is usually the dominant group that defines what is to be a "legal" war and what is considered to be a terrorist operation, condemning only actions not in their interests.

This discussion of "legal" and "illegal" terrorism brings back to focus the struggle between the in-group and out-group. Many individuals in the European, Latin American, and Arab cultures believe the American presence in their land is an act of terrorism. To them, America is the oppressor, using its unchallengeable military power to coerce American policies on the local population. This is highly contrary to what we are led to believe by our American media and politicians; justifying our presence as a means of spreading democracy and preventing further terrorist attacks on American soil. As Americans, we also understand that the 9/11 attacks were a major contributing factor to our operations in the Middle East. However, we must note that between 1983 and 1998, there were over 2,400 attacks on American citizens, facilities and interests, of which America responded only three times.[41] This is a clear example of the dominant group condemning and retaliating only when the interests are in their favor. This does not mean America is a terrorist state, as some claim, it just serves as an example of the unbalanced power scale we are exposed to in modern international relations. Clearly, the differences in culture dictate how individuals define terrorism.

Western mass media tend to label individuals "terrorists" when they are fighting for liberation, and the same people "statesmen" when they succeed in liberating their country. Two examples are Nobel Peace Prize winners like Menachem Begin (former head of the anti-British Zionist underground group the Irgun Gang and former Israeli Prime Minister) and Nelson Mandela (former anti-apartheid armed resistance member and first President of liberated South Africa). For cultural or political reasons, even states that are close allies can disagree if members of a particular group should be considered terrorists. For instance, even though the Irish Republican Army used violent methods against the UK, some American leaders refused to label IRA members as "terrorist," simply because of the Irish-American lobbying efforts and several pro-IRA Congressmen. In the UK, however, the IRA was and continues to be labeled as a "terrorist group."[42]

In modern times, terrorism has gone into a grey area of definition. Depending on the culture, terrorist activities can be viewed in a positive or negative light. The task of condemning terrorism can only be assigned to those groups that submit positive solutions to the problems that breed terrorism.[43]

Is there a difference between terrorists and freedom fighters? The change of label is an attempt to portray a different message to the public; however, there are actual distinctions between a freedom fighter and a terrorist. Freedom fighters tend to be more regional. The Palestinian Liberation Organization (PLO) was labeled as a terrorist organization, however, its goal to repossess Palestine was regionally oriented. The PLO engaged in violence in order to gain attention — from Israel, the global media, and the world. Once they were politically recognized, the PLO agreed to meet with Israel. While the negotiations may not have always produced positive and peaceful results, the PLO willingly used diplomacy and negotiations.

On the contrary, al-Qaeda bears different methods and goals. Al-Qaeda has no interest in negotiations. Their goal is total annihilation of the "infidels." Reasoning, diplomacy and negotiation — all lack meaning to this terrorist organization. They will not be stopped until they have destroyed their enemy by whatever means necessary. Both PLO and al-Qaeda have caused the deaths of thousands of civilians, however, al-Qaeda shows less interest in the loss of human life if it furthers its cause.

Some media agencies, such as the BBC and Reuters, aside from attributed quotes, avoid using the phrases "terrorist" or "freedom fighter," in order to steer clear of their political repercussions. The BBC did, however, refer to the Catholic Irish Republican Army (IRA) as terrorists, while members of the Protestant armed groups in Northern Ireland were usually referred to as "paramilitaries" instead of terrorists. The IRA was formed by the political group Sinn Fein in 1969 as a legal political movement determined to remove the British presence from Northern Ireland and unify the entire country. Based on Marxist principles, the IRA operated under the leadership of the Army Council. Hundreds of fighters struck from small cells distributed throughout Ireland. They gained strong support from sympathizers in the Irish Catholic population, and even received financial support from citizens of the United States. While their operations are reported to have training grounds in Libya, with funding and influence from the PLO and possibly the ETA, they have isolated their attacks to focus on the British government. Their activities have ranged from bombings and assassinations to kidnappings and robberies. Targets have included numerous senior British officials, Northern Irish Loyalist paramilitary groups, police, and military. Members of the IRA are touted by many supporters to be freedom fighters because of their open, political goals. The IRA declared a ceasefire on July 19, 1997, when it was promised entry into negotiations regarding Northern Ireland's political future. While all acts of violence and unrest failed to cease, the hard 17-month "terrorism" campaign led by the IRA ended, and a notable decrease in violence was recorded.[44]

Still, there are several organizations with blatant terrorist intentions. The Japanese Red Army (JRA), founded by Fusako Shigenobu in 1971, stemmed from the Red Army Faction of the Japanese Communist League, also known as the Anti-Imperialist International Brigade (AIIB) or the Nippon (Japan) Sekigun. While the group only reached around 400 members at its peak, it was once considered one of the best-known armed leftist groups. The stated goals of the JRA were to overthrow the Japanese government and instigate a revolution. Their tactics intentionally disregarded any actions that would lead to negotiation. The JRA was responsible for the hijacking of the Japanese Airlines Boeing 727 on March 31, 1970, before breaking away from the Japanese Communist League. Eight terrorists carried a bomb onto the plane, which was carrying 129 people.

Through and through, just as people can be positive world citizens, so too can people detrimentally influence the world. The Japanese Red Army not only struck domestically, but it took its war abroad. Two years after the plane hijacking, the terrorist group was tied in with the machine gun and grenade attack on the Lod Airport (now Ben Gurion International Airport) in Tel Aviv, Israel. This action cost the lives of 26 people, and injured 80 others. Suicidal terrorist actions aim to attract attention and/or to stir up fear. They offer no deals to governments. In 1974, the Shell facility in Singapore was attacked while a simultaneous assault was launched against the Japanese embassy in Kuwait. Release of hostages taken was negotiated only after a high ransom and safe passage was granted to the terrorists. In 1988, five people were killed in a bombing at the United States military recreational (USO) club in Naples, Italy.

There is not a clear winner and loser when a group utilizes terror tactics. Although recognition is usually the achieved goal, the historical records show terrorism to be a mixed bag in the ultimate cause of that particular group. The only real victimization in terrorism is the loss of innocent life, which highlights the humanitarian significance of terrorism. Here, being mindful helps in identifying the problem and the sense of world citizenship provides the means for managing this global challenge.

Business and the global economy

The demise of the Soviet Union and the end of the Cold War accompanied a period of flourishing global free-market trade, which had been facilitated by the technological boom. Among many developing nations, there is a sense of urgency in competing for investment capital from developed countries. New advances in technology have lessened the communication gap between nations around the world. The introduction of the internet along with e-commerce allows a network of global businesses to interact on a real-time basis. Also, MNCs are now able to have multiple operations and markets around the globe, all operating from a single headquarters. All of these factors resulted in what is known as globalization, an umbrella term explaining the complex interrelated processes, structures, forces, agents, and effects of the global economy.[45] There is much discussion about globalization in the modern business world, especially the viability of a global economy. Although scholars are unable to predict the future, they do acknowledge globalization is occurring and many businesses and nation-states are embracing it with open arms.

Since the 1990s the term "globalization" has become a common buzzword, frequently used in the mass media, political propaganda, and among intellectual circles. However, globalization is not a completely new phenomenon, as its main characteristics can be found in other periods throughout history.

Global trade characteristics, such as the free movement of capital, technology, ideas, human resources, and goods were apparent as early as the ancient era of the Silk Road, which connected Asian trade to Europe via the Middle East. What differentiates modern globalization from its past is the immense impact of new technologies of the communication revolution. Collectively, these technologies and their interactions are producing a knowledge-based economy that systematically changes how people conduct their economic and social lives.[46]

Today, globalization is the system that governs international affairs. Nations are increasingly interconnected with one another. Moreover, there are more windows of opportunity and communication through these growing interconnections. While globalization in itself is neither naturally "good" nor "bad," it bears potential for great influence depending on the way it is used. If it is abused, coercion through globalization bears negative effects, whereas treaties, charities, and unions can bring nations greater opportunities. Journalist Thomas Friedman, in his book *The Lexus and the Olive Tree*, wrote: "[Globalization] can be incredibly empowering and incredibly coercive. It can democratize opportunity and democratize panic. It makes the whales bigger and the minnows stronger. It leaves you behind faster and faster, and it catches up to you faster and faster. While it is homogenizing cultures, it is also enabling people to share their unique individuality farther and wider." Globalization is constantly met with different receptions. Businesses are finding that the international market presents an opportunity to offset cutbacks in profit on the domestic market. The United States exports a fifth of industrial production and a third of its farm products. More and more businesses are supported by exports from multinational corporations. In fact, about one fifth of economic growth activity is attributed to exports — which leads pro-market experts to suggest that "trade is the engine of growth." Globalization expands economic freedom and encourages business competition, which in turn raises the standards of living and productivity. However, it has also caused the loss of jobs, the increase of pay cuts, and the vulnerability of organizations as more and more businesses move abroad.

McDonald's epitomizes a globalized business. With over 31,000 restaurants in more than 119 countries on six continents, and employing 1.5 million people, McDonald's is one of the most recognized brands in the world, with its prominent golden arches and friendly clown, Ronald McDonald. Its impact has been immense, with one out of eight Americans having been employed at some point by the corporation. Sometimes, its effect is referred to as "McDonaldization" of society. Selling its inexpensive hamburgers, chicken nuggets, carbonated beverages, French fries and, most recently, fruit and salads, McDonald's offers the community a quick meal on the run.

Despite the success of McDonald's global business, anti-globalism protesters view McDonald's expansion as culturally invasive. As it moves into different communities, it brings the American mindset with it. To this end, McDonald's has been viewed as being culturally imperialistic. But at the same time, McDonald's has standardized service in various countries such as East Asia, where it was the first restaurant in Hong Kong in 1975 to offer consistently clean facilities and restrooms (see Chapter 7 for an analysis of the McDonald's logo). It also erased some social taboos in countries such as Japan, where it was socially unacceptable to eat and walk at the same time. But its influence has also caused it to be the subject of many heated debates, ranging in topics such as corporate ethics, consumer responsibility, obesity, the environment, intellectual property, and animal rights.[47] Concern is not only over the brand influence, but over the brand products as well, and the physical impact on consumers has been raised by numerous activist groups and organizations.

Despite the controversy over products, the brand and its business practices, McDonald's remains sensitive to the cultures it penetrates. It varies ingredients and menu choices depending on the country. In India, for example, McDonald's does not offer a beef hamburger, and has removed the beef tallow it normally used when cooking its fries. The McDonald's in Israel offers a kosher menu that respects the Jewish Shabbat, and in Egypt and Saudi Arabia, the menu items are *halal*, permissible according to Islamic law. This mindfulness, while it has not deterred all criticism, has enabled McDonald's to successfully integrate into the countries' societies.

The corporation has surpassed the simple business, profit-oriented mindset and pushed into philanthropic activities such as its Ronald McDonald House charity. Its largest annual children's fundraiser, World Children's Day, is celebrated in over 100 countries and raises funds for children's charities. Famous celebrities such as former football player Emmitt Smith and the Duchess of York, Sarah Ferguson, participate in the fundraiser by serving at the counters in various McDonald's restaurants or making public service announcements regarding the event. In Japan, pop stars Tatsuya Ishii and Maki Ohguro were featured at a fundraising concert; Mexico-based McDonald's sold World Children's Day anniversary T-shirts. Over 31,000 restaurants help to raise support for its 260 Ronald McDonald Houses. The Ronald McDonald House Organization also brings awareness to the needs of many children throughout the world.[48] To date, McDonald's charities have raised over $440 million to improve the lives of children. So, in the mixed bag of globalization, while McDonald's intrudes on different societies with its own values and ideas, it also brings some positive values and ideas that can produce a positive impact while remaining profitable as a global business.

The fundamental rule of economics states that as the demand grows, prices and supply will eventually increase in correlation. Therefore, when businesses aim to maximize profit, they search to find the cheapest places to produce and the most profitable places to sell their goods and services.[49] Technological advances in communication and transportation entices businesses to increasingly expand their search on both dimensions globally. The developed nations benefit from the expanding business of their firms via tax and stocks, to name a few. Developing nations also benefit by receiving a relatively trained workforce, better infrastructure, economic gain, and political stability, as long as they are willing to play by the rules. When these requisitions are met, then MNCs transfer resources, allowing the developing nation to join in the global economy. Needless to say, international and intercultural factors are at play to make this possible for all.

However, globalization does have fallacies that must be addressed. There is an increasing concern about the effects of a global economy; particularly that globalization will ultimately result in a single global economy. This view portrays the new-world global system as being monolithic and hegemonic, ultimately resulting in a single dominating power penetrating both economic and social cultures.[50] The resulting totalitarian power will attempt to impose its logic and policies for the rest of the world to adopt, essentially destroying state sovereignty. Also, there is a concern about the widening disparity between the available resources for the rich and poor. Today, about half of the world's population lives on under US$2 a day.[51] The low labor rate in developing nations is a highly lucrative factor when MNCs review expansion opportunities. In fact, there are no signs of the income disparity closing, more accurately the gap is actually widening on a global scale.

As discussed in the previous section, the issue of terrorism not only affects political organizations, but the business economy of nation states. As globalization increases and nations open their borders to the international community, vulnerability to terrorist strikes also increases. After the attacks of 9/11, businesses and the economy suffered severe hardships as people became reluctant to travel. Well-known businesses and government installations were essentially placed on lock-down from the public and security was severely heightened in order to preserve the feeling of safety. As we know from Maslow's Hierarchy of Needs, safety and security is extremely important to an individual. Therefore, if one feels unsafe to go out and conduct business, the economy suffers. The airline business presents an example of a business greatly affected by globalization.

In one sense, airlines have immensely benefited and profited from increased globalization. The industry has acted as an anchor for international businesses to travel from state to state. More than two billion people fly every year and the number continues to increase, with cargo transportation by air alone taking in more than $3.2 trillion annually.[52] However, global events can also damage an industry. After the terrorist attacks of 9/11, 50 percent of the United States' airline industry; including Delta, Northwest, and United Airlines, filed for bankruptcy. Nearly a decade after 9/11, most airlines have recovered. Although airports have improved security, they also added a long, frustrating list of new "dos and don'ts" for travelers. The United States government instituted the Transportation Security Authority (TSA) to address new issues in light of the terrorist events, and charged the new transportation authority with the job of screening all passengers and protecting planes and airports from attack. This affects the bottom line for travel agencies, airports, airlines, and the government. The costs of employing TSA agents, the additional security force, screening machines, and even the training drains from the profits of the company or organization.

Nothing destroys the reputation of a tourist destination or travel industry like a failure in security or safety. While many tourists and travelers are still unaware of numerous safety warnings or new travel regulations, the moment there is a slack in either security or safety and a slip-up occurs it carries a detrimental effect on the travel or tourist industry. As technology continues to improve, allowing business trips to be replaced by the option of video conferencing, electronic communication, and phone conferences, travelers may be more inclined to avoid the hassle and risk. In a globalizing world, these are the factors and challenges that tourism and travel businesses face. Along with improving the perception and reality of security, such industries struggle to remember that hospitality still plays a huge party in providing that sense to their guests — because if a guest does not feel cared for, their perception about the business' ability to provide quality service and security will be diminished. Therefore, hotels and airlines have a delicate balance to achieve in order to win and retain clientele.

A strange reality is that as globalization and business opportunities increase for travel and tourism, so do the opportunities and potential for crime and terrorist attacks.[53] Businesses will continually have to devote a substantial amount of finances toward safety and security. Crisis management has become an essential part of any industry in the globalizing world. A larger security force and numerous backup plans are present at theme parks and airports. These forces must be culturally sensitive because of the variety of cultural habits that their customers possess.

People are becoming increasingly aware of terrorism as global travel has increased. Tourism in a globalizing system is at the mercy of a double-edged sword in many ways. On one hand, globalization has brought increased business to developing countries that desperately need the income. In fact, tourism is the third largest global industry after the huge commodities of oil and narcotics. For instance, Bali (Indonesia) attracts more than a million international guests each year. Moreover, technology allows tourist destinations to communicate to potential guests. On the other hand, tourism presents an enticing target for terrorists seeking to make a political statement. Plus, technology also allows bad news to travel more quickly. Tourists represent the West and its ideology; tourism is the symbol of capitalism. Therefore, by attacking state-sponsored tourism, terrorists feel as though they are making a political statement. Tourism also faces the risks of war and recession. All three of these factors greatly hinder tourism. While civil wars are rare among more developed countries, tourist destinations in the developing world, such as Kenya, Egypt, or Bali, are far more vulnerable to terrorism.[54]

Through globalization, individuals of different cultures interact with each other on a daily basis. While the caravans of the Silk Road took years to bring messages from one corner of the world to the other, now it takes a second to do so. This promotes knowledge-sharing among individuals and a better understanding between cultures producing more mindful global citizens. The effects of globalization can be seen everywhere in our daily lives, whether it is chatting on the internet or receiving merchandise from eBay. If it is used in a mindful fashion, globalization can ultimately produce an atmosphere of mutual understanding and relative peace among all humans. Contrarily, if its power is left unchecked, then we may be faced with a totalitarian global authority, resulting in the demise of domestic economies, the loss of control over state sovereignty, and destruction of rival cultures around the world. Thus, better international communication again plays a significant role for a win-win global situation.

MEDIA IMPACT
Converged Wireless Communication and Computing Devices Stirs a New Social Revolution and Puts Power in the Hands of the Masses

As more and more individuals across the globe increasingly use converged wireless communication devices, capable of multimedia tasks and computing, new forms of engagement with other individuals throughout the world are available. The way people create projects, share ideas, meet with one another, work, and even govern has changed and is progressively transforming right before our eyes. What is most interesting about the fact that more citizens are using multimedia mobiles is that it gives people more than one way to take part in collective action using their very own handheld devices.

An example of mobile communication use and collective action was seen in the Philippines when political activists engaged in an attempt to overthrow a repressive regime by using text messages via mobile phones to take part in collective action. Their plan succeeded on January 20, 2001, when the "smart mob" made President Joseph Estrada of the Philippines the first leader to ever lose power to collective wireless communication action. Over one million Manila citizens mobilized and communicated via text messaging to assemble together to bring down the regime. On Epifanio de los Santos Avenue, also know as "Edsa," tens of thousands of Filipinos came together after all receiving a text message reading, "Go 2EDSA, Wear blck." More than a million people gathered over a period of four days and for the most part, were wearing black.

This is just one example of the social revolution that multimedia mobiles have initiated, bringing new forms of power to ordinary citizens. In November 1999, autonomous protesters of the World Trade Organization's meeting used laptops, websites, and mobile phones to win the "Battle of Seattle." In September 2000, a massive number of citizens in Britain, angered over skyrocketing gasoline prices, took advantage of SMS, mobile phones, laptops, and CB radios to communicate with one another and block fuel delivery to certain stations. Although these are just a few, brief examples, there have been many other instances, and we are likely to see even more in the future.

It is important to note that this cooperation and collaboration of the masses using mobile technology has many implications, with both positive and negative dimensions. After all, large-scale coordinated outbreaks catalyzed the collapse of communism. With our connected world and numerous open lines of instant communication, human beings can share a "collective intelligence." As more and more people use mobile technology, we become more and more dependent on technology. People then use these technologies or new media to create new forms of their own, whether it be within the entertainment industry, commerce, or any other area. As people have a greater relative advantage with the ability to organize with many across the globe via communication and information technology, it is evident that collective action, whether good or bad, becomes much easier and more eminent. With the use of such technology among ordinary individuals, their level of power increases and their overall awareness of who they are communicating to and what actions they make, are more important than ever.

Sources: Howard Rheingold, *Smart Mobs: The Next Social Revolution* (Cambridge, MA: Perseus Publishing, 2002), pp. 157–82. Eric P. Bucy, *Living in the Information Age: A New Media Reader*, 2nd ed. (Australia: Wadsworth/Thompson, 2005), pp. 231–9.

Preservation, sustainability, and the environment

It is impossible to separate development and globalization from environmental concerns, since all human activity impacts our environment, without which we cannot survive as a species. How humankind will transform its economic growth into an environmentally sustainable system for living on this delicate planet is presently unknown and in some circles is in considerable doubt. Nations choosing a rapid economic development approach usually set environmental issues aside while concentrating on growth. For instance, China is currently overwhelmed with many environmental and health concerns and is a victim of its own unchecked modernization progress. Some observers may even argue that the environment has become a strain on human progress.[55] It is only in recent years that international environmental issues such as global warming and the loss of the ozone layer have come to the attention of the masses, as well as policymakers. When issues of environmental sustainability span across borders, the mediation of the situation involves different cultures. Many times, the differences in culture and attitude prohibit these issues from becoming fully resolved. Often, the breakdown of cross-cultural communication and the lack of understanding allow the problems to persist, while the damaging effects on nature continue to occur.

Global tourism serves as a fine example in illustrating problems that allow cultural differences to affect the environment. The new transportation methods allow tourists to travel to exotic places around the world. Tourism provides a strong opportunity for cultures to learn about one another. The tourists' perceptions of a destination depend on the experience they encounter during the visit. Tourism offers an opportunity for individuals to act as citizen diplomats. The Disney World parks (in Florida) provide examples of places where numerous ethnic groups representing various cultures come to taste one aspect of American culture. Entire families and many times, multiple generations, visit the Sunshine State to meet Mickey Mouse. From January through

March 2005, Florida alone saw 23.8 million visitors.[56] Theme parks that once were a day experience, have now become a week-long experience due to their strategic repositioning in the market. Advertising encourages longer visits in order to experience all that the theme parks offer. Besides increasing the revenue gained from the tourists' extended visit, the visitors are also receiving an extended cultural experience. During these tourist visits, people build on their knowledge of what is for them a foreign culture.

In eco-tourism, popular tourist destinations enjoy a strong and unique environmental ecosystem — the quality that tourists seek. These destinations usually have a delicate ecosystem that has yet to be affected by human development. The environmental challenges arise when members of a foreign culture, who are either unaware or just inconsiderate in manner, do not respect the local traditions and end up damaging the environment in the process. A good example is San Felipe, Mexico, which has become a very popular tourist destination in recent years. This small coastal fishing village was once a major colony for a rich variety of seabirds and immense mangrove areas.[57] The past decade saw this fishing village transform into a tourist Mecca, primarily with all-terrain-vehicle enthusiasts. The tourists who come here enjoy riding their ATVs along the beach, finding great enjoyment in driving though pelican colonies. The vehicles, however, have caused soil loss and long-term soil erosion along with damages to the bird colonies. As a result, the tourists have gradually destroyed the special features of the ecosystem that attracted them to visit in the first place.

Florida is well known for its everglades and mangrove swamps. There are estuaries, plants, and animal species in Florida that cannot be found anywhere else in the world. Hawaii boasts floral beauties and creations that can only be enjoyed on one of the many volcanic islands in the Pacific Ocean. Residents of these tourist destinations can influence visitors by interacting and sharing their enjoyment and pride for the natural beauty of their region. This also requires governments to proceed carefully to market the environmental beauties; and to limit the number of tourists; in order to minimize their environmental impact. There must always be a sensitivity to preserve wildlife in its natural setting. Balancing the preservation of the environment and the material benefits of tourism is a difficult and delicate task.

There are also challenges in the eco-tourism industry at an international level. International guests are often accustomed to certain minimum amenities for an eco-trip. Some cultural groups are used to more modern amenities, even in the outdoors format, than the primitive necessities provided by the hosts. Of course, it is not easy to balance the environmental concerns and the site investment cost. Economic growth is necessary for eco-tourism to be successful. Globalization of information can help in this area by communicating and informing the special features of each site. Nowadays, formerly obscure tourist destinations (like Thailand beaches) market themselves as new, quiet, and beautiful vacation destinations. In conjunction with such advertising campaigns, the governments invest resources to clean up the beaches, develop resorts, and organize special sites in order to entice visitors. Amidst their beauty, the jungle roads are improved to ease the visitors' access to the country's natural beauties.[58]

Eco-tourism's focus on the environment and conservation also improves cultural understanding. The challenges of learning to adapt to different cultural backgrounds can eventually be eased as more visitors arrive and an understanding is developed between the guest and the hosts. The natural aspect of eco-tourism provides the visitors with a sense of a "pure," enriching vacation, free from the superficiality of heavily commercialized tourist destinations.[59] Whether through urban tourism, theme park experiences, or eco-tourism host nations can utilize the opportunities to serve as citizen diplomats.

Beyond these experiences of mindfulness, individuals have the opportunity of influencing the representatives of other cultures right at home. Warren Griffith, a Southern Baptist missionary "journeyman," founded Mission to Japan in 1993. After living and teaching in Japan for two years, Griffith brought back six Japanese students to the United States so they could experience the American culture first-hand. This way, he established the first home-stay program. Seeing the need to minister to Japanese students and the opportunity for cross-cultural communication when American families became involved, Warren and his wife (Yukari Takeda, the eldest daughter of a Japanese pastor) set out to work full-time in this ministry. On a voluntarily basis, Mission to Japan seeks to bring the "gospel to Japan through mission trips and 'home stay' programs." The ministry is concerned that Japan has an exceptionally high suicide rate, especially among young people.[60] That is why Griffith focused on ministering to students ranging from 16 to 22. It was during these exchanges that the host American families interacted with visiting Japanese students and both sides learned about each other's culture.

The main location in the United States for these particular home-stay programs is Orlando, Florida. Therefore, many foreign students are exposed to American culture, English language classes, local wetlands, nearby beaches, and Disney World and other theme parks. Japanese students are often impressed with the quality hospitality and love that they experienced from their American hosts.[61] The connections promote a stronger sense of understanding between the two cultures. It also provides the American family a chance to act as a cultural ambassador without ever leaving home, because they represent America to the Japanese students. Much of what the students experience in America is due to the efforts and forethought of the host family.

So far, over 600 students have participated in the Mission to Japan home-stay program. During the program, American high school and college students volunteer to befriend the Japanese students. While they help teach the Japanese students how to speak English, the American students learn more about their guests' culture, traditions, and world view. Thus, this exchange program establishes cross-cultural friendships, and it is also educational. Such a set-up promotes communication between two diverse cultures, and improves individual relationships, which are the building blocks of better and more comprehensive ties between American and Japanese people at the national levels.

While traveling to another country, the individuals subconsciously represent their home country and culture. Even amidst environmental and humanitarian crisis, like the 2010 Haiti earthquake, people are fully aware of their own background and their differences with the foreign volunteers. Robert Smith, Founder and President of Agathos Foundation, understands this notion as he strives to improve the lives of thousands in Africa. The Agathos Foundation's mission states it aims:

1. To act as a pillar of support to the Agathos structure in providing care for orphans and widows by providing teams to work in physical, spiritual, and cultural functions on a short- or long-term basis.
2. Bring the living gospel of Christ into the mission field through direct contact with the community in both a long- and short-term setting.
3. Educate people on the current pandemic facing the peoples of South Africa by direct contact with the crisis and equipping them to educate others in their local communities, thus enhancing global awareness.[62]

The Agathos Foundation is passionately spreading awareness of the dire African situation and formulating plans and actions, considering that over 20 million people have died worldwide due to AIDS. The majority of them were living in Africa, and they were survived by 14 million AIDS orphans. Over 40 million are currently living with the virus in Zambia and South Africa, with a 19.95 percent HIV adult prevalence rate, and the death toll continues to climb. During his travels, Smith learned that 47.1 percent of Zambia's total population is under the age of fifteen. That awareness turned to action. The Agathos Foundation believes caring for the poor, orphans, and impoverished communities are a global responsibility. Individuals that contribute or work with the organization act as global citizens. They have moved beyond a simple state of mindfulness and have committed their lives to involvement on the world stage. Children in such regions face incredible suffering and death on a daily basis. The loss of parents strips away their source of security and comfort. Children are left to raise children, so education is not a realistic possibility. Exploitive and abusive situations are incredibly high. In fact, the high death tolls are affecting the economy of sub-Saharan Africa, as much of the working population dies off at increasingly alarming rates. Healthy, educated, able-bodied, and motivated workers are becoming scarcer, and the national wealth of such states continues to drain as the poverty rate continues to climb.

To address the situation, Agathos Foundation members have developed a system to provide "a highly cost-effective, easily replicable support system for the unique needs of orphans and the elderly."[63] The foundation follows the old Chinese Proverb, "Give a man a fish and you feed him for a day; teach a man to fish and you feed him for a lifetime." Agathos establishes farming communities in order to provide families a way of sustaining themselves in the future. By cooperating with US and regional charities, non-governmental organizations, local churches, and cities, the organization provides the necessities for the maintenance of such farms. These farms provide the desperately needed capital for other necessities such as housing, education, and marketable skills.

Workers in the fields are literally acting as cultural ambassadors in the areas where Agathos is operating. These visiting teams get to know the local people and work with them in the fields. As understanding and trust is built between the ambassadors and the community; the teams begin to operate. From this stage, a manual labor team is able to begin the construction of farms and orphanages. This is only possible because solid relationships have formed between the visitors and hosts to improve the quality of life for the villagers. Eventually, Agathos aims to build self-sustaining villages and farms that provide an educational and moral foundation for the children in the community. Their main goal is to be fully independent from the international aid.

To make a difference in a community, one does not need to travel; one can make change in their own local community. Candy Lightner and Cindy Lamb founded Mothers Against Drunk Driving or the MADD (originally called Mothers Against Drunk Drivers) organization over 25 years ago following the tragic death of Lightner's 13-year-old daughter Cari, when she was hit by a drunk driver while she was walking to a church carnival in May of 1980. Shortly before that, in November of 1979, Lamb and her six-month-old daughter, Laura, were hit by a drunk driver on their way to the grocery store, and Laura became the nation's youngest quadrapeligic. Laura later died of complications at the age of seven. Lightner started the MADD organization in her daughter's old bedroom shortly after her death. By September 1980, she had met Lamb, who then started a Maryland chapter of MADD. In the 1980s, drinking and driving was frequent social behavior even though tens of thousands of people died at the hands of drunk drivers. At the time, states were failing to pass DUI bills. On October 1, 1980, Lightner and Lamb riveted the nation during a national press conference on Capitol Hill that created a shift in drunken driving legislation and united mothers around the country.

Over the next 25 years, MADD continued to grow and fight for victims of drunk driving, educate the public, and push for further legislation. Today, the organization has over two million members and supporters. MADD has been able to change laws and social behaviors. It is no longer common in the United States for someone to "grab one for the road" and the term "designated driver" has become a household term. MADD continues to fight for victims of drunk driving, to change the laws that make it easy for minors to purchase alcohol, and they vow that as long as people continue to drive under the influence, they will continue to fight. The MADD organization is a terrific example of a grass-roots effort to effect change at a local level. The efforts of a few mothers has became a nationwide organization that has changed government policy as well as social norms and behavior. As a result of their persistence, hundreds of thousands of lives have been saved.[64]

Another successful example is Rescue a Million, established by a young woman named Julie Butler who used her entrepreneurial mind to make a global difference. She operates as a global citizen to "educate, inspire, and empower millions of people to invest their time, talent, and resources to save the children and the environment." Rescue a Million sets out to plant a million trees and rescue a million children from poverty by 2015. The organization works with various project partners. On the environmental side of the organization, they plant trees to preserve the earth's precious resources for our future. During this process, the organization follows the example of the Grameen Bank by donating to provide families with micro-credit loans. Every 7 to 10 years, the trees are ready for harvest. Some trees are used for lumber so families can rebuild their homes or sold to fund Rescue a Million, while other trees are used for conservation and reforestation projects around the world. Thus, the program has a self-perpetuating support system.

On the humanitarian branch of the organization, Rescue a Million hopes to slow the horrific effects of poverty on the lives of children. Currently, poverty claims the lives of 22 children every minute.[65] Small micro-credit loans are given to families to start small businesses. This allows families an opportunity to improve the quality of life for themselves by providing them with the basic necessities to get a home or business started. The loans are used in areas such as animal husbandry, agricultural products, craft, kiosks, and snack shops.[66] Eventually, as the families become more self-sufficient, the loans are paid back and another family is aided.

The members of organizations are working to be global citizens, and to duplicate their experience in the lives of others who do not enjoy the same fortunate situation. The Orphan Rescue Fund within Rescue a Million partners with families and businesses to support orphans throughout the world. Funds from this organization support vocational training, education, and micro-credit loans. In the US, students are taught to be mindful of other cultures and learn where they can make a difference through the Every Child a Hero program. This program engages children in service and academic learning, teaching them to be involved in their community in the hope that they will begin to take an interest in the world community in the future.

It is through the passions of individuals like Robert Smith (with his Agathos Foundation) and Julie Butler (with her Rescue a Million) that mindfulness gradually evolves into global citizenship. With their vision and efforts, they move beyond impacting their own local communities to influencing larger environments, like their country and the world. Such actions indicate how the local and global environments are interconnected.

Last Remarks

We began this book by explaining the dramatic shifts in the nature of international communication and intercultural relations in the twenty-first century. We have repeatedly shown how the world has shrunk, mainly due to the technological revolution in computers, transportation, and telecommunication. Indeed, there are increased interactions among more local, national, and international actors in our global community than ever before in human history. In the global work environment, more interactions mean more chances for conflict and/or cooperation. People often take cooperation for granted, but they are rightfully concerned about conflicts, which lead to wasting time, energy, and other scarce resources in addition to creating uneasy human relations. To avoid unwanted and unintended conflict, we proposed that one should be mindful of intercultural communication, which contributes to conflict just as economic rivalry and security threats have traditionally done.

Our modern world requires a modern humankind: one who can see beyond national citizenship; one who thinks globally while acting locally; one who recognizes that it is hard if not impossible to separate many domestic and international problems; and one who realizes that managing many current international challenges requires abilities beyond the control of only one nation, no matter how powerful that nation is. Considering such factors, we propose that an effective professional may think like a global citizen in the contemporary global work environment. We do not necessarily see a contradiction between practicing global citizenship and acting as a national of any country. No one is expected to ignore his/her homeland, ethnic group, religion, or national identity. In fact, we live in a world where states like the USSR, Yugoslavia, and Czechoslovakia disintegrated to smaller units, where the new states are organized around fewer nationalities. Thus, nationalism, national citizenship, and national loyalty are still important factors in the twenty-first century, despite the growth of integration schemes such as the European Union (EU), North American Free Trade Agreement (NAFTA), Economic Cooperation Organizations (ECO), Association of South East Asian Nations (ASEAN), and Asia Pacific Economic Cooperation (APEC), to name a few.

Practicing global citizenship involves being aware of our global environment, responsibilities, and rights beyond our individual, local, and national commitments. From a legal-political perspective, this is not a difficult task for US citizens, since they are used to keeping a balance between their national citizenship and identification with their own home state. In this regard, global citizenship does not require formal status, since it is only a state of mind. In other words, it is just an informal commitment suitable for living in a global village. Human beings are flexible enough to naturally switch from one role to another in the right environment. All such role-playing exercises require that we become self-aware that our environment has changed. Such self-awareness allows us to interact differently with our parents or our friends, simply because we recognize that the nature of the relationship is different: this is not a value judgment but the statement of a fact.

First and foremost, acting as a global citizen requires self-awareness and mindfulness. We must recognize there is a bigger picture of life beyond our immediate surroundings. This consciousness is vital since the larger world always affects our small portion of the globe, whether we realize it or not, and whether we like it or not. Second, we should realize that the cultural values and social rules of conduct are perhaps different from those of our own. Third, we need to discover the common characteristics of the two worlds as a starting point of an effective mode of intercultural communication. Fourth, we must attempt to identify the key cultural values of others, so we can avoid unintended disrespect and unwanted conflict. Finally, we need to build a mutually cooperative and beneficial relationship based on established culturally clear and comprehensive lines of communication focused on common interests packaged in sound solutions.

In the twenty-first century, it is time for a change of how global citizens interact in a growingly global environment. The cues for such changes are all around us, especially in popular culture. It is amazing to see how even Superman has changed his message and goals. In the 1940s, Superman stood for "Truth, Justice, and the American Way." In the 2006 *Superman Returns* movie, he stands for only "Truth and Justice," since even this alien American-adopted immigrant does not want to impose "the American Way" on all other nations in the world. That said, we should certainly learn from Superman in his endeavors of improved mindfulness and global citizenship, both of which advance the quality of intercultural communication as well as international relations.

References

1. Ellen J. Langer, *Mindfulness* (Reading, MA: Addison-Wesley, 1989), pp. 61–79.
2. Chris Brown, *Understanding International Relations*, 3rd ed. (New York: Palgrave Macmillan, 2005), p. 6.
3. Nancy Gibbs, "Persons of the Year," *Time*, December 2006, p. 44.
4. Andrew Sullivan, "The Year We Questioned Authority," *Time*, December 2006, p. 190.
5. Gibbs, p. 44.
6. Amanda Ripley, "From Rags to Riches," *Time*, December 2006, p. 77.
7. Gibbs, p. 45.
8. Ripley, p. 77.
9. Bill and Melinda Gates, "Letter from Bill and Melinda Gates," Bill & Melinda Gates Foundation, www.gatesfoundation.org/AboutUs/OurValues/GatesLetter.htm, 2006, accessed November 12, 2010.
10. Gibbs, p. 44.
11. Josh Tyrangiel, "The Constant Charmer," *Time*, December 2006, p. 55.
12. Michael Mink, "The Very Soul Of Compassion Act With Courage: Mother Teresa Dedicated her Life to Caring for the Forgotten," *Investor's Business Daily*, September 2006, A03.
13. Invisible Children, www.invisiblechildren.com/pages/our-story, accessed November 12, 2010.
14. MSF-USA, "New from Bolivia," Doctors Without Borders, www.doctorswithoutborders.org/news/country.cfm?id=2277, accessed December 22, 2010.
15. MSF-USA, Doctors Without Borders.
16. T. Kumar, "Trade with Vietnam," in *CQ Congressional Testimony*, Capitol Hill Senate Hearing, (Washington, DC: July 2006).
17. Grameen Communications, "A Short History of Grameen Bank," Grameen Bank, www.grameen-info.org/index.php?option=com_content&task=view&id=19&Itemid=114, accessed November 12, 2010.
18. Abu N. M. Wahid, "The Grameen Bank and Poverty Alleviation in Bangladesh: Theory,

Evidence, and Limitations," *American Journal of Economics and Sociology,* (January 1994), p. 6.

19. "Micro-credit Can Play a Vital Role to Eradicate Poverty," Nationwide International News, *The Pakistan Newswire* (November 2006).

20. Farhan Haq, "Microcredit Reaches More Poor Women," TWN, www.twnside.org.sg/title/micro-cn.htm, accessed November 12, 2010.

21. Tyrangiel, p. 5.

22. "Microfinance: A Key Tool in the Fight against Poverty and the Empowerment of the World's Poor — Especially Women," DATA (Washington, DC: October 2005).

23. Giosue Alagna, "Bono's DATA, Rocking the Development World," Devex, August 28, 2008, www.devex.com/en/articles/bonos-data-rocking-the-development-world, accessed November 12, 2010.

24. The International Council of Central Florida, http://iccfvip.com/index.html, accessed November 12, 2010.

25. R. J. Rummel, "International Actor and Situation," in *Understanding Conflict and War, Volume 4: War, Power, and Peace* (Los Angeles, CA: Sage, 1979).

26. Samuel P. Huntington, "The Clash of Civilizations?" *Foreign Affairs*, (Summer 1993).

27. Huntington, p. 32.

28. John Esposito, *The Islamic Threat: Myth or Reality?* (New York: Oxford University Press, 1999).

29. Betsy Pisik, "Arab-Israeli Conflict Fueling Climate of Fear: Annan; If Security Council Cannot End Crisis, Respect for the UN Will Decline, He Warns" *The Straits Times* (Singapore) September 2006.

30. David Saperstein, "Criticism of Israeli Policy v. Anti-Semitism," *The Washington Post*, February 26, 2007, http://newsweek.washingtonpost.com/onfaith/david_saperstein/2007/02/criticism_of_israeli_policy_v.html, accessed March 27, 2007.

31. Fiona Meredith, "What the Papers Say," *BBC News*, July 25, 2006, http://news.bbc.co.uk/2/hi/uk_news/northern_ireland/5212398.stm, accessed November 10, 2010.

32. Mithre J. Sandrasagra, "Politics: Arab-Israeli Conflict Feeds Muslim-West Rift," Inter Press Service English News Wire, November 14, 2006.

33. Josef Joffe, "The Perils of Soft Power," *The New York Times*, May 14, 2006, p. 15.

34. "Faith, Reason and the University Memories and Reflections: Lecture of the Holy Father," www.gees.org/documentos/Documen-01416.pdf, accessed November 12, 2010.

36. John James, "Pope's Comments Provoke Controversy," *Niagara Falls Review*, September 12, 2006, B5.

37. CNN, "Pope Invites Muslim Envoys to Meeting," http://abclocal.go.com/kabc/story?section=news/national_world&id=4589590, accessed December 22, 2010.

38. Huntington, p. 48.

39. *The American Heritage Dictionary of the English Language,* 4th ed. (Boston, MA: Houghton Mifflin Company, 2000).

40. Paul Butler, "Foreword: Terrorism and Utilitarianism: Lessons from, and for, Criminal Law," *The Journal of Criminal Law and Criminology*, Autumn 2002, 1–22.

41. Fernando Reinares, "The Empire Rarely Strikes Back," *Foreign Policy*, January–February 2002, 92–4.

42. "Northern Ireland," in Queen's University Belfast School of Law, p. 17.

43. Bilal al-Hasan, "Who has the Right to Condemn Terrorism?" *Journal of Palestine Studies* (Spring 1986), 150–1.

44. The Institute for Counter-Terrorism, "The Irish Republican Army," in *International Terrorism*.

45. Richard L. Harris, "Introduction: Globalization and Globalism in Latin America: Contending Perspectives," *Latin American Perspectives*, November 2002, 5–23.

46. Lester C. Thurow, "Globalization: The Product of a Knowledge-Based Economy," *Annuals of the American Academy of Political and Social Science*, 570, July 2000, 19–31.

47. Carolyn Walkup, "An Overarching Influence: McDonald's Changed the Way People Thought About Fast Food and Has Remained a Dominant Trailblazer Throughout Its 51-Year History," *Nation's Restaurant News*, January 29, 2007, http://findarticles.com/p/articles/mi_m3190/is_5_41/ai_n27135989/pg_2, accessed November 12, 2010.

48. "Children's Day at McDonald's to Benefit Children Around the World," *Asia Pulse, Nationwide International News*, November 16, 2006.
49. Thurow, p. 148.
50. Douglas Kellner, "Theorizing Globalization," *Sociological Theory*, 20 (November, 2002), 285–305.
51. Craig N. Murphy, "Global Governance: Poorly Done and Poorly Understood," *International Affairs*, 76, (October 2000), 789–803.
52. Giovanni Bisignani, "Think Again: Airlines," *Foreign Policy*, January 4, 2006, www.foreignpolicy.com/articles/2006/01/04/think_again_airlines, accessed November 12, 2010.
53. "Lessons Tourism Chiefs Must Learn," *Western Daily Press*, September 8, 2006, p. 12.
54. Paul Groves, "Terror and Travel: Terrorism Expands in our Shrinking World," *Birmingham Post*, December 10, 2005, p. 45.
55. Robert Goodland, "The Concept of Environmental Sustainability," *Annual Review of Ecology and Systematics*, 26 (1995) 2.
56. "Florida Visitor Numbers Increase Across the Board in 1Q," *Tampa Bay Business Journal*, www.bizjournals.com/tampabay/stories/2005/05/16/daily32.html, accessed October 14, 2006.
57. R. Chuenpagde, "Community Perspectives Toward a Marine Reserve: A Case Study of San Felipe, Yucatan, Mexico," *Coastal Management*, 30 (2002), 183–91.
58. Jim Algie, "Acting Natural," *The Nation* (Thailand) February 4, 2006.
59. Ibid.
60. J. Sean Curtin, "Suicide Also Rises in the Land of the Rising Sun," *Asia Times* (Japan) July 28, 2004.
61. Mission to Japan website, http://missiontojapan.org, accessed November 23, 2006.
62. Project Teams Purpose, *Agathos Foundation*, www.agathosfoundation.org/project_teams, accessed November 27, 2006.
63. Agathos Foundation, "One Church One Village," www.onechurchonevillage.org, accessed November 12, 2010.
64. Mothers Against Drunk Driving, www.madd.org, accessed April 18, 2007.
65. Rescue a Million website, www.rescueamillion.org, accessed November 28, 2006.
66. Ibid.

Index